MASKED BALL AT THE WHITE CROSS CAFÉ

THE FAILURE OF JEWISH ASSIMILATION

Janet Kerekes

IGUANA

Copyright @ 2005, 2020 Janet Kerekes

Published by Iguana Books
720 Bathurst Street, Suite 303
Toronto, ON M5S 2R4

All rights reserved. No part of this publication may be reproduced, stored in a retrieval system or transmitted, in any form or by any means, electronic, mechanical, recording or otherwise (except brief passages for purposes of review) without the prior permission of the author.

Publisher: Meghan Behse
Front cover image:

ISBN 978-1-77180-391-5 (paperback)

Originally published by University Press of America, Inc.

This is a second print edition of *Masked Ball at the White Cross Café: The Failure of Jewish Assimilation.*

Table of Contents

Preface — v

Introduction — 1

SECTION 1 From Toleration to Liberalism

Chapter 1 The Era of Toleration — 17

Chapter 2 The Enlightenment — 37

Chapter 3 From Ideals to Praxis: The Emergence of Liberalism — 65

SECTION 2 Hungary 1867-1920

Introduction — 83

Chapter 4 The Emancipation Process — 95

Chapter 5 Assessing Assimilation after 1867 — 111

Chapter 6 A Case of Ritual Murder — 119

Chapter 7 The Politics of Assimilation after Tiszaeszlar — 133

Chapter 8 Issues of Assimilation — 147

Chapter 9 1914-1920 — 179

Conclusion — 205

SECTION 3 The Basis for Comparison: Britain 1830-1920

Introduction — 215

Chapter 10 The Emancipation Process 1830-1858 — 219

Chapter 11 Alienage after Emancipation — 225

Chapter 12 Jews in Business — 245

Chapter 13 The Prewar Years — 253

Chapter 14 The First World War — 259

Chapter 15 Anti-Alienism in Postwar Britain — 267

Conclusion — 275

SECTION 4 **Hungary and Britain: A Comparison**

Analysis — 281

Conclusion — 287

Bibliography — 291

Index — 321

Preface

Between the covers of this book lies a world that may be as foreign to the reader as it was to newly emancipated Jews in Europe. This world was the non-Jewish world, where Christians were living for the first time with Jews as part of their society, and not separate from them. And for many Christians, this was an experience that provoked disappointment, frustration, and bitterness. This study examines Christian Hungarian and British societies' response to the presence of emancipated Jews in their respective countries between 1867 and 1920. As such, it constitutes a chapter of Hungarian and British history. In the course of my research, I found that the issues which were raised during this period revolved almost exclusively around assimilation in its many aspects; and that a significant number of the populace in both nations had concluded that Jews had failed to satisfactorily assimilate.

In order to understand this phenomenon, I found that I had to keep reaching further back in history, eventually arriving at the early Middle Ages, a time-consuming exercise. Staying faithful to the content in the primary sources—resisting the impulse to apply present-day norms and definitions—took great effort on my part. Just as challenging was the necessity to divest myself of all the usual ways of thinking about Jews in European society—from both the pro- and anti-Jewish perspectives—and become imbued with those prevalent over those many centuries. This was an arduous task, one that forced me to suspend my own identity in order to carry out this work with integrity.

Likewise, the reader will have to make the same efforts, in order to be open to another way of looking at the post-emancipation period of history, one that is not fixated on the Holocaust and which works its way backwards to formulate explanations for that tortured era. The approach used here is the idea of moving forward in history, and it does seem to indicate that there is an inextricable link between European Jews' failure to assimilate in prescribed ways and the Holocaust. Thus, the reader will find that the stock explanations often found in the literature are absent. Some consider these to be serious omissions.

For example, there are historians who acknowledge that assimilation was incomplete, but they argue that the reasons for this are important and should not have been omitted. I would argue otherwise. While any such 'reasons' may be true, they are not germane to this work. The aim of this book has been to *understand* the perspective of the host society, which was being asked to accept Jews into their society as co-citizens for the first time in its history. Others have observed that the Jewish perspective on assimilation is missing. Only when Jews weigh in on this discussion, they argue, can one assess whether or not Jews were truly assimilated. Again, I must underscore that it is the perspective of the host society which is our interest here, not the Jewish one. In fact, it is the Jewish perspective on this topic that has held sway for many years. A preponderance of Hungarian Jews, and British Jews for that matter, have vociferously maintained (and still maintain today) that Jews were indeed assimilated.

Which brings me to the next omission. I have done away with the use of the term 'anti-Semitism' as far as possible. The term has erected an almost impassable roadblock to the past, providing little in the way of explanation. Whether writ large as 'prejudice' or reduced to the "banality of evil," both are merely opposite ends of the spectrum of 'anti-Semitism', which lamentably have served to reduce the parameters of the Holocaust to the lessons of Auschwitz. But to be faced with a work concerning Jews in Europe between emancipation and the Holocaust where anti-Semitism is not the organizing principle, is to throw some readers into a panic and verges on heresy. If not anti-Semitism, then what? However, as will be discussed, use of the term anti-Semitism has hindered rather than helped to understand this era.

Then there is the purported omission of the contributions Jews made to the modernization of Hungary, and Britain as well, seen by some as a necessary addition to any historical work dealing with the post-emancipation period. They are not relevant. The subject of the book is Jewish assimilation, and the Jews' failure to assimilate along prescribed lines. Thus, I cannot see how listing these 'contributions', as they are called, would have aided the discussion in any way. Furthermore, and ironically, these 'contributions' would probably not have happened had Hungarian Jews assimilated in the ways they were enjoined to.

Lastly, it has been observed that sources testifying to the existence of congenial relations between Jews and Christians are missing. I have one response to this. It was a common phenomenon that Christians spoke of having Jewish friends, yet felt there was a 'Jewish Problem.'

I, too, saw an omission in the literature encompassing the post-emancipation era. My research into the contemporary records made it absolutely clear that, after emancipation, to enter into a discussion about Jews meant that, in one way or another, the parties were discussing the issue of assimilation—and frequently, the lack thereof. Yet, this fact has not been reflected in the histories which address this time period.

I must say a word about the language barrier concerning the part of the project related to Hungary. I do not speak Hungarian at all well. I was totally dependent on my translators which, needless to say, created its own subset of problems. That being said, I owe a tremendous debt of gratitude to my husband in particular, Sandor Kerekes, who carried out most of the Hungarian research and translated it into English for me. My research debt extends as well to Gyorgy Kozma who also aided in researching and translating primary source material. They further merit my special thanks for their support in what was otherwise a rather lonely endeavor.

May I add that two recent trends have made a second edition of this book timely. The first trend may be observed in Hungary and is the assessment of Christian Hungarians' role in the deportation of Hungarian Jews to the death camps. Simply put: do they share guilt with Nazi Germany (and to what degree) in carrying out the Holocaust? Did they play an active role as collaborators; or play no role at all as bystanders; or did they oppose Nazi Germany's aims? Each of these possibilities needs to be qualified. In the first case, does "they" imply the whole population? In the second case, should bystanders be considered guilty because they did not try to stop the deportations? In the third case, those who claim they opposed Nazi Germany's aims, is there any evidence for such a claim? Of course, this is only the tip of the iceberg; I can only hope that such nuances will be taken into account as Hungary faces its wartime history. Although such self-examination is not welcomed by everyone, it could be valuable if done circumspectly, and this book provides valuable historical context.

The second trend has no possible merit attached to it; quite the contrary. This is the lamentable resurgence of anti-Jewish sentiment on both sides of the Atlantic. This 'resurgence' is not just expressed as hate; it is expressed in the form of many issues – and they are the same issues, in fact, that Hungarians and others raised as long ago as the Enlightenment concerning their Jewish populations. While it is not at all well known, the Jews having a homeland has long been a controversial issue; now that it has been established, it is simply more provocative than it was in the past. But rest assured, this, and other issues have a long history, adding to the timeliness of this book.

The idea for this book has no direct lineage. I can only state that a background in Jewish studies, my status as a Western European historian, and a belated and incidental interest in European Jewry aided in the fermentation of what evolved into my approach to and interpretation of Jewish assimilation in the post-emancipation era in Hungary and Britain, and by extension, Europe.

Janet Kerekes
Budapest
November 2019

Introduction

In 1945, George Orwell noted, "One effect of the persecutions in Germany has been to prevent anti-Semitism from being seriously studied." We need not take Orwell's use of the word "anti-Semitism" too literally; in fact, we shouldn't. But his overall point is one we should pay heed to. Orwell's observation remains essentially correct; not only "the persecutions in Germany" but other factors have inhibited the study of the era which led up to the Holocaust.*

The first factor that has acted as a barrier to the study of this era is one that all historians face: the challenge of refraining from applying current sensibilities and standards when assessing original sources. By current standards, Werner

---

* The historiography on anti-Semitism is voluminous; therefore, I have confined my introductory comments to trends that have particular relevance to this study. The parameters of this overview are further narrowed because I chose not to address the works of Hungarian historians. My reason for this decision is that no comprehensive body of historiographical works on nineteenth- and twentieth-century anti-Semitism in Hungary currently exists. Generally speaking, anti-Semitism has not been a 'topic for discussion' there for decades. In the immediate aftermath of the Second World War, Hungarians quickly took the position that the deportation of their Jewry was the responsibility of the Nazis alone. Further removing this topic from the public eye was the invisibility of Jews during the Communist era. This kind of public identification was censured by the Communists in fulfillment of the Communist ideal of solidarity. In line with this notion of solidarity, the Soviet Union imposed its view of the war upon all its satellites: the party line was that this war had been a war against Fascism; everyone who died during the war was a martyr in the fight against this evil. Singling out the Jews by discussing their attempted extermination would have run counter to this monolithic rendering. Of the few books on anti-Semitism written after 1946, either the Soviet imprint is clearly evident or they were historically distant enough not to represent a challenge (Judith Kubinszky's *Politikai antiszemitizmus Magyarorszagon 1875–1890* [Political Anti-Semitism in Hungary 1875–1890] published in 1976, for example). Following the 'change' in 1990, the possibility has existed for Hungarian historians to write freely about anti-Semitism. And they have: the most observable trend is works on the Holocaust. However, it is my opinion that not enough time has elapsed for these historians to sufficiently come to grips with issues related to anti-Semitism, thus making it appropriate to challenge them. There are also a number of books on this subject that have been written over the years by historians who were born in Hungary but have lived for decades in America and elsewhere. While their work has value, it cannot be said to be representative of *Hungarian* analyses of anti-Semitism. Produced in a non-Hungarian environment, it cannot fill in the gap created by Hungarians' renderings of the extermination of their Jewry, along with decades of censorship.

Sombart's The Jews and Modern Capitalism (1902) is a typical anti-Semitic tract. Yet M. Epstein, who translated the book into English in 1909, described Sombart's work as having "received universal recognition for its brilliance," "though his work has not always been accepted without challenge."[2]

Beyond this, there is a tendency to inadvertently erect another kind of barrier, by squeezing facts out of shape, or sacrificing them altogether. Like many, historian Robert Wistrich accepts the popular view that society became secularized over the nineteenth century; religiosity is therefore downplayed or disregarded as a factor in determining attitudes towards Jews. Therefore, he writes: "It was this social functionality of anti-Semitism along with its protean quality and ability to fuse with a whole series of other views which, among other things, distinguished it from traditional Jew-hatred and gave it a distinctly modern quality."[3] The idea that religion-based anti-Semitism predeceased political (ethnic or national) anti-Semitism is a mistaken notion. R. W. Southern has made the point that far from being outmoded, "the identification of the church with the whole of organized society" persisted throughout the nineteenth and into the twentieth century:[4] In Hungary, the Roman Catholic Church fostered the creation of a Catholic political party in 1895, and Christians of all denominations worked to make the Christian Socialist Party a success following its formation after the First World War. In nineteenth-century England, all state occasions (royal marriages, funerals) were celebrated in the Church of England. It is a mistake to take their form and content for granted. In point of fact, they were part-and-parcel of the theater of power, one which adhered to a Christian vision of political and social organization.

With reference to the Jewish Question, historian Gershom Scholem views the emancipation of the Jews as a point of demarcation. According to him, emancipation exacerbated the Jewish Question, as relations between Jews and Christians actually worsened because the occasions for contact were vastly increased in the cultural, intellectual, political, and economic spheres.[5] While this observation about emancipation is correct, the implication that there had always been a Jewish Question is not. The historic marginalization of the Jew in the ways described by Scholem was not the result of a problem or a question but the concrete expression of Christian theology which dictated a separate and inferior role to the Jews. The Jewish Question arose only when Jewish emancipation was being considered. Use of this expression is appropriate provided it follows contemporary use, that is, in debates on emancipation; or on discussions pertaining to the immigration of Eastern European Jews to Western Europe (which was in itself part of the emancipation debate); or thereafter.

Historian Michael Marrus looked at contingencies, seeing what provokes anti-Semitism or causes it to recede as opposed to the "ideological approach" where, "throughout history, anti-Jewish feeling works its way as a virus, scarcely altering its basic form, always ready to infect vulnerable societies."[6] Hannah Arendt's focus was on how contingency relates to the eruption of political anti-Semitism: "Anti-Jewish feeling acquires political relevance only when it can combine with a major political issue, or when Jewish group interests come into open conflict with those of a major class in society."[7] Bearing a family resemblance to contingency theories is Michael Bernstein's theory of "sideshadowing", which grew out of his rejection of determinist histories. Using the expression "foreshadowing" to describe the notion of a "closed universe in which all choices have been made," Bernstein advocates "sideshadowing": the examination of "sideshadowed ideas and events, on what did not happen," serving as a caution to the historian to remain open-minded, lest he or she conclude that "the future was inevitable simply because it happened."[8] These three examples share the same fundamental weakness. Placing the accent of contingency on ideas and events that might (reasonably) happen as a tool in historical analysis leads one away from 'history'. That is to say, there was no element of contingency in the ever-increasing anti-Jewish sentiment of the post-emancipation era. It was well-grounded in certain causes that this work will explore. Where the element of contingency *did* exhibit itself was in the way this sentiment would be manifested.

The influence of Marxism to derail sober historical investigation is apparent among certain historians who were attempting to answer the following question: "Were figures in the past acting as Jews or as members of other collectivities?" Marxist theoreticians, of course, favored the latter option, arguing that "class and class consciousness [were] the determining features of [Jewish] economic and social life."[9] However, this assertion is made at the expense of the universal identification of the Jew *as* Jew, possessing no other designation. Therefore, the Jew could not possibly have been acting as a member of "other collectivities."

Another example where theory holds sway over fact is the interactive theory, advanced by David Feldman: "We need to shift the initial historical question away from the problem of why men and women objected to the Jews, to the question of what they meant when they were doing so." A sample of this is provided by Feldman: "Because the Englishness of English history was bound to the language of rights, the argument for Jewish emancipation constituted an argument about the nation as well as the individual."[10] As the legislators were contemplating the emancipation of the Jews, there may well have been visions of national importance dancing in their heads, and "the idea of individual liberties protected by the law" was certainly a concern, but there were also visions of Jews, and most of them were not very pleasant ones.

The interactive theory was a stepping-stone for the many historians who began to stress contextualization.[11] Pierre Birnbaum and Ira Katznelson contend that "no useful comparative history of this [emancipation] process can be written if Jewish history is segmented from the histories of the many different societies to which Jews belonged, since their identities and practices were affected distinctively by the configuration of each case."[12] Hence, the rebellion against "ghetto" histories,[13] as they are called, where the existence of a 'history of the Jews' was presumed, and moreover, that there was a universal pattern to the historic relationship between Christians and Jews. "Realist" histories seek to rectify these errors by placing the Jews in context, that is to say by placing them within the history of the host society. Thus, if one dips into historian George Mosse's book, Toward the Final Solution, one finds: "When anti-Semitism awakened in Poland toward 1880, it was largely due to a Catholic reaction against scientific positivism, as well as to a more general fear of capitalist development among the population. . . . Catholicism and Protestantism drew sustenance for their anti-Semitism from their rural roots, from the 'unchanging countryside'—which in reality was changing only too quickly.... All over Europe, the agricultural crisis of the fin de siecle used the Jew as the symbol for the hated city, for uprootedness, and for modernity.... The principal anti-Jewish riots in Germany (1819, 1830, 1844, 1848) were partly due to economic causes such as famine and the decline of handicrafts."[14]

While I wholeheartedly concur that "ghetto" histories were missing the perspective of placing Jews within the history of the host society, the picture painted by these regional histories is problematic. The fundamental issue is that contextualization, having given rise to regional histories of anti-Semitism, has obscured the universal reasons for the historic relationship between Christians and Jews, to the detriment of such studies. The national context has not substantively affected any country's response to its Jews. Rather, a comparative study of national contexts shows that each host society drew from a common pool of reasons for marginalizing the Jews. The conditions in the host society simply determined which of these would be highlighted. Thus, the English accentuated crime (an example of the Jews' immorality); the French, usury (an example of the Jews' greed, obsession with money, and hatred of Christians); the Hungarians, the unwillingness of Jews to undertake Magyarization (an example of the force of Judaism on its adherents).

As a consequence of this drive to contextualize history, history itself has taken a beating in the last few decades. In Hungary, for example, contemporaries' comments such as 'Jews are monopolizing the economy' have been judged by historians to be incorrect and unjustified, and therefore not properly part of Hungarian history because they are not 'true'—not true in the sense that, as historian Raphael Patai characteristically describes, the development of Hungary along modern, industrialized lines was undertaken by Jews, for these were "tasks the Christian Hungarians were unable, or rather unwilling to shoulder."[15] (Other historians have provided different explanations.) *This* is history. Contemporary Hungarians' grounds for resentment having thus been shown to be historically illegitimate, their comments are then relegated to the anti-Semitic trash bin. However, to render this judgment is to take a liberty that is outside the mandate of the historian. The truth of a nation's history is not only derived from historical analyses such as Patai's but also from the viewpoints and perceptions articulated by the people who, being present and active at the time made that history. That they may be considered unpalatable must not exclude them from use in historical analysis.

But the greatest problem is the framing of all discussions on the post-emancipation era in terms of anti-Semitism. We may start with statements such as this one by historian Asher Cohen:

> The 'fantasy' element was strong in this nineteenth-century genre of plebeian anti-Semitism—and its mythical quality (transcending theological hatred of Jews which sounded medieval and reactionary) was strengthened by the new emphasis on 'race'—a concept which conveniently lent itself to all kinds of mystification in spite of its modern 'scientific' ring. The very abstractness of

the anti-Semitic 'ideology'—itself largely the creation of semi-radicalized, frustrated, intellectual misfits and some sensation-mongering journalists—succeeded in activating the sense of an ideal world beyond the social atomization, the class antagonisms, and the decadence of contemporary bourgeois society. The diffuse radicalism expressed by this diffuse mythology offered a kind of anchor for the psychologically unhinged, the economically insecure, the social misfits, the unemployed intellectuals, and the bankrupt aristocrats, as well as serving the material interests of the 'respectable' professional middle classes suddenly confronted by unwelcome Jewish competition.[17]

The conviction persists that anti-Semitism is prejudice, discrimination, racism, false accusations, and an irrational hatred, whose adherents are misfits, and it has been so since the middle of the nineteenth century. The reality is, that between emancipation and the Holocaust, what is called anti-Semitism was the public discourse on the failure of Jews to assimilate, and the negative effects that this failure was having on society. Coincident with this conviction, one of the hallmarks of liberalism, a pronounced 'philo-Semitism', surfaced: "this feeling that anti-Semitism is something sinful and disgraceful, something that a civilized person does not suffer from."[18] It is an error not only to perceive Christians' feelings towards Jews before the mid-nineteenth century as anti-Semitic, but then to see in this an evolution: from religious to political anti-Semitism; an explicit political creed that possessed a catechism that was novel and born of nineteenth-century nationalistic trends. On the contrary, Jews as aliens, as a separate race, as a nation, and as enemies who are conspiring to gain hegemony over Christians or harm or destroy them were, in fact, perpetual concerns.

And we must call into question the idea that the anti-Semite is dressed in black, not because we applaud or support hatred of Jews, but because what historians label 'anti-Semitism' are actually convictions that were widely conceived and on which there was a consensus amongst the majority of Christian European society. Even though J. W. Parkes consistently condemned anti-Semitism, he did allow that, "in the loose sense of everyday speech, anti-Semitism, whatever its particular cause may be in any particular place, is 'instinctive,' and as such is the common inheritance of a common past."[19] Looking at this issue from a different perspective, the eminent Hungarian Bishop Ottokar Prohaszka and others wanted to prevent the breakdown of Christian society; prevent the Judaization of Hungary; and help the well-intentioned and nationalist Jews to unite with the national Christian society. Why, then, Prohaszka asked, does this make us anti-Semites?[20] (Interestingly, both Wistrich and Prohaszka would agree that anti-Semitism is an irrational hatred.) It cannot be emphasized enough how much the persistent use of the term 'anti-Semitism' is one of the greatest barriers to exploring and understanding this period.

There is yet another barrier to the study of this period, one that is far more emotionally charged. For the most part, as much as we care to envision the ancestors of Jews, or, if you are Jewish, your forebears, Hollywood, the Yiddish theater, and various authors have helped us along by providing us with stereotypes. Fathers were fiddlers on the roof, and mothers were *meine Yiddishe mamas*. It is time to face some unpleasant truths. We cannot expect that these

Jews, who had been marginalized for centuries, repeatedly expelled, forced to live in ghettos, and who at times survived by committing illegal acts, actually conformed to the images churned out by those awash in nostalgia. That unflattering characteristics may have been due to the marginalization and isolation of Jews over the centuries—which some Europeans from the Enlightenment on did believe—the fact remains that they did not want these influences infiltrating their society. Furthermore, after emancipation, new issues arose and eroded this sympathetic explanation for negative Jewish traits. A number of Jews remained strongly traditional, and were even opposed to assimilation, while others were 'modern' Jews, edgy, and iconoclastic, and in fact, spearheaded revolutionary movements. Traditional or modern, they were socially cohesive, and still stood out from mainstream society.

In looking back at the literature predating the Holocaust, one will find endless references to the Jews' need to assimilate, and, following their emancipation, the failure of Jews to satisfactorily assimilate. In fact, the issue of assimilation was the cornerstone of anti-Semitic sentiment. Beginning with the Enlightenment, it was hammered at, that is, until the Holocaust. I would not say the subject was neglected for the last seventy years. I would rather say it became taboo. And why? Because nobody wanted to admit into the historical record the rather popular opinion that European Jews had failed to assimilate. To do so would be to indict the Jews as instruments in their own destruction, and this was an unthinkable proposition after the horrors of the Holocaust. At the same time, the image of Europeans as unwilling to live with Jews who were unassimilated indicted the Europeans in the Holocaust. An equally unacceptable proposition. Nor did anyone want to admit into the historical record that already before 1900, this failure and its likely disastrous consequences were clear to a number of people. "A new unrest is perceptible throughout the civilized world on the subject of the Jewish Question," wrote the Englishman Arnold White, in 1899. "The conclusion, therefore, seems obvious, that either the situation must be dealt with – i.e., by Europe as a whole – or an alarming outbreak against the race . . . and the clock of civilization thus be thrown back for a hundred years."[21] The best thing was to bury the whole issue of assimilation, for it implicated everybody. Only several decades after the Holocaust did it come out of the closet, so to speak —but completely revised and bearing little resemblance to contemporary records of years gone by.

Another barrier to the study of this period, and by extension, the Holocaust, is the fairly recent but by now universally held belief that we can derive the benefit of a lesson from the Holocaust, namely, that the Holocaust contains lessons for mankind, warning each of us of the lethal dangers of prejudice and discrimination. For example, in 2005, the fiftieth anniversary of the Holocaust, Auschwitz was the messenger of this lesson, and we were saturated with the lessons we must learn. Now, if prejudice and discrimination were the sole reasons for the Holocaust, it might make sense to speak of educating people on how to overcome these pernicious biases. But these cannot be considered the fundamental reasons, and therefore, there is no lesson to be learned. This focus has had the ramification of expunging the specificity of the Holocaust, thereby increasing the comfort level of both Jews and non-Jews.

Now merely a generic example of the consequences of prejudice and racism—albeit the supreme one—non-Jews are released from their historic responsibility, while many Jews have supported this shift in the misguided belief that by working towards eradicating prejudice and discrimination generally, this will somehow put an end to hundreds and hundreds of years of anti-Jewish sentiment.

Finally, one last factor must be considered, which has obscured the interconnectedness between the post-emancipation era and the Holocaust. This is the idea that the Holocaust is a unique and unfathomable event in history. Elie Wiesel, for instance, holds this view in its extremity. Thus, he has reservations about subjecting the Holocaust to historical examination.[22] While acknowledging the legitimacy of both these points, this work is guided by another imperative. It draws on Julian Barnes's statement that "history is by its nature an act of hindsight, of understanding, or understanding better, what was understood less well at the time, or of understanding again what has been temporarily forgotten."[23] The problems concerning the Jews have always been very well understood at the time. Thus, the accent of this work is on "understanding again what has been temporarily forgotten."

By means of a structure of toleration (Section I), which had its origins in Christian theology, Christian society maintained a state of equilibrium in its relations with Jews. Intrinsically ambivalent, the term 'toleration' at times has a positive connotation, at other times, a negative one. I have adhered to the negative or 'restrictive' use of the word, which has implicit in its meaning no idea of acceptance but rather putting up with. The constrictive and precarious existence of Jews who dwelled in Christian countries reflects such an interpretation. Acceptance could be achieved, but one way and one way only: through conversion to Christianity. The Enlightenment heralded a new era whose ideology emphasized humanistic universalism: the notion of the equality of all human beings—including the Jews. Historians in general have paid little attention to Enlightenment thought as it pertains to the Jews: Arthur Hertzberg, Isaac Barzilay, and Adam Sutcliffe stand out as exceptions.[24] The burgeoning scholarship on the Enlightenment (which coincided with the revival of Theodor Adorno and Max *Horkheimer's Dialectic of Enlightenment* [1944)]) has often assessed Enlightenment thought negatively, thereby quashing, to some extent, the once popular notion that the ideal of universal humanism prompted positive feelings towards Jews and advanced their emancipation. At the same time, this scholarship has done much to promote the idea that the Enlightenment thinkers were anti-Semitic. However, it is possible, by eliminating the foregone conclusion that anything negative said about the Jews presumes an anti-Semitic frame of mind and further, by adopting the perspective of the Enlightenment thinkers when examining their statements, to see that they approached the matter of applying universal humanistic ideals to the Jews honestly, sincerely, and realistically. In uniform agreement that the Jews were in a degenerate condition, the Enlightenment thinkers—*philosophes*, theologians, politicians, and literary figures—then examined each and every concern pertaining to the feasibility of Jewish emancipation. This in turn prompted the formulation of a number of reforms—what I term the 'Enlightenment ideals specific to the Jews.' That these reforms became and remained the criteria by which the efforts of Jews to become assimilated were judged says much about the wholeheartedness and thoroughness of this effort.

As the Enlightenment gave way to the era of liberalism, efforts were made to implement certain general Enlightenment ideals. Thus, liberalism, in its nascent, tentative stage begins with the *Toleranzpatent* of Joseph II (1781-83), which also included a number of measures designed to put the Jews on the path to reform. Within ten years, a muscle-bound version proclaimed the rule of liberalism in France and emancipated the Jews in its wake. However, the results of this French gesture of fraternity were seen as less than acceptable; Jews were continuously criticized for failing to reform and to transform themselves into Frenchmen. Napoleon's extension of political parity to Jews in other European countries was revoked in the wake of his defeat, and elsewhere, the condition of Jews remained precarious. Therefore, many Jews were disabused of the hope that they might share in the benefits of Enlightenment thought. In such an inhospitable climate, it is not surprising that some Jews looked to other options. The two major trends that evolved were Zionism and migration—and both meant getting out of Europe.

Despite the justified pessimism of many Jews, the ideal of universal humanism increasingly became a prod to consider the emancipation of the Jews. During the early pre-emancipation period, the debates revolved around *if* and *to what extent* the status of the Jews should be improved, and the debaters emphasized reform, the Enlightenment ideals specific to the Jews, as the key to 'successful' emancipation in much the same way as their Enlightenment forebears had. However, while the Enlightenment thinkers had been weighed down by one burden—how to reconcile their humanitarian impulses with the current state of the Jews—liberals were being weighed down by another: the liberal ethos. Consequently, it was not long before liberals opted to emancipate the Jews in Central and Western Europe, without waiting until the process of reform was fully manifest, a process that some considered to be well underway, and others felt was far from complete. The year 1867 may be considered the benchmark for emancipation in Central and Western Europe: the year Hungary and Austria emancipated its Jews, countries with substantial Jewish communities, it is also proximate in time to their emancipation in Britain, Germany, and Italy.

Whatever efforts Jews made to reform after their emancipation, Christians in Central and Western Europe considered them largely unsuccessful. The Jews had not become 'just like us.' Their reform foundered because most Jews failed to grasp that essential condition of their emancipation: the imperative to fulfill the Enlightenment ideals specific to the Jews, the outcome of which would be their assimilation into the nation they inhabited. Jews were perceived to have fallen very short of the mark, as shown by their embrace of Zionism; their supranationality; their persistent cosmopolitan image; the coupling of cosmopolitanism and Zionism with an enthusiastic nationalism (an irritating and impossible combination according to many, if not most Europeans); their saturation of the professions; their monopolization of fields ranging from the theater to the press to capitalist enterprises; their lopsided participation in the economy; their unequal notable contributions to the social sciences, for example; their "Judaization" of society (Austria, Hungary); their disproportionate involvement in radical politics, particularly the Socialist and Communist movements; their stunning financial successes in times of economic distress for others; and lastly, their 'Jewishness', which still seemed so obvious to so many and was heightened by ongoing migration from Eastern to

Western Europe. All of which led to the conclusion that the Jews had not really assimilated and become 'like us.' The 'Jewish Question' became a pervasive one as much of Hungarian society determined that Jews had failed to assimilate in the prescribed ways. Random attacks, government-sanctioned raids, and legislation all signal that the emancipation of the Jews had begun to come undone.

Thrown into sharp relief in this work is the existence of a continuum—the acceptance of the Jew only as a *non*-Jew—historically achieved through conversion and reconfigured by the Enlightenment thinkers as a series of reforms culminating in assimilation. Its rupture—the emancipation of the Jews, which failed to prompt the vast majority of Jews into conforming to these requirements—created the conditions that eventually led to the Holocaust. In making this assertion, I am relying on the role of contingency in one respect. By 1920, complaints against the Jews in Hungary had so escalated that violence against them became common and legal measures limiting the rights of Jews were implemented. But the attitude towards Jews in other countries was similar. Therefore, had Hitler never existed, then perhaps this pervasive anti-Jewish sentiment might have expressed itself in the following scenarios: in Poland, a program of pogroms and mass expulsion; in Russia, continued eradication of the Jewish intelligentsia and a policy of ethnic marginalization, forcing the Jews to choose between the abandonment of their religion or living as pariahs; in Romania, a continuation of the Jews' third-rate status coupled with expulsions and pogroms; in Hungary, continued application of quotas in education and subsequently, in all areas of endeavor, coupled with continued violence against the Jews; in Germany and Austria, an atmosphere of hostility that would gradually ease Jews out of influential positions in culture and business; and in Britain, under the combined mantle of anti-Zionism, anti-Bolshevism, and anti-domination, the increased targeting of Jews as aliens. Common to all these possible scenarios would have been increased conversion and an attitude of stoicism on the one hand, as well as a steady stream of emigration and a growing Zionist movement on the other. How far the objections to the Jewish presence would have gone is, of course, unknown. Would they have remained regional in nature? Would the migration of Jews have provoked its own subsection of discontents? But the idea that without Hitler the situation of the Jews in Europe after the end of the First World War would not have been dire is inconceivable. It is that unpredictable element of contingency which assigned Jews their particular fate.

Hungary is a particularly good choice for an analysis of Jewish efforts to assimilate (Section II), for nowhere have Jews been more vocal in claiming the success of their assimilation into 'the historic nation,' which they saw as an amalgam of St. Stephen and Sandor Brody.[†] Especially between 1867 and 1914, many Jews believed they were enjoying the 'golden era of Hungarian Jewry.'[25] But this was a 'Brodian' rendering of Jewish life in Hungary after emancipation.

[†] St. Stephen was not only the founder and first king of the Hungarian state, he also introduced Christianity to Hungary. Sandor Brody (1863-1924) was a prominent Jewish author, journalist, and playwright in *fin-de-siecle* Hungary. A chronicler of urban life, he also detailed the plight of the urban poor and in his plays dealt with social conflict. He would have considered himself a completely assimilated Jew.

In St. Stephen's Hungary, there was the Tiszaeszlar ritual murder trial (1882-83) which exposed the profound animosity towards emancipated but unassimilated Jews; the formation of the National Anti-Semitic Party (1883); vociferous objections to the *Recepcio* (1895), which placed Judaism among the 'received' religions; the founding of another political party, the Neppart (1896), whose agenda included the circumvention and destruction of Jewish monopolies; and thousands of articles and pamphlets decrying the negative influence of the Jews upon Hungarian society. Despite such widespread demonstrations of hostility towards Jews, the belief that this period was the 'golden era of Hungarian Jewry' persists. There is still resistance to accepting the implications of these events, indicating a preference for this mythologized version. Those who challenge it are accused of making *a posteriori* arguments (foreshadowing) and relying on the benefit of hindsight. However, such a golden era never existed, and most certainly not in the minds of non-Jewish Hungarians.[26]

While this study turns on an examination of Hungary between the years 1867 and 1920, it gains force by making a similar examination of Britain (Section III). "This sceptred isle" was a country with a liberal reputation for civility and progressive government. Jacob Katz is just one historian who has argued that the treatment and status of Jews in England differed from that in continental Europe. Like others, he maintains that apart from the inability to become naturalized, any further disabilities endured by Jews were also applied to everyone not belonging to the Church of England. Hence, "These restrictions were not aimed against Jews but against non-Anglican Christians, so that the Jews had no reason for feeling discriminated against."[27] This is not the conclusion I have come to. By comparing the response to emancipated Jews in England and Hungary (Section IV), one will see that the similarities far outweigh the differences; it was only a matter of degree. The Jewish effort to reform and thereby assimilate into the host society was similarly unsuccessful in both Britain and Hungary. Christian Europe responded uniformly to the presence of unreformed Jews in its midst.

This study, while it has relevance for Jews, is actually a chapter of European history. Almost exclusively, non-Jewish sources written between the period of the Enlightenment and 1920 were used. Comments by Jews have been employed very selectively. Their use is simply to corroborate the intensity of the attitudes towards Jews, for it was the case in both post-emancipation Britain and Hungary that Jews were at pains to hush up or downplay hostility and only spoke out when the situation was considered grim. This perspective—that of the host society—as the Jew made the transition from being a 'tolerated' Jew to an 'emancipated' Jew has been lacking to date. Historians have been reluctant to consider this approach in deference, I suspect, to the long history of Jewish persecution, the Holocaust, and their liberal sensibilities.

For the Jew, it raises the possibility of never having been accepted as an equal and indistinguishable member of society while remaining a Jew. To those Jews who would contest this statement and argue that they have successfully assimilated, I would respond in the following way. "There are no Jews in Szeged any more," wrote Kalman Mikszath in 1879, meaning that Jews had abandoned the peoplehood aspect of Jewishness: "The younger generation in Szeged may even think of Jehovah as an old man wearing a Hungarian short coat with gold lace."[28] There *are no Jews in Szeged* now. Eliminated is a Jewish population that was composed of traditional Jews who fought against assimilation and those who were spinning their wheels to achieve an assimilation that was perhaps beyond their capabilities and at the same time beyond the apprehension of most. There are so few Jews left now in need of reform. This, together with the fact that Western society is still somewhat chastened by the attempted extermination of the Jews has allowed for the claim that Jews have successfully assimilated into the nations in which they reside. Any assessment of this post-Holocaust phase of assimilation must take these two facts into account.

This study may also prick the conscience of those Jews (and I suspect there are many) who have understood that acceptance 'allows' for an assimilation which is not a condition for acceptance, but rather the inverse: being permitted to assimilate is in itself a sign of acceptance. In such a paradigm, assimilation can only evoke a positive response. Any ability to assess the implications of assimilation is completely suspended, and while one's Jewishness appears to be neither significantly nor intrinsically threatened, in fact, it is.

Non-Jews must still ask the question: what are the grounds on which acceptance of the Jew *as* Jew can be forged?

NOTES

1. George Orwell, "Antisemitism in Britain," in *The Collected Essays, Journalism and Letters of George Orwell*, ed. Sonia Orwell and Ian Angus (London: Martin Secker & Warburg Limited, 1968), 336.
2. Werner Sombart, *Jews and Modern Capitalism*, "Translator's Introductory Note," trans. M. Epstein (1902; repr., New York: Collier Books, 1962), 7.
3. Robert S. Wistrich, *Between Redemption and Perdition* (London and New York: Routledge, 1990), 38.
4. R. W. Southern, *Western Society and Church in the Middle Ages* (Harmondsworth, UK: Penguin Books, 1970), 16.
5. Gershom Scholem, "Jews and Germans," *Commentary* 42 (November 1966): 33.
6. Michael R. Marrus, "The Theory and Practice of Anti-Semitism," in *The Nazi Holocaust: The Origins of the Holocaust*, ed. Michael R. Marrus (Westport, Conn.: Meckker Corporation, 1989), 2:174-76.
7. Hannah Arendt, *The Origins of Totalitarianism* (New York: Harcourt, Brace, 1951), 28.
8. Michael Andre Bernstein, *Foregone Conclusions: Against Apocalyptic History* (Berkeley and Los Angeles: University of California Press, 1994), 23, 7, 27. German historians raised the same issue in what has become known as the Historians' Debate (1986-87). Their argument also reflected the influence of the *Annales* School, in that they advocated a long-term view of the Nazi era. See Peter Baldwin ed., *Reworking the Past: Hitler, the Holocaust, and the Historians'Debate* (Boston: Beacon Press, 1990).
9. David Feldman, *Englishmen and Jews: Social Relations and Political Culture, 1840–1914* (New Haven, Conn.: Yale University Press, 1994), 36-40.
10. Feldman, *Englishmen and Jews*, 36-40. For the articulation of this idea in Hungary, see George Barany, "'Magyar Jew or Jewish Magyar?' (To the Question of Jewish Assimilation in Hungary)," *Canadian-American Slavic Studies* 8, no. 1 (Spring 1974): 5-6.

11. See also Feldman, *Englishmen and Jews*, 14; Alan E. Steinweis, "The Holocaust and Jewish Studies," in *Lessons and Legacies*, ed. Peter Hayes (Evanston, Ill.: Northwestern University Press, 1999), 3:31; Raphael Patai, *The Jews of Hungary: History, Culture, Psychology* (Detroit: Wayne State University Press, 1996), 512-13; Nathaniel Katzburg, "Hungarian Antisemitism: Ideology and Reality (1920-1943)," in *Antisemitism Through the Ages*, ed. Shmuel Almog, trans. Nathan H. Reisner (Oxford: Pergamon Press, 1988), 342.

12. Pierre Birnbaum and Ira Katznelson, "Emancipation and the Liberal Offer," in *Paths of Emancipation: Jews, States, and Citizenship*, ed. Pierre Birnbaum and Ira Katznelson (Princeton: Princeton University Press, 1995), 11.

13. The foremost example of "ghetto" histories is Heinrich Graetz's eleven-volume *Geschichte der Juden*, written between 1853 and 1876.

14. George L. Mosse, *Toward the Final Solution: A History of European Racism* (New York: H. Fertig, 1978), 133-36.

15. Patai, *Jews of Hungary*, 360.

16. Asher Cohen, "The Attitude of the Intelligentsia in Hungary Toward Jewish Assimilation Between the Two World Wars," in *Jewish Assimilation in Modern Times*, ed. Bela Vago (Boulder, Colo.: Westview Press, Inc., 1981), 58. It should be mentioned that Szabo's popularity was in no way tied to his "anti-Semitic" views. Furthermore, he is only the first of many individuals to be mentioned in this study who were of high standing and also "anti-Semitic."

17. Wistrich, *Between Redemption and Perdition*, 38.

18. Orwell, "Antisemitism in Britain," 336-37. Putting this philo-Semitism into practice, historians have rallied to excavate archives and other sources in an attempt to prove the untruth of statements contained in works such as Werner Sombart's *The Jews and Modern Capitalism* or to present his information in a different light.

19. J. W. Parkes, *The Jew and His Neighbour* (London: International Student Service, 1930), 47, 49. Leo Pinsker expressed a similar idea in his work *Auto-Emancipation*, published in 1882. Arthur Hertzberg, *The Zionist Idea* (New York: Atheneum, 1973), 186. In examining the provenance of the term 'anti-Semitism', we find that Wilhelm Marr, while he is credited with coining the term, had no intention of establishing either a new lineage for anti-Jewish sentiment or creating a fundamentally new approach to the Jews (i.e., political anti-Semitism). In various works written by Marr in 1879, Moshe Zimmermann found that Marr's occasional use of 'Semitism' was, like 'Aryanism', simply a substitute for the words 'Orientalism' and 'Germanism'. When pressed, Marr made use of the term anti-Semitism to set atheists (anti-Christians) like himself apart from Stoecker's Christian-social movement which declared itself specifically anti-Jewish (in the religious sense) in September 1879. Not only did his book, *The Victory of Judaism over Germanism* not employ this term, there is no evidence of it in his newspaper, *Deutsche Wacht*, the monthly of the Anti-Jewish Association that was published for five months beginning in November 1879. The decision to incorporate the term anti-Semitic into the name of the Anti-Semitic League—which actually catapulted the term into general use— did not rest with Marr alone, but also Hector de Grousillier, who set up the League and invited Marr to be part of it. Moshe Zimmermann, *Wilhelm Marr: The Patriarch of Anti-Semitism* (New York and Oxford: Oxford University Press, 1986), 89-92.

20. Zoltan Bosnyak, *Prohaszka es a zsido kerdes* [Prohaszka and the Jewish Question] (Budapest: A Magyar Kulturliga kiadasa, 1938), 12-13.

21. Arnold White, *The Modern Jew* (New York: Frederick A. Stokes Company, 1899), 273-75.

22. Elie Weisel, "Looking Back," in *Lessons and Legacies*, ed. Peter Hayes (Evanston, Ill.: Northwestern University Press, 1999), 3:18.

23. Julian Barnes, "Always True to France," *New York Review of Books*, 12 August 1999.

24. I am indebted to both Arthur Hertzberg and I. E. Barzilay, who are among the very few historians who have emphasized the Enlightenment in relation to the Jewish Question. While their arguments are not ones to which I subscribe, their works provided necessary sources on Enlightenment literature as it pertains to the Jews, thus easing my task.

25. T. D. Kramer, *From Emancipation to Catastrophe: The Rise and Holocaust of Hungarian Jewry* (Lanham, Md.: University Press of America, 2000), 7. This notion is so entrenched among Hungarian Jews that in the memorial service on the 50th anniversary of the liberation of the Budapest ghetto, Chief Rabbi Robert Frolich spoke of the period between 1867 and 1914 as the "Golden Age for Jews."

26. Janos Gyurgyak calls mass assimilation of the Jews then and now an "illusion shared by many." *A zsidokerdes Magyarorszagon* [The Jewish Question in Hungary] (Budapest: Osiris Kiado, 2001), 18.

27. Jacob Katz, *Out of the Ghetto* (Cambridge, Mass.: Harvard University Press, 1973), 12. This is also the position of V. D. Lipman, among others. *A History of the Jews in Britain since 1858* (Leicester: Leicester University Press, 1990), 3-4.

28. Kalman Mikszath, quoted in Jeno Zsoldos, ed., *Magyar irodalom es zsidosag. Koltoi es prozai szemelvenyek* [Hungarian Literature and the Jews: Selected Poetry and Prose] (Budapest, 1943), 84-85.

SECTION 1

FROM TOLERATION TO LIBERALISM

Chapter 1
The Era of Toleration

The Jewish Condition

Until emancipation, toleration (in the narrow sense of the word) was the context that determined the historical relationship between Christians and Jews and through this mechanism, a state of equilibrium was maintained between the two religious groups. This position began to evolve early in the second century and was firmly in place by 400 CE. Foremost, "The Jews, having murdered Jesus, had placed themselves outside humanity; spiritually and physically, they were marked as perpetual aliens."[1] Sarah Pearce provides this summary, distilled from numerous contemporary sources:

> ... that the Jewish people have lost their status as the Chosen People of God because of their failure to recognize Jesus as the Messiah, the Christ; that failure, and especially alleged Jewish responsibility for the death of Christ, is seen as the final act in a long series of rebellions and rejections of God on the part of the Jewish people; Jews did not understand the true, spiritual meaning of their own Scripture which, read properly, would lead them to Christ; and the recent catastrophes of 70 CE (the destruction of the Temple) and 135 CE (the expulsion of Jews from Jerusalem and its vicinity) represented the divine punishment of the Jews for the killing of Christ.[2]

Still, it was acknowledged that the two faiths were interconnected. This was expressed by the Augustinian view that "Jews were in the past depositories of divine revelation; they are, in the present, witnesses to the faith preached by their fathers. . . . our very enemies bear witness to our faith."[3] Furthermore, their continued existence was ordained by God for the purpose of acting as witnesses to the truth of Christianity forecast in the Old Testament. So, while papal bulls canonized Jews as inferior and their condition as one of "perpetual servitude"[4] and restrictions were introduced to limit the occasions where Jews might exert influence or authority over Christians "befitting a deicide people," at the same time they were protected: the murder and excessive persecution of Jews was specifically forbidden.[5] Canon law also not only allowed for but guaranteed the rights of Jews to practice their religion: "In accordance with a Divine Mandate [we] are obliged to permit them to observe their law."[6] Never did the Church produce any literature against the continued existence of the Jewish people or their right to practice their religion.

Yet we see that the official position of the Church was at times ignored. During the Crusades, pontiffs' proclamations ordering both the Crusaders and the common people to refrain from inflicting violence upon the Jews fell on deaf ears. Religious zeal inspired extreme interpretations of Christian teachings *vis a vis* the Jews and prompted the Dominicans (followed by the Franciscans) around 1231 to categorize converted Jews who covertly practiced Judaism as heretics; they then became subject to the authority of the Inquisition.[7] Jews were later blamed for the Black Death, which broke out in 1348, and as a result, they were massacred, tried, tortured, and executed, and their quarters continually sacked. Entire communities were wiped out; this, in spite of the fact that in July of 1348 and again in October Pope Clement VI issued a bull which proclaimed the Jews' innocence. Likewise, the charge of ritual murder, also the occasion for widespread attacks, was repeatedly refuted by ecclesiastical authorities.[8] There was also a move to burn and confiscate the Talmud. Yet Pope Innocent IV had recognized the Talmud as that book without which "they are unable to understand the Bible and other ordinances of their Law according to their faith."[9] The implication of these contraventions of formal Church policy for the Jews is that they destabilized the entire theologically based framework of toleration, and, one would have to say, worsened the condition of the Jews.

Over the course of centuries, a litany of complaints was added to this doctrinal position of the Church, underscoring the need to segregate the Jewish community. They mocked and blasphemed the Christian religion in their evil books, insulted it by spitting on and defiling its sacred statues and objects of veneration, and profaned the sacred host.[10] They spread heresy; entered churches and disputed over matters of religion; impeded conversions to the true faith; scandalized Christians by eating meat during Lent; and contaminated "Christian ears by their over-loud psalmody."[11] They employed Christian nurses and servants who, being in such close proximity to Jews, were bound to come under their negative influence.[12] Jews were evil, perpetrators of every kind of crime. Conspiring with human as well as satanic enemies to harm the Christian cause and Christian nations, they were awaiting the coming of the anti-Christ. Decried above all was the purported use of Christian blood (primarily that of children) for ritual or magical purposes. The charge of ritual murder had an enormous impact on the entire Jewish community and was often the provocation for mass burnings at the stake and/or expulsion. It would be difficult to find a Jewish community that was not subjected to this charge at one time or another.

Papal statutes, decrees, enactments, and regulations such as those ultimately passed by the Third and Fourth Lateran Councils of the Catholic Church further concretized the exigencies of Jewish existence. Having legal and social aims, these measures ensured that Jews would be forbidden to be admitted to any judicial function or hold public office; speak or act in a way that cast aspersions on Christianity; profane the Christian Sabbath; hire Christian servants; publish anti-Christian literature; convert Christians to Judaism; hamper proselytizers; or engage in social intercourse with Jews.[13] Especially this last prohibition was facilitated by the introduction of the mandatory Jewish badge.

Marginalization reached its apex in the creation of ghettos. The Church gave the following reasons for the establishment of the ghetto in Rome:

> Since we have learned that in Rome and other places under the control of the Church, the impudence of Jews has reached such proportions that they dare not only to live among Christians but to be seen near churches without distinguishing dress, and that they rent houses on the principal streets and in the principal squares, buy and hold property . . . we find ourselves forced to take the following measures.[14]

The layout of the Rome ghetto was typical: congregated in one street, there was only a single exit, which was gated, and locked at night. Into this space were collected not only all the Jews of Rome but the Jews from the outlying vicinity as well. Ghettos were invariably terribly congested, with little prospect for maintenance or improvement, and the lives of Jews within these walls were heavily regulated.[15]

Coupled with these legal measures was 'ritualized humiliation:' Jews were forced to play a prominent role in the carnival games at Agone and Testaccio (Rome), for example—as the object of mockery and violence. In the sixteenth and seventeenth centuries, they were made to perform naked in the Palio of Siena; and each year during Passion Week, Umbria's Jews were ritually stoned.[16] These humiliations, which had their counterparts in other countries, may be said to have been at once a response to the presence of the "perfidious" Jew and an indirect way of inducing Jews to convert.

The Jew had only one option to escape this tolerated status: conversion was the sole means through which a Jew could gain acceptance into society. Conversion was a step for which Christians fervently prayed. In the meantime, the presence of Jews, and particularly their reluctance to convert, produced a degree of tension within the Church itself as it sought to balance its negative view of Jews with its reverence for them as having once been the vessel of God's word.

The early Church's assessment of the Jews remained in effect and incontrovertible; however, during the ninth and tenth centuries, the burgeoning of national monarchies meant that the fate of the Jews now resided in a revised schematic whereby toleration was exercised at both the religious and secular levels. An additional, secular code of law determined the legality of their presence in any given community. Residency became a matter of royal privilege and was acquired through a charter issued by the king or local potentate. Charters had three major characteristics: they were provisional in nature; they defined Jews as *servi nostrae camerae* (the king's serfs), rendering them chattels or private property; and they demanded certain considerations of a financial nature while offering a measure of protection—the right to practice their religion, albeit in a constricted fashion, and juridical autonomy (recourse to Talmudic law).[17]

The secular basis for toleration was the proviso that Jews be of economic benefit to the host country. Whenever it was perceived that they had become an economic liability, whether through underperformance (i.e., being unable to meet the monetary obligations imposed upon them, inadequately performing their role as moneylenders, or failing to stimulate the economy when it was needed) or overperformance (i.e., being overly competitive with the Christian merchants or charging excessive rates of interest), a reduced level of tolerance was the outcome. While everyone—from monarchs to the masses—tended to uphold the Church's position on refraining from contact with Jews in every other respect, contact with them in the economic sphere was one they were loath to forego. This exceptive approach to the marginalization of the Jews was an ongoing source of tension between every stratum of Christian society and the Church, which not only forbade contact, but stipulated that opportunities should not be given to Jews, "whom their own sin has condemned to eternal servitude."[18]

In assuming ownership of the Jew, monarchs (and in some cases, noblemen) implemented one of the key components of the Jewish condition. The charter outlining the Jews' terms of residence in England is representative of the thousands that were issued over the centuries, identifying the Jews as the king's chattels upon whom he bestowed certain privileges. It granted protection from "misusage" (they were answerable to the king alone, with free recourse to the king's justice and responsible to no other); freedom of movement; relief from ordinary tolls; permission to retain land taken in pledge as security; and special provision to fair trial—all "existing for the king's advantage."[19] Rights of ownership also entailed the disposition of Jewish property at any time. This concept also insinuated itself into the matter of debts owed to Jews, any portion of which could be canceled. It further included the right to sell, pawn, present as a gift, or exchange the Jews themselves. Henry III, for example, once pawned his Jews to Richard of Cornwall and on another occasion gave them over to his son, Edward, who in turn pawned them to their rivals, the Cahorsins.[20] These laws concerning Jews-as-property extended to the most intimate aspects of the Jews' lives. In 1750, Frederick the Great passed a law that in Cleves only the eldest Jewish male was allowed to marry and maintain residence in that town. Such legislation was also in effect throughout most of the eighteenth century in Alsace and much later in Moravia.[21]

Conversionism was practiced both by the Church and the secular authorities. Methods ranged from inducements in the form of monetary rewards, belongings, and even help in establishing converts in a trade[22] to public sermons, which Jews were regularly forced to attend. (In 1584, the Catholic Church institutionalized this approach to conversion.) Public disputations were also staged: debates between a Christian and a Jew, experts in their respective theologies, with the Jewish community in attendance, who were gathered to witness the "defeat of Jewish theology."[23] Recently baptized Jews (whose numbers swelled during the Crusades and the Inquisition) were a fundamental part of the Church's conversion efforts. Whether of their own volition or acting under pressure, these converts gained a reputation as vociferous envoys of the ecclesiastical establishment and public denouncers of Judaism. It is not surprising to learn, then, that the first charge of blood libel (William of Norwich in 1144) was brought forward by a converted Jew, now known as the monk Theobald of Cambridge.[24]

It may be observed that whenever Christians' hopes for conversion were high, toleration was more expansive. The period of the Reformation is a prime example of this. Protestants were convinced that their new, pure version of Christianity would overcome all previous reticence on the part of the Jews and bring about their mass conversion.[25] Consequently, the phenomenon of philo-Semitism swept over seventeenth-century England, forming a significant part of the context in which the readmission of Jews to Britain would be considered. Conversely, when hopes for conversion were minimal, toleration reached a low point. Thus, King Lajos I of Hungary expelled the Jews in 1360 because his campaign to convert them had failed, and Martin Luther, who had initially held out great hopes that a reformed Church would be a natural invitation to the Jews to convert, was bitterly disappointed when it did not. Luther proclaimed that Christians

> should throw brimstone and pitch upon them; if one could hurl hell fire at them, so much the better . . . and this must be done for the honor of Our Lord and of Christianity, so that God may see that we are indeed Christians. Let their houses also be shattered and destroyed . . . let their prayer books and Talmuds be taken from them, and their whole Bible too; let their rabbis be forbidden on pain of death, to teach henceforth anymore. Let the streets and highways be closed against them. Let them be forbidden to practice usury, and let all their money and all their treasures of silver and gold be taken from them and put away in safety. And if all this be not enough, let them be driven like mad dogs out of the land.[26]

Equally, when the sincerity of the conversion was in doubt, toleration plummeted. A striking example of this occurred in Spain. Commencing in the thirteenth century, restrictive laws, a policy of social marginalization, pogroms, and forced conversions prompted thousands to voluntarily convert: between 1412 and 1419, 15,000 to 20,000 Jews found their way to the baptismal font in Aragon alone. After a while, the sincerity of these conversions came under question. "New Christians" were suspected of "Judaizing" (an expression used at the time referring to Jews who were still practicing Judaism in secret) or making efforts to reconvert to Judaism, often with the help of the Jewish community. Furthermore, it was observed that they had kept up certain links with the Jewish community: kinship and other traditional networks, friendships, and the continued use of Hebrew. The Spanish Inquisition was introduced in Castile in 1478 specifically to identify and prosecute these insincere converts.[27]

Forced conversions were always a possibility during the era of Toleration. Sometimes individuals were targeted: the Mortara case of forced conversion involving a Jewish child in Bologna in 1858 is only the most publicized case of its kind.[28] Occasionally, mass conversions were decreed, as occurred in Portugal in 1497, where the entire Jewish population was converted.[29] Forced conversions were an ongoing problem in Hungary throughout the eighteenth century, and the Empress Maria Theresa felt called upon to issue her own prohibition of this act in 1763. It had little impact, and subsequently, the municipal authorities stepped in, threatening to punish anyone who baptized a child without the consent of its parents.[30]

Expulsions were occasionally generated by the Jews' recalcitrance in the matter of conversion, but more often by economic over- or underperformance. England was the first country to expel its Jews (1290) and its decision to keep them out for hundreds of years was far from unique. Spain followed the same pattern: Jews were forbidden there from 1492 until the mid-nineteenth century. In France, the Jews were expelled in 1394 (with the exception of Provence, which expelled them at the end of the sixteenth century). "Jews, known under the name of Portuguese, otherwise called New Christians" began to arrive there shortly after 1492, but only in 1638, with the conquest of Alsace, did France acquire self-confessed Jews again.[31] The situation in Russia was similar. Expelled under Ivan IV (1533-84), measures were taken by successive tsars to keep Jews out. They were the unhappy baggage acquired during the partitioning of Poland (1772, 1793, and 1795). Far into the eighteenth century the practice of expelling Jews continued. In a few cases, such as Sweden and Norway, the issue of expulsion was bypassed by not admitting Jews until 1774 and 1851 respectively. In most jurisdictions, expulsions lasted only a few years. As soon as the need arose, Jews were invited back; and it often happened that Jews would reinhabit a town several times. This phenomenon highlights the Jew as an economic entity, whose sole value was based on his ability to enhance the economic well-being of various sectors of the population. Whenever there was a dispute between the parties, as sometimes happened between the monarch and the merchants, as long as the Jews were performing to the king's advantage, they were permitted to stay. The Church's extremely negative attitude towards usury coupled with the fact that Jews were prohibited from practicing most occupations meant that Jews became heavily involved in this profession, so much so, that it was designated a Jewish profession.[32] Almost as valuable as the function of moneylending were the taxes extracted from Jews. In every country, Jews were considered an automatic source of revenue, and it was their inability to pay these taxes that was a frequent cause of expulsion, as occurred in England.

The contours of the 'Jewish Condition' were established by the Church's theological structure of marginalization. They were both adapted and compromised by the appearance of national monarchies: adapted by the monarchs' introduction of the notion of ownership; compromised by their violation of the Church's stand of ostracizing the Jews in order to enrich themselves. Still, it was recognized that the official nexus between Christians and Jews could only be the Jews' conversion. Until then, the state of degradation would persist, and a policy of conversionism would be pursued. Expulsion was a solution employed by both religious and secular authorities whenever conversionism or economic over- or underperformance became significant issues. With the Enlightenment, the framework of toleration would come under examination.

Hungary

In Hungary, the Christianization of the inhabitants and the emergence of a national monarchy more or less coincided. Having undergone baptism, King István I (r. 997-1038) was most enthusiastic to see Christianity entrenched and he ordered all Magyars baptized, by force, if necessary. Despite the fact that Hungary was now a Christian nation, the Church's framework of toleration towards the Jews was not applied during Istvan's reign, and even the Council of Szabolcs (1092) issued laws which only prescribed punishment for the following: marriage to Christian women, owning Christian slaves, and working on Sunday. The reason for this non-application of Church doctrine may be that since the end of the ninth century, when Magyars settled in the Carpathian Basin, they had coexisted peacefully as pagan and Jew. Altering the parameters of this relationship would not occur immediately.

In 1096, the Crusaders arrived in Hungary and, as elsewhere, they plundered and attacked not only the Jews but also the Christian population. Hungary launched an energetic and successful campaign against the Crusaders—seeking to protect the Christian population and only incidentally the Jews. Mistakenly, then, Hungary gained the reputation of being a haven for Jews and attracted many who were fleeing from the Crusaders. This influx quickly prompted further decrees circumscribing the place of Jews in Christian society. A relatively timid process in the beginning (with the exception, perhaps, of wearing an identifying badge), it was not until 1251 that the status of the Jews really became codified under King Bela IV (r. 1235-70). Borrowing from the Jewish Laws of Frederick II the Bellicose (1244), this meant that the Jews in Hungary, Austria, and Germany enjoyed approximately the same status.[33] In adopting these laws, Bela clearly favored a financial policy that would enable the Jews to perform at a high economic level. What he did not favor was the duplicity of those who had converted to Christianity only to obtain public office, yet remained to all intents and purposes Jewish. In 1235, he vowed to "exterminate the false Christians with all [his] might."[34] King Lajos I the Great (r. 1343-82) was also confronted with the attachment Jews had to Judaism. Approaching their conversion in a manner consistent with the Church's format, he first employed persuasion, in conjunction with incentives and rewards such as full tax exemption.[35] When this tactic failed, Jews were compelled to listen to sermons by the Church prelates exhorting them to convert and when this tactic, too, failed to achieve the desired outcome, "Ludovicus [Lajos] in his religious zeal ... since he could not carry this intention of his ["to win them for Christ"] because of the Jews' headstrong stubbornness, liberated all the Jews in the whole of the kingdom of Hungary and ordered their expulsion" in 1360.[36] Why Lajos readmitted the Jews after only a four-year absence must be explained by his grim financial situation and the need to raise funds to counter the threat posed by the Turks.[37]

Not all the Jews accepted his invitation to come back; there were pros and cons to returning. On the other hand, the rate set by the city of Pressburg for borrowing money was 43.33 per cent annually for larger loans and 86.75 per cent for smaller ones under one pound; and seventy-five years later, King Sigismund's (1385-95 [as consort], r. 1395-1436) letter patent stated that if a Christian took out a loan, in general, unless there were specific terms, the Christian borrower had to pay two denars weekly per hundred denars borrowed, an annual interest rate of 100 per cent.[38] On the other hand, when the need arose, the king modified his laws to increase the Jewish contribution to his revenue.[39] Subsequent monarchs, King Laszlo V (r. 1453-58), King Matthias Corvinus (r. 1458-90), and King Lajos II (r. 1516-26) all pursued policies similar to that of Sigismund.

As elsewhere, a Jew who was willing to jettison his formal adherence to the Jewish community was capable of attaining immense fortune, power, and position, thus extricating himself from the pervasive Jewish condition. Such a Jew in Hungary was Shneur Zalman (1460?-1525), known as Szerencses (Fortunatus) after his conversion. Providing large loans to the treasury proved extremely lucrative and in time, he became very influential at the royal court, where he gained the favor of the king and queen. He was then appointed sub-treasurer of Hungary while serving as advisor to both Laszlo Szalkay, who acted for the king, and the current state palatine. Eventually, his role in public office was to the degree that he was appointed a member of the council of state.

Fortunatus's death preceded by one year what is regarded as the most cataclysmic event in Hungary's history: its defeat at the hands of the Ottoman Turks at Mohacs in 1526. Known as the Mohacs Disaster, the Ottomans went on to capture Buda (which they made the capital of their newest province) and gained complete control of the central part of Hungary by 1541, an occupation that would last in parts of the region until 1715. The conquest divided Hungary into three parts: Royal (Habsburg) Hungary in the west and the north, Turkish Hungary in the middle, and the Principality of Transylvania in the east (established by the sultan in 1541), and this division had a number of ramifications for the Jews. In the region under Ottoman occupation, the millet system was put into place. Millets were autonomous, non-Muslim communities whose inhabitants were permitted the free exercise of religion and unrestricted pursuit of economic activities while being obligated to fulfill rigorous tax requirements. This peaceful subjugation created reasonably favorable conditions for the Jews, unknown to them under the Hungarians, and brought about the transfer of these Jews' loyalty to their Turkish rulers. It was also the motivating factor for a number of Jews to move from Transylvania and Royal Hungary to the Ottoman-occupied territory, a move that did not go unnoticed by the Austrian authorities.[40]

Those Jews living in the Principality of Transylvania—more precisely, in the city of Gyulafehervar—for they were excluded everywhere else, experienced such harsh treatment that the Prince of Transylvania was often called upon to intercede on the Jews' behalf. Still, as was usual, certain Jews obtained the highest of positions at court. The attitude towards the Jews in Royal Hungary may be evidenced by the desire of the Diet to expel all those who remained under their authority. While this resolution was annulled, expulsions did take place, including from the two most important cities in Royal Hungary, Sopron and Pressburg, as well as two towns that were the site of blood libel cases. Seen as a trend, the leaders of Hungarian Jewry communicated with Pope Paul III, appealing for protection. In response, he issued an encyclical which condemned the blood libel, affirmed the privileges extended to the Jews by the Church, and ordered that the clergy protect the Jews.[41]

During the reconquest of Buda in 1686, punishment for their displaced loyalty to the Ottoman Turks was meted out to the Jews: approximately half of the city's 1,000 Jews were massacred and the other half were captured and held for ransom. Along with this, the Jews' homes and property were looted and destroyed. Reformation Protestants, a significant number in Hungary, now advocated the complete removal of the Jewish population, while the Royal Hungarian Lord Lieutenancy wanted at least to limit Jewish immigration. However, pragmatism determined their future treatment. The Habsburgs saw some value in their presence as suppliers of money and provisioners to complete the rout of the Ottomans; and they could further help repopulate Hungary, whose numbers had dropped from a pre-invasion figure of about four million in the latter half of the fifteenth century to 3.5 million in 1729 (while Europe as a whole during the same period had risen from 80 to 130 million). The treasury, in particular, saw the Jews as a needed source of income to be generated through taxes and services. The Church, in its capacity as landlord, along with the landed estate owners, supported the settlement of Jews, for both were familiar with the equation that more Jews meant more money.[42]

The following picture emerges of eighteenth-century Jewry in a reunited Hungary. The practical consequence of the expulsions, combined with the general devastation in central Hungary over the course of Turkish rule, had been to locate increasing numbers of Jews on the estates of the great magnates, but laws of residency also contributed to this trend. They were generally banned from the Royal Free cities—and emphatically so from the mining towns and its environs. As of 1749, Jews resided in only nine of the thirty-seven Royal Free cities. It was in 'private cities,' in reality no more than villages located on a magnate's estate, that most Jews lived. There, many of them derived their income from acting as middlemen between the magnates and the peasants. Typically, they ran flour mills, managed the sale of agricultural produce, and collected tolls. They also bought up some of the peasants' wares and in turn peddled merchandise to them (such as wool, wine, candles, and soap) on the estates and throughout the country. In the wine trade and as liquor distillery lessees they played a major role, in spite of the fact that it was illegal for them to do so. Upwards of twenty-five per cent of the Jews made their living as innkeepers and publicans. While this description applies to the majority of Jews, there was an upper stratum of import and export traders and a certain number who were permitted to practice manual trades and work as artisans in order to fulfill the needs of the Jewish community.[43]

A typical 'tax profile' may have looked something like this. In 1735, a Jewish family living in the village of Boldogasszony had to pay 40 florins to the village; 12 florins for the use of the pasture to the village; 150 florins to the manor in Magyarovar; 40 florins to the Cistercian order; and 12 florins to the Chapter of the Cathedral in Gyor.[44] Beyond this, Jews became obligated to pay a Toleration Tax: an annual head tax in the amount of two florins instituted by the Empress Maria Theresa (r. 1740-80).*

---

* In the first year the Toleration Tax was applied, 20,000 florins were collected from the Jewish community; by 1812, this amount had risen to 160,000 florins. And in 1813, the tax was doubled. Not only do these figures show that the Jews substantially added to the coffers of Vienna, they also reflect the steady increase in the Jewish population throughout the eighteenth century, from 10,000 in 1749 to almost 80,000 around 1810. Patai, *Jews of Hungary*, 201-2.

In assessing the situation of the Jews between the reunification of Hungary and the end of Maria Theresa's reign in 1780—and taking into account that the post-Ottoman period was one of intense adjustment—one may say that life was somewhat easier and more predictable for the Jews, for the following reason. Those who were strongly opposed to a Jewish presence kept them out. Expulsions dotted the eighteenth-century landscape: Jews were expelled from Dalmatia, Croatia, and Slavonia in 1729. The question of Jews living in Buda continued to be a sensitive one, and in 1746, Jews were once again expelled, temporarily, at the instruction of Maria Theresa.[45] Those who could make use of the Jews treated them well enough to ensure that they would be of value. The Jewish community itself has provided us with a self-portrait which describes their condition at this time.

> To our greatest pain, we have been despised until now, but not because of our own fault; here and there they treated us not as is customary to treat human beings and the inhabitants of the same country but like slaves, not to say draft oxen. We have been driven from city to city, from village to village, often exposed to the ridicule, derision, insult of the mob, even on the highways and the crossroads, though it is necessary that every traveler should have secure and safe journey on them, the mischievous youths not infrequently threw stones at us, unpunished.[46]

Britain

A generally prosperous existence was maintained by the Jewish community for some time after they arrived in England around 1066. The privileges granted in the royal charter ensured this, notwithstanding a pattern of fining Jews on any pretext, occasional accusations of ritual murder, and violent actions against them during the Crusades. This lasted until the reign of King John (r. 1199-1216), after which, and applied with even greater vigor by King Henry III (r. 1216-72) who followed him, Jews were systematically fined and taxed. Reaching extortionist levels, the economic stability of the Jewish community was almost ruined. The final blow was delivered by the nobility who were extremely indebted to the Jews: they destroyed the debt records and furthermore engaged in looting, rioting, and executions.[47] In an attempt to undo the collective damage wreaked upon the Jews, King Edward I (r. 1272-1307) tried, through radical reforms, to resuscitate the Jewish community to the point where it could once again function as the Royal 'milch-cow'. He was unsuccessful. With the terms of toleration abrogated—"No Jew shall remain in England unless he serve the king," stated Henry III, and, as the Patent Roles of 1274 indicate, a number of Jews were in arrears with respect to taxes[48]—coupled with pressures from the Church, there was no justification for a continued Jewish presence in England. Edward I thus ordered their expulsion in 1290. The Jews would not be legal residents of England again until the mid-seventeenth century.

The restoration of King Charles II in 1660 provided a window of opportunity for Jews who would "promise themselves the effects of the same favour as formerly they have had, soe long as they demeane themselves peaceably and quietly with due obedience to his Majesties Lawes and without scandall to his Government," "in and about Your Majesties City of London" (22 August 1664).[49] A tiny number of Spanish and Portuguese crypto-Jews who had taken up residence in England then came forward to identify themselves as Jews, and with this, Jewish resettlement formally commenced. While the Sephardi Jewish settlers felt their presence in England to be tentative,[50] it was not fraught with continental perils; and so, with each persecution in Europe there was a transfer of some Eastern European Jews to the British Isles. Thus, between 1664 and 1768, the Jewish population went from zero (officially) to approximately 7,000, of whom more than two-thirds were Ashkenazi Jews. The next thirty years saw a further diluting of the Sephardi community as the total Jewish population swelled to 21,000.[51] Like all other European countries, Britain now evidenced the typical two-tiered nature of the Jewish community: a narrow stratum of Jews who possessed great wealth and an impoverished majority.*

In the immediate post-readmission era, representations of Jews were derived from late seventeenth-century playwrights who regularly employed medieval imagery;[52] reports from abroad that depicted Jews negatively, such as the kidnapping of a potential convert by his coreligionists;[53] and those few Sephardi merchants who lived in London.

> As for Jews, they may well bear somewhat extraordinary, because they seldom eat and drink with Christians, hold it no disparagement to live frugally and even sordidly among themselves, by which way alone they became able to under-sell any other Traders, to elude the Excize, which bears but according to men's expenses; as also other Duties by dealing so much in Bills of Exchange, Jewels, and Money, and by practising of several frauds with more impunity than others; for by their being at home everywhere and yet nowhere they become responsible for almost nothing.[54]

Privileges, not legal rights, sustained the Jewish community's presence: hence, the repeated suggestions that they be segregated as they were before the expulsion and a judge's refusal in 1667 to allow a Jewish plaintiff to bring forward a suit for the recovery of a debt, for, in the judge's words, the Jews were "perpetual enemies."[55] Their religious status was also fragile: their right to public worship was regularly challenged, and in 1685, nearly half of London's Jews were arrested for not attending Church (based on a resurrected Elizabethan statute). Jews were further elected to the office of Churchwarden—a position they could neither protest nor hold—and exemption from which was the payment of a

---

* While this structure seems to resemble that of non-Jewish society, there is a crucial difference. Whereas the wealth of the nobility was derived from the very structure of society and largely accumulated through various kinds of sanctioned appropriations from the peasants in the form of taxation, crops, and labor, Jewish wealth was generated by financial interactions conducted outside of the Jewish community.

heavy fine. The pattern of encouraging Jews to convert persisted, indicated by the regular publication of pamphlets and books on the subject.[56] Jews who criticized Christianity were the objects of sharp censure. When they "presumed to correct Christian misreadings of sacred scriptures, and when they had the audacity to even ridicule Christian articles of faith and recall those embarrassing disagreements among Christians themselves, they had crossed the line of civility and proper Jewish behavior."[57]

The disproportionate incidence of criminality among Eastern European (Ashkenazi) Jews who had recently arrived in England was a prominent issue late in the eighteenth century.[58] An explanation for this deviant behavior was proffered by the police magistrate of London, Patrick Colquhoun, in *A Treatise on the Police of the Metropolis*.

> If the superstitious observance of institutions, with regard to meat not killed by Jews, and to the Jewish Sabbath, shall exclude these youths from being bound to useful employment, and mixing with the mass of the people, by becoming servants or apprentices; surely it is proper some care should be taken that they shall not become public nuisances; an evil that must inevitably arise from a perseverance, in the system which now prevails, in the education and habits of this numerous class of people; and which is directly hostile to the interests of the State, and to the preservation of morals.[59]

A complete overhauling of Jewish practices conjoined with "useful and productive labour [for] the numerous youths of that persuasion who are at present rearing up in idleness, profligacy, and crimes" would improve this "depraved race."[60]

In comparison to these destitute immigrants, the original Sephardi settlers (consisting of no more then one thousand Jews) had been able to bear the levy of a poll tax on top of another tax of £100,000, plus a forced loan, and the imposition of alien duties by King William III in order to accomplish his Glorious Revolution in the late 1680s.[61] By the Restoration period (1660-1685), the Venetian trade was predominantly in the hands of Sephardi Jews. They had garnered a number of army contracts: Solomon de Medina was referred to as "the King's great Jewish army contractor." By 1712, they were the primary suppliers of gold to the Bank of England. At the payment of the sixty-fifth half-yearly dividend in 1726, the largest proprietor of bank stock was the Sephardi Jew, Francis Pereira.[62] An obituary of Joseph Salvador described him as "formerly a most eminent merchant in England, being one of those who furnished that Government with a million of money in two hours' notice, during the rebellion in the year 1745."[63] By the mid-1700s, two of the twelve guarantors of the Bank of England were Jews; Jews subscribed twenty-five per cent of government loans and further bolstered the stability of the Government by importing bullion. In fact, it was regarded as a "Jewish specialty,"[64] as was the export of coral from Leghorn to India. They dealt extensively in the diamond trade and largely managed the West Indian silk and cotton trade.[65] It is the opinion of Werner Sombart that "Jews played, if not the most decisive, at any rate a most prominent part" in colonial expansion.[66]

In 1732, the British ambassador to Portugal wrote that the "greatest dealers to Portugal in our woollen goods are the Jews in London."[67] Historian Harold Pollins acknowledges that verifying this statement with any precision is difficult because, on the one hand, due to the Inquisition in Portugal, Anglo-Jewish traders were compelled to hide their Jewish identity so that their goods would not be confiscated, and on the other hand, they sought to protect family members still living there as *conversos* who were also involved in this trade. The obvious solution was subterfuge: the falsification of names coupled with the use of Christian, mostly English-speaking correspondents in Lisbon. However, a study mentioned by Pollins disputes the English ambassador's claim because of the paucity of Jewish names listed as signatories of memorials of trade. Discounting the good reasons for this, Pollins has supported this study and attempted to discredit the ambassador. He has done the same thing with regard to Jewish involvement in the tobacco market, which rose to the extent that in 1774, Joshua and Jacob de Fonseca Brandon of London were reported to be the "greatest Tobacco Brokers in England." This claim, too, is disputed by Pollins, who writes that it has no basis in fact. I would suggest that such revised versions which minimize Jewish involvement in the economic sphere stem less from a desire to 'set the record straight' than from a perceived need to redeem the Jew in history. If it can be proven that the Jews in London were not the "greatest dealers to Portugal"—after having considered how many Jewish traders there were in total; what share of the trade they controlled; and, out of the total number of dealers in woolen goods, what the percentage of Jews was—the influence of Jews in the economy may be minimized and perhaps serve as ammunition to undercut one of the main arguments used by 'anti-Semites': that Jews have always had economic power far beyond their numbers. Other historians may wish to challenge these examples of Jewish monopolies not on the ground that they are false but that they are not representative of the Jewish community as a whole. I would argue that representativeness was not among the concerns of the contemporary society. That any Jews had, or were believed to have had a monopoly over one or more areas of trade and commerce—this was the source of their concern and proof that Jews played an instrumental role in domestic and international markets. The uproar over the Naturalization Bill, known as the Jew Bill—which was passed in May 1753 and repealed in December of the same year—produced bounteous evidence of the perceived economic influence of the Jews at this time.[68]

Not surprisingly then, in many eighteenth-century plays, poetry, novels, and satirical essays, the image of the Sephardi Jew revolved around his money.[69] Initially, he hoarded it. Later, this miser began to put his money to many uses: bringing about indebtedness among the population; satisfying his appetite for Christian women; attempting to buy his entry into society; and transforming himself into a dandy.[70] While pursuing such endeavors, he was still speaking a jargon form of English and was dirty.[71] Arthur Murphy's play *The Temple of Laverna* (1752) is only one of many written during the mid- to late-eighteenth century which makes the point that Jews possessed considerable economic power. In the minds of many Englishmen, this power naturally led to Jews contemplating entry into the political arena: "We are told, Sir, that you intend to offer yourself as a Candidate for Middlesex . . . everybody is surprised that a gentleman of your fortune does not get into Parliament." While this Jewish gentleman does not want a political career for himself (perhaps for his son), such Jews are "the very Atlas of the state! Our ministers have recourse to him in all their distresses, and are never able to carry any point, I mean in the money-way, but when he co-operates with them."[72] Driven by "their unquenchable thirst for wealth," such Jews were compared unfavorably with "the generality of Englishmen [who] know where to stop and repose themselves in the bosom of affluence, unannoyed by the cares of trade, [while] the Jew studies the arithmetic of infinites incessantly and never delays his progress one instant."[73]

As the eighteenth century drew to a close, Jews still perceived their political status in terms of privileges rather than rights. In 1787, the Jews of England wrote this response to the Jews of Rome who had inquired as to the condition of their brethren in England.

> The privileges of the Jews in this country must not serve as a rule for their privileges in other countries, as the government is very different. Where sovereigns are absolute, the Jews may enjoy advantages to a greater or lesser extent, but in this kingdom, even if his Majesty wished to favour them, he could not do so without the consent of Parliament, consisting of 500 or 600 Nobles and Commons. This makes it very difficult to obtain the privileges we need, and which would be very useful to us. The only privileges enjoyed by our nation are equal to all those enjoyed abroad, and these consist of the free exercise of our religion and the security of our property.[74]

The Bedford Charity case of 1818-19 shows that in the eyes of some legal authorities the theologically based position towards the Jews was still applicable. The court was charged with deciding the eligibility of Jews as recipients of a fund (which provided a variety of benefits to the inhabitants of Bedford) established in the reign of King Edward VI. The Solicitor General, in explaining his decision against the Jews, acknowledged that they were permitted to live in England at this juncture, but "though born in this country, yet professing Judaism, the law distinguished them as alien enemies;" "nor can it be supposed that Edward the Sixth, a most religious monarch, designed to found an establishment for the support of infidels by letters patent."[75]

Jews aspiring to enter the legal profession found their former indemnity from the sacramental test (a requirement before being called to the bar) nullified in 1828,[76] and until that year there had been a quota on Jewish stockbrokers. The repeal of the Tests and Corporation Acts, also in 1828, enabled Dissenters to participate in the political life of the nation; however, the operative phrase in the new bill, "on the true faith of a Christian," excluded Jews.* Jews were further

---

* Katz, *Jews in the History of England*, 384. David Katz has argued that their status thus seemed worse than before because, prior to 1828, this political disability was shared with Nonconformists. However, Melvin Scult has pointed out that even before the formal repeal, the comparison between Jews and Dissenters would be inaccurate because Indemnity Acts had been passed annually for some time enabling Dissenters to hold office. "Conversion of the Jews," 241.

excluded from the 'Freedom of the City'—the right to engage in retail trade within London's borders—until 1828, when it was extended to converted Jews, and then in 1830 to practicing Jews. Attempts were made to hamper the Jews' right to practice their religion as late as 1829.[77] Isaac D'Israeli's lament in 1797 was accurate concerning the prohibition against owning land (although it was not stringently enforced); as late as 1830, the Solicitor General determined that legislation was needed in order to clarify this aspect of Jewish rights, and the law was not formally struck down until 1846.[78] The very legality of Jewish settlement itself was only resolved that same year.

Obligated to support their own hospitals and to provide for their poor, at the same time, "the poor's rates and the various other parish assessments are levied without distinction to Jew or Gentile, to bond or free, but the inmate of the workhouse is exclusively confined to one class."[79]

> They are incapacitated from the advantages and rights which others enjoy. Thus, whilst they are compelled to serve on juries, to act as Constables and Headboroughs, any step in the honourable profession of law is strictly denied to them; they cannot take place at the Bar; they dare not aspire to the Bench; from these as well as from all other offices of dignity or value they are effectually shut out, either by the nature of the oaths proposed or by the mode of administering them; but neither of these means avails them to escape from the minor offices, the drudgeries which all would be glad to avoid; in those cases, when their services are desirable, the oaths are so altered, both in substance and in the mode of administering them, as to be accordant with their religious principles.[80]

The ability to gain an education was made almost impossible by the stricture forbidding the Jewish community to financially support its own schools, on the one hand, and by exclusionary regulations in the public schools or the mandatory Christian component, on the other. They were also barred from entering most professions: law and medicine were the exceptions, that is, if the aspiring medical student could find placement outside the universities, from which he was excluded.[81] The few Jews who became prominent in fields restricted to Christians did so by converting. Such a man was Isaac D'Israeli.

> They [the Jews] groaned in ages of persecution, and in ages of toleration they are degraded. In England it is doubtful whether the Jews be citizens, they are merely tolerated inhabitants; even this express is too gentle. . . . This British land, which when the slave touches it he becomes free, retains the child of Jacob in abject degradation. The Jew cannot purchase the house which he inhabits, and is not permitted to elevate himself among his horde by professions which might ennoble his genius and dignify his people. [*Vaurien* (1797)][82]

Notes

1. Todd M. Endelman, *The Jews of Georgian England 1714–1830* (Philadelphia: Jewish Publication Society of America, 1979), 87.

2. Sarah Pearce, "Attitudes of Contempt: Christian Anti-Judaism and the Bible," in *Cultures of Ambivalence and Contempt: Studies in Jewish-non-Jewish Relations*, ed. Ian

Jones, Tony Kushner, and Sarah Pearce (London: Vallentine Mitchell, 1998), 59-60. See also Gerhard Falk, *The Jew in Christian Theology: Martin Luther's anti-Jewish Von Schem Hamphoras*. . . . (Jefferson, N.C.: McFarland & Company, Inc., Publishers, 1992), 5.

3. St. Augustine, quoted in Melvin Meyer Scult, "The Conversion of the Jews and the Origins of Jewish Emancipation in England" (Ph.D. diss., Brandeis University, 1968), 1-5, 7, 15.

4. Papal bull issued by Pope Innocent III in 1205, quoted in Anna Foa, *The Jews of Europe after the Black Death*, trans. Andrea Grover (1992; Berkeley and Los Angeles: University of California Press, 2000), 27.

5. James W. Parkes, *The Jew in the Medieval Community: A Study of his Political and Economic Situation* (London: Soncino Press, 1938), 101-4.

6. Pope Innocent IV writing in 1247, quoted in Foa, *Jews of Europe*, 32.

7. Foa, *Jews of Europe*, 29-30.

8. Foa, *Jews of Europe*, 13-21.

9. Pope Innocent IV, quoted in Foa, *Jews of Europe*, 32.

10. Parkes, *Jew in the Medieval Community*, 86, 124; Patai, *Jews of Hungary*, 75.

11. Cecil Roth, *A History of the Jews in England* (Oxford: Oxford University Press, 1941), 59. Concerning "over-loud psalmody," the proximity of the synagogue in Pozsony, Hungary (now Bratislava in the Slovak Republic) to a Cistercian monastery resulted in a complaint being lodged against the Jews, and in 1335, Pope Benedict XII ordered the destruction of the synagogue. Sandor Scheiber, *Magyarorszagi Zsido Feliratok: A III Szazadtol 1686-ig* [Jewish Inscriptions in Hungary from the Third Century to 1686] (Budapest: Magyar Izraelitak Orszagos Kepviselete kiadasa, 1960), 67.

12. Roth, *History of the Jews*, 59.

13. Roth, *History of the Jews*, 163.

14. Papal bull issued by Pope Paul IV in 1555, quoted in Foa, *Jews of Europe*, 138-39.

15. Foa, *Jews of Europe*, 140-41.

16. Foa, *Jews of Europe*, 46.

17. Jacob Katz, *Exclusiveness and Tolerance: Studies in Jewish-Gentile Relations in Medieval and Modern Times* (New York: Schocken Books, 1962), 5-7; Guido Kisch, *The Jews in Medieval Germany: A Study of Their Legal and Social Status* (New York: Ktav Publishing House, 1970), 135. See Parkes, *Jew in the Medieval Community*, chaps. 4-6 for a thorough description of Jewish life under the charter system.

18. Pope Urban IV, quoted in Patai, *Jews of Hungary*, 57. "The Bishops have no concern with our Jews," English civil authorities aggressively pronounced to the Church. Quoted in Roth, *History of the Jews*, 40-41.

19. Quoted in Roth, *History of the Jews*, 6.

20. Parkes, *Jew in the Medieval Community*, 116-22.

21. Arthur Hertzberg, *The French Enlightenment and the Jews: The Origins of Modern Anti-Semitism* (New York: Columbia University Press, 1968, 1990), 113; Michael Laurence Miller, "Rabbis and Revolution: A Study in Nineteenth-Century Moravian Jewry" (PhD diss., Columbia University, 2004), 160-63.

22. Scult, "Conversion of the Jews," 10-11. Such help was reasonable in light of the fact that in the act of converting the neophyte erased his previous life: Jews therefore lost title to everything they owned but also, it should be mentioned, the obligation to repay any debts they owed. Patai, *Jews of Hungary*, 82.

23. Quoted in Foa, *Jews of Europe*, 45, 88-89.

24. *Thomas of Monmouth*, in *The Life and Miracles of St. William of Norwich*. . . ., trans. and ed. A. Jessop and M. R. James (Cambridge: Cambridge University Press, 1896), 93.

25. Scult, "Conversion of the Jews," 45-51; Roth, *History of the Jews*, 149; James W. Parkes, "Jewish-Christian Relations in England," in *Three Centuries of Anglo-Jewish History: A Volume of Essays*, ed. V. D. Lipman (Cambridge: Jewish Historical Society of England, 1961), 154-55.

26. Martin Luther, quoted in Falk, *Jew in Christian Theology*, 67-68. In this book, Falk has produced the first translation of Luther's foremost tract on the Jews, *Vom Schem Hamphoras und vom Geschlecht Christi* [Of the Unknowable Name and the Generations of Christ] written in 1543. On Luther, see also Elisabeth Maxwell, "Silence or Speaking Out," in *Cultures of Ambivalence and Contempt: Studies in Jewish-non-Jewish Relations*, ed. Sian Jones, Tony Kushner and Sarah Pearce (London: Vallentine Mitchell, 1998), 86.

27. Foa, *Jews of Europe*, 83-89.

28. Foa, *Jews of Europe*, 210.

29. Solomon Grayzel, *A History of the Jews from the Babylonian Exile to the Present* (1947; repr., Canada: Meridian / Penguin Books Canada Limited, 1984), 365-67.

30. Patai, *Jews of Hungary*, 189, 203.

31. Quoted in Foa, *Jews of Europe*, 177-80.

32. By the early thirteenth century, it was made a sin for Christians to engage in moneylending at any rate of interest. The Jews, however, were prohibited only from charging immoderate usury at the Fourth Lateran Council in 1215. Foa, *Jews of Europe*, 17-18, 35, 39-40, 110-118, 124-25; Patai, *Jews of Hungary*, 63, 69, 73-74, 76, 81, 88, 93-94. See Parkes, *Jew in the Medieval Community*, part 3, "The Royal Usurer," 267-382, for a comprehensive discussion of usury and the Jews' role in it.

33. Patai, *Jews of Hungary*, 40-41, 47-51.

34. King Bela IV, quoted in Patai, *Jews of Hungary*, 46.

35. Patai, *Jews of Hungary*, 82.

36. The chronicler, Janos Turoczi, quoted in Patai, *Jews of Hungary*, 56. As property of the king, until Jews were "liberated", they were unable to leave the country.

37. Patai, *Jews of Hungary*, 60.

38. Regarding usury, two points should be made here. One is that usury was legal; the Law Book of Buda only remarks that the usurer "will be responsible for it on the Day of Judgment." The other is that while the city of Pressburg set the interest rate formally, the Jewish moneylenders actually pre-set it by refusing to lend money below a certain rate of interest. Quoted in Patai, *Jews of Hungary*, 65, 72-73.

39. To cultivate the goodwill of the cities, King Sigismund initiated the practice of "letter killing," which exempted Christians from paying interest on the loans owed to Jews. For the same purpose, he issued a decree endowing the barons of the realm the right of "keeping and owning Jews." To keep the Jews performing at a high level, he agreed to reaffirm the 1251 Jew Law of King Bela IV, which had been ignored by the municipalities and later—the Jews having paid him a huge sum to do so—Sigismund granted them new privileges. Quoted in Patai, *Jews of Hungary*, 69.

40. Coincident with one of the attempts by the Austrians to recapture Buda, a rumor was circulating in Padua in 1684 that the Buda Jews had bribed the pashas not to enter into peace negotiations with Austria. Patai, *Jews of Hungary*, 164-66, 177, 186.

41. Patai, *Jews of Hungary*, 113-14, 202.

42. Patai, *Jews of Hungary*, 187-89, 201-3.

43. Raphael Mahler, *A History of Modern Jewry* (London: Vallentine, Mitchell & Co. Ltd, 1971), 277; Patai, *Jews of Hungary*, 154-57.

44. Istvan Veghazi, "The Role of Jewry in the Economic Life of Hungary," *Hungarian Jewish Studies* 2, ed. Randolph L. Braham (New York: World Federation of Hungarian Jews, 1966-1973), 52-54.

45. Patai, *Jews of Hungary*, 201-2.

46. Quoted in Patai, *Jews of Hungary*, 219. This excerpt was part of an application (1790) to the Hungarian Diet written in the name of "the community of the Jews living in Hungary" requesting an improvement in the conditions of the Jews.

47. Roth, *History of the Jews*, 32-37, 43-73; Parkes, "Jewish-Christian Relations," 149-50; Bernard Glassman, *Anti-Semitic Stereotypes Without Jews: Images of the Jews in England, 1290–1700* (Detroit: Wayne State University Press, 1975), chap. 1.

48. King Henry III, quoted in Parkes, *Jew in the Medieval Community*, 108; Roth, *History of the Jews*, 68.

49. Sir Henry Bennett, quoted in David S. Katz, *The Jews in the History of England 1485–1850* (Oxford: Oxford University Press, 1994), 140-42.

50. There were a number of proposals to expel the newly readmitted Jews. Bernard Glassman, *Protean Prejudice: Anti-Semitism in England in the Age of Reason* (Atlanta: Scholars Press, 1998), 148-49; Glassman, *Anti-Semitic Stereotypes*, 136-37.

51. Roth, *History of the Jews*, 223, 233.

52. See Esther L. Panitz's book, *The Alien in Their Midst: Images of Jews in English Literature* (East Brunswick, N.J.: Associated University Presses, Inc., 1981).

53. Glassman, *Protean Prejudice*, 167-70, 175.

54. Sir William Petty, "A Treatise on Taxes and Contributions," in *The Economic Writings of Sir William Petty, 2 volumes in 1* (1662; repr., Fairfield, N.J.: Augustus M. Kelley Publishers, 1986), 84.

55. Quoted in Roth, *History of the Jews*, 180-81.

56. Parkes, "Jewish-Christian Relations," 164; Glassman, *Anti-Semitic Stereotypes*, chap. 6.

57. Anglican cleric Anselm Bayly, quoted in David B. Ruderman, *Jewish Enlightenment in an English Key* (Princeton: Princeton University Press, 2000), 182-83.

58. John Corry, in a satirical presentation of London wrote that while a few Jews may be "honourable", "the majority are notorious sharpers. Their adherence to the Mosaic law prevents them from mixing with the rest of their fellow citizens; hence, they absolutely subsist on the industry of others, and become public nuisances." Quoted in Katz, *Jews in the History of England*, 292-93.

59. Patrick Colquhoun, quoted in Katz, *Jews in the History of England*, 317.

60. Patrick Colquhoun, quoted in Katz, *Jews in the History of England*, 317.

61. Glassman, *Protean Prejudice*, 147.

62. J. H. Clapham, *The Bank of England: A History* (New York: Macmillan Company, 1945), 1:134. With a holding of £104,625, only the aggregate holdings of the late Duke of Marlborough, of Duchess Sarah, and of Sarah and Godolphin exceeded Pereira's. Just some thirty to forty individuals had holdings of more than £20,000.

63. *Charleston Morning Post*, quoted in Albert M. Hyamson, *The Sephardim of England: The History of the Spanish and Portuguese Jewish Community, 1492–1951* (London: Methuen & Co. Ltd., 1951), 118.

64. Clapham, *Bank of England*, 1:279, 282.

65. Harold Pollins, *Economic History of the Jews in England* (East Brunswick, N.J.: Associated University Presses, Inc., 1982), 50; Hyamson, *Sephardim of England*, 97.

66. Sombart, *Jews and Modern Capitalism*, 28. Sombart's assertion is fleshed out in Chapter 4, "The Foundation of Modern Colonies."

67. Pollins, *Economic History of the Jews*, 50-51.

68. For a detailed discussion of the Jew Bill, see Thomas W. Perry, *Public Opinion, Propaganda, and Politics in Eighteenth Century England: A Study of the Jew Bill of 1753* (Cambridge, Mass.: Harvard University Press, 1962).

69. Edgar Rosenberg, *From Shylock to Svengali: Jewish Stereotypes in English Fiction* (Stanford: Stanford University Press, 1960); M. J. Landa, *The Jew in Drama*

(1926; repr., Port Washington, N.Y.; Kennikat Press, 1968); M. F. Modder, *The Jew in the Literature of England* (1939; repr., Philadelphia: Jewish Publication Society of America, 1944); David Philipson, *The Jew in English Fiction* (1889; repr., New York: Robert Clarke & Co., 1918); H. R. S. Van der Veen, *Jewish Characters in Eighteenth Century English Fiction and Drama* (1935; repr., New York: Ktav Publishing House, Inc., 1973); Esther L. Panitz, *The Alien in Their Midst* (East Brunswick N.J.: Associated University Presses, Inc., 1981).

70. Edgar Rosenberg, "Tabloid Jews and Fungoid Scribblers," in Van der Veen, *Jewish Characters*, 45.

71. Panitz, *Alien in Their Midst*, 79, 85, 89, 162-70. Panitz's thesis, based on her reading of English literature from Chaucer to the twentieth century, is that the Jew is consistently portrayed as an alien. See also Rosenberg, "Tabloid News," 33, 45.

72. *The Temple of Laverna*, quoted in Rosenberg, "Tabloid Jews," 17-18.

73. *Gentleman's Magazine* (1810), quoted in Endelman, *Jews of Georgian England*, 97.

74. Quoted in James Picciotto, *Sketches of Anglo-Jewish History* (London: Trubner & Co., 1875), 197.

75. Commenting on the case, Lord Chancellor Eldon, who was also Solicitor General, "apprehend[ed] that it is the duty of every judge presiding in an English Court of Justice, when he is told there is no difference between worshipping the Supreme Being in chapel, church, or synagogue, to recollect that Christianity is part of the law of England." Quoted in Picciotto, *Sketches*, 363-65. This decree was removed in 1842.

76. Abraham Gilam, *The Emancipation of the Jews in England, 1830–1860* (New York and London: Garland Publishing, Inc., 1982), 11-12.

77. Gilam, *Emancipation of the Jews*, 10; Katz, *Jews in the History of England*, 325.

78. V. D. Lipman, "The Age of Emancipation, 1815-1880," in *Three Centuries of Anglo-Jewish History: A Volume of Essays*, ed. V. D. Lipman (Cambridge: Heffer, 1961), 78; James Parkes, "The History of the Anglo-Jewish Community," in *A Minority in Britain: Social Studies of the Anglo-Jewish Community*, ed. Maurice Freedman (London: Valentine, Mitchell & Co., Ltd., 1955), 38; W. D. Rubinstein, *A History of the Jews in the English-Speaking World: Great Britain* (London: Macmillan Press Ltd, 1996), 48; Gilam, *Emancipation of the Jews*, 10-11.

79. An anonymous pamphleteer (1834), quoted in Gilam, *Emancipation of the Jews*, 12.

80. Bernard van Oven, quoted in Gilam, *Emancipation of the Jews*, 13.

81. Ursula R. Q. Henriques, *Religious Toleration in England, 1787–1833* (Toronto: University of Toronto Press, 1961), 180.

82. Isaac D'Israeli, quoted in Picciotto, *Sketches*, 197.

Chapter 2
The Enlightenment

Concepts of the Enlightenment*

The tolerated status of the Jew was promulgated by all Christian denominations and remained in place until certain pivotal ideas of the Enlightenment forced an examination of this tenet. At the center of Enlightenment idealism was the doctrine of progress: the belief in the historical evolution of man from a primitive and barbaric past to a scientific and perfect future.[1] Proclaimed by Johann Gottfried Herder, Condorcet, and others such as the Scottish philosophers Adam Ferguson and John Millar, the proof of human progress lay in the advancement much of mankind had already achieved from a state of "savagery" to "civilization" and from "rudeness" to "refinement".[2] The yardstick by which to measure this evolution, according to Herder, was the degree to which universal humanitarianism had been embraced.[3] Concerning this cherished ideal, an anonymous merchant from London wrote:

> In our conception of man we should always accustom ourselves to look on the human race, however scattered and dispersed, as one and the same grand republic of which God is the common father, amongst which equity, generosity and humanity ought ever to prevail. Each country should not be considered as independent of others, but [as] the human race—as one indivisible one, we should not be limited to the love of our countries only, or the love of the Protestants only—that is a narrow, selfish and contracted principle. The Englishman's heart should be more enlarged by a universal friendship and confidence between man and man and between nation and nation.[4]

Condorcet distilled into three points the essential hopes of humanists: "the destruction of inequality between different nations, the progress of equality in one and the same nation, and lastly the real improvement of man."[5]

---

* This section is a brief review of certain ideals that we refer to as 'Enlightened' ideals irrespective of their place of origin and time of conception. Not only would it be difficult to trace the development of Enlightenment thought along strictly chronological lines, such a task would further be hampered by the fact that these concepts were not the domain of one country or one nationality alone. Therefore, I have privileged thematic over diachronic analysis.

Deism, a religion to which many but by no means all of the *philosophes* adhered was also influential in promoting reflection of these concepts.

> [Deists] told men of their great inheritance and opportunity: they emphasized their unity and their progressive development towards perfection and urged them deliberately to hasten the advance towards a happier, freer and more equal society. Without this conception 'the march of science' was a meaningless accumulation of the less interesting kinds of knowledge.[6]

Immanuel Kant's work was another cornerstone of Enlightenment thought, and in particular, it promoted a spirit of toleration for the 'other'. Propounding the notion of the private realm, which drew a distinction between 'public' and 'private', Kant argued that while reason must prevail unfettered in the public domain, restrictions in the private realm—as in the matter of religious belief—were permissible and did not compromise the overall principle.[7]

As well, John Locke continued to have an impact. Applying utilitarianism to political thought, he had argued that the commonwealth was solely "a society of men constituted for the procuring, preserving and advancing of their own civil interests;" therefore, "there is absolutely no such thing as a Christian Commonwealth." "Neither pagan, nor Mohammedan, nor Jew ought to be excluded from the civil rights of the Commonwealth because of his religion," because "the care of everyman's soul belongs unto himself and is to be left unto himself."[8]

Discussion of these ideals was not restricted to the notables whom we generally identify with the Enlightenment, such as Voltaire or Diderot. Apart from the *philosophes*, theologians, scholars, literary figures, lawyers, and other professionals—politicians, state administrators, and individuals who had no special designation (the anonymous merchant from London is one such example) also participated. And they voiced a multiplicity of understandings over the span of a hundred years. An anonymous writer noted in 1790 that there were no common definitions of the word 'enlightenment'; each person forwarded his own ideas so that all discussion had become no more than "a war of all against all."[9] However, as Roy Porter has pointed out, the variegated quality of the Enlightenment did not undermine the existence of at least one crucial tenet held in common. Paraphrasing Peter Gay, Porter writes,

> They shared a general commitment to criticizing the injustices and exposing inefficiencies of the ancien regime; to emancipating mankind, through knowledge, education and science, from the chains of ignorance and terror, superstition, theological dogma, and the dead hand of the clergy; to instilling a new mood of hope for a better future . . . and to practical action for creating greater prosperity, fairer laws, milder government, religious tolerance, intellectual freedom, expert administration, and not least, heightened individual self-awareness.[10]

The Enlightenment as it was Applied to the Jews

In 1775, French lawyer Louis Lacratelle maintained (in a legal case where he was challenging the exclusion of Jews from newly created places in the guilds) that under one category or another Jews ought to qualify or "else we are excluding them from the human race;" "let us receive them, if not as compatriots, at least as men," for "reason has raised its radiant head in our century."[11] This assertion, that Jews should be considered part of the human race, finds its origin in the Enlightenment ideals of reason, progress, and universal humanism. This was the context for all discussions on the Jews and it created an atmosphere that was conducive to a reconsideration of their status.

However, the connection that is often made between the ideals of the Enlightenment and the emancipation of the Jews is overstated. The *philosophes* drew on the general concepts discussed above to bring the Jew into the human family; but such statements as "the Jew is even more man than Jew"[12] did not point to the automatic inclusion of Jews into the body politic. At best, Jews were in need of improvement; at worst, they had to be "humanized".[13] This meant fundamentally reconfiguring the Jew in order to bring him into society. On this point, there was absolute agreement among Enlightenment thinkers.

Those who were optimistic about the prospect of change among the Jews, like Jean Baptiste Nicolas de Lisle de Sales, believed that the basis for their degenerated condition lay in their harsh treatment at the hands of Christians over the centuries. Since a "Jew is a man before being a member of a sect, before being a usurer, even before he is a Jew," the solution was simple: "If we want him to stop trading deceitfully and believing in a ridiculous cult, let us behave like men towards him."[14] Those who were pessimistic about the prospect of change saw the faults of the Jews as an inevitable product of their adherence to the Jewish religion and they argued that until such time as Jews substantively reformed their religion—or abandoned it—the acquisition of political rights ought to be denied them. However, this disagreement as to the cause of the degeneracy was relatively minor in relation to the consensus that Jews needed to reform themselves.

There thus evolved a revised, secular formula for the acceptance of Jews into society in place of the theologically based one of conversion. Identifying each and every concern pertaining to the feasibility of emancipation in turn prompted the identification of an area in which Jews needed to reform themselves—what I have termed the 'Enlightenment ideals specific to the Jews.' Successfully undertaking these reforms would result in their regeneration, rehabilitation, amalgamation, or, what later came to be called assimilation. One may imagine a pyramid, at the top of which was assimilation; the reforms constituted building blocks to assist in the process. Reform leading to assimilation was the essence of the Enlightenment thinkers' concerns; extending equality to the Jews as an innate right, based on the common humanity of all men (without making the requisite changes) was not considered.

Whether or not Jews could meet the requirements sparked vociferous debate. There were those like Orientalist scholar Johann David Michaelis who believed that while civic equality for the Jews was theoretically possible, the process of moral reform would take so long as to make the enterprise pointless; in the meantime, the country would be overridden by that segment of Jews which was undesirable.[15] A second group felt that any or all of the following factors spoiled Jews as suitable candidates for citizenship: Jewish character traits were too deeply embedded in the Jewish personality, or were in fact immutable; being a national entity ruled out the possibility of political integration; and extensive religious reform or conversion was unlikely. A third faction was in favor of civic equality, but felt that the process of reform should precede the legal act. The justification for this sequence included the idea of equality as a reward and proof that Jews were not only willing but also capable of reforming themselves, thereby deserving equal status. Those in the fourth camp were equally supportive of civic equality, but were distinguished from the third group by their belief that the sooner disabilities were removed the sooner Jews would reform themselves and assimilate. Indeed, the fourth group considered equality a necessary condition of successful assimilation. In the fifth group were those such as Johann Gottlieb Fichte, German philosopher and founder of ethical idealism, who believed that Jews could never fulfill the requirements of citizenship. However, "They must have human rights, even if they will not grant them to us [meaning that the Jews hate Christians and behave immorally and deceitfully towards them]. For, they are human . . ."[16]

These points of view were represented in an essay contest sponsored by the Royal Society for Arts and Sciences in Metz in 1785 and awarded in 1787. The society requested the submission of essays on the topic, "Are there means of making the Jews happy and more useful in France?" In seven of the nine essays, the view was expressed that such a possibility existed, and all concurred that "*les juifs sont hommes commes nous, et, à ce titre, susceptible d'être Français.*"[17] One of the three successful submissions was authored by lawyer Adolphe Thièry,[18] a second by Zalkind Hourwitz, a Polish Jew who had long been vocal about the need for Jewish emancipation,[19] and the most prominent essay in this contest was by Abbé Henri Grégoire, a Jansenist, entitled *Essai sur la régénération physique, morale et politique des Juifs*. He fused his commitment to traditional humanitarian Enlightenment ideals with his hope that "the granting of religious liberty to the Jews would be a great step forward in reforming and, I even dare say, in converting them, for truth is most persuasive when it is gentle," to support an improvement in the status of the Jews. (Abbé Grégoire would be one of the foremost advocates for Jewish emancipation in the revolutionary *Assemblée*.)* That Abbé Grégoire's submission enjoyed the greatest popularity shows the degree to which his views resonated with the public.

---

* Barzilay, "Jew in the Literature," 102. Abbé Grégoire's hope for the conversion of the Jews was reiterated in his book, *Histoire des sectes religieuses*: "The Catholic Church maintains its sweet hope that the Jews will enter its bosom." Abbé Grégoire, quoted in Hertzberg, *French Enlightenment*, 264-65. It is opportune to point out the prominence of clerics in the Enlightenment movement in Britain, France, and Germany. It is evidence that Voltaire's (and a number of other *philosophes*) views on religion were not the

A degree of urgency was lent to the task that Abbé Grégoire and other Enlightenment thinkers set before themselves. This was due to the phenomenon prevalent throughout the eighteenth century of overestimating the number of Jews living in Europe. In 1714, the well-known Irish Deist, John Toland, wrote that the Jews were more numerous than either the Spaniards, for instance, or the French. French Protestant theologian and historian Jacques Basnage's contention that at the end of the seventeenth century "there are still near three millions of people who profess this religion," was more or less proportionate to Abbé Grégoire's exaggerated calculation of four and a half million eighty years later. According to Diderot, the Jewish population in Amsterdam exceeded 100,000 by the latter half of the eighteenth century. The *Cahiers* from Alsace repeatedly used the expression *"Nous sommes environnés des Juifs,"* with some estimating the number of Jews there in excess of 50,000 families.[20] (In fact, there were approximately two and a half million Jews worldwide at the end of the eighteenth century.[21]) This purported 'demographic fact' further emphasized the need to bring Jews into conformity with the surrounding civil society.

The Constituent Parts of Reform

The Character Traits of Jews

Constantly held up as an obstacle to the removal of civil disabilities was the immoral character of the Jews. In 1803, German Professor Kosmann compiled a list of character traits needing reform that is typical and reasonably comprehensive: "rapacity, group prejudice, vindictiveness, excessive racial pride, timidity mixed with guile and cringing, idleness, suspicion."[22] Most traits were derived from the Jews' primary impulse "to grab the purse" of non-Jews, according to Goethe.[23] The Enlightenment period is filled with literature—from philosophic tracts to dramatic pieces, from pamphlets to works of fiction[24]—that tells how, in business, Jews cheated, robbed, stole, and extracted usurious amounts of interest; how they were driven by their greed for money. Michaelis claimed that Jewish mendicants, vagrants, or outright villains outnumbered their German counterparts by a ratio of 25:1.[25]

Baron Adolf von Knigge, considered by Jacob Katz to be "one of the brilliant figures of the German Enlightenment," advised the well-educated how to behave towards all kinds of people with whom they might come into contact in

---

authoritative Enlightenment views, contrary to popular understanding. It is also proof that the ideals of the Enlightenment were not eschewed by practicing Christians—neither Roman Catholics nor Protestants. George Mosse, for example, wrote, "For the Enlightenment, Judaism, like all religions, was a dead issue." *Germans and Jews: The Right, the Left, and the Search for a Third Force* (London: Orbach & Chambers Ltd, 1970), 39.

his manual, *Über den Umgang mit Menschen.* In the chapter entitled "On Jews and how to treat them," a number of character traits he attributed to Jews are revealed. Presuming that the only contact a Christian would have with a Jew was through business, von Knigge described the Jew as the ubiquitous businessman, always putting himself forward with a great efficiency and with indefatigable efforts that were not only circumstantially motivated but also innate. Lacking any ethics—gain being his only aim—the Christian was at great risk of falling prey to the Jews' cunning ways, which were evident not only in the peddler but amongst the wealthier sort as well. Rich or poor, von Knigge told his readers, both found it terribly hard to part with their money.[26]

The Order of the Asiatic Brethren (a group of Freemasons) admitted Jews at least by 1783.[27] On a certain occasion, one of its members felt called upon to defend his order's decision to admit German Jews. Yet, in his defense, he allowed that they adhered to "many superstitious opinions, to many useless and ridiculous customs." Even enlightened Jews were not sociable; those who were successful were disdainful of their poorer brethren, though the difference between the two was only in exteriors. Only business—bills of exchange, pledges, mortgages, and the interest to be derived therefrom—occupied them; and never would the intonation (*sington*) "in the German dialect of the Israelites [or] their inclination (*hang*) to stand out as a distinctive crowd" be gotten rid of. "Perhaps," he mused, "the nation of the German Israelites [has] itself contributed not a little to the fact that many people cannot yet entirely free themselves from prejudice against them."[28]

Jews were said to hate Christians, yet they lusted after Christian women: "They love fair women though they be Christians. . . . They are as fond of money as beauty."[29] They were said to be cowardly[30] but also possessed a "fiery nature," which was only one of the Jews' "customs and manners" that is "so different from ours that it is hard to conceive that they could change to such an extent that they would integrate in our society."[31] Jews might be integrated into a commercial state, perhaps, but not an agricultural one. Once viewed indifferently, the social cohesiveness of the Jews was now perceived to have all the earmarks of a character trait which, in the context of integrating the Jews into the general society and the *Spectator's* more far-reaching goal of conversion, presented a major obstacle.

> For they live all in a body, and generally within the same inclosure [sic]; to marry among themselves, and to eat no meats that are not killed or prepared their own way. This shuts them out from the most agreeable intercourse of life; and by consequence, excludes them from the most probable means of conversion.[32]

Pessimists among the Enlightenment thinkers were convinced that history had proven that the impulse to change, to progress—unlike all other peoples— was absent in Jews. Although Fichte, on principle, supported civic improvement, he was certain that if Jews attained this goal, their unassimilable character and nature would corrupt society.[33] Optimists like Christian Wilhelm von Dohm believed that the "moral education" (one of the expressions for the reform of character traits) and "enlightenment" of the Jews was possible in response to state-sponsored programs aimed at teaching the Jew "to develop his reason by the clear light of knowledge, the science of nature and its great creator."[34]

Moral Reform . . . Connected to Occupational Reform

The occupations that Jews were engaged in persisted unchanged for centuries. The enlightened community shared with the general public contempt for these pursuits as well as the belief that Jewish business practices were immoral, often illegal, and aimed at taking advantage of Christians. What was novel in their discussions was the connection many of them made between the Jews' debased state and the narrow range of occupations available to them. This, in turn, led them to conclude that "it is primarily the limitation of the Jews to commerce which has had a detrimental influence on their moral and political character."[35] From there, it was a simple step to inquire into the possibility of moral reform through occupational reform, also called 'economic integration.' Jews branching out into agriculture and handicrafts came to be the solution proposed by virtually everyone who considered the matter. As Dohm pointed out, negative character traits had been absent in Jews "as long as their only occupation was agriculture." He was particularly enthusiastic about the virtues of artisanship:

> The sedentary way of life and the quiet industry exacted by these [activities related to artisanship] are contrary to the restless wanderings of the Jewish trader; the peaceful enjoyment of the present, the contentment with small gain are contrary to his greed for profit and his speculation on the ups and downs of the money market.[36]

By eliminating occupational restrictions, he expected that Jews would spontaneously gravitate to the various fields of endeavor proportionate to their numbers: "When no occupation will be closed to Jews, then they should, in all fairness, not have a monopoly on any occupation in preference to other citizens."[37]

However, whether Jews would actually be able to make this transition was a source of much dissension. Since many were convinced that Jews were unethical and driven by greed, and gain their only aim, it seemed unlikely that Jews would turn away from those occupations which satisfied these traits. Herder remained unconvinced because, "Since their emergence on the stage of history, the Jews were a parasitic growth on the stem of other nations, a race of cunning brokers all over the earth. They have caused great evil to many ill-organized states, by retarding the free and natural economic development of their indigenous population."[38] Distinguished Berlin jurist Karl Wilhelm Friedrich Grattenauer raised the problematic issue of economic domination over Christians; this had occurred in Berlin, Vienna, and Prague.[39] Condorcet concurred, noting the domination of Jews over the native populace in Eastern Europe.[40] On two counts the preacher Schwager considered Jews poor candidates as farmers: one was their proclivity towards trade; the other was the issue of Sabbath observance. Having observed Saturday as their day of rest, they would naturally work on Sunday, but as work was forbidden on the Christian Sabbath, Jews would suffer the loss of a day's work, rendering agricultural pursuits both unappealing and impractical. Furthermore, he said, the interdependence that was a hallmark of agricultural communities would not be at play due to the antipathy of the Christian farmers towards the Jews.

Regardless of whether the Enlightenment thinkers were optimistic or pessimistic about the prospect of occupational change, there was a significant segment within the enlightened community that was enthusiastic about the results produced by the Jews' concentration in urban-based financial and commercial activities. "It is again to the Jews that we are indebted for the establishment of the banks at Bayonne and Bordeaux,"[41] gushed Abbé Grégoire. Although the merchants of Bordeaux strenuously objected to the Jews' presence and requested their removal, this request was flatly rejected by Cardinal Fleury: "We rather wish they could be indulged with more and larger privileges, that thereby greater numbers might be invited to leave other countries and settle in France with their families and effects."[42] Diderot spoke of "the Jewish refugees in Holland [who], by their example, taught the Dutch to form establishments along the coast of Berbery and the Levant."[43] "They are disseminated through all the trading ports of the world, that they are become the instruments by which mankind are knit together by a general correspondence. They are the pegs and nails in a great building, which, though they are but little valued in themselves, are absolutely necessary to keep the whole frame together:" such was the assessment of the *Spectator*.[44] Toland lauded the economic virtues of Jews: "This one rule of More, and Better, and Cheaper, will ever carry the market against all expedients and devices."[45] "Throughout the world," wrote Montesquieu admiringly, "wherever there is money, there are Jews."[46] In fact, Toland and Montesquieu both agreed that "experience has shown the error of the expulsion of the Jews from Spain."[47] Hand in hand with these testimonials went recommendations to relax all restrictions that impeded the Jews' full participation in the economy.[48]

Lauding the concentration of Jews in trade, commerce, and money-related businesses that yielded riches to the nation they inhabited, Enlightenment thinkers simultaneously condemned it as contemptible and integral to the immoral character of the Jews. If today we look upon this as an incongruous combination, there seems to be no evidence that it was considered so at the time. We must remember that this dichotomy was firmly entrenched: the Church's dim view of the Jews' occupational activities and the secular world's enthusiasm for the benefits that accrued from these activities had coexisted for centuries, even though the two occasionally came into conflict.

Religion

Hindering all attempts to bring Jews into civil society was the Jewish religion itself.[49] "Mosaic Law," declared Michaelis, "makes the full naturalization and fusion of the Jews with other peoples virtually impossible."[50]

> So long, therefore, as the common man among the Jews is not prepared to listen to and accept reasons that make clear to him that this or that law, this or that ceremony do not belong at all to the essence of religion; so long as he cannot bring himself to see that the essence of religion suffers in no way from discarding many a law and many a custom; so long as he cannot understand that so many religious institutions are as unsuitable for our times as a costume of another climate and other time; so long can there be no hope for a general improvement.[51]

Diderot likewise abhorred the Jews' stubborn adherence to Mosaic Law, believing that it contravened the enlightened spirit of the times and that it sanctioned them "to steal the goods of Christians, to regard them as savage beasts, to push them in a precipice. . . . to kill them with impunity and to utter every morning the most horrible imprecations against them."[52]

Fichte was in favor of tolerance in general, in the sense that no one should be persecuted for his religious beliefs: "Let the poisonous air of intolerance stay as far from these pages as it is from my heart."[53] However, tolerance for Mosaism, a religion whose foundation was nationalism and hate and whose ideals were devoid of such notions as freedom and equality was out of the question.[54] Even the theology which allowed for Jews as part of the divine plan did not go so far as to excuse the Jews' spitefulness towards the Christian religion and their hatefulness towards Christ.[55]

Deists, prominently represented by Voltaire, drew on a theory of Judaism and its origins formulated by the Christian Hebraists, an English fundamentalist group, to support their denunciation of the Jewish religion.[56] Thus, Voltaire attacked the Jewish Bible as no more than a tribal saga filled with irrational and primitive customs that fostered Jewish exclusivity. In contradistinction to the Hebraists, however, he accepted the Jews' claim of divine revelation, but he used it to serve as one more source of criticism: any religion based on revelation, rites, observances, and ceremonies, was no more than superstition.

Voltaire was equally critical of Talmudic Judaism. Believing it to be filled with superstition and immorality, it affected the Jews' character forever. As long as it exerted any influence on the Jews, their potential to reform intellectually, religiously, and socially was jeopardized.[57] Having found reinforcement for his views in the classicists such as Cicero and Tacitus,[58] still, Voltaire was ready "to sit down at one table and share his meal with a Turk, a Chinese, a Hindu and . . . even a Jew, provided the Jew frees himself first of his hateful Jewish superstitions and prejudices."[59] This criticism was also levied by Montesquieu, even though he decried persecution on the grounds of religion, thought highly of biblical Judaism, and believed that religion had an indispensable role to play in strengthening social values. Turning his attention to the rabbis who were responsible for the transmission of the Talmud, Montesquieu declared, "One can hardly find two among them who have the least common sense."[60] Abbé Grégoire was equally critical: "Instead of expanding the horizons of the human spirit, they have consecrated its errors and declared as dogmas the false offspring of a delirious imagination."[61] Wilhelm Meister's portrayal of a rabbi struck a chord of recognition in Goethe.

> Nobody ever portrayed the caricature of a rabbi better than he. The fanatic zeal, the repulsive enthusiasm, the wild gesticulations, the confused murmuring, the piercing outcries, the effeminate movements, the sudden ups and downs of exaltation and the queerness of an ancient nonsense—all these he grasped so acutely that the presentation of his distasteful scene could make happy every man of taste as long as it lasted.[62]

The very practical reason for condemning the Jewish religion as it was currently practiced was that its laws precluded assimilation. "As long as Jews keep the laws of Moses," wrote Michaelis, "as long as for instance they do not take their meals with us . . . or with simple folk over a glass of beer are not able to make friends they will never fuse with us like Catholics and Lutherans, Germans . . . and Frenchmen living in the same State."[63] Dohm, however, was optimistic that Jews would "reform their religious laws and regulations according to the changed times and conditions, and [would] find authorization to do so alone in their Talmud" once they enjoyed a "life of normal civil happiness." Since historic exclusion had caused the "timid and petty spirit of ceremony" and the "sophistic speculation" of the Jewish religion and made Jews "forget the relation of their law to the state," once they became part of the body politic, their "clannish religious opinions" would then fall by the wayside, and this improvement would engender the greatest sense of patriotism—out of sheer gratitude.[64] But in his optimism, Dohm set his sights even higher: once Jews had bettered themselves, they would naturally prefer another confession—Deism, the religion he practiced, is the one he had in mind—and convert to it.[65]

Other Enlightenment thinkers—not only believing Christians but also secularists—had their own rationales for promoting conversion as the best or even only method to ensure reform among the Jews. According to Friedrich Traugott Hartmann, conversion was perhaps the only way to overcome the hatred every nation felt towards the Jews, the cause of which was the Jewish religion itself, as well as the authority of the rabbinic courts which demanded obedience to a separate set of laws, thereby subverting the uniform mentality and spirit that contributed to the well-being of the state.[66] According to Charles Malesherbes (who was behind the edict which extended a number of rights to the non-Catholic French population), conversion might be the antidote to the Jewish communal organizations, "a powerful body which often uses its power in a way which is prejudicial to society."[67]

The Jansenists urged conversion strictly on theological grounds and they exerted considerable influence on discussions concerning the future treatment of Jews in France. Ardent millenarians, they believed that the conversion of the Jews was essential; however, it was being held back by those who treated Jews badly, "persecutors [who] strike fear and impede the progress of the Gospel by their cruelties and their tricks."[68] Johann Caspar Lavater is an example of a millenarian upon whom the Enlightenment had an increasing influence; it eventually supplanted his millenarian beliefs although not his conversionist convictions. Twice he tried to convert Jewish philosopher Moses Mendelssohn, first in 1770, and then again in 1782. His millenarian beliefs framed his first appeal. By 1782, he used rationalism to argue his case: it was primitive, with outward manifestations that substituted for true religiosity; it was a theocracy controlled by despotic clerics. Christianity, on the other hand, was "a liberal system for the more reasonable worship of God." What was therefore complementary to Christianity had been retained: "veneration for the only God, obedience to the divine commandments given through Moses, and the assembling of the nations into one flock under the common scepter of one Messiah whose coming had been announced by the words of the prophets."[69]

The Enlightenment thinkers also considered different approaches that might encourage Jews to convert. Abbé Antoine Guenée, an enlightened *religieux*, employed a strategy that had often been used by Churchmen. His *Lettres de quelques Juifs portugais et allemands à M. de Voltaire* (1769) included a republication of Isaac de Pinto's *Apologie pour la nation juive* (1762)[70] along with a comprehensive rebuttal of de Pinto's points. Where de Pinto argued for respect for Judaism, Abbé Guenée reserved his respect only for Biblical Judaism, and urged conversion. Where de Pinto praised the Jews' commitment to their faith at the expense of economic advancement, Abbé Guenée rebutted: "No one is inviting them to make business with their religion but rather to open their eyes to the Light. One can have compassion for them and forgive them but one should not praise them."[71] Wilhelm Friedrich Hezel, a theologian and Professor of Biblical and Oriental literature suggested a different reading program, one that would successfully reeducate the Jews to enable them to appreciate Christianity and thereby convert.[72] There was also a suggestion by German Lutheran theologian Friedrich Schleiermacher that was intended to help Jews attain political equality more easily. His idea was to organize a new Jewish sect which would incorporate only those customs and tenets that were conducive (as he saw it) to fulfilling one's civic duties in a Christian state. Those Jews who were willing to modify their beliefs should achieve full political equality, but all others would remain unemancipated.[73]

Goethe used a 'soft-sell' approach in the matter of conversion. Reflecting on a collection of poems written by the Polish Jew Issachar Falkensohn Behr in German in 1772, he wrote how "extremely praiseworthy [it was] for a Polish Jew to give up business in order to learn German, to polish verses and devote himself to the Muses. But if he can do no more than a Christian *étudiant en belles lettres*, then he does wrong, we think, to make such a fuss about being a Jew."[74] While Kant stopped short of advocating conversion, it was his conviction that Judaism would have to undergo purification—by which he meant that it would then be based on the teachings of Jesus while subject to Jewish interpretation.[75] However, amongst the Enlightenment thinkers there were some who felt that not even conversion would help. Grattenauer was scornful of Christians who celebrated any addition to their numbers for so embedded were the Jews' immoral character traits that even conversion could not overcome them. Sharing Grattenauer's skepticism, an anonymous writer suggested that every potential convert should be on probation for six years so the sincerity of the act could be judged.[76]

Given that many of the Enlightenment thinkers were practicing Christians, their reliance on conversion as a way to overcome the degenerate state of the Jews is not surprising. But why would those who considered Christianity an impediment to the advancement of enlightened ideals, not to say an enemy of the Enlightenment, put conversion forward as an effective method to bring about the Jews' reform? The answer may lie in the fact that for secularists, conversion had less to do with wanting Jews to become Christians, and more with finding a way for them to become assimilated as quickly as possible. Conversion circumvented the need for Jews to make all the requisite reforms and immediately rendered them assimilated—at least in theory—culturally and politically with the majority living around them. Other secularists took a more long-term view of the benefits that would accrue through conversion: this tactic more than any other was envisioned to have the efficacy to break down social exclusivity; overcome the adverse effects of the Jewish religion; modify negative character traits; and dissolve membership in the Jewish polity. Moreover, even though secularists had rejected many of the formal trappings of Christianity (or Christianity altogether), they did acknowledge that it was a cornerstone of European civilization and political culture: "It is not the baptism that counts but that the Jew, by saying 'Baptize me', says at the same time: I obey the laws of the country, I submit myself to the institution you have created, I fulfill all the obligations laid upon me at all times."[77]

Acculturation

While the issue of acculturation only becomes a dominant one after emancipation, the general view of the Jews' attempts to become acculturated is reflected in Grattenauer's comments below and formed part of his argument against granting political rights to Jews.

> Those Jews who had become acculturated only appeared so. Their dress, however splendid it may be, has nevertheless retained certain Jewish traits as has their physiognomy. Their language is still the wretched stammering jargon which, though they try to modernize it in conversation with Christians, they still use among themselves; filth and uncleanliness prevails among them and they cannot cover it with their great pomp—that they are in Vienna and Berlin complaisant towards Christians and even attempt some gallantry, is done for gain.[78]

Jews needed to become "equal partners . . . in the common culture of humanity," wrote Herder,[79] but this was an impossible aspiration as long as they remained "so obstinately loyal" to their particularistic and nationalistic law.[80]

The injection of a small but steady number of religious Eastern European Jews into Western Europe heightened the impression that Jews were failing to become acculturated. Government legislation and polemical literature written on this subject (Goethe's works are a prime example) invariably described these Eastern European Jews as uncivilized and uncultured.[81]

The Political Status of Jews

Much of the critique of the Jews revolved around their relation to the state: Jews as a political and not a religious entity; as a mighty state; as a state within a state; as a nation that had a homeland elsewhere; and in references to the application of the principle of separation of Church and state and the Christian character of the state. Abbé Jean Sieflein Maury elevated the nationalist aspect of Jewry to the degree that he proclaimed it was "not a sect but a nation having laws that it has always followed and that it wished to follow. . . . Jews have traversed seventeen centuries and not mixed with other nations."[82] Likewise, Kant made no allowance for Judaism as a religion: Jewry was a political community plain and simple—*staatlich-politische Gemeinschaft*.[83] Taking this one step further, Fichte popularized the idea that Jewry was "A powerful, hostilely disposed nation [that] is infiltrating almost every country in Europe."[84]

The view that Jews were a nation was reinforced by their persistence in speaking the Yiddish language. Abbé Grégoire referred to it as "this kind of dialect, the German-Hebrew-Rabbinical Jargon, which is current among German Jews and understood only by them. . . . [and] is used only to spread ignorance or to conceal their knavery." Goethe repeatedly commented on the Yiddish language: "There is something pathetic in the *Judensprache*"—"*naseweises Nestquackelchen*"*—and he agreed with Abbé Grégoire that it was the means by which the rabbis spread their anti-Christian message.[85] In abjuring Yiddish and learning to speak the language of the country in which they resided, it was believed that Jews would at once loosen their ties with fellow Jews abroad and draw nearer to the native population. Hence, the inclusion of a clause in Joseph II's *Toleranzpatent* (1781-83) which "explicitly forbid their use [Hebrew and Yiddish] in all public transactions in and out of the courts."[86] Louis XVI of France followed his lead with a similar clause in the *Lettres Patentes* (1784).

Status in statu, the idea that Jews formed a state within a state, was also spread through the works of Fichte[87] and it became a stock item in the debates concerning the removal of civic disabilities.[88] Ernst Traugott von Kortum, while seeming to qualify the parameters that would constitute a state within a state—"according to my humble opinion, a *Status in Statu* is constituted, when a larger or smaller society within the state will, in the case of a conflict between its laws and the laws of the state, repudiate the laws of the state and only observe its own"—nonetheless declared the following:

> The esprit de corps of the Jews, coupled with the spirit of their theocratic laws, enables them, in every country where their numbers are appreciable, to constitute a *Status in Statu*, and this is tolerated, even though this same manifestation arouses zealous opposition elsewhere. As for the dangerous Jesuits, the fact that their Order constituted a state within a state was considered a crime. They were destroyed. Yet no one has undertaken an unbiased study to determine whether the Jewish *Status in Statu* is not equally harmful, or even worse.[89]

---

* In applying this expression to the Yiddish language, Goethe was drawing a comparison between the language and a spoiled child who is the last one left at home: impudent and saucy, but at the same time wishing to remain dependent.

Only when the Jewish nation was dismembered and reconstituted as individuals could Comte Stanislas de Clermont-Tonnerre entertain the idea of granting civic equality to the Jews. He made this clear in his speech to the French National Assembly on 25 December 1789.

> The Jews should be denied everything as a nation, but granted everything as individuals; they must disown their judges, they must have only ours; they must be refused legal protection for the maintenance of the supposed laws of their Jewish corporation; they must constitute neither a state, nor a political corps, nor an order; they must individually become citizens; if they do not want this, they must inform us and we shall then be compelled to expel them. The existence of a nation within a nation is unacceptable to our country.[90]

H. E. G. Paulus, a liberal Protestant theologian, agreed with Clermont-Tonnerre in opposing group rights, but stipulated that even the extension of individual rights should rest on personal merit.[91] The position of Baron Schroetter on this matter was similar, but as a member of the Prussian cabinet in 1804, he had been more concerned about the economic hegemony of the Jews, and on this basis was reluctant to approve reforms ameliorating their status, for "the greatest capital sums are in the hands of the Jews; for to the Jews all means are the same in order to attain their objective." Four years later, while he still affirmed that "the tendency of their spiritual makeup is trade, and its aim, money . . . from the richest to the poorest [this] has become a national matter," as a state within a state, they posed an even greater threat. He thus directed his energies towards the formulation of a new constitution that would "undermine their nationality, destroy it, and thus gradually induce them no longer to aim at forming a 'State within a State.'"[92]

Further advancing the notion that Jews were a state within a state was the matter of textual references to Zion. On this issue, a virtual consensus obtained among the Enlightenment thinkers.[93] Their homeland was not the country they inhabited, "which they hope one day to leave to their great happiness, and return to Palestine." "A people that has such hopes," argued Michaelis, "will never entirely feel at home or have patriotic love for the paternal soil."[94] The English philosopher, physician, and psychologist David Hartley enumerated several factors that supported this conviction. Fifteen centuries of oppression and persecution had not eliminated the Jewish identity or way of life. Jews possessed a national language. They had a communal structure, which could facilitate the move to their own state. They had mobility by virtue of the fact that Jewish wealth was concentrated in "money and jewels" rather than "inheritance of land."[95] Hartmann believed that this issue was insuperable because "the greater part of the Jews . . . will never be able to settle as citizens and will never be as loyal to the homeland as others who have no article of faith compelling them to flee when an impostor gives the danger signal."[96] Here, Hartmann was referring to Messianism (and specifically false messiahs): the belief in a Messiah who would herald the ingathering of the Jews to the land of Israel (Zion).[97]

Enlightenment thinkers who were in favor of political equality tended to soften the literal interpretation of Zion, giving it symbolic overtones. Dohm wrote that this hope was of a spiritual-mystical nature, similar to the Christians' belief in the Second Coming.[98] Abbé Grégoire interpreted the Zionist aspiration according to Mendelssohn:

> In times of suffering, when misfortune weighs heavily on the Jew, when trembling he eats his bread of affliction, he sighs perhaps for the Messiah. . . . His coming, however, would be less welcome to our Israelite if the humaneness of the people would allow him to breathe in peace and live happily in his home. . . . Very often do the advantages of the present life make one forget the promises of the future. In this sense, the Jew is not in any way different from us. His hopes would by no means make him give up those comforts that would be within his reach.[99]

The separation of Church and state to meet the goal of secularization was a desideratum for many—but not all—Enlightenment thinkers. Wilhelm von Humboldt was a tireless proponent of this principle (despite his position as head of the department for religious affairs in the Prussian administration). As a severed Siamese twin, the new role of the state would be a passive one. It should do no more than "reverse the inhuman and prejudiced way of thinking that judges a man not according to his origin and religion and conceives of him—in contradistinction to all notions of human dignity—not as an individual but as one belonging to a race and sharing certain characteristics as of necessity."[100] How the state could best effect this reversal was "by declaring in no uncertain terms that the State will no longer recognize any difference between Jews and Christians."[101] Ismar Freund describes Humboldt's approach as surgical: complete indifference on the part of the state to the religious affiliation of its inhabitants, which meant that Jews would automatically be granted political equality. Following this move, Humboldt anticipated the Jews' complete integration into society: occupationally, morally, and culturally. Only the religious distinction would remain and that was not the business of the state.* Not so, said Grattenauer, and he sounded an alarm in his second book, subtitled "A Word of Warning to all our Christian Co-citizens" (1803):

> Grant the Jews full right of citizenship . . . they will reward you royally, for you will stand and tend the flocks of the Jews; your sons and daughters will become the slaves and handmaiden of the Jews; you will work in the sweat of your brow, but the Chosen People of God will enjoy the fruits and live grandly!!! This prophecy is written in the Talmud; allow it to happen, so that the prophecies of the rabbis will come true.[102]

---

* Humboldt's formally articulated position was actually at odds with his personal views. According to Freund's interpretation of Humboldt, institutional decline would be followed by a corresponding lapse in personal observance, but simultaneously, the Jew, "driven by the innate human need for a loftier faith," would undoubtedly embrace Christianity. I. Freund, quoted in Katz, *Out of the Ghetto*, 78.

As far as Grattenauer was concerned, the state did have an important role to play in protecting and promoting its own well-being and that of its citizenry, and that was to not grant the Jews citizenship. A number of Enlightenment thinkers of course opposed any suggestion of separation between Church and state; however, along with those who favored this separation, they did support application of this principle when it came to the Jews. Separation between Church and state as it was to be applied to the Jews meant the elimination of the peoplehood (or community or nation or state) aspect of Jewishness, leaving only the religious component intact.

Advocating the separation of Church and state did not necessarily mean rejecting the notion of the Christian character of the state. On the contrary, to Hartmann, this Christian character was so much a part of the fabric of the state that even the lowest level of political empowerment—the civil level—was beyond the reach of the Jews. "All the divisions that exist between the burgher, peasant, and nobleman, city-dweller and countryman, warriors and unarmed scholars are not divisions that can be compared with those existing between Christians and Jews;" and therefore, the reciprocity necessary between tradesmen (among whom Jews would have been counted) and those engaged in agriculture could never be established.[103] An appreciation of Christianity also gave impetus to preserving the Christian character of the state. Among the Enlightenment thinkers were those who had never been seduced by Voltaire and Deism but remained faithful to the traditional churches.[104] Porter's image of a typical English Enlightenment thinker was a "scientific parson of the Anglican Church:"[105] Warburton, "the irascible English bishop," according to B. W. Young, was one such example.[106] A whole generation had absorbed the tenets of the Enlightenment and they applied reason to justify their Christian beliefs. As Grattenauer proclaimed, "I am a Christian, not in name but from true conviction. My reason tells me that Christian morality is in exact harmony with my vocation as a human being and its exercise makes me happy and satisfied."[107] The rational approach stimulated the movement to harness Christianity "as a semi-secularized agency of cultural assimilation:" emphasis was laid on the positive offshoots of the Christian religion, such as its ability to set the cultural and moral tone of society.[108] The state continued to support reference points which only the Church could provide: a system of ethics and morality; holidays through which to orient the calendar; ritual as a way to regulate one's life; and observance of life passages (birth, marriage, death). At the very least, in contradistinction to the infidel Turks or the pagan Africans, one was 'Christian', signifying not only a religious designation but also a civilized one.

Apart from the theoretical aspects of the Jews' relation to the state, there were two practical concerns. The first was the employment of Jews in the government. Dohm challenged those who were opposed to this, although he was, in fact, equivocal; Jews who were capable should have this right, but "I think, however, that in the next generations this capability will not yet appear frequently, and the state should make no special effort to develop it." On several counts the present condition of the Jews precluded this profession as a good choice in the near future: the Jews' lack of appropriate education; the unsuitability of the bureaucratic profession as a corrective to the "too mercantile spirit of most Jews;" and the requirement that civil servants be "far removed from any suspicion of misdemeanors due to greed." But even when a Jew was a suitable candidate, if there was a Christian who was also suitable, "the obvious right of the majority in the nation" meant that the Christian should have preference.[109]

The other issue revolved around the Jews' ability to serve in the military. The general reasons that stood in the way of civic improvement were the same reasons why Jews would not be able to fulfill their military obligations. The Jews' adherence to traditional Judaism was of particular concern to Michaelis: "The might of the state does not rest entirely on gold and silver, but to a much greater extent on arms and legs, on soldiers; and that one will not get from the Jews, as long as they have not changed their current religious thinking."[110] Yet Dohm was convinced otherwise, assured that they "will fulfill the obligation to defend the society which gave them equal rights." However, Dohm then proceded to undercut his own argument by adding that their lack of "physical fitness," one of the two requisites of military service, would be overcome by "discipline and training;" "personal courage," the other requisite, "is in today's kind of warfare no longer so very essential."[111]

A 'Neutral' Society:
Moses Mendelssohn and the Salons

Jacob Katz uses the expression "neutral society," "the human one—to which members of both religions could belong," to describe the budding relationship between some Jews and Christians during the period of the Enlightenment.[112] The success of Moses Mendelssohn—from both the professional and personal standpoint—and the vibrant salon life facilitated by Jewish hostesses in several European cities seem to challenge the broad application of Enlightenment ideals specific to the Jews and instead provide proof that Jews were included under the umbrella of the general Enlightenment ideals. Both warrant further scrutiny.

It is possible to argue that beyond Mendelssohn's contributions to philosophy and his genial personality, those philosophical tracts which addressed Jewish theological matters were a factor in the degree of acceptance he garnered. Based on them, it was clear to Christian *philosophes* that they had captured him for themselves. There are two examples which indicate that Mendelssohn had made a fundamental shift away from traditional Judaism and into the Christian-enlightened fold. The first was his deviation from the traditional Jewish basis for toleration. Whereas the Jewish understanding (as expressed by Rabbi Jacob Emden [1697-1776]) was that Gentiles shared with Jews a faith in revelation and the Bible and therefore could not be excluded from salvation, Mendelssohn abided by the Enlightenment version, which based tolerance (here the word is interchangeable with acceptance) "on the common humanity of all those led by reason to live in accordance with the Law of Nature which, [as] the philosophy of Rationalism taught, was both good in essence and innate in every human being."[113] The second reconfiguration was the transformation of Judaism from revealed religion to revealed law. In making this change, Jewish law would retain its power as a moral instrument, but one that was now invested in man rather than in God.*

It is only logical that the *philosophes* awaited the next step in Mendelssohn's enlightenment: his conversion. This did not occur, despite repeated challenges to explain his ongoing adherence to Judaism by Lavater, Balthasar Kolbele, and the anonymous author 'S'.[114] The stumbling block (apart from any others) that stood in the way of Mendelssohn's conversion—as the author of 'enlightened' Judaism he could hardly detach himself from it—was not an obstacle for future generations. The logical progression in enlightenment, from Jew, to enlightened Jew, to baptized Jew could be pursued by the next generation. Salomon Bartholdy could state in all sincerity to Mendelssohn's son, Abraham, that while "you say you owe it to the memory of your father [to remain Jewish]," conversion "is rather a form of homage which you and all of us are rendering to the efforts of your father in behalf of true enlightenment."[115]

The salons, in their time, served much the same purpose as the scholarly exchanges Mendelssohn engaged in throughout his life. There, Hannah Arendt asserts, Jews were able to meet with Christians on a more or less equal footing, drawn together by their desire for individual as opposed to political freedom, the need to escape from the constraints of family, and the common condition of being "socially homeless."[116] However, Arendt exaggerates the element of commonality in the condition of social homelessness, for Jews not only suffered from intellectual and cultural alienation but were also denied class membership and political status in their country of residence and their religion differed from that practiced by everyone else. Furthermore, the idea that these cultural associations fostered by the salon life created a 'neutral' society is a dubious one. The salons were solely in the homes of Jews, and there is no sign that mutuality was the operating principle.[117] Even those who most actively promoted an improvement in the status of the Jews had a general view of the Jewish people that was critical in the extreme. Therefore, as Katz maintains, they served no purpose beyond a curiosity, a distraction, or a temporary interest for some enlightened Germans.[118]

However, for Jews interested in improving their status, the salons performed a vital function. The reasons for this were twofold. Since only the state had the power to alter the condition of the Jews—and there was no indication that it was about to undertake such a move—the goal of equality not only had to be downsized but attainable through individual effort. A social association with intellectual and cultural overtones was construed as the only venue whereby these Jews could, through their own efforts, elevate their status. But should a public debate prod the government into changing its stand, it was understood that it would apply universal emancipation. From the time this prospect began to be discussed, many of the 'Jewish intelligentsia' or otherwise aspiring Jews believed that

---

* Katz, *Exclusiveness and Tolerance*, 180. While Mendelssohn staunchly maintained that none of his reconfigurations could lead to the dissolution of Judaism, in the opinion of many Jews, they would have exactly that effect.

being lumped in with the reviled Eastern European Jews reduced their chances of being accepted into the host society. Therefore, the salons became a deliberate substitute for the promotion of emancipation.

When emancipation seemed to be on the verge of reality—with Napoleon's victory over Prussia in 1807, reforms in the laws pertaining to Jews commenced—salon life imploded. With the prospect imminent that Jews were to become their equals, many of the mainstays of the Berlin intelligentsia turned their backs on the Jewish salons. It is a matter of speculation whether this occurred because emancipation encompassed all Jews (Arendt[119]); because the hothouse environment of the salon was an artificial one that never did nor could have engendered equality between Jews and Christians (Katz); or if it was a combination of these factors. Some Jews tried to find their way out of this situation by converting;[120] others, like Adam Müller, continued to oppose Jewish emancipation. A member of the Berlin Jewish intelligentsia, Müller felt the necessity of writing a dissuasive letter to Metternich in 1815, when the Treaty of Vienna was being forged and the reinstitution of German-Jewish emancipation was under discussion. "Every legal or political measure for the emancipation of the Jews," he warned Metternich, "must necessarily lead to a deterioration of their civic and social situation."[121]

****

In assessing Enlightenment thought as it pertained to the Jews, it requires a great deal of effort on the part of the reader who comes equipped with twentieth-century sensibilities to refrain from describing these Enlightenment thinkers as 'anti-Semitic'. The image of the Jew, for both religious and secular Enlightenment thinkers was a very flawed one. It is not the place here to go into detail about this. Suffice to say, that a people which had been marginalized for centuries, repeatedly expelled, boarded up in ghettos, held in the lowest possible esteem by the host society, taxed beyond endurance, and forced into quasi-legal or outright illegal acts simply to survive were probably, on the whole, most unappetizing figures. The same is true even of those Jews who were in a position to become to some extent involved in the general society (*Schutzjuden* [protected Jews] or those who were accepted into the order of the Asiatic Brethren, for example). It is highly unlikely, given the centuries of segregation and marginalization, that their first forays into society were anything but awkward. One need only be reminded that the Enlightenment thinkers who promoted civic improvement for the Jews considered them degenerate and in need of reform. Though Jean Baptiste Nicolas de Lisle de Sales and the member of the Asiatic Brethren may have disagreed somewhat as to the cause of this condition, both had the same poor impression of Jews. Acting in the spirit of universal humanism, Wilhelm von Humboldt had helped forge the Prussian *Judenedikt* of 1812 (which gave Jews citizenship although not the right to become officials) and he was a staunch advocate for them at the Congress of Vienna,[122] yet he wrote shortly thereafter, in 1816: "I love the Jew really only *en masse*; *en détail* I strictly avoid him."[123]

When considering the Jewish religion, secular Enlightenment thinkers condemned it as superstitious and subversive when they juxtaposed it to rational thought. While they reached the same conclusion about Christianity, one must be careful not to confuse their lambasting of the Christian religion with the criticisms leveled against Judaism. They were not of the same ilk. The secular *philosophes* described the Church in very negative terms, but they did not impute negative character traits to Christians as a consequence of their adherence to Christianity. However, they did assert that Judaism had a profoundly negative affect on the character of its followers.

With respect to the state, the overarching issue was that of loyalty. While cognizant that the quality of loyalty cannot be presumed of anyone who exists outside the body politic and whose very residence is tenuous, the Enlightenment thinkers had a list of issues which might reasonably be thought to foster incivism. In everyone's estimation (both the Jews and the host society), Jews were a separate people and not just followers of a religion.* According to many of the *philosophes*, they were more than this: they were a political entity. This gave rise to the description of Jewry as a *status in statu*; and if this were the case, then Jews would automatically adhere to their own laws rather than the laws of the state, especially if the two conflicted. On the issue of textual references to Zion, there was a large measure of agreement that the Jews' expectation to return one day to Palestine set limits on their patriotism. Preserving the Christian character of the state posed a different problem. While it obviously remained important to those who were believing Christians, even many who no longer considered themselves religious found it difficult to imagine how European civilization could be apprehended or appreciated without this imprint.

There is little foundation for labeling these issues brought forward by the Enlightenment thinkers as manifestations of 'anti-Semitic' sentiment. As they regarded the Jews, who had never been part of Christian Europe—not in the political, cultural, or social sense; who had never been on 'intimate' terms with that society—in the sense of 'breaking bread' with them or marrying them; and whose day-to-day rhythm was so at variance with the Christian rhythm, the fundamental issue was whether or not Jews were capable of change—or changing enough. Grappling with the distinctiveness of the Jew in its numerous manifestations, they applied themselves to the question of what would be required to make the Jew fit into society at large. Despite the harshness of many of their criticisms, this was done in the spirit of 'equity, generosity and humanity.'

This 'common humanity' argument was, however, only one side of the Enlightenment coin in relation to the Jews. The other side of the coin was the requirement that Jews would have to put into practice a specific set of Enlightenment ideals that applied only to them. That being said, it is clear just how much

---

* As the emancipation debates heated up in the nineteenth century, reform-minded Jews scrupulously eradicated all references to Jews as a people and vociferously protested such a designation. Jews were not a people, they argued, but only members of a religion. (The degree to which reform was undertaken as a way to promote emancipation rather than being self-initiated is an open question.)

conversion was central to the discussions, and economic utility was the chief means of assigning value to Jewish existence. These observations do not undermine the insistence on reform as a prerequisite to acceptance nor its status as the primary vehicle by which to gain it. In the 'Enlightenment primer' on the regeneration of the Jews, neither conversion nor economic utility was counted among the reforms that would engender assimilation. The high esteem in which economic utility was held and the particular merit of conversion to enhance the process of assimilation do, however, cast doubt on reform as a sufficient effort through which to join society. Similarly, the efficacy of reform was undermined by the battle for the identity of the state: should it be Christian or secular? A protracted struggle, it could not but add to the fundamental difficulties inherent in the mandate to reform. What would be the consequence of being a Jewish citizen in a state whose symbols, civilization, and ideology were Christological? What would be the repercussions of Jews siding (inevitably) with the secularists who were, withal, Christians at birth, making this in fact a family squabble? And, given the frequently expressed hope that reform of the Jewish religion would be the first step leading to conversion, would not their support of secularism still classify them as opponents of Christianity?

Despite these inconsistencies, the Enlightenment ideals specific to the Jews came to frame all subsequent discourse concerning the Jews. Eventually, they became the criteria by which the efforts of the Jews to assimilate were judged in the post-emancipation era.

Notes

1. Kingsley Martin, *French Liberal Thought in the Eighteenth Century: A Study of Political Ideas from Bayle to Condorcet* (London: Phoenix House, 1962), 286-87.

2. Roy Porter and Mikulas Teich, eds., *The Enlightenment in National Context* (Houndmills, Basingstoke, Hampshire, UK and New York: Palgrave, St. Martins Press, 2001), 16.

3. Isaac Eisenstein Barzilay, "The Jew in the Literature of the Enlightenment," in *Emancipation and Counter-Emancipation: Selected Essays from Jewish Social Studies*, ed. Abraham G. Duker and M. Ben- Horin (New York: Ktav Publishing House, Inc., 1974), 93. Johann Gottfried Herder was a German poet, critic, and preacher who came to have a great deal of influence on German Romanticism.

4. Published not long after the furor over the Jew Bill in 1753, *A Letter to the Right Honourable Sir Thomas Chitty, Lord Mayor of London* (London, 1760), 80.

5. Condorcet, quoted in Barzilay, "Jew in the Literature," 93. Numerous others wrote on this topic, including Bacon, Pascal, Bossuet, Fontenelle, Voltaire, Turgot, and Volney.

6. Martin, *French Liberal Thought*, 305.

7. Immanuel Kant, "What is Enlightenment," quoted in William V. Rowe, "Difficult Liberty: The Basis of Community in Emmanuel Levinas," in *From Ghetto to Emancipation: Historical and Contemporary Reconsiderations of the Jewish Community*, ed. David N. Myers and William V. Rowe (Scranton, Ill.: Scranton University Press, 1997), 65.

8. John Locke, "A Letter Concerning Toleration," in *The Works of John Locke* (London, 1823), 6:9, 23, 38, 52.

9. Quoted in James Schmidt, ed., *What is Enlightenment?* (Berkeley and Los Angeles: University of California Press, 1996), 2-11.

10. Roy Porter, *The Enlightenment* (Houndmills, Basingstoke, Hampshire and New York: Palgrave, 2001), 4-5, 7. Taken from Peter Gay's *The Enlightenment: An Interpretation*, 2 vols. (New York: Knopf, 1966-69).

11. Louis Lacratelle, quoted in Hertzberg, *French Enlightenment*, 55-58.

12. Christian Wilhelm von Dohm (1751-1820), *Concerning the Amelioration of the Civil Status of the Jews*, [*Übber die bürgerliche Verbesserung der Juden*] trans. Helen Lederer (1781; repr. in English, Cincinnati: Hebrew Union College-Institute of Religion, 1957), 14. In 1783, Dohm's book was republished along with a second volume in which he clarified his views and responded to his critics.

13. J. G. Herder, quoted in Barzilay, "Jew in the Literature," 91.

14. From Jean Baptiste Nicolas de Lisle de Sales's *De la philosophie de la nature*, quoted in Hertzberg, *French Enlightenment*, 307.

15. Katz, *Out of the Ghetto*, 92-93.

16. Johann Gottlieb Fichte, quoted in Mendes-Flohr and Reinharz, *Jew in the Modern World*, 309. Philosopher and legal scholar H. F. Diez also advocated complete equality, even though he was convinced that, due to their religious practices, Jews would never be as good citizens as Christians. Liberles, "From Toleration to *Verbesserung*, 13.

17. Abbé Henri Grégoire, *Essai sur la régénération physique, morale et politique des Juifs* (n.p., 1789).

18. Adolphe Thièry hinged his arguments on Montesquieu's conviction that freedom and equality were the due of all men, including the Jews, as well as on his own belief in "the basic goodness of human nature," to eventually bring about the betterment of the Jews. Quoted in Hertzberg, *French Enlightenment*, 298.

19. Critical of "the seductive eloquence of Voltaire and all the other celebrated writers who are sworn enemies of all their fellow men who pray to the Supreme Being in Hebrew" and Christians who had treated the Jews badly over the centuries, Zalkind Hourwitz was equally scathing in his remarks about the Jews: particularly the rabbis and the lay leaders were in desperate need of reform. Quoted in Barzilay, "Jew in the Literature," 298, 102; Frances Molino, "The Right to be Equal: Zalkind Hourwitz and the Revolution of 1789," in *From East to West: Jews in a Changing Europe, 1750-1870*, ed. Frances Molino and David Sorkin (Oxford: Basil Blackwell, 1990), 93.

20. Jacques Basnage, quoted in Barzilay, "Jew in the Literature," 109-110; John Toland, *Reasons for Naturalizing the Jews in Great Britain and Ireland, on the Same Foot with other Nations. Containing also, A Defence of the Jews Against All vulgar Prejudices in all countries* (London: Printed for J. Roberts in Warwick-lane, 1714), 40.

21. Jacob Katz, *Jewish Emancipation and Self-Emancipation* (Philadelphia, New York, and Jerusalem: Jewish Publication Society, 1986), 4.

22. Kammer-Assessor Professor Kosmann, *Für die Juden* (1803), quoted in H. D. Schmidt, "The Terms of Emancipation," *The Leo Baeck Institute Year Book* 1 (1956): 34. (henceforth referred to as *LBIYB*).

23. Goethe, quoted in Barzilay, "Jew in the Literature," 103.

24. The following list of such pieces of literature was composed by Barzilay: Lessing's *Juden*, Eisenmenger's *Entdecktes Judentum*, Defoe's *Roxanna*, Smollett's early novels, Richardson's *Sir Charles Grandison*, Dejob's citations in "Les Juifs dans la Comédie au XVIII Siècle," Herbert De Witt Carrington's *Die Figur des Juden in der dramatischen Literatur des XVIII. Jahrhunderts*, and Fanny Burney's *Cecilia*. "Jew in the Literature," 104, 113.

25. Katz, *Out of the Ghetto*, 92-93.

26. Katz, *Out of the Ghetto*, 81-83.

27. Jacob Katz, *Jews and Freemasons in Europe 1723-1939*, trans. Leonard Orschy (Cambridge: Harvard University Press, 1970), 38.
28. Quoted in Katz, *Out of the Ghetto*, 84-85.
29. Diderot and Jacques Basnage, quoted in Barzilay, "Jew in the Literature," 104, 114.
30. Barzilay, "Jew in the Literature," 104.
31. Schwager, a preacher, quoted in Barzilay, "Jew in the Literature," 103.
32. *Spectator*, 495, Saturday, 27 September 1753; 84.
33. Barzilay, "Jew in the Literature," 108.
34. Dohm, *Concerning the Amelioration*, 66. Dohm was a councillor in the department of foreign affairs and a "semi-prominent member of the Enlightenment scene in Berlin." He became involved in the debate on the status of the Jews out of his connection to Jewish philosopher Moses Mendelssohn, who had been asked by the Jews of Alsace to write a tract which would not only refute François Hell's current work criticizing the Jews but would also advocate improvement in their legal status. Mendelssohn passed on the task in part to Dohm who, from that time, had an avid interest in the situation of the Jews. In his tract, he described the circumstances Jews lived under and the historical reasons for this, why these conditions were not warranted, and how to go about ameliorating them. Writing of the disruption of family life, heavy tax burdens, the restricted means of earning a living, and the necessity to engage in the practice of usury, Dohm's rendering of "these unfortunate asiatic [sic] refugees" was a sympathetic one. *Concerning the Amelioration*, 2-3. His description was a composite, drawn from the varying conditions under which Jews existed in all parts of Europe at that time. However, everywhere one thing was consistent: these conditions were based on the extension or withdrawal of privileges, not a system of rights. Jacob Katz is of the opinion that the publication of Dohm's tract in 1881 triggered the widespread contemplation of the status of the Jews. Jacob Katz, "The Term 'Jewish Emancipation': Its Origin and Historical Impact," in *Emancipation and Assimilation: Studies in Modern Jewish History*, ed. Jacob Katz (Westmead: Farnborough, Hants, UK: Gregg International Publishers Limited, 1972), 26-29.
35. Dohm, *Concerning the Amelioration*, 60-61. Johann August Schlettwein, the leading physiocratic thinker in Germany at the time, was in the minority when he identified the economic stability of the Christian consumer rather than the moral rehabilitation of the Jew as his rationale for promoting occupational reform. He felt that rerouting the Jews into manual skills and manufacturing could bring an end to the cycle whereby the business activities that Jews were restricted to all had the effect of increasing the cost of goods to the Christian consumer. Liberles, "From Toleration to *Verbesserung*," 6.
36. Dohm, *Concerning the Amelioration*, 60, 51-54, 61-62.
37. Dohm, *Concerning the Amelioration*, 60.
38. J. G. Herder, quoted in Barzilay, "Jew in the Literature," 103.
39. Katz, *Out of the Ghetto*, 85-86.
40. Liberles, "From Toleration to *Verbesserung*," 15-16.
41. Abbé Grégoire, *Essai sur la régénération*, 83.
42. Cardinal Fleury, quoted in *Letter to the Right Honourable Sir Thomas Chitty* (London: 1760), 43-44
43. Diderot, quoted in Barzilay, "Jew in the Literature," 103.
44. *Spectator*, no. 495. Saturday, 27 September 1753: 82.
45. Toland, *Reasons for Naturalizing the Jews*, 40.
46. Charles Louis Montesquieu, *Lettres Persanes*, Texte établi et présenté par Elie Carcasonne (1721; repr., Paris, 1929). Letter lx.
47. Montesquieu, *Lettres Persanes*, Letter lx; Toland, *Reasons for Naturalizing the Jews*, 6; *Letter to the Right Honourable Sir Thomas Chitty*, 43, 63-64.

48. Toland, *Reasons for Naturalizing the Jews*, 41. The English anonymous merchant, who was a staunch supporter of the Enlightenment and a proponent of putting Jews "on the same footing as the old inhabitants" "in all respects relating to trade," was at pains to reassure the Lord Mayor of London that "none of them [would] be permitted to be of His Majesty's privy council or a member of either house of parliament, or to hold any office or place of trust either civil or military under the government—all these should be reserved for the old inhabitants." *Letter to the Right Honourable Sir Thomas Chitty*, 80.

49. Schmidt found that, without exception, in the thirty years following the publication of Dohm's tract all writers advocated religious reform. "Terms of Emancipation," 31.

50. J. D. Michaelis, quoted in Liberles, "From Toleration to *Verbesserung*," 13.

51. An anonymous writer of the period, quoted in Katz, *Out of the Ghetto*, 131.

52. Diderot, quoted in Barzilay, "Jew in the Literature," 100.

53. J. G. Fichte, quoted in Mendes-Flohr and Reinharz, *Jew in the Modern World*, 309.

54. Gustav Mayer, "Early German Socialism and German Emancipation," *Jewish Social Studies* 1, no. 4 (October 1939): 413-14.

55. Mosse, *Toward the Final Solution*, 129.

56. Reaching back to the time of the Jews' enslavement in Egypt, the Hebraists determined that imitation of the Egyptians was actually the foundation for what Jews claimed was revealed religion. John Spencer's *Legibus Hebraeorum* (1685) was one of the main vehicles advancing this idea. Edward Breuer traces in detail the history of Christian scholarship of the Hebrew Bible in *The Limits of Enlightenment: Jews, Germans, and the Eighteenth-Century Study of Scripture* (Cambridge, Mass.: Harvard University Press, 1996), chap. 3. See also David S. Katz, "The Hutchinsonians and Hebraic Fundamentalism in Eighteenth-Century England," in *Sceptics, Millenarians, and Jews*, ed. David S. Katz and Jonathan I. Israel (Leiden, N.Y.: E. J. Brill, 1990), 252-55.

57. Hertzberg, *French Enlightenment*, chap. 9, 253-58; Jay R. Berkovitz, *The Shaping of Jewish Identity in Nineteenth-Century France* (Detroit: Wayne State University Press, 1989), 33-34.

58. Hertzberg, *French Enlightenment*, 299-308.

59. Voltaire, quoted in Barzilay, "Jew in the Literature," 62.

60. Montesquieu, quoted in Barzilay, "Jew in the Literature," 101.

61. Montesquieu and Abbé Grégoire, quoted in Barzilay, "Jew in the Literature," 101.

62. Goethe, quoted in Barzilay, "Jew in the Literature," 101.

63. J. D. Michaelis, quoted in Katz, *Out of the Ghetto*, 91-92.

64. Dohm, *Concerning the Amelioration*, 80.

65. This comment of Dohm's may be found in his second volume, *Über die bürgerliche Verbesserung der Juden, II* (1783) which, unfortunately, is rarely referred to. Ruprecht-Karls-Universitat Heidelberg, Germany. Call No. SWB 02442963. See 171-87, 214-15, 222-24, 236-46, 259-62, 290-94, 358-60. See also Katz, *Out of the Ghetto*, 64.

66. Katz, *Out of the Ghetto*, 94-95.

67. Quoted in Hertzberg, *French Enlightenment*, 323; Molino, "Right to be Equal," 90-91. Charles Malesherbes recommended granting Jews permission to use public legal registers for their personal status and other issues. This would undermine the communal organizations while helping to draw Jews closer to the general society, which in turn, would reduce antipathy towards them. The ultimate outcome of this process, he anticipated, would be their conversion.

68. François Malot, a scholarly churchman writing in 1776, quoted in Hertzberg, *French Enlightenment*, 260-63.

69. Johann Casper Lavater, quoted in Katz, *Out of the Ghetto*, 107-8.

70. The complete title of Isaac de Pinto's work was *Apologie pour la nation juive, ou réflexions critiques sur le premier chapitre du VIIème tome des oeuvres de M. de Voltaire au sujet des Juifs. Par l'auteur de 'Essai sur le luxe.'*
71. Abbé Antoine Guenée, quoted in Hertzberg, *French Enlightenment*, 291.
72. Katz, *Out of the Ghetto*, 108-9.
73. Katz, *Out of the Ghetto*, 118, 123. Schleiermacher may have come to this idea because he was extremely wary about the effects of mass conversion, which to his mind would have brought about a Judaization of the Church.
74. Goethe, quoted in Howard M. Sachar, *The Course of Modern Jewish History* (1958; rev. ed., Vintage Books / New York: Random House, Inc., 1990), 148.
75. Katz, "The Term Jewish Emancipation," 22.
76. Katz, *Out of the Ghetto*, 123.
77. F. T. Hartmann, quoted in Katz, *Out of the Ghetto*, 94-95.
78. K. W. F. Grattenauer, quoted in Katz, *Out of the Ghetto*, 85-86.
79. J. G. Herder, quoted in Barzilay, "Jew in the Literature," 108.
80. Johann Gottfried Herder, "Bekehrung der Juden," *Herders sämtliche Werke, herausgegeben von Bernhard Suphan* (Berlin, 1883), 14: 61-75.
81. Barzilay, "Jew in the Literature," 92.
82. Abbé Maury, quoted in Katz, *Out of the Ghetto*, 100.
83. Mayer, "Early German Socialism," 416.
84. J. G. Fichte, quoted in Katz, *Jewish Emancipation and Self-Emancipation*, 80-81.
85. Abbé Grégoire and Goethe, quoted in Barzilay, "Jew in the Literature," 102.
86. Joseph II's *Toleranzpatent*, quoted in Mendes-Flohr and Reinharz, *Jew in the Modern World*, 39, 37.
87. When François Hell coined the expression *status in statu* in 1779, it was not used in connection with the Jews. A modification made by Johann Heinrich Schulz in 1784 resulted in the standard application of the expression, which Fichte popularized. Jacob Katz, "State Within a State," in *Emancipation and Assimilation*, ed. Jacob Katz (Westmead, Farnborough, Hants, UK: Gregg International Publishers Limited, 1972), 48-56.
88. Katz, "State Within a State," 56-58, 61, 65-70.
89. Ernst Traugott von Kortum, quoted in Katz, "State Within a State," 64.
90. Count de Clermont-Tonnerre, quoted in Berkovitz, *Shaping of Jewish Identity*, 71.
91. Hannah Arendt, "Privileged Jews," in *Emancipation and Counter-Emancipation: Selected Essays from Jewish Social Studies*, ed. Abraham G. Duker and Meir Ben-Horin (New York: Ktav Publishing House, 1974), 57.
92. Baron Schroetter, quoted in Katz, *Out of the Ghetto*, 102.
93. David Hartley, quoted in Barzilay, "Jew in the Literature," 105. Barzilay mentions Basnage, Toland, Diderot, Voltaire, Herder, and Michaelis as some of the other *philosophes* who held this view.
94. J. D. Michaelis, quoted in Katz, *Out of the Ghetto*, 91-92.
95. Barzilay, "Jew in the Literature," 105.
96. F. T. Hartmann, quoted in Katz, *Out of the Ghetto*, 94-95.
97. Traditionally a core belief in Judaism, it is counted among the "Thirteen Articles of Creed" of Maimonides.
98. Barzilay, "Jew in the Literature," 106.
99. Abbé Grégoire, quoted in Barzilay, "Jew in the Literature," 106.
100. Ismar Freund, quoted in Katz, *Out of the Ghetto*, 76-78. Freund was a contemporary of Humboldt's and wrote a good deal on his work in *Die Emanzipation der Juden in Preussen unter besonderer Berücksichtigung des Gesetzes vom 11. Marz 1812*.
101. Ismar Freund, quoted in Katz, *Out of the Ghetto*, 76-78.

102. K. W. F. Grattenauer, quoted in Katz, *Out of the Ghetto*, 101.
103. F. T. Hartmann, quoted in Katz, *Out of the Ghetto*, 94.
104. Breuer, *Limits of Enlightenment*, 17. As Ole Peter Grell and Roy Porter have pointed out, religion retained its preeminence in European society during the eighteenth century, despite deists' relentless condemnation of it as institutionalized, ritualized, superstitious, clerically driven, and inauthentic, having supplanted the natural religion of morality. The self-appointed task of deists was one of reform: to excise bigotry and superstition and put in their place a god of reason and nature. "Toleration in Enlightenment Europe," in *Toleration in Enlightenment Europe,* ed. Ole Peter Grell and Roy Porter (Cambridge: Cambridge University Press, 2000), 1-2. Still, one should not minimize the influence of or the receptivity to deistic thought. The fate of Robert Dodsley's (noted poet, playwright, bookseller, and promoter who died in 1764) *The Oeconomy of Human Life Translated from an Indian Manuscript written by an Ancient Brahmin to which is Prefixed an Account of the Manner in Which the Said Manuscript was Discovered in a Letter from an English Gentleman now Residing in China, to the Earl of* **** was that within fifty years more copies of it would be sold than any other book published in the 18th century, with the exception of the Bible. Translated into every Western language between 1750 and 1800, two hundred editions were published on the continent and forty-eight editions in the United States. Masked as a Taoist, or perhaps Brahmin text, it was written in the Biblical style, presumably to assure its reception and digestion, and it promoted the values of deism. Ruderman, *Jewish Enlightenment*, 95.
105. Roy Porter, "The Enlightenment in England," in *The Enlightenment in National Context,* ed. Roy Porter and Mikulas Teich (Houndmills, Basingstoke, Hampshire, UK and New York: Palgrave / St. Martins Press, 2001), 4, 6.
106. B. W. Young, *Religion and Enlightenment in Eighteenth-Century England: Theological Debate from Locke to Burke* (Oxford: Clarendon Press / New York: Oxford University Press, 1998), 167-212.
107. K. W. F. Grattenauer, quoted in Katz, *Out of the Ghetto*, 88.
108. Katz, *Jewish Emancipation and Self-Emancipation*, 23, 113; Katz, *Out of the Ghetto*, 106-7.
109. Dohm, *Concerning the Amelioration*, 65-66.
110. J. D. Michaelis, quoted in Liberles, "From Toleration to *Verbesserung*," 14. Some of the impediments to serving in the military were the Sabbath, the many Jewish festivals, and dietary restrictions.
111. Dohm, *Concerning the Amelioration*, 75-83. Since Jews would not be able to serve in the army immediately, "Therefore, nothing will be more justified than to require them to pay a special tax for non-fulfillment of that obligation."
112. Jacob Katz, *Tradition and Crisis: Jewish Society at the End of the Middle Ages* 1958 (Hebrew); 1961 (English); repr., New York: Schocken Books, 1971), 254-55. Addressing this topic in his doctoral thesis in 1935, Katz believed that a "neutral society" had been established. Later, he would revise this to a "semineutral society," at best. *Out of the Ghetto*, 231; David Cesarani, "Introduction," in *The Making of Modern Anglo-Jewry,* ed. David Cesarani (Oxford: Basil Blackwell, 1990), 4-5.
113. Katz, *Exclusiveness and Tolerance*, 173-74.
114. Katz, *Out of the Ghetto*, 51-54.
115. Salomon Bartholdy, Abraham Mendelssohn's brother-in-law, quoted in Sachar, *Course of Modern Jewish History*, 151.
116. Arendt, "Privileged Jews," 68, 70, 73. Since Arendt's writing, it has become clear that the German proponents of the *Aufklarung* were not mainly members of the bourgeoisie, in the sense of being engaged in finance, trade, and commerce, or as merchants and businessmen. Rather, as the sources used here show, many were professionals: doctors

lawyers, and especially state administrators.

117. Katz, *Out of the Ghetto*, 231.
118. Katz, *Jewish Emancipation and Self-Emancipation*, 69.
119. Arendt, "Privileged Jews," 70.
120. Arendt, "Privileged Jews," 70, 72. A memorandum written by German Jew David Friedlander at the time indicates that ten per cent of this group converted between 1806 and 1810. Raphael Mahler, *A History of Modern Jewry 1780-1815* (London: Vallentine, Mitchell & Co. Ltd., 1971), 217. This figure or an even higher one has been posited by Deborah Hertz, "Seductive Conversion in Berlin, 1770-1809," in *Jewish Apostasy in the Modern World*, ed. Todd M. Endelman (New York: Holmes & Meier Publishers, Inc., 1987), 54-55.
121. Adam Müller, quoted in Arendt, "Privileged Jews," 85.
122. Mayer, "Early German Socialism," 409.
123. Wilhelm von Humboldt, quoted in Arendt, "Privileged Jews," 56.

Chapter 3
From Ideals to Praxis: The Emergence of Liberalism

For anyone who enters the arena of liberalism, the task of distilling its common elements is a challenging one. Arriving at a definition that is satisfactory to everyone is even more difficult.* It is inevitable that Steven Beller's definition of liberalism as "the political expression of the Enlightenment"[1] would be challenged; as James Schmidt has pointed out: "We forget that many *Aufklärers* were not liberals, [and] that some of the more ardent liberals were by no means well disposed toward the Enlightenment."[2] Beyond the difficulties of identifying common elements in and formulating a definition of liberalism is the problem that many individuals found in the liberal camp do not belong there.

There were individuals who called themselves liberals but for whom this term encompassed only those principles with which they were comfortable. In some circles, identifying oneself as a liberal had a certain cachet attached to it; by paying lip service to 'liberal' values, one's status automatically rose. In the common parlance of the nineteenth century, those who wanted to be considered 'progressive'—politically, socially, or intellectually—often described themselves as liberals. Expediency drove others into the liberal camp, particularly in politics. Wherever the Liberal Party was in ascendance, we find aspiring politicians legitimizing themselves by pronouncing popular liberal values—this, in spite of the fact that their own views were contrary to liberal ones (at least on certain issues). In fact, it seems that everyone could lay claim to being a liberal, if they so desired. The breadth of views that could be accommodated under the liberal mantle is well-illustrated by Gyozo Istoczy, considered the preeminent anti-Semite in Hungary during the latter third of the nineteenth century. A Liberal member of Parliament for many years, he only resigned from the Party in 1882 and shortly thereafter founded the National Anti-Semite Party in 1883.[3] Historians have tended to take these claims too seriously. Holding these individuals up to a standard that they have determined as normative liberalism, historians have then undertaken to critique their 'liberal' views.[4]

We may thus settle on Rustem Vambery's very generic definition of liberal-

---

* One may begin with J. A. Hobson, who divided nineteenth-century liberalism into two distinct phases: the old *laissez-faire* liberalism and the new one based on a "policy of social reconstruction." *Crisis of Liberalism* (London: P. S. King & Son, 1909), 3.

ism, which considers it the legitimate child of the French Revolution and Napoleon's 'new order.' Liberalism, despite an absence of orthodox tenets, possessed "positive aims:" "Dignity of the individual, freedom of the mind, search for the common good according to Lord Morley, these were the objectives of liberalism."[5] There is one aspect of liberalism that does deserve special consideration, however. This is the fundamental dichotomy inherent within liberalism, stated in the following manner:

> There is 'dogmatic' toleration—the true acknowledgment of all expressions of faith as equal. Then there is 'political' toleration—the pragmatic concession of equality within the political commonwealth. Interesting consequences derive from that distinction: political toleration, being part of the political realities of a society, tends to abrogate concessions of toleration as soon as the initial political conditions change. The history of the Edict of Nantes could serve as an appropriate illustration in this regard.[6]

A. A. van Schelven's construction gives rise to a more cynical definition of liberalism than Vambery's: liberalism is what emerged after the altruistic rhetoric of the Enlightenment was digested and filtered through the sieve of pragmatism.

'Dogmatic' toleration was expressed in the concept of universal emancipation that was central to the *weltanschauung* of the nineteenth century.[7] Jewish emancipation* was advanced by the state in fulfillment of this concept. This meant that the debate among the Enlightenment thinkers as to whether emancipation should precede reform or follow it would be settled in favor of emancipation first, after which it was expected that Jews would undertake reform and soon assimilate. This two-pronged approach to the emancipation of the Jews was among the credentials of any self-confessed liberal. Like the Jewish Oral Law of Biblical times that was considered binding and was to be applied in harmony with the Written Law (the Torah), the 'Oral Law of Assimilation' was to work in tandem with the 'Written Law of Bills of Emancipation.' However, once politicians donned the liberal mantle and confirmed that reform would not be a condition of emancipation but reduced to an expectation, liberals would become liable for the failure of Jews to assimilate in accordance with the Enlightenment thinkers' detailed prescription and further, the multiple negative affects on society caused by their expanded presence in it. At this point, people expressed their

---

* While it has now become the norm to apply the term 'emancipation' to all efforts to improve the status of the Jews, this term was not in use during the Enlightenment or the early years of the liberal era. After the publication of Christian Wilhelm von Dohm's seminal work, *Concerning the Amelioration of the Civil Status of the Jews* (1781), Enlightenment thinkers typically spoke of self-betterment, civic betterment or improvement, amelioration, or the removal of civic disabilities. The actual provenance of the term seems to date from 1828, at which time the movements to relieve English Catholics and Jews of their civic disabilities coincided. The expression 'Catholic Emancipation' was quickly adapted, and the expression 'Jewish emancipation,' immediately taken up by the press, replaced all former terms. Katz, *Jewish Emancipation and Self-Emancipation*, 78.

dissatisfaction not only with the Jews but also with liberalism as the author of this untenable situation. This, in turn, led to accusations that the liberals were in the pocket of the Jews. However, at their pragmatic best throughout most of the nineteenth century, liberals defended the ideals of egalitarianism and freedom that had been promoted under the rubric of 'dogmatic' toleration. This avoidance of "political realities" continued for several decades, but eventually, liberals proceeded to "abrogate concessions of toleration," exposing the dichotomy inherent in liberalism.

Nascent Liberalism: Joseph II's *Toleranzpatent*

Relying on Emperor Joseph II's statement that "tolerance is an effect of that beneficial increase of knowledge which now enlightens Europe, and which is owing to philosophy, and the efforts of great men,"[8] many historians have claimed that those regulations in Joseph II's *Toleranzpatent* (1781-83) directed at the Jews reflect an attitude of tolerance (according to its generous meaning) towards them. Therefore, they pinpoint the *Toleranzpatent* as the beginning of the end of centuries of discrimination against the Jews, thus paving the way for emancipation.[9] Yet, the new regulations governing the lives of the Jews were called "favors", and the first lines stated explicitly that it was not to be understood as an expansion of Jewish rights.

> It certainly is not at all Our supreme wish herewith to grant the Jews residing in Vienna an expansion [of rights] with respect to external tolerance [*Duldung*]. On the contrary, it will remain that they do not constitute an actual community under a designated leader from their own nation, but as hitherto each family, considered separately, will serenely enjoy the protection of the laws of the land in accordance with the tolerance [*Duldung*] specifically given it by Our government of Lower Austria.[10]

The regulations themselves were geared to eliminating Jewish particularities,[11] that is to say, reform along the lines of the Enlightenment ideals specific to the Jews: "Our goal [is] to make the Jewish nation useful and serviceable to the state, mainly through better education and enlightenment of its youth as well as by directing them to the sciences, the arts and the crafts."[12]

To this end, the use of Hebrew and "the so-called Jewish language" (Yiddish) in public and commercial records was prohibited; after a two-year transition period, any legal instruments drawn up in either of these languages would be null and void.[13] Concerning education, Jewish children were permitted to attend Christian primary and secondary schools. The option to establish Jewish primary schools was also available provided that three suitable young people had been trained by the administration in "acceptable pedagogical practice;" the school was administered in the same way as state-sanctioned primary schools; and all religious material was inspected and approved by the superintendent of schools.[14] Both instruction in and the practice of any kind of craft or trade was now permitted to the Jew should there be mutual willingness between a Jew and a Christian to forge an apprenticeship agreement, although not up to the level of master craftsman. The free arts such as sculpting and painting were also permitted.[15] Economic utility was given prominence: Jews could engage in commerce and they might continue to invest in factories and manufacture "that benefit the public." Even the proscription against living in the rural regions of Lower Austria was suspended for those who "wish to establish a factory or pursue a useful trade."[16]

Apart from the *Toleranzpatent*, there was an ongoing process of adding to the body of law directed at the Jews. These laws would remain in force beyond the life of the *Toleranzpatent*, which the emperor all but rescinded shortly before his death in 1790.[17] The Imperial Chancery offered this rationale for these laws: "The Jews through their religious prejudice, their closed union, and their separation from other believers, through their aversion for bodily exertion, and their desire for rapid gain are harmful rather than helpful members of civil society."[18] All edicts, then, from 1781 onward were issued with a twofold purpose: to make it difficult or even impossible to maintain a distinctive Jewish way of life; and to correct the faults of the Jews and put them on the path of assimilation.

Examples of the former include the abolition of rabbinical juridical autonomy (1784)[19]; a special tax on ritually slaughtered meat (1784) which was periodically increased; and a candle-lighting tax (1797)—to be collected weekly before the Sabbath—which rose to two and a half times its original amount.[20] Counted among the laws meant to promote the "integration" of the Jews was the obligation to serve in the military (1787).[21] A year later, it became mandatory to Germanize both personal and family names that were preselected by the government.[22] Passed in 1806, a court decree mandated that all elected officials of the Jewish community have an understanding of German. This decree was amplified in 1810 to include all Jews who wished to vote in Jewish communal elections; moreover, it stipulated that they not only understand, but also speak and write German. To further entrench German as the *lingua franca*, Jewish couples, before being permitted to marry, were required by decree (1812) to pass an examination in German on a Jewish religious-moral text. An imperial decree was also issued in 1820 setting a target date by which time synagogue worship would have to be conducted in either German or the language spoken by the local populace.[23] Behind the passage of the law forbidding Jews from the occupation of innkeeping (an almost exclusively Jewish enterprise in many places)[24] was the idea of moral reform connected to occupational reform. It was the immorality of the Jewish innkeeper that provided the peasants with so much alcohol that eventually resulted in their indebtedness to the Jew as well as harming the peasants' families. Thus, the *Toleranzpatent* should be seen as a document that bears the clear imprint of the Enlightenment ideals specific to the Jews. Any amelioration of the Jews' condition was simply a byproduct of these measures.

'Prometheus Unbound:'
The Emancipation of Jews in France

In comparison to Joseph II's Jewry that was offered only the Enlightenment ideals specific to the Jews, the Jews of France were beneficiaries of both these and the general Enlightenment ideals. 'Dogmatic' toleration drove the revolutionaries to consider the emancipation of the Jews. But this "true acknowledgment of all expressions of faith as equal," to quote van Schelven, was not sufficient impetus to emancipate them. The rubric under which this did occur more closely resembles 'political' toleration. Under the direction of the National Assembly, Louis XVI passed the "Law of Jewish Emancipation" on 27 January 1790, giving full civic rights to the Sephardi Jews of Balogne, Bordeaux, and Paris.[25] The general willingness to admit these Jews to the French polity was undoubtedly due to their significant contribution to the economy and their somewhat neutral status as Jews: most of them had originally entered France as 'New Christians,' and as such had never reclaimed certain distinctive dimensions of Jewishness. Ashkenazi Jews living in Alsace (often referred to as German Jews), who formed the vast majority of French Jewry, possessed neither of these qualifying features. Rather, they were considered to be both unassimilated and usurious. Abbé Maury and Jean François Rewbell, a Jacobin deputy from Alsace were among the many who wanted to withhold citizenship from these Jews. Abbé Maury blamed the Jews' tenacity to their religion for keeping them in an alien and morally degenerate state while Rewbell felt that it had contributed to the creation of certain Jewish social and political doctrines that were at odds with French civil law.[26] Given the bitter fight that ensued in the National Assembly for the next year and a half, it is clear that the extension of emancipation to the Alsatian Jews (28 September 1791) was an act performed to maintain the consistency of the revolutionary pledge: to create in France an atmosphere of *liberté, fraternité*, and *égalité* (what van Schelven calls the "the pragmatic concession of equality within the political commonwealth"). Excluding the Alsatian Jews would have compromised this principle.

Not long after universal emancipation, signs of retraction began to appear, revealing that, as far as the French were concerned, the Alsatian Jews had not (yet) taken the Enlightenment ideals specific to the Jews to heart. Foreclosures that put the newly purchased properties of many thousands of peasants into the hands of Jewish creditors between 1802 and 1804 were blamed on the Jews' usurious practices. This crisis became part of the Royalists' arsenal in their drive to revoke the revolutionary emancipation.[27] Jewish usury was also one of the main issues that impelled Napoleon to convoke an assembly of Jewish notables, to whom he submitted a series of questions, the answers to which were meant to determine the Jews' credentials as suitable citizens. The outcome was the Imperial Decree of 30 May 1806: two clauses were related to the establishment of a Central Consistory to administer French Jewry and the third clause, known as the 'Infamous Decree,' effectively reduced the emancipated status of the

Jews. Bearing more than a passing resemblance to the *Toleranzpatent* of Joseph II, it indicated a pulling back to the nascent, pre-emancipatory period of liberalism.[28]

The government also contemplated withdrawing the right of citizenship (at least temporarily) from Alsatian Jews and commissioned an inquiry to look into the matter. In the event, nothing was done, but the pamphlet produced for the inquiry by lawyer Louis Poujol was extremely critical of the Jews. Poujol cited the Jews' continuation of usury, nonattendance at public ceremonies, nonfulfillment of military obligations, and failure to take to agriculture and the trades. Moreover, their animosity towards Christians made them enemies of the state. On a grander scale, their desire for world domination was embedded in their very religion and was their ultimate goal. In order to achieve the betterment of the Jews, he advocated not only firm control over their economic activities but also religious reform. Only when Jews abandoned their peculiarities could they be assimilated into French society.[29] In all the points mentioned by Poujol, we see the clear imprint of the Enlightenment ideals specific to the Jews.

Emancipation granted under the banner of '*liberté, fraternité, égalité* for all' seemed to provide little incentive for French Jews to wave their own banner of 'complete assimilation.' Some details are available about the situation in Alsace after 1810. A letter from the Central Consistory noted that out of 3,700 Jewish children of school age, only 348 were attending public schools. As another letter to a *Conseiller d'Etat* explained, "Christians are annoyed to see their children mingle with Jews in the educational institutions," and so school directors refused to allow them to attend.[30] On the other hand, this same letter made the point that Jews were failing to reform: "Their religious prejudices, their usages and customs keep them from our schools."[31] In an effort to help "this class of persons" whose "moral destiny" was at stake, the Minister of the Interior suggested organizing special schools for them alone.[32] This suggestion was in fact taken up; however, these special Jewish schools did not fare well. The statistics on graduates illustrates their marginal success: between 1843 and 1851, 156 girls had been trained in a girls' school in Paris; in Strasbourg, only eighty-five boys had gone through one of the most notable *écoles de travail* between 1833 and 1845; and between 1845 and 1856, the Mulhouse school only accommodated between ten and twenty-two students annually. In total, only several hundred children ever attended such schools, in spite of a potential capacity to train many more.[33] These few children experienced a very uneven education: in some localities "only Hebrew reading and writing are ordinarily taught," wrote one inspector; "the children . . . learn nothing of what a French citizen should know," wrote another. The pattern of low attendance in the secular schools continued. Paula Hyman cites a letter (1831) from the Administrative Commission of the Strasbourg Jewish Community that attributes the low rate to "apathy", and she further supplies a number of sources describing Jewish parents' resistance to modern education. In 1833, the *département* of the Lower Rhine assessed that there were 4,000 Jewish children of primary school age but only 365 were registered.[34]

Jews continued to believe in the Messiah, maintain their attachment to Zion, and remain obedient to a separate legal system. Particularly this last point was the object of much criticism. It was said to foster social exclusiveness and promote a dual standard of morality. Agricole Moreau's tract, De *l'incompatibilité entre le Judaisme et l'exercise des droits de cite et des moyens de rendre les Juifs citoyens* saw religious law intruding into the civil realm, compromising the loyalty of the Jew and causing conflict, particularly in the areas of habits, customs, behavior, and morality.[35] Adherence to such a system believed to be of divine origin also came to mean that the Jews were 'uncivilized'. French historian and statesman François Guizot popularized a new dimension to the word 'civilization' when he drew a connection between it and the idea that "we are called upon to reform, perfect, and regulate all that is. We feel able to act upon the world and to extend throughout it the glorious empire of reason."[36] Jews, in maintaining their religious beliefs, were failing to apply reason and thus reform their religion. The French were disappointed in their expectations in other ways. The extension of Jewish residence from the original ten *départements* to forty-four does not truly represent demographic trends. Jews tended to gravitate to communities they had previously inhabited.[37] Occupational change, too, was marginal. Rather, new circumstances simply added a twist to age-old occupations. All these issues were placed on the front burner by another essay contest in 1824, asking questions not unlike those posed prior to the French Revolution. Whether in favor of emancipation or not, all the contestants evaluated Jews and Judaism negatively. The winning submissions considered the following points to promote *régénération*: religious reform, economic diffusion, education, and restrictive legislation for recalcitrant Jews.*

The case of France is instructive. As a chronological exception, it provides a preview of the pattern of reaction to Jewish emancipation that would be repeated as each country, in turn, emancipated its Jews. French Jewry's emancipation was succeeded by charges—some easily supportable, such as the resistance to gravitate to agriculture and the crafts, the withholding of children from secular schools, and the pattern of living concentrated in certain areas; others less so, as in the charges of ongoing usury and social exclusivism—that Jews were failing to implement the Enlightenment ideals specific to the Jews.

---

* Berkovitz, *Shaping of Jewish Identity*, 11-15, 57, 117-18; Hyman, *Emancipation of the Jews*, 21-24. I would say that this left French Jews with three options. One, they could intensify their efforts at reform. Two, they could follow in the path of the Jew Theodore Ratisbonne, a professor of philosophy, who initially was a strong advocate of religious reform, then a convert to Catholicism in the 1820s, and ultimately a priest with pronounced conversionist leanings. Or, three, they could join various movements such as the prototypical socialist Saint-Simonians which seemed to look beyond class, social standing, and ethnic origins. Although, to be sure, Zosa Szajkowski is emphatic that French socialist literature from Saint-Simon to Drumont was devoid of any "sympathetic references to the Jews." "The Jewish Saint-Simonians and Socialist Antisemites in France," *Jewish Social Studies* 9, no. 1 (1942): 60.

Radical Departures

Zionism

It is clear from the date—1798—of an anonymous letter entitled a "Letter to the Brethren" written by an Italian Jew, that the practical intent to resettle in Palestine begins at least from this time. Due to the unrelenting animosity towards Jews, writes the author, the only solution to the Jewish plight was to become a nation once again.

> O my Brethren, what sacrifices ought we not make to attain this object? We shall return to our country, we shall live under our own laws—we shall behold those places where our ancestors demonstrated their courage and their virtues. Already I see you all animated with a holy zeal. Israelites! the end of our misfortune is at hand. The opportunity is favorable—take care that you do not allow it to escape!*

This idea quickly gained momentum, much to the dismay of some of their co-religionists. David Friedlander spoke for Jewish reformers.

> [The Jewish people] has lost the feeling for the value of reason and the understanding of the higher truths. . . . On top of all this, the idea of a Messiah was added which has totally confused the heads and has prevented them from a free judgment. . . . This expectation of the Messiah and of the return to the Promised Land has necessarily strengthened the inclination to concentrate all the diligence and contemplation on the ancient history, on the service in the Temple, on the sacrifices and the ceremonial law.[38]

David Levi (Levy) stated the case for traditional Judaism: restoration of the Jews was in God's hands; until such time as God chose for the ingathering of His people, Jews were to remain dispersed throughout the Diaspora.[39]

Five phases can be discerned in the Jewish literature concerning the restoration of the state of Palestine. In the first phase, the underlying rationale of unrelenting misfortune is preeminent, although a sense of buoyancy is also apparent, whether due to the expected coming of the Messiah that Friedlander

---

* Quoted in Franz Kobler, *Napoleon and the Jews* (New York: Shocken Books Inc., 1976), 30-32. Far from being an obscure piece, which would not be surprising, this document was widely circulated. It was republished in several literary magazines in both French and English in 1798: *Courier de Londres, La décade philosophique, littéraire et politique,* the *St. James Chronicle,* and *The Monthly Visitor and Pocket Companion.* Generally, a distinction is made between Zionism as an intellectual movement and Zionism as a mass movement, the implication being that only when it became a mass movement (which is usually tied to Theodor Herzl) was there really any practical intention to settle in Palestine. The writings of the following 'Zionists' seem to refute such a distinction.

referred to or because the "opportunity is favorable" as the anonymous writer alluded to. In the second phase of such writings, the theme of restoration as redemption becomes prominent—after the failure of the first round of Jewish emancipation and after persecution of the Jews intensified in Russia in 1825. Rabbi Yehuda Alkalai spoke of it in a booklet called *Shema Yisrael* (Hear, O Israel) published in 1834 and in another work published nine years later, entitled *The Third Redemption*. "A Natural Beginning of the Redemption" was the title of one of the chapters in Rabbi Zvi Hirsch Kalischer's book, *Seeking Zion* (1862).

A third theme may be detected from the mid-nineteenth century on: Jewish restoration to Palestine couched in nationalistic terms. Sensing that the reestablishment of Palestine was within the realm of possibility in this age of ethnicities struggling for nationhood, Rev. (Rabbi) Isaac Leeser of Philadelphia asked in an editorial: "And if ancient Germany again becomes a nation—if Poland throws off successfully its chains of mighty oppressors—if fair Italy takes a rank as one people . . . why should not the patriotic Hebrew also look forward to the time . . . when he may again proudly boast of his own country."[40] Also approaching the idea of a return to Palestine from the nationalistic perspective, Moses Hess, author of *Rome and Jerusalem* (1862) came to passionately affirm the existence of a Jewish nationality, "which is inseparably connected with my ancestral heritage, with the Holy Land and the Eternal City."[41] However, Hess's nationalism was expressed in a way that reflected his continental perspective.

> As long as the Jew denies his nationality . . . his false position must become ever more intolerable. What purpose does this deception serve? The nations of Europe have always regarded the existence of the Jews in their midst as an anomaly. We shall always remain strangers among the nations. . . . Religious fanaticism may cease to cause hatred of the Jews in the more culturally advanced countries; but despite enlightenment and emancipation, the Jew in exile who denies his nationality will never earn the respect of the nations among whom he dwells.*

The outbreak of pogroms in Russia in 1880 provoked the publication of a great number of pamphlets from 1881 on. Lwow lawyer Moses Shrenzel wrote a booklet entitled *The Solution of the Jewish Problem* in 1881 that remained fairly obscure while Dr. Leo Pinsker's tract, *Auto-Emancipation*, along much the same lines, became quite popular. In it, we see a fourth theme: the Jew as alien.

---

* Excerpt from Moses Hess's *Rome and Jerusalem*, quoted in Hertzberg, *Zionist Idea*, 121. The mid-nineteenth century is the point at which liberal nationalism in the mold of the American and French Revolutions (and upon which Leeser relied) and conservative nationalism, exemplified by Gobineau's *Essai sur l'inégalité des races humaines* (1853) (which appeared not long before Hess wrote his tract), overlap. Hertzberg, *Zionist Idea*, 38.

[The Jew] is not a guest, much less a welcome guest. He is more like a beggar; and what beggar is welcome?. . . The *general law* does not apply to the Jews, as strangers in the true sense of the word. On the other hand, there are everywhere *laws for the Jews*, and if the general law is to apply to them, this fact must first be determined by a *special law*. . . .

. . . Generally, he is treated as an adopted child whose rights may be questioned; *never* is he considered a legitimate child of the fatherland. . . . The *legal emancipation* of the Jews is the crowning achievement of our century. But *legal emancipation* is not *social* emancipation, and with the proclamation of the former the Jews are still far from being emancipated from their exceptional *social position.*[42]

Furthermore, by its nature, legal emancipation is "a postulate of logic, of law, and of enlightened self-interest;" it is never an expression of "human feeling." For this, "social emancipation" is required. Emancipation "remains a rich gift, splendid alms, willingly or unwillingly flung to the poor, humble beggars whom no one, however, cares to shelter, because a homeless, wandering beggar wins confidence or sympathy from none."[43] Also written in 1882 was *Ein Zukunftsbild*, a piece by Edmund Eisler, a native of Tyrnava (located in today's Slovakia). Eisler painted a dramatic picture of Jewish migration to Palestine similar to the exodus from Egypt. In this tract, the fifth and final theme emerges: a Jewish state as a worldwide necessity because the Jewish problem had become a worldwide problem.*

Migration

Alongside these many writings, schemes, and practical efforts to bring about the restoration of the Jews to Palestine, large-scale Jewish migration from Europe was not only being suggested by Jews and non-Jews alike but being undertaken by thousands upon thousands of Jews. This trend is usually associated with Russia, which not only lacked an agenda to emancipate its large reservoir of Jewry but whose policies prompted a massive exodus from the latter part of the nineteenth century on. But decades earlier, this trend was prevalent in Central and Western Europe, where Jews would be emancipated shortly.[44]

Several points are worth noting about this phenomenon. First, the ebbs and flows of migration are a barometer of both public sentiment and the progress of legal emancipation. In the post-Treaty-of-Vienna climate, prominent members of the German *Verein für Kultur und Wissenschaft der Juden* wrote in 1822 to Mordecai Noah, a Jewish resident of Albany, New York that a massive emigration of European Jews to the United States was the only solution "to escape end-

---

* Mark Wischnitzer, *To Dwell in Safety: The Story of Jewish Migration since 1800* (Philadelphia: Jewish Publication Society of America, 1948), 55. Not only were Jews seeking protection through the establishment of a Jewish homeland, so was Fichte, as he wrote in 1793: "I see no other way to protect ourselves from the Jews, except if we conquer their promised land for them and send all of them there." Quoted in Mendes-Flohr and Reinharz, *Jew in the Modern World*, 309.

less slavery and oppression."[45] Twice (1832 and 1840) Baron A. M. Rothschild of Frankfurt was approached by one Bernhard Behrend to acquire an area in North America or Palestine for mass settlement by Polish and German Jews.[46] With Sir Moses Montefiore, plans for mass migration became more defined. While he personally favored Palestine, his schemes were not particularly Zionist in motivation; it was only one of several possible destinations.[47] Noah, who had gone on to be a diplomat, civil servant, writer, and traveler, published *Discourse on the Restoration of the Jews* in 1844, a plea to both Americans and other free peoples of the world to aid in a scheme to resettle the Jews in Palestine.[48]

In the wake of the 1848 Revolutions, persecution of the Jews intensified, as this Christian observer wrote:

> In several of my letters, I expressed the opinion that the Jewish people are hastening very fast toward a fearful persecution. In this opinion I have been much corroborated by late events and daily occurrences. Scarcely a day's paper appears without the news of some new excess against the Jews, in some part of the civilized world. And, moreover, I have come to the full persuasion, after having for years past closely watched the movement, that the more the Jews wedge themselves into Christian affairs and legislature, the more they fraternize and make common cause with Deists, Atheists, and Republicans of the day, the more do they expose themselves to the hatred of those very persons.[49]

This further deterioration provided even stronger impetus to emigrate, and it was in this context that the formation of the first emigration societies took place. They sprang up in Vienna, Pest, Prague, and Lwow (Lemberg), for example, on the Continent,[50] and in London, where the Jewish Emigration Society was formed in 1853 at the instigation of the Ladies Benevolent Loan and Visiting Society as a way to handle the ever increasing arrival of destitute Jews.[51]

The second point is that on each occasion when Russia was asked if it would agree to 'release' its Jews, it responded in the affirmative. In 1846, Jacob Isaac Altaras, scion of a famous Sephardi family in Marseilles, went to Russia himself and presented the government with a plan for colonizing large numbers of Jews from Russian Poland in Algeria. The Russian government agreed. No obstacles would be put in the way; emigration passports were offered free of charge, the only stipulation being that these Jews would cease to be Russian subjects. Altaras then took the matter up with the French Minister of War, Marshal Nicholas Soult, who authorized an official mission to Algeria to determine the feasibility of such a plan. Soult, however, was overruled by François Guizot, now Foreign Minister: "Do you intend to judaize [sic] Algeria?" he asked.[52] Again, early in the 1890s, the Russian government displayed receptivity to the idea of mass Jewish emigration, with Palestine as the destination. Russian Foreign Minister N. K. de Giers agreed to an international conference if the American government would propose it, but no such conference was ever held.[53]

The third point that may be extrapolated from the data on migration not only brings the Russian Jews but all Eastern European Jews into the Central-Western European orbit. Their ever-increasing migration to Central and Western Europe was either a matter of intention or because they found themselves stranded there.[54] It was the presence of these Jews that gave rise to the notion of 'our' Jews and 'those' Jews. It was 'our' Jews who were being assessed as to the feasibility of emancipation and around whom the emancipation debates revolved. Yet, the Eastern European Jews had a direct bearing on the proceedings because, since the Enlightenment, their presence was universally considered a major obstacle to social assimilation when the Jewish community as a whole was being looked at.⁵⁵

****

In only seven years, liberalism evolved from a tentatively articulated set of laws under Joseph II to a full-blown political system during the French Revolution. This system was characterized by 'political', not 'dogmatic', toleration in its approach to governance, and right from the beginning, the dichotomy inherent in liberalism became fully exposed. In the heated atmosphere of the French Revolution, amidst proclamations of *liberté, fraternité, égalité,* it may appear that the Enlightenment ideals specific to the Jews had been discarded and that Jews were emancipated under the umbrella of 'dogmatic' toleration. However, one must take note of the reluctance to emancipate the Alsatians, the bulk of French Jewry. Their emancipation was rather "part of the political realities;" and when more compelling realities surfaced, that is, when the Alsatian Jews provided little evidence that they were assimilating, "concessions of toleration" were abrogated, and the "pragmatic" decision was made to consider placing limitations on the Jews' political rights: the Imperial Decree of 1806; the inquiry into the removal of rights extended to Alsatian Jews; and the exclusion of Jewish children from the secular schools in Alsace. The popular judgment was that the Jews had not reached a level which warranted citizenship. Had Jewish emancipation not been proposed in the heat of revolution, there is no doubt that it would never have been approved at this time.

The emergence of Zionism and migration were responses to the legal, then qualified emancipation in France; the reversal of emancipation throughout the Napoleonic Empire (sanctioned by the great powers);[56] and the fact that although "the happy sun of all Europe [the Enlightenment] has arisen, so to speak, so that there is no longer anyone so savage and uneducated as not to know those duties that man naturally owes to man," Jews were not going to have a "minute share in the happiness."[57]

This chapter has described the early years of the liberal era, but it bears little resemblance to many accounts of this period which maintain that nineteenth-century liberalism allowed for the integration of Jews *as* Jews.[58] Moreover, these accounts present the process of Jewish emancipation as the essential plot of the period. Actually, impending emancipation was rather the sub-plot; it was the age-old framework of toleration that was the pervasive condition of Jewish existence throughout much of the nineteenth century. Jews were not patiently waiting in the wings for their cue to step on stage as emancipated Jews. In fact, there was extreme resistance to the idea of putting Jews on the stage at all.

Still, the 'spirit of the age' was prompting discussion of the emancipation of the Jews. In the early decades of the nineteenth century, the centerpiece of most of these discussions was the program for the reform of the Jews and its feasibility. As the philosophy of liberalism increasingly took hold, to be 'liberal' meant to favor emancipation, and so the dictates of 'political' toleration meant that the debaters increasingly advocated the immediate emancipation of the Jews.

NOTES

1. Steven Beller, *Vienna and the Jews, 1867–1938: A Cultural History* (Cambridge: Cambridge University Press, 1989), 122.
2. Schmidt, *What is Enlightenment?* 12.
3. In Hungary, in Alice Freifeld's estimation, liberalism "had an emotional resonance throughout the population, with virtually every political party calling itself liberal." This pervasive liberalism grew out of Hungary's subservient position to Austria: "Hungarian liberalism identified its conservative rival with the alien Royal court and thus discredited conservatism as a viable alternative." *Nationalism and the Crowd in Liberal Hungary, 1848–1914* (Washington DC: The Woodrow Wilson Center Press, 2000 / Baltimore: Johns Hopkins University Press, 2000), 19, 229, 240. Laszlo Tokeczki's *Magyar liberalizmus* [Hungarian Liberalism] (Budapest: Szazadveg, 1993) is a work that provides a good selection of representative writings on this subject. For contemporary views on the state of Hungarian liberalism, see Count Sandor Karolyi, quoted in Miklos Szabo, "Uj vonasok a szazadfordulo magyar konservativ politikai gondolkodasaban" [New Features in the Hungarian Conservative Political Thinking at the Turn of the Century] in *Szazadok* (1974): 108; Endre Ady, "A mennyeknek orszaga," [The Realm of Heavens] in *A Zsidosagrol* [About Jewry] (1903) [articles written between 27 August 1901 and 12 April 1903]; repr., Nagyvarad, 1919). In Britain, many who called themselves liberals only superficially embraced a commitment to the liberal ethos of tolerance (in the expansive sense of the word), according to W. Williams. With respect to the Jews, for example, he states that there was no "validation of the Jewish identity per se" nor any indication of the "demise of older anti-Semitic traditions which continued to travel freely along the informal channels of communication." British liberals practiced "the anti-Semitism of tolerance." "The Anti-Semitism of Tolerance: Middle Class Manchester and the Jews 1870-1900," in *City, Class and Culture*, ed. Alan J. Kidd and K. W. Roberts (Manchester: Manchester University Press, 1985), 78.
4. See for example, Barany, "Magyar Jew or Jewish Magyar?" 6; Randolph Braham, *The Politics of Genocide: The Holocaust in Hungary* (New York: Columbia University Press, 1981), 1:1, 3, 8; Maria M. Kovacs, *Liberal Professions and Illiberal Politics: Hungary from the Habsburgs to the Holocaust* (Washington, DC: Woodrow Wilson Center Press, 1994), 27.
5. Rustem Vambery, *Hungary—To Be Or Not To Be* (New York: Frederick Ungar Publishing Co., 1946), 90-91. Vambery was first a lawyer, then an appeal court judge, and later, a professor, publicist, and member of the Hungarian Academy of Sciences.
6. A. A. van Schelven, quoted in Hans J. Hillerbrand, "Religous Dissent and Toleration. Introductory Reflections," in *Tolerance and Movements of Religious Dissent in Eastern Europe*, ed. Bela K. Kiraly (New York and London: East European Quarterly, Boulder, Colo. / Columbia University Press, 1975), 2.
7. Liberty is the "soul of the age," proclaimed Hungarian poet Daniel Berzsenyi early in the nineteenth century. Quoted in Kalman Benda, *One Thousand Years: A Concise History of Hungary*, ed. Peter Hanak, trans. Zsuzsa Beres, trans. revised Christopher Sullivan (Budapest: Corvina, 1988), 96.
8. Joseph II, quoted in T. C. W. Blanning, *Joseph II and Enlightened Despotism* (London: Longman Group Limited, 1970), 80.
9. For example, the editors of *The Jew in the Modern World,* Paul Mendes-Flohr

and Jehuda Reinharz place the *Toleranzpatent* within the chapter entitled "Harbingers of Political and Economic Change."

10. *Toleranzpatent*, quoted in Mendes-Flohr and Reinharz, *Jew in the Modern World*, 37.

11. Joachim Whaley, "A Tolerant Society? Religious Toleration in the Holy Roman Empire, 1648-1806," in *Toleration in Enlightenment Europe*, ed. Ole Peter Grell and Roy Porter (Cambridge: Cambridge University Press, 2000), 87.

12. *Toleranzpatent*, quoted in Mendes-Flohr and Reinharz, *Jew in the Modern World*, 37.

13. This law was extended in 1814 to include all the provinces of the empire. Raphael Mahler, "The Austrian Government and the Hasidim During the Period of Reaction 1814-1848," *Jewish Social Studies* 1, no. 2 (1939): 196.

14. *Toleranzpatent*, quoted in Mendes-Flohr and Reinharz, *Jew in the Modern World*, 37-40. These German-Jewish schools had a short shelf life; they were abolished in 1806. This came about due to a Concordat between Francis I and the Roman Catholic Church in 1805, which restored the management of the schools to the clergy. It was also feared that an overly 'enlightened' Jewish populace might come to oppose absolutism and clericalism. Mahler, "Austrian Government," 196.

15. Mendes-Flohr and Reinharz, *Jew in the Modern World*, 39.

16. *Toleranzpatent*, quoted in Mendes-Flohr and Reinharz, *Jew in the Modern World*, 38-39.

17. The decrees remaining in force were those concerning religious toleration, the monastic orders, and the abolition of perpetual serfdom.

18. Quoted in Mahler, "Austrian Government," 197.

19. Mendes-Flohr and Reinharz, *Jew in the Modern World*, 40.

20. Mahler, "Austrian Government," 195.

21. From the late eighteenth century on, military service was generally viewed by the state as a primary agent in the transformation of the lower classes. Discipline and training "daily transformed the peasant lad into a worthy soldier." Dohm, *Concerning the Amelioration*, 75-83. British politicians in the late nineteenth century saw military service as an ideal way to instill in this generally unreachable class values they considered important to being good citizens in the modern state.

22. Mendes-Flohr and Reinharz, *Jew in the Modern World*, 40.

23. Mahler, "Austrian Government," 196.

24. These laws were not entirely successful; as late as 1830, one quarter of the Jews scattered throughout the villages of Austria were still engaged as innkeepers. Mahler, "Austrian Government," 197.

25. Solomon V. Posener, "The Immediate Economic and Social Effects of the Emancipation of the Jews in France," *Jewish Social Studies* 1, no. 3 (July 1939): 271-73.

26. Hertzberg, *French Enlightenment*, 342, 351, 354-56.

27. Sachar, *Course of Modern Jewish History*, 43-45.

28. The points of the 'Infamous Decree:' 1) mandatory adoption of surnames 2) refraining from the use of Hebrew in commerce 3) mandatory registration of occupations 4) no immigration of foreign Jews unless they were property owners, established a business, or performed military service 5) the inapplicability of the constitutional right to substitutions for military service 6) prohibition of movement between the *départements* of Alsace—those who owned property and engaged in agriculture were exempted 7) prohibition against establishing any new Jewish communities in Alsace 8) prohibition against loans to Christian married women or minors unless their husbands agreed; in the case of soldiers, with the consent of their officers. Interest not to exceed five per cent and loans calculated at a higher rate could be invalidated 9) the requirement for all Jewish

merchants to obtain a patent in order to operate a business. These patents, granted by the prefect, were dependent upon the receipt of certificates of good conduct from both the local municipal council and the newly established Central Consistory. The Imperial Decree was put in force for a period of ten years (although not strictly), at which time it was to be reconsidered. In 1818, it was allowed to lapse, despite the objections of the General Councils of Alsace. Paula E. Hyman, *The Emancipation of the Jews of Alsace: Acculturation and Tradition in the Nineteenth Century* (New Haven and London: Yale University Press, 1991), 17-18.

29. Berkovitz, *Shaping of Jewish Identity*, 41-42.
30. Quoted in Posener, "Immediate Economic and Social Effects," 310-11.
31. Quoted in Posener, "Immediate Economic and Social Effects," 311-12.
32. Minister of the Interior, quoted in Posener, "Immediate Economic and Social Effects," 312.
33. Berkovitz, *Shaping of Jewish Identity*, 109, 105, 107, 108.
34. Quoted in Hyman, *Emancipation of the Jews*, 98-103, 124.
35. Berkovitz, *Shaping of Jewish Identity*, 40-43, 46-56.
36. F. Guizot, quoted in Berkovitz, *Shaping of Jewish Identity*, 47-48. Guizot was also emphatic about the role of education, which had additional application in the case of the Jews: "Instructing a nation is the same as civilizing it; stifling learning in it means leading it back to the primitive state of barbarity. . . . Ignorance is the lot of the slave and the savage."
37. Posener, "Immediate Economic and Social Effects," 281-93.
38. David Friedlander wrote this letter on behalf of "several heads of families of the Jewish religion." Quoted in Kobler, *Napoleon and the Jews*, 89-91.
39. David Levi (Levy) published his views in his three-volume work entitled *Dissertations on the Prophecies of the Old Testament, Containing All Such Prophecies as Are Applicable to the Coming of the Messiah: The Restoration of the Jews and the Resurrection of the Dead; Whether so Applied by Jews or Christians* (1796-1800).
40. This excerpt was taken from one of a series of articles Leeser wrote between 1848 and 1849. Quoted in Salo W. Baron, "The Impact of the Revolution of 1848 on Jewish Emancipation," in *Emancipation and Counter-Emancipation: Selected Essays from Jewish Social Studies*, ed. Abraham G. Duker and Meir Ben-Horin (New York: Ktav Publishing House, Inc., 1974), 185-86.
41. Excerpt from Moses Hess's *Rome and Jerusalem*, quoted in Hertzberg, *Zionist Idea*, 119.
42. Leo Pinsker, quoted in Hertzberg, *Zionist Idea*, 187.
43. Leo Pinsker, quoted in Hertzberg, *Zionist Idea*, 187. Readers of this tract will find more than a passing similarity to Herzl's *Der Judenstaat*.
44. It is impossible, within the confines of this study, to cover the extensive plans to relocate Jews to more hospitable countries or to trace their migration. Mark Wischnitzer's *To Dwell in Safety* is the only book I came across that treats this subject in a comprehensive manner, and I would refer the reader to it.
45. This letter was published 4 October 1825 in the *Albany Daily Adviser* and it is not unexpected in light of the fact that shortly before, Noah had issued an appeal to the Jews everywhere to come and live in Albany, New York, which he called 'Ararat', this city of refuge.
46. Wischnitzer, *To Dwell in Safety*, 17.
47. Over the course of the century, Jews would seek havens and also attempt to establish autonomous Jewish settlements in such places as Cyprus, Turkey, Egypt, the Sinai Peninsula, El Arish, Palestine, Uganda, Mesopotamia, Canada, United States, Australia, Cyrenaica in North Africa, Angola, the Caribbean Islands, and most countries in Central and South America. Wischnitzer, *To Dwell in Safety*, 134-39.

48. Wischnitzer, *To Dwell in Safety*, 14-16. The publication of Noah's tract more or less coincides with an 1841 petition brought forward by Rabbi Hirsch Fassel on behalf of the Jews of Moravia to overturn laws which continued to make their lives unbearable: among them, the Familiants Laws (which permitted only the eldest son in the family to marry), severe restrictions on practicing handicrafts, and the prohibition against purchasing agricultural land in order to take up farming. Miller, "Rabbis and Revolution," 160-63.

49. *Jewish Intelligence* 14 (1848): 217. This paper was the organ of the London Society for the Promoting of Christianity Amongst the Jews.

50. Wischnitzer, *To Dwell in Safety*, 19-21.

51. Israel Finestein, *Anglo-Jewry in Changing Times: Studies in Diversity 1814–1914* (London: Vallentine Mitchell, 1999), 32-33.

52. F. Guizot, quoted in Wischnitzer, *To Dwell in Safety*, 27-28.

53. Wischnitzer, *To Dwell in Safety*, 86. Apart from the willingness of the Russians, in 1882, three countries that we know of offered to admit Russian Jews as settlers: the Dominican Republic, Chile (according to a report in the Russian paper *Voskhod*), and Santo Domingo. "We shall receive them with open arms," said General Gregorio Luperon, the provisional president. Why none of these offers materialized is unknown. General Gregorio Luperon, quoted in Mark Wischnitzer, "The Historical Background of the Settlement of Jewish Refugees in Santo Domingo," *Jewish Social Studies* 4, no. 1 (1942): 50. As well, at the strong urging of the American consul general in Romania, the government in Bucharest issued an official decree in 1872 putting into motion a program for the mass emigration of its Jews. In this case, it was the Romanian Jewish leaders who put a halt to the plan, arguing that it would circumvent the critical issue of granting civic rights to the Jews. Wischnitzer, *To Dwell in Safety*, 65-66, 22-25.

54. Finestein, *Anglo-Jewry*, 32-33; Zosa Szajkowski, "How the Mass Migration to America Began," *Jewish Social Studies* 4, no. 4 (October 1942): 307. See also Zosa Szajkowski, "The Alliance Israelite Universelle and East European Jewry in the '60s," *Jewish Social Studies* 4, no. 2 (April 1942): 139-60; Wischnitzer, *To Dwell in Safety*, 29-30.

55. Western and Central European Jews were cognizant that the presence of Eastern Jews in their communities posed a real obstacle to the improvement of their political status, but American Jews, although they were already emancipated, felt a similar trepidation. Even before the Russian pogroms of the 1880s, they feared that an inundation of these Jews might threaten their position. Wischnitzer, *To Dwell in Safety*, 31. See also Max J. Kohler, "The Board of Delegates of American Israelites," in *Publications of the American Jewish Historical Society* (1925), 29:91, 101-2.

56. The forging of the Treaty of Vienna in 1815 provided an opportunity to restore the political rights of Jews living within the Napoleonic Empire that had been cancelled with Napoleon's defeat. Jews from Frankfurt and the Hansa towns sent delegates to the Congress to plead the cause of Jewish emancipation. Hardenberg and Metternich were in support of such a measure (hence Adam Müller's letter, above) and Tsar Alexander I was not adverse to some concessions to the Jews. The end result was not the hoped-for one, however: the Redaction Committee made a minor substitution in the wording at the last minute, nullifying the efforts of those who had worked to reinstate the emancipated status of the Jews of Germany. Protests by supporters had no effect. If there was any doubt about the permanence of this reversal, it was eliminated at the Congress of Aix-La-Chapelle in 1818. Lucien Wolf, *Notes on the Diplomatic History of the Jewish Question* (London: Spottiswoode, Ballantyne & Co. Ltd., 1919), 12-15.

57. From an appeal by the Jewish community to the Hungarian Diet of the Upper Chamber, quoted in Patai, *Jews of Hungary*, 219-223.

58. David Sorkin, "Emancipation and Assimilation: Two Concepts and their Application to German-Jewish History," *LBIYB* 35 (1990): 29.

SECTION 2

HUNGARY 1867-1920

Introduction

The efforts of Jews to assimilate, both before and after emancipation, generated much discussion among historians not long ago, so much so, that a historiographical bottleneck occurred. The first trend that may be observed is the emphasis placed on the element of reciprocity as a component of assimilation. Elevated to a primary position, some historians have gone so far as to exclude the concept of "being absorbed within" that James Parkes, from an earlier generation considered to be the main aspect of assimilation.[1] As George Schopflin asserts, "the contention that Hungarian Jews were . . . assimilated to a degree achieved by no other community in Central and Eastern Europe—is true insofar as it was extensive—but it was not intensive—and—it was based on a false premise—lack of the necessary reciprocity for successful assimilation."[2] Nor was reciprocity present in Germany according to Enzo Traverso, where Judeo-German culture "took the form of a *Jewish monologue*."[3] Similarly, David Sorkin has put forth the view that "emancipation and assimilation denoted reciprocally dependent processes which had been under discussion since the 1780s. They represented the inseparable halves of a *quid pro quo*, the two clauses of a complex contract."[4] However, neither the terms nor the idea of "reciprocity" or "contract"—both of which connote an involvement by both parties—can be found in the literature of the time. The ingredient of reciprocity, like the idea of a contractual relationship, has been added retroactively.

The second prevalent trend, expressed by historian Marian Kaplan, among others, is that the nineteenth-century use of the term "assimilation" is the equivalent, today, of the term "acculturation".[5] David Feldman also prefers this term because it provides "a more positive and nuanced evaluation of Jewish history."[6] Such historians "have restored assimilation by the Jews to its original narrow acceptation, arguing that in the nineteenth century it was the equivalent of what contemporary parlance calls 'acculturation,'" acculturation being the "adoption of some characteristics of the major group—without renouncing other religious or cultural differences."[7] Yet, historian Janos Gyurgyak advises extreme care in the use of these two terms and consistently argues in his book that "assimilation", not "acculturation", was what was demanded of the Jew.

> Before all, I make the distinction between assimilation and acculturation . . . under assimilation I understand the social and cultural process during which a certain social group or individual loses national ethnic or cultural identity and trades it in for another one. In this respect, I am following Istvan Szabo, according to whom complete and final it is, if 'the assimilant without any reservation has donned the new *volk* consciousness of his identity, and his lost identity is henceforth as indifferent to him as any other alien identity.'[8]

Gyurgyak is also following Peter Agoston, who wrote one of the seminal works on the Jewish Question in Hungary in 1917. Whereas assimilation implied that Jews would pick and choose from the whole population, Agoston asserted that, instead, they tended to help only their coreligionists and had a low rate of intermarriage—in fact, their numbers were increasing. Even purportedly assimilated Jews had not really understood the meaning and goal of emancipation, which was a device of equalization. It did not mean the continuation of differences: the preservation of memories of different origins; the practice of customs that separate; keeping together, and favoring each other in preference to others.[9] If currently there is a tendency to interchange the term "assimilation" with "acculturation"—implying that the only demand on the Jews was the adjustment to certain norms in the country they inhabited—no reading of the contemporary literature can support such a modification. As this benign euphemism is unable to be stretched so far as to include the demand that Jews reform every facet of their Jewishness—because Jewishness in and of itself was considered harmful or unwelcome to the general society—it is of limited use. Both the injection of overtones of acculturation as part of the meaning of assimilation and the inclusion of reciprocity as one of its elements highlight the larger problems of which revisionism is the product: the difficulty of suspending current sensibilities and, ironically—because their intentions are to the contrary—the tendency to look at events, phenomena, and trends from the Jewish perspective.

While these problems have led some historians to a confusion between acculturation and assimilation, they have led others along a different path. Ignoring the view held by Christian European society, that the assimilation of the Jews was a positive act, they have framed assimilation in negative terms:

> One of the greatest spiritual temptations of modern existence is to surrender one's precious identity to an elite group or cultural milieu, a charismatic leader, a proximate social class, or, above all, to some ideological fundamentalism; and Jews, since the beginning of the Emancipation have provided abundant and painful examples of the various strategies of surrender.[10]

Also giving it a somewhat negative caste is Traverso, who sees assimilation in terms of an assault on the "suspended, frozen world of Judaism," after which there was a "fusion of Judeity with the German world, based on the abandonment of a past and distinct identity."[11] Summarizing this view, Sorkin has written, "There has been a strong temptation not only to make both [emancipation and assimilation] pejoratives, but to conflate them, so that emancipation has no other possible outcome than self-destruction or destruction by others."[12]

Apart from discussing the nature of assimilation, some historians have turned their attention to the failure of Jewish assimilation, a subject on which there is an increasing consensus among the scholarly community. Katz enumerates four obstacles that stood in the way of successful assimilation after emancipation: the persistence of "typical traits" (thinking, bearing, appearance); Christians' awareness of these "typically Jewish traits;" the power of Jewish symbolism even on those who had the most superficial ties to Judaism; and a self-consciousness of their minority position.[13] That the process of assimilation took place over a relatively short period of time and many Jews still had religious family members or had themselves grown up in religious or quasi-religious households is mentioned by Beller.[14] However, once again, it is the Jewish perspective that has been applied: to the host society, these considerations could appear as nothing more than excuses.

Some historians have undertaken to analyze the failure of Jewish assimilation by regions; this is not surprising given the trend to contextualize the Jewish experience. Thus, in Hungary, "The problem was that, from a socioeconomic [Hungary was a gentry-peasant society] as opposed to a nationalist point of view, the Jews could not be absorbed."[15] Instead, as Schopflin and Asher Cohen defined the actual outcome, "The Jews assimilated into a social vacuum. The failure of the process was therefore predetermined, deriving from the socio-political structure of Hungary."[16] The problem with this approach is that it is incomplete: while regional circumstances may have added to the difficulties of assimilating, the issues inherent in the mandate to assimilate have been bypassed.

In one respect, many historians have reached beyond local particularities to identify one common factor that inhibited the successful assimilation of Jews everywhere. This is the phenomenon of nationalism, which Katz defines as "the transforming of ethnical facts into ultimate values" and "the elevation of national attributes such as attachment to one's birthplace, clinging to the mother tongue, and a certain preference for one's ethnic group members to supreme, perhaps even sole values."[17] The nationalist impulse is credited with highlighting or even identifying Jews as a separate nation or ethnic group or race, thus providing the impetus for a restructure of anti-Semitism along political rather than religious lines; or, adding one more dimension to anti-Semitism; or, being a component part of 'modern' anti-Semitism:[18] historians have many ways of assessing the effect of the nationalistic movement in Europe on attitudes towards Jews.

It cannot be stressed enough that the concept of Jewry as a nation does not date from the time of nascent nationalism in Europe. Throughout the medieval period, the peoplehood aspect of Jewry was never detached from Jewishness; they were the Jewish people, an ethno-national group (although this fact had no application at the time). When naturalization of the Jews in Britain was being considered (Jew Bill: 1753), then Jewry as a nation became problematic, raising fears that naturalization would lead to almost unlimited Jewish power, both economic and political. Enlightenment thinkers identified Jews as an ethno-national entity and stipulated that this aspect of Jewishness be eliminated. It was the conviction of many of them that the revamping of Jewry was impossible or uncertain precisely because Jews are a separate nationality; they constitute a *status in statu*; they are a theocracy, whose laws would preclude assimilation; and they have a homeland in Palestine. When the French debated the merits of the Jews *vis a vis* citizenship, they discussed this national aspect of Jewishness—with a view to breaking it down. After emancipation was granted in Hungary, the acknowledged fact that Jews were a separate national entity was now raised as a problem, whose only solution was complete assimilation.

> May those who wish to stay among us in Europe, for whatever reason, cease forming a state within the state and abandon forever all the politics of extermination. May they, without any *arrière-pensée*, embrace our customs, reconcile sincerely with the Christian civilization, and assimilate into us, becoming one with us in body and soul. Then we shall welcome them in our midst with heartfelt joy.[19]

The emergence of nationalism in Europe during the nineteenth century did no more than increase the sensitivity to Jews as a people.

Those who do not subscribe wholesale to the idea that Jewish assimilation failed, posit that there was a time in Hungary between emancipation and the First World War called the 'Golden Era,' when the Jews there were assimilated. They point to the Jews' stunning success in countless enterprises as proof of this assertion. Ezra Mendelsohn has challenged this claim to the extent that he sees this assimilation as a tentative and temporary accomplishment. Hungarian Jews could only be considered assimilated . . . as long as identification of the Jews with Magyarization in the ethnically mixed regions did not explode . . . as long as the nexus between the Jews and the ruling elite, an elite which was antidemocratic and reactionary despite its pro-Jewish policy, did not explode in their face . . . as long as the Jews' conspicuous role in Hungarian life, particularly the economy, was seen to be beneficial . . . as long as the percentage of Jews was an important factor in maintaining the rule of gentry liberals over the non-Magyar majority.[20] Mendelsohn's 'as long as list' was sustained by the catchy slogan, "In growing Hungary, there is a place for everybody."[21] Yet in all but one of Mendelsohn's criteria it is the value of the Jews to Hungarian society that is being identified—mistakenly—as a sign of assimilation. Those who claim that Jews were considered assimilated during the 'Golden Era' have made the same mistake. Whether or not Jews met the real criterion for assimilation—reform along the lines of the Enlightenment ideals specific to the Jews—is left unaddressed. Furthermore, so many of these successes were economic in nature, and intensification of capitalistic endeavor ran directly counter to the reform concerning occupational change. As Jozsef Patai observed early in the twentieth century,

> the hatred of the Jews, by the way, appeared everywhere along with emancipation. As long as the Jews were only pariahs, there was rather contempt for them, which became compassion among the noble-minded of the people [liberals], and ultimately led to the liberation of the Jews. . . . [Anti-Semitism grew] parallel with the growth of the territory the Jews occupied [were able to occupy after emancipation] in agriculture, commerce, industry, art, and politics, with their toilsome work and their steadfast application.[22]

****

This section relies heavily on a collection of newspaper clippings called the *Judische Delikatessen*[23] that was assembled by one Istvan Bonyhadi Perczel. Between the years 1880 and 1887, Perczel cut out thousands of articles on the

Jews from the newspapers to which he subscribed. These varied over time, but by the end of 1881, the *Fuggetlenseg** becomes the most common source. Some detail about the newspaper's publisher and editor, Gyula Verhovay, and the newspaper itself, is required.

Verhovay completed his legal studies in the 1870s and in short order, became renowned as a publicist, with views that were in line with the ultra-left Independence Party. By the age of twenty-six, both the style and content of his articles had brought him countrywide fame and earned him the affectionate moniker, *kis Kossuth*—little Kossuth. At the time of the Russian Turkish War (1878), he organized and participated in street demonstrations, for which he was jailed. This only increased his popularity; three electoral districts chose him to be a candidate for the Independence Party in the 1878 election. Now an MP, he took up a position with the *Egyetertes*, the official organ of the Independence Party and he used this venue to criticize both the foreign and domestic policies of the government and to take a stand on behalf of the workers. Within a year, antagonism between Verhovay and fellow party members first resulted in his leaving the *Egyetertes* and not long after, the Party. In the interim, he founded the *Fuggetlenseg*, a political, economic, and social daily, the first issue of which came out in December 1879. It was not long before his articles against the *Nemzeti Kaszino* (National Magnates Club) provoked such animosity that he was called upon to fight a duel and was severely injured. This increased his popularity to such a degree that spontaneous street demonstrations involving thousands gathered in front of the *Kaszino* for days to show their support for Verhovay and, upon his recovery, he was received triumphantly in cities across the country. He addressed the Jewish Question through the *Fuggetlenseg* with the same passion as he supported all his other causes. Late in 1883, Verhovay was accused of being involved in embezzling the funds of a charitable collection. While he was eventually exonerated, he and his paper were almost ruined. In 1887, he lost his seat in Parliament and at the same time, the *Fuggetlenseg* ceased publishing.[24]

The tone and content of the articles on Jews in the *Fuggetlenseg* may lead one to conclude that it was an 'anti-Semitic rag.' That is not the case. On the one hand, the biography of Verhovay shows that he did not conform to the typical—or imaginary?—idea of a seedy, vengeful, marginal character whom some might assume to be the editor of such a paper. On the other hand, an inspection of this paper shows that it was on a par with other reputable newspapers in all respects. What did distinguish it from other reputable papers was the prominence it gave to the Jewish Question. The liberal press was decidedly neutral in its treatment of Jewish issues. This is not surprising, given that the position of liberals was to deny the existence of a Jewish Question and further, that the liberal press was heavily controlled by Jews. Thus, the subject was mostly avoided, and this is

---

* *Fuggetlenseg* is translated as 'independence', and through his newspaper, Verhovay was seeking to capitalize on the sentiments of the large constituency that had not given up on separating from the Austrian monarchy.

why there is a noticeable absence of negative views towards Jews in the liberal press. (This lack has served as reinforcement for those who wish to support the claim of Jewish assimilation in Hungary to conclude, without taking the former point into account, that there was little anti-Jewish sentiment in Hungary.) Equally, one cannot detect a philo-Semitic bias in the liberal press. The reason for this, I would suggest, is that the readership would not have been receptive to such a viewpoint.

A concerted effort was made to find literature that detailed the acceptance of Jews into the host society, thereby showing that they had successfully assimilated. Hampering this effort is the truism that it is generally the case that 'good news' stories do not make the headlines. It is beyond doubt that some Jews and Christians enjoyed good relations with each other, including marriage. (For most of the period under discussion that would have involved conversion on the part of one of the spouses.) Some newspapers made efforts to show accord between Christians and Jews, although it must be said that their coverage was of ceremonial occasions.[25]

However, with the fewest of exceptions,[26] declarations of wholehearted acceptance of the Jews were belied by some kind of qualification. For instance, Christians submitted letters to the *12 Ellen Ropirat*, a Jewish periodical started up to counter assertions being made against Jews in an anti-Semitic periodical. They say as much about Christians' traditional attitudes towards Jews as their neighborly relations with them.

> The city of Arad, especially with the presence of so many converted families, is competing with Nagyvarad in the cordial even friendly treatment of our Jewish compatriots, and neither Istoczy, nor other more professional prophets shall succeed in disturbing this accord. We do have Jewish and Christian moneylenders equally, and can see that the latter are not at all better. We detest both and we like the Jew if he is not it. If there is any shortcoming that needs correction, we do not want it done like this gent, but with Christian love, with consideration, and whomsoever shall cast stones at us we shall give bread in return to oblige him to gratitude.[27]

> It can be said that there was nobody amongst the Christians who performed towards the suffering Christians [after the great flood in Szeged] as assiduously as did a substantial number of the Jews of Szeged. For example, Mrs. Naschitz herself supplied food and drink for weeks to a number of the unfortunate, and organized more members for the Budapest Women's Association of the Red Cross in Szeged and environs than others did in three counties. I am convinced that in other cities the Jews practice the same charity, wherever there is need and has its place.[28]

Exactly why did the Jews outperform the Christians in helping to overcome the effects of the great flood in Szeged?*

---

* It would appear that this overextending of aid was actually a trend among Jews, one that was deliberately promoted. Rabbi Hirsch Fassel, for example, repeatedly and strongly

Introduction

The grave situation provoked by the Tiszaeszlar ritual murder case* impelled Gusztav Beksics to write a book asserting that Hungary's Jews were indeed assimilating. He began by applying Count Istvan Szechenyi's criterion of "thinking, writing, and creating in Hungarian" as the primary way of becoming Hungarian. To this he added the idea that "wealth has its own assimilating force in this country. Capital and land turns its owner into a Hungarian."[29] However, Beksics cobbled together his theory rather poorly. First, he used Szechenyi's model of Magyarization—language—but Szechenyi was convinced that no agent of assimilation would work with the Jews, whom he said were only interested in acquiring profit. Second, Beksics's view that wealth accumulated in the form of capital and land ownership would turn Jews into Hungarians ran completely counter not only to prescribed Enlightenment thought but also the perception of most Hungarians. Furthermore, by his own admission, Beksics was less interested in the "national interest" than in the "national ideal [which] is to promote the Hungarian identity,"[30] yet, it was exactly the national interest that was at stake and which was reflected in the demands that the Jews reform themselves. This is the scope of the literature: if it seems no more than a grudging and qualified support of the Jews, that is because it was. Therefore, I am relying on the same newspapers as Perczel did in assembling his collection of clippings.

Only in the Jewish literature do we find paeans proclaiming the success of Jewish assimilation, but in the absence of convincing corroboration from Christians, it is difficult to rely upon them. Rarely did Jews who were not Zionists—but like them saw that Jewish assimilation was problematic—express this thought publicly. Three such Jews were Jozsef Steiner, an otherwise unknown Hungarian Jew, who wrote thirteen years after emancipation; Czech philosopher Hugo Bergmann, who wrote just before the First World War; and famous playwright and novelist Arthur Schnitzler. Steiner wrote:

> Whatever a Jew is doing, it raises attention; if he becomes Hungarianized, he is a danger to the State. If not Hungarianized, he is attacked as being Germanized —if he votes for the Government he is a 'realist'; if he votes for the Opposition, he lacks gratitude. If he goes to the Hungarian theater, people complain about 'too many Jews here' (as I hear in the National Theater frequently). So, whatever a Jew does in Hungary, he is unable to satisfy everybody. They don't like us, that's for sure; we cannot do anything, but before emancipation we were harassed less, having lived in peace with the people and the people with us.

---

urged the Jews of Prosnitz in Moravia during the 1840s to help their Christian neighbors who were enduring the consequences of floods, fires, and the like. He considered this to be a method that would not only build better relations between the two groups but also dispel the impression that Jews were indifferent to the plight of their non-Jewish neighbors while willing to go to great lengths to help their coreligionists wherever they lived. Miller, "Rabbis and Revolution," 158-59.

* The Tiszaeszlar blood libel case started with the disappearance of Eszter Solymosi, a fourteen year-old servant girl, a week before Easter, 1882, in the village of Tiszaeszlar. The subsequent investigation and trial developed into the battleground around which the pro- and anti-emancipation forces clashed.

We were constrained to be merchants and accused of cheating and theft . . . Now that Jews have embarked on scientific careers, they claim we force others out. If the Jew is a merchant or scientist, both are bad, oh God, what should we do? I prophesied the appearance of anti-Semitism, and it did happen—alas—a sad fact of life.[31]

Bergmann wrote:

These gifted Jews are pioneers of atheism and materialism, revolutionaries and demagogues. . . .
[They] march at the head of the agitation against marriage and the family, participating as leaders and in all the perversities of contemporary, urban society. . . . they have not grown organically into European culture but simply appropriated its results as they existed in 1789 or 1848. Hence they have no understanding for the history of this culture and hence they undermine its foundations.[32]

Schnitzler wrote that Jews had the option "of being counted as insensitive, obtrusive and cheeky; or of being insensitive, shy and suffering from feelings of persecution." "How beautiful it is," he penned longingly in his *Tagebuch*, "to be an Aryan and be at peace with your abilities."[33] That is to say, to be assimilated; that is to say, not to be a Jew.

This section concentrates on the years 1880 to 1884. One of the reasons for this is, admittedly, that these are the years Perczel was busiest cutting out his clippings. And as I have mentioned, there were thousands to cut out; Jewish issues were prominently in the public eye. The question will then undoubtedly be asked, with particular reference to the *Judische Delikatessen*: are these samples, collected over such a short period, representative of the sentiments of the general population? Perhaps this is not the right question to ask.

One should first keep in mind the following facts. The majority of Hungarians were faithful Christians who subscribed to their Churches' teachings, which stated clearly that there was no room for the Jew *as* Jew in society. Additional grounds for antagonism towards the Jewish religion were being forged as it continued to be examined from the perspectives of 'rationalism', 'progress', and science. Perceived as overly generous, laws passed by the 1839-40 Diet to improve the condition of the Jews were immediately revised, and even the revised laws were often circumvented. A petition for Jewish emancipation presented to the 1843-44 Diet was defeated by a large majority. Prior to the opening of the 1847-48 Diet, circulars advocating emancipation were distributed by Jews; the general reaction to them was very negative. During the 1848-49 Revolution, the people rioted against, attacked, expelled from their towns, and pauperized a substantial number of the Jewish population. Finally, fostered by the policies of the Bach regime (put in place by Austria to administer Hungary for ten years after the Revolution), the atmosphere in Hungary continued to be one that marginalized the Jews socially and politically.

Emancipation was legislated less than a decade later (1867). It would be naïve to imagine that the passage of a bill modified the views of those who had shown such strong opposition to the prospect of civic improvement for the Jews.

As for that segment of the population that did favor emancipation, they had done so in the belief that it would bring about the assimilation of the Jews. By the 1880s, it was apparent to almost all Hungarians that one way or another Jews were maintaining their Jewish traits. Therefore, the representativeness of the *Judische Delikatessen* is not a crucial question. Rather, one should be concerned with the question Hungarians were asking: How is the assimilation of the Jews going to be accomplished?

This question was central in the emancipation debates during the early years. But as in other European countries that experienced the upheaval of 1848, the course of parliamentary debate in Hungary was not a progressively evolving one. Interrupted by the 1848-49 Revolution, it was only in 1860 that the emancipation debates resumed their 'natural' course. In short order, liberals were able to add Jewish emancipation to their list of progressive legislation, assured that Jews were theoretically capable of carrying out the mandate to reform. However, this supposition was soon challenged. Concerns about the probity of Jewish efforts to assimilate escalated into a national upheaval when some Jews were accused of committing ritual murder in the village of Tiszaeszlar in 1882. The extreme nature of the accusation conjured up an image of Judaism as a demonic force and served as dramatic proof that Jews were failing to reform. The charge brought in its wake demands that Jewish emancipation be revoked. The Liberal government's unequivocal stand was to defend its decision to emancipate the Jews, but not due to the belief that Jews had completed the process of assimilation; indeed, many Liberals expressed the idea that this task still lay ahead of the Jews. Rather, in defending Jewish emancipation, they were defending one of the hallmarks of liberalism. In the face of sustained agitations that at times escalated to a point where the government could not control them, the Liberal government still insisted that there was no Jewish Question.

However, the issues that gave rise to the conviction that there was a Jewish Question—the failure to assimilate at both the individual and institutional levels—continued to be raised. By the time of the *Recepcio* in 1895, which conferred the status of a 'received religion' upon Judaism, the shelf life of assimilation as a realistic possibility had pretty well expired. As with the charge of ritual murder thirteen years before, challenges to the bill brought in tow objections that Jews were not 'just like us,' and beyond this, they were dominating and Judaizing society. The ethnic minorities (whose proportion in the population approached fifty per cent) had their own subsection of discontents.

The First World War summoned numerous charges that Jews were unpatriotic, but the boundaries for complaint and discussion were quickly expanded to include the Jewish Question. Confining itself to the issue of loyalty, the government sanctioned certain steps meant to control and punish Jews for perceived unpatriotic behaviors. Austria-Hungary's defeat in 1918 resulted in the collapse of the Empire and with it Hungary's system of government. Following in rapid succession, various forms of government were attempted, but the most infamous one was the declaration of Hungary as a Soviet Republic. It provoked outrage among significant numbers of the population who were subjected to a ruthless, although brief Communist regime under a leadership that was largely Jewish. The demise of that regime was the occasion for carrying out atrocities against

Communists—particularly Jewish ones—and for demands that the Jewish Question be settled. The first step in that direction was the formulation of a law in 1920, known as the *Numerus Clausus*.

NOTES

1. Parkes, *Jew and his Neighbour*, 189.
2. George Schopflin, "Jewish Assimilation in Hungary: A Moot Point," in *Jewish Assimilation in Modern Times*, ed. Bela Vago (Boulder, Colo.: Westview Press, Inc., 1981), 75.
3. Enzo Traverso, *The Jews and Germany* (Lincoln and London: University of Nebraska Press, 1995), xx.
4. Sorkin, "Emancipation and Assimilation," 18.
5. Marian Kaplan, quoted in Sorkin, "Emancipation and Assimilation," 30. Sorkin himself favors the term 'integration'.
6. Feldman, *Englishmen and Jews*, 5-6.
7. Sorkin, "Emancipation and Assimilation," 27, 25.
8. Gyurgyak, *A zsidokerdes Magyarorszagon*, 18-19. Istvan Szabo was a very distinguished professor of Hungarian history at the Debrecen University from the 1920s on. In Gyurgyak's opinion, what did occur amongst Jewry in nineteenth-century Hungary was "acculturation": "the idea of becoming culturally similar."
9. Peter Agoston, *A zsidok utja* [The Way of the Jews] (Nagyvarad: A Nagyvaradi Tarsadalomtudomanyi Tarsasag, 1917), 290-95. Agoston was professor of law at Nagyvarad and a social democrat.
10. Robert Alter, quoted in Michael R. Marrus, "European Jewry and the Politics of Assimilation," in *Jewish Assimilation in Modern Times*, ed. Bela Vago (Boulder, Colo.: Westview Press, Inc., 1981), 6.
11. Traverso, *Jews and Germany*, 3.
12. Sorkin, "Emancipation and Assimilation," 24-25.
13. Katz, *Emancipation and Assimilation*, 7-9.
14. Beller, *Vienna and the Jews*, 13.
15. Ezra Mendelsohn, *The Jews of East Central Europe Between the World Wars* (Bloomington, Ind.: Indiana University Press, 1987), 91.
16. Cohen, "Attitude of the Intelligentsia," 70-71. Schopflin used the term "void" because, with ethnic minorities making up slightly more than half of the population in Hungary, no homogeneous society existed "toward which Jews could assimilate." "Jewish Assimilation," 75-76.
17. Katz, *Jewish Emancipation and Self-Emancipation*, 89.
18. Like Wistrich (above), David Kertzer writes of 'modern' anti-Semitism: "Modern anti-Semitism rises directly out of older Church views; the Jews' emancipation is the catalyst that transforms the earlier forms into the new." *The Popes Against the Jews: The Vatican's Role in the Rise of Modern Anti-Semitism* (New York: Alfred A. Knopf, 2001), 145.
19. Gyozo Istoczy, a Hungarian parliamentarian in the latter third of the nineteenth century, quoted in Andrew Handler, *An Early Blueprint for Zionism: Gyozo Istocsy's Antisemitism* (East European Monographs Boulder, Colo. / New York: Columbia University Press, 1989), 49.
20. Mendelsohn, *Jews of East Central Europe*, 94-95. See also Oscar [Oszkar] Jaszi, *The Dissolution of the Hapsburg Empire* (Chicago: University of Chicago Press, 1929), 174.

21. Popular slogan before World War I, quoted in Istvan Deak, "Hungary," in *The European Right: A Historical Profile*, ed. Hans Rogger and Eugen Webber (Berkeley and Los Angeles: University of California Press, 1966), 368.

22. Jozsef Patai, *Harc a zsido kulturaert* [Struggle for Jewish Culture] (Budapest: Mult es Jovo jubileumi kiadasa, 1937), 189-93.

23. This collection may be found in the Orszagos Szechenyi Konyvtar (OSZK) [Szechenyi National Library] 730. Oct. Hungary. It contains seventy-five volumes, of which numbers 1, 2, 3, and 55 are missing.

24. Judit Kubinszky, *Politikai antiszemitizmus Magyarorszagon 1875–1890* [Political Anti-Semitism in Hungary 1875-1890] (Budapest: Kossuth Konykiado, 1976), 62-64, 159-61, 221-23; *A Pallas Nagy Lexicona* [The Great Lexicon of Pallas] (A Pallas Irodalmi es Nyomdai Rt., 1893-1897).

25. For example, a bishop was present at the consecration of a new synagogue. *Neues Pester Journal*, 31 August 1880.241. At the burial of MP Fleischer, both a rabbi and a priest gave speeches; Crown Prince Jozsef accepted membership in the community organization, the *Chevrei Kadishe*; and His Royal Highness sent money to a Jewish charity. *Magyarorszag*, 4 September 1880.245, 28 October 1880.299; *Pesti Naplo*, 7 April 1881.96.

26. A pamphlet published in Nagy Kanizsa in 1880, entitled *To the Jewish Question*, authored by "A Christian," stated that there was "no difference between people," everyone was equal, and the Talmud was just defensive. *Judische Delikatessen*, Book 6.

27. *12 Ellen Ropirat* [12 Counter Pamphlet]. II Fuzet. 1 December 1880: 62-63.

28. *12 Ellen Ropirat*. II Fuzet. 1 December 1880: 62-63.

29. Gustav Beksics, *Magyarosodas es magyarositas: kulonos tekintettel varosainkra* [Becoming Hungarians and Turning Them into Hungarians: With Special Regard to our Cities] (Budapest: Az Atheneum R. Tarsulat kiadasa, 1883), 7-8, 37. Beksics was primarily a journalist and historian, but he had also been admitted to the bar and was an official at the Royal Court. He was elected as a Liberal MP in 1884 where he assumed the post of secretary of the Prime Ministerial Office.

30. Beksics, *Magyarosodas*, 57, 51-52.

31. Excerpt of a letter by Joseph Steiner, *Magyarorszag*, 24 August 1880.231.

32. Excerpt of a letter by Bergmann to Professor Carl Stumpf in 1914, quoted in Wistrich, *Between Redemption and Perdition*, 97. Ironically, Bergmann has identified the very same 'qualities' that could have been utilized to implement the Enlightenment ideals specific to the Jews. Atheist: this shows the Jews' willingness to modify his religion. Materialistic: this reflects the Jews' understanding that his value in the non-Jewish world still lay in his ability to be of economic utility, neither overperforming nor underperforming in the economic sphere. Revolutionary: embedded in this quality is the ability to envision a radical change in one's condition (from a ghetto existence to an emancipated one). Demagogue: a good deal of demagoguery would be required to galvanize the Jews into transforming themselves.

33. Arthur Schnitzler, quoted in Wistrich, *Between Redemption and Perdition*, 99.

Chapter 4
The Emancipation Process

What was at issue and hotly debated during the pre-emancipation years was whether Jewry could satisfactorily conform to the Enlightenment ideals specific to the Jews: as individuals, as a people, and as a religion. While this chapter is devoted to an outline of these debates in Hungary, some of the more important trends in Germany should be touched on first, because of the pollination of ideas generally, and specifically, because of the strong link between Germany and Austria, and Austria's link to Hungary.

German Trends

Religion-based arguments against emancipating the Jews persisted and in fact received a boost from a most unexpected quarter in Germany. The treatment of the origins of Christianity at the hands of certain German-Jewish historians deeply affronted many Christians.[1] Abraham Geiger argued that not only was Jesus a Pharisee who had simply radicalized this Jewish sect, thereby establishing links of continuity between Judaism and Christianity, but that early Christianity was syncretic and rife with paganism, thus nullifying twice over all claims to revelatory transmission. Heinrich Graetz emphasized Christianity's superstitious, miraculous, and magical elements, saying that these elements had struck a chord with pagans and the lower classes of Jews, and this client base had practiced "intolerance, foolhardiness, and a maltreatment of Jews" ever since.[2]

The Christian community's response was an indictment of Judaism, on the one hand, and a minimizing of the relevance of the Old Testament, on the other. Placed before the public in a large variety of publications, Adolf von Harnack, for example, argued that the Pharisees had "weighted, darkened, distorted, rendered ineffective, and deprived of its force by a thousand things ["the spring of holiness"] which they also held to be religious and every whit as important as mercy and judgment," Christianity was "the spring burst forth afresh, [which] broke a new way for itself through the rubbish."[3] Karl August von Hase, in his well-known *Das Leben Jesu* (1829), contrasted the historically framed and hence particularistic nature of Judaism with the universalism of Christianity, as did David Friedrich Strauss in his book, also entitled *Das Leben Jesu* (1835).[4] In assessing the impact of this dispute, one must conclude that it did not interfere directly with the emancipation process. However, the works of these Jewish historians provided fresh arguments for defining Judaism in negative terms and may thus have added weight to the calls for reform of the Jewish religion.

The Pietist movement predated this historically oriented dispute and extended beyond it. It, too, fostered the idea that the source for Christian revelation did not lie in Judaism. Along with its ideals of community, the unity of man and of the universe, Pietism forged a strong connection to the fatherland. "He who does not love the fatherland which he can see, how can he love the heavenly Jerusalem which he does not see?" proclaimed leading Pietist, Justin Moser, in 1774.[5] Pietism was yet another approach to framing the character of the state in Christian terms.

The suspicion throughout the pre-emancipation period that the conversion of many German Jews was insincere led some to consider these converts still Jewish.* This suspicion gained proof as some prominent baptized Jews were not adverse to admitting this openly: "If I could have made a living by stealing silver spoons without going to prison," wrote Heinrich Heine, "I would never have been christened."[6]

New, popular arguments "from the standpoint of natural science" were marshaled to oppose emancipation. Noted Jewish historian Salo Baron makes reference to a theory publicized in 1848 by a man whom he refers to only by his surname, Cscherich. Baron summarizes his theory as follows: "Both the biological history of the Jewish people and the anatomical structure of each Jew proved that the relationship of Jews to all other races, including primitives, resembled that of weeds to other plants. Hence their ubiquity and indestructibility!"[7]

In 1860—the same year Hungary would recommence discussions on emancipating the Jews—German First Minister Lamey, a member of the Liberal government made a statement acknowledging that there was no popular consensus for emancipating the Jews.† However,

---

* This suspicion was not unfounded. In an article entitled "Results of Jewish Emancipation on the Continent" by the London *Jewish Chronicle*, it noted the large number of reconversions of baptized Jews in Prussia after their (temporary) emancipation. 5 (November 1848): 45.

† This lack of public consensus would undermine the effectiveness of emancipation. As F. von Schuckmann described, "For one thing, the inner content of human actions—tone and gesture—cannot be challenged before a court of law; for another, at the present stage the large majority of the newly accepted Jews would undeniably be lacking in the requisite civic capabilities." Furthermore, "A sudden mixture of the Jews with the rest of the citizens would probably fail to relieve their situation of its oppressiveness; driven by deep-rooted prejudice the citizens would still not accept them as brothers. . . . What can decrees avail against prejudice. . . . So long, then, as the nation as a whole looks upon the Jews as an inferior kind of people and takes offence at being treated on a par with them; so long as prejudice against them rules the hearts of the greater part of the constituted Christian authorities and of the clergy who guide the people." Quoted in Reinhard Rurup, "Jewish Emancipation and Bourgeois Society," *LBIYB* 14 (1969): 72-73.

the structure of our state does no longer tolerate that a group of citizens, because of a feature of as little relevance as an outwardly professed belief should be excluded from a number of legal powers.... Even if they were below the Christian population from the human point of view, their exclusion from general law would be an injustice, as it would also concern the educated, the honest, the hardworking among them, for the sake of some bad ones; while in the Christian population the numerous rude and indecent people for the sake of the better ones have the same rights.[8]

Hungary

The commencement of the debates on improving the Jews' status may be tied to the reconvening of the Diets in 1825, at which time Hungary entered upon the Age of Reform.[9] It was in this new climate that an 1827 gubernatorial rescript indicated a willingness to admit qualified Jewish students to the university law faculties (although as of 1840, none had been admitted at the University of Pest[10]) and four years later, one of the cherished acts of being established in a country—owning one's own home—was permitted to Jews fifteen years after they had reached maturity.[11] On the other hand, *Hitel* (Credit) (1830), the first work of Hungary's greatest statesman, Count Istvan Szechenyi, took a very harsh view of the Jews in relation to their participation in the economy. Predicated on their being an alien nation, Szechenyi asserted that "the Jews paid no attention to economic interests and the good of the country, being only interested in acquiring profit; they are one of those alien nations living in Hungary whose multiplication will lead to its decline."[12]

The real debates began when the Diet of 1839-40 was called into session, and the public contributed to them generously in the press and by publishing numerous pamphlets. The debates reflected three different positions regarding the emancipation of the Jews. Amongst those who insisted that Jews should be emancipated immediately, some did so on altruistic, liberal grounds: freedom was the natural right of all human beings. Others affirmed it from a pragmatic standpoint: by incorporating the Jews as Hungarians, the Magyar element in society would be augmented and Hungarians would have greater leverage over the nationalities. At the other end of the spectrum were those who were completely opposed to emancipation. They cited the Jews' lack of nationalist sentiment; their adherence to a religion that stimulated negative attributes among its believers; and issues revolving around assimilation, including the conviction that Jews were incapable of assimilating and the idea that Hungary could not afford to assimilate the Jews because their numbers were too great. In the middle were those who identified emancipation as both a political and a social act. As a political act, they were in favor of equality in principle; but as a social act— whose fulfillment rested on the Jews—there were grave reservations about the Jews' willingness and capability to undertake social assimilation.[13]

This Diet was the first to entertain motions to improve the political status of the Jews by abolishing the Toleration Tax and extending civil rights that were on a par with other inhabitants who did not belong to the nobility.[14] (One deputy from Pest proposed the extension of rights similar to those soon to be enjoyed by the serfs: the right to purchase their freedom along with their plot of land.[15]) "I already now know, in the Plain, Jews who with regard to language have totally become Magyars," declared Count Aurel Dessewffy, the new leader of the young conservatives in the Upper Chamber. But as far as immigration was concerned, he stated that it should be restricted, "otherwise the country will be flooded with a multitude of immigrant beggar Jews . . . which is in the interest of neither the country nor the homeland's Jewry."[16] Only those who could offer "some guarantee regarding [their] wealth, morality and professional competence" should be considered for immigration.[17] Even the up and coming liberal leader of Hungary's reform movement, Lajos Kossuth, referred to these Jews as "the dregs of the Maramaros Jew crowd . . . from whose crimes we cannot protect the country," although he still advocated that they be considered one group along with the Hungarian Jews.[18]

The issue of immigration was often conjoined to discussions on Jewish emancipation, but it was a concern among Hungarians as early as 1798. Count Laszlo Tolnai Festetich received a letter from poet, writer, and Paulist monk Benedek Virag in which he complained, "The Jews arrive loudly. . . . These followers of Moses are like a boil on an anthill. Wait a little while; they will become more than the sons of Arpad; they rarely buy and are always enriching themselves."[19] Between 1805 and 1840, the number of Jews in Hungary increased by eighty per cent, mostly due to emigration from Galicia. Usually dubbed 'Hasidic', they were in fact a cross-section of traditional Jewry, for as Gustav Mahler observes, early in the century there was "rapprochement in the face of a common enemy" as all Jews who opposed the efforts of the *maskilim* gathered together under the Hasidic mantle.[20] About these Hasidic Jews, the provincial governor wrote in 1827: "He goes about with a bare throat, with rolled up sleeves, and usually is very dirty and shabbily dressed. The commonest Jews belong to this sect. They attach themselves to no profession, are usually common inn-keepers, swindlers, and cheats." The Lemberg police commission in 1838 described them as "idlers, given to drink, hypocrites, lazy fanatics and beggars."[21] They were known for their refusal to use the official government courts; evasion of military service and the government prohibitions against the sale of liquor in villages and transferring money abroad; and circumvention of all laws that involved the payment of a tax. As one official piece of correspondence noted—and from the above list, it would appear to be a gross understatement—the 'Hasids' did not "demand reverence and obedience to the laws and the authorities."[22] While this reputation preceded the Hasids' arrival in Hungary, there is no basis for concluding that Hungarians simply adopted the viewpoint of their neighbors. Hungarians' perceptions of Galizianers or Khazars, as these immigrant Jews were called in Hungary, were grounded in their own experience of them.

By the end of the Diet of 1839-40, the following had been agreed upon: abolition of the Toleration Tax (actually withdrawn in 1846); the right to reside throughout Hungary, mining towns excluded; professional freedom; conditions similar to the serfs with respect to the purchase of property; and the immigration of Jews who had ample means and reasonable education. Vociferous objections by the city inhabitants to the King brought about immediate concessions in the form of the 1840 Bylaw XXIX, which overturned the original proposal in four respects. First, any "complaints against him [the Jew] or his moral behavior" were grounds for expulsion. Second, that section of Joseph II's *Toleranzpatent* concerning the mandatory use of the vernacular in official and business documents and the adoption of preselected personal and family names was reinstituted. Third, Jewish tradesmen were forbidden to hire Christian assistants; and fourth, Jewish immigration was curtailed. Even the terms of the revised law were met with non-compliance as Hungarians sought to keep Jews out of the cities, and in some cases, a county *en bloc* refused to admit them. The ongoing complaint that Jews were guilty of overperformance in the economy manifested itself in several ways. Jewish manufacturers and merchants were compelled to put a sign over their door identifying themselves as Jews. The guilds pressured shopkeepers not to hire Jews[23] and they were particularly influential in hampering the Jews' professional freedom. So, although Jews now had permission to cultivate and lease land, work as tailors, tanners, masons, carpenters, cabinetmakers, painters and sculptors, and to engage in manufacturing—"to try their hands gainfully in a wider field in order to become useful citizens of the state" as it was said—the guilds resisted employing Jewish apprentices and refused to admit recently graduated Jewish masters into the guild. In practice, then, Jews could take little advantage of any easing of occupational restrictions and gain employment beyond the Jewish community.[24]

The Diet of 1839-40 coincided with the publication of the most important tract favoring the emancipation of the Jews: *A zsidok emancipacioja* (The Emancipation of the Jews), by author, scholar, and politician Baron Jozsef Eotvos. Eotvos is most often credited with spearheading the movement to emancipate the Jews in Hungary and has the reputation of being the foremost Enlightenment thinker in Hungary.[25] Yet one may note the late date—1840—of his tract, indicating that Hungary had come under the effect of the Enlightenment very late, long after other countries in Europe had concretized its ideals, and slid into the liberal era. Eotvos is actually an excellent example of how liberalism (using as its starting point the common humanity of all beings, while making use of all the arguments of those *philosophes* who stressed how the betterment of the Jews would occur all the sooner if they were emancipated) came to inform thinkers in the nineteenth century, and therefore, despite the common assessment of Hungarians to classify Eotvos as a figure of the Enlightenment, I have included him here as a liberal.

Etvos wrote about a hypothetical country, saying that, if it had disappeared, one could mourn this loss; but how much sadder it is for a country to be vanquished, but alive and dispersed, as the Jews are. This situation was once due to the fanaticism of religion; those days are past, but Jews are still persecuted, and in these times, this is due to prejudice.

Eotvos then summoned a number of the classic arguments against emancipating the Jews. First among them was the historic superiority of Christians over Jews. Mockingly, he asked: what would happen to the lowly trades if Jews also practiced them; and if Jews owned property, would Christians still be able to make a living? In order to maintain this superiority, perhaps it was enough that Jews would help defend the homeland, breathe the same air, and be buried in the same size grave. In fact, why be a Christian if it is not advantageous?[26]

The second reason not to emancipate the Jews was that they were corrupt. Recounting examples of the crop rotation of utility and persecution, comparing it to fattening cattle then slaughtering them, Eotvos stated it was no wonder the morals of the Jews were corrupt.[27]

The third charge leveled against the Jews was that they were preoccupied with money. Eotvos did not dispute the charge, but said that it was society's fault for no other means of advancement had been offered to them; anyone who knew the facts realized that Christians had cultivated this fault in them. If trading were the reason for Jewish immorality, then emancipation would allow them to choose other professions. And even if it were true, why should it preclude Jews from having civic rights?[28] To the fourth argument, that "Jews, based on their religion, consider themselves a separate nation," even their duty, and therefore, they "cannot reasonably expect and could not possibly gain the rights, whose main condition is to belong to the nation," Eotvos summoned three counterarguments. "Liberty is not a thing, that for merit, we can give as a reward; that is the birthright of every person, of which, without fault, cannot be deprived by anyone; we can say: if anyone abuses civil rights, to exclude a whole class of people, is not sufficient cause."[29] The acceptance of all nationalities was in the interest of the nation, like the health of all parts was in the interest of the body. Moreover, how could the emancipation of a few Jews hurt the Hungarian nation which has survived so much adversity?[30]

Yet one cannot say that this summary of Eotvos's tract is completely representative of his views. An additional quote that has been extracted from a diary entry made in 1868 reads as follows: "The historical mission of the Jewish people is to represent the ideal of a single God. It is my conviction that in the moment that this ideal becomes universal, the Jewish people as a separate national identity will cease to exist."[31]

During the next Diet, held in 1843-44, not only was the hearing of a Jewish petition for emancipation delayed until the end of the session, it was defeated by a large majority (thirty-five to thirteen).[32] The Jews' failure to undertake religious reform was a primary reason for this outcome. The delegate from County Ugocsa argued that "the Jews should not be emancipated until they chisel off the trappings from the formalities of their religion;" the one from County Komarom declared that "the eccentricities of the Jews in religious matters should be smoothed away;" and the representative from County Gyor believed that the Jews ought to "contradict the principles of their religion."[33]

The liberal reformer, Lajos Kossuth, wrote at length about this issue in his paper, *Pesti Hirlap*. First, he stated that no one should be excluded from civil rights on the basis of their religion, and "the Jews in our country are a religious denomination." However, they are clearly more than this:

> Moses was not only a creator of a religion; he was also a civil legislator....
> The Jews therefore cannot be emancipated, because their religion is a political

institution based on theocratic foundations, which cannot be reconciled politically with the existing governmental order. . . . Yes, let us look around and we must admit regretfully that sympathy for Jewish emancipation has constantly diminished since 1840.[34]

Emancipation would not relieve Jews of the burden of inequality, for emancipation had two independent components: the political and the social; removal of legal restrictions would not engender social emancipation. Therefore, Jews should "convene a universal conclave, which should determine what in their faith is religious dogma." It was up to the Jews to "lay the cornerstone of social amalgamation," and this would primarily be achieved by religious reform; responsibility lay with the "more spirited Jews" to make "appropriate reforms" that would ensure that Jews were a separate religion only and not a separate people.[35] A rebuttal to this article by Leopold (Lipot) Low, a prominent and reform-minded rabbi, elicited from Kossuth further clarification of what he meant by "social amalgamation."

> As long as the Jews cannot eat together with their fellow citizens of other religions a little salt, a piece of bread, cannot drink one wine with them, cannot sit at one table, so that these and other similar things hinder the social amalgamation of the various religious denominations, as long as these things are not declared not to belong to the essence of Jewish religion—not only by the practice of the more educated ones, who thereupon are considered by their coreligionists bad Jews, but by solemn ecclesiastical declaration of faith—the Jews will not be emancipated socially, even if they should be emancipated politically a hundred times.[36]

That the Jews had not been pursuing the course of reform may be seen from several pieces of correspondence that are not generally considered and which were written at the outset of the 1848 Hungarian Revolution. Jonas Kunewalder, a very prominent Jewish community leader wrote that "Meanwhile, let us provide the most public clarification of what was hitherto kept in the mysterious dark concerning our religious and communal constitution, so that we could at least . . . commence upon the most radical reforms." Immediately, reform societies sprang up in Pest and several provincial towns. As a German-Jewish correspondent noted, "Elsewhere, for instance in Hungary, where spiritual movements of every tendency were at a standstill, now the religious [sphere] has been stirred up by the political." Looking at the situation from a somewhat different perspective, a communication from the reformers of Arad to Samuel Holdheim of Germany on 23 April 1848 stated that the "useful reforms of institutions and external practices of the Jewish religion are desirable from a political and social viewpoint as well."[37]

Szechenyi highlighted the unassimilability of the Jew—a trait that had particularly negative ramifications in the Hungarian national context—in a speech to the 1843-44 Diet.

> The English nation can afford to emancipate the Jewish race. Because, if for instance I pour a jar of ink into a large lake, its water will not spoil and everybody can drink it without any harm. In the great English element the Jew can

dissolve. The same is true for France. But if the ink is poured into the Hungarian soup, that soup will be spoiled and no human can eat it. I shall bring another example too. If my own child and someone else's are sitting in a rowboat with me, when taking on water, and being unable to keep both children; if I toss out my own child the newspapers will praise me for it. But I shall rather choose to keep my own child and toss the others out. In this respect, liberalism is clearly to the detriment of nationalism. And this is not just an opinion, because it can be proven that every such favor is to the detriment of the Nation.[38]

Despite the obvious resistance of this Diet to improve the status of the Jews, the abolition of the Toleration Tax followed soon after in 1846 and was considered a victory by the Jews in their battle for emancipation. They were thus optimistic about a positive outcome during the upcoming 1847-48 Diet. Before it commenced in November, the Permanent Committee of Hungarian Jews sent circulars to all county assemblies and Royal Free boroughs, in which they requested that the deputies promote the emancipation of the Jews. Most of the Royal Free boroughs and the county assemblies chose rather to instruct their deputies "to oppose effectively Jewish emancipation condition" and to lobby for the termination of Jewish immigration.[39] The deputies of the Royal Free boroughs spoke on behalf of the burghers who felt frustrated by the economic competitiveness of Jews. The Jewish religion continued to be attacked: it was a "pagan faith" which ought not to be favored in any way—but if they had to put up with the Jews, the very least that had to be done was "to accustom them to civilization, and . . . make them aware of the principles of Christianity."[40] A liberal-minded correspondent of the *Pesti Hirlap* noted that in the course of the proceedings of this Diet "extreme and unjust declarations against the Jews were received with great ovations."[41]

When the Hungarian Revolution of 1848 broke out, some Jews who identified themselves as the 'Jewish Leadership of Transylvania and Hungary' pronounced: "We are Hungarians and not Jews, not a separate nation, because we are only distinct when we pray to the Almighty in our houses of worship and express our deepest indebtedness for the benevolence bestowed on our homeland and ourselves; in every other respect we are exclusively patriots, exclusively Hungarians."[42] Such a self-perception accounts for Lajos Schnee's request to Kossuth on 31 March 1848 to declare a law emancipating the Jews. To which Kossuth responded: "There are impediments which not even the gods can overcome at certain moments. To regulate the Jewish question [through emancipation] at this point would mean placing a great many of these people at the mercy of their enemies' fury."[43] Kossuth was right; Schnee's timing was very poor. Extensive rioting against the Jews had already commenced in the cities and towns.[44] At the behest of the Jewish leadership, due to the excited state of the citizenry, Prime Minister Lajos Batthyany ordered that the Jews in Pest and Pozsony be relieved of their duty to serve in the National Guard and those already serving be decommissioned.[45] At the same time, at the insistence, it seems, of the German population, Batthyany ordered increased vigilance in the application of the law curtailing Jewish immigration to the Free Royal cities.[46]

The defeat of two separate bills on Jewish emancipation (19 July 1848 at Pest and 12 May 1849 at Debrecen) was therefore not unexpected.

> As far as point c) [Paragraph 3-ik c) 1840: XXIX] is concerned, we opposed any addition because the status of the Jews, besides being special, the quoted section does not change anyway and otherwise it would not be proper to tie the hands of future legislators. And, on the other hand we report that towards the Jews this Parliament seems to be extremely irritated, to the extent that we have not much hope left that towards this neglected class they will be willing in their orders to express any fatherly intentions.[47]

Lack of fatherly intent was reflected in Upper House member Count Janos Berenyi's suggestions that all past and future debts incurred by Christians to Jews should be annulled and a special tax levied on the Jews in the amount of 10,000,000 florins to pay for the construction of new roads.[48]

In the event, on 28 July 1849, the revolutionary government, now headed by Kossuth, did pass an emancipating decree, the Bill About the Jews, Act IX: 1849. Its major points included equal rights to all "residents [born in Hungary or legally settled there] of the Mosaic faith" and the right to legally enter into marriages with Christians—plus the following clause:

> Those of the Mosaic faith should convene an assembly of their clergy and elected representatives, partly in order to declare—or reform—their articles of faith, and partly in order to effect improvements in their future ecclesiastical organization conforming to the wishes of the age [so that] those of the Mosaic faith should be led to the practice of handicrafts and agriculture through suitable rules.*

While the government's stated reasons for delaying emancipation were fear that it would precipitate more riots in the cities which were vehemently anti-Jewish and insufficient time to prepare a bill of such sensitivity,[49] the passage of this Bill might also be viewed as the dying gasp of a revolutionary government soon to be in retreat and no longer having to answer to the people.

Austria applied harsh measures against both the Hungarians and the Jews in retaliation for the Revolution.[50] (It goes without saying that legislation passed by the revolutionary government—including the emancipation of the Jews—was revoked.) Against the Jewish community a penalty tax of 2,300,000 florins was

---

* The Bill About the Jews, Act IX: 1849, quoted in Patai, *Jews of Hungary*, 276. This bill of Jewish emancipation may be the only one that coupled emancipation with a number of the reforms stipulated by the Enlightenment thinkers. It indicates that these politicians had moved beyond the Enlightenment thinkers who had envisioned either-or scenarios—reform before emancipation or emancipation first as a way to bring about assimilation quickly—but that they were not yet firmly in the grip of liberalism. This demand, that Jews undertake reform, had also been included in the 1848 petition to emancipate the Jews submitted by Minister of Internal Affairs Bertalan Szemere. Zsoldos, *Magyar irodalom es zsidosag*, 217-21.

levied by the Viennese Council of Ministers, for "the greatest part of the Israelites living in Hungary promoted, by their feelings and evil manner of acting, the revolution in that country, which without their participation could never have attained such dimensions."[51] Having thus punished the Jews, a number of decrees were passed by the Bach regime with a view to improving their economic utility. Compensation was provided for Jewish businesses that had been destroyed during the revolution (1850). The government decreed that nobody could be excluded from engaging in commerce and industry on the basis of religion, nationality, or birth (1851) and the Factory Act of 1859 removed all religious distinctions. In 1860, Jews were permitted to engage in dispensing pharmaceuticals, the distilling of spirits, the milling of flour, and settling in the mining towns. However, three more laws were introduced over this period which, when looked at in conjunction with the above laws, approximated the *Toleranzpatent*. The Imperial Patent of 1853 rescinded the right of Jews to acquire landed property and reintroduced the recitation of the ancient Jewish oath when a Jew appeared before a court of law; and in 1863, supervision of Jewish schools was taken out of the hands of the clergy and claimed by the state as one of its mandates.[52]

Between 1859 and 1860, the absolutist policy of Emperor Francis Joseph suffered a number of blows, making it necessary to offer Hungary certain political concessions. With the Oktober Diploma (1860), as it was called, liberalism again began to make inroads in Hungary. Agoston Trefort, who was to play a prominent role in the Liberal government after emancipation was among those who, in 1861, considered the idea of selective emancipation for Jews who met certain qualifications. The government went so far as to consult with Jewish leaders (a number of whom agreed to this idea), but Parliament was dissolved before anything further could come of the matter.[53] Trefort suggested another format for emancipating the Jews only a year later, based on the following observation. Jews in Hungary were German both in language and culture, but in contrast to their counterparts in Germany and elsewhere, they upheld the status quo and there was little difference between them and Christians—that is, the wealthier, upper stratum of Jews, although they possessed a weak sense of honor, were superficial, reluctant to do heavy physical work, and displayed a lack of cleanliness. However, "Harmful is the influence on the people of those lower-class Jews whom, selling the worst merchandise expensively, wandering door to door, demoralize the people in a hundred different ways." Therefore, Trefort wanted to strike a bargain with the wealthier Jews: "So let's emancipate the Jews, but let us not keep secret for the sake of liberal modesty their faults, but demand from them that they give up their old views, and we must demand from the upper Jewish classes that they effect the transformation of the lower classes."[54] Two things should be noted here. First, as late as 1862, there were some among the liberal fold who grasped the real issues surrounding the emancipation of the Jews and had not succumbed to "liberal modesty." The second point, which stems from the first, is that the Jews' faults, their old views, must be given up.

However, when Parliament convened again in 1865, the little discussion that took place concerned details. Ferenc Deak, a prominent Liberal politician and architect of the compromise which established the Dual Monarchy (1867), desired to change the phrase "without distinction between the legally-received religions" to "without any religious distinction." This would have eliminated the need for a special piece of legislation, which he was opposed to. Minister of Justice Boldizsar Horvath wanted to combine naturalization and emancipation in one bill. But a consensus had been reached: no conditions would be attached to Jewish emancipation; this went against the liberal ethos. And, in any case, the objectives of religious reform and assimilation had partially been accomplished. Amongst some liberals, reform of the Jews was now expressed as a hope: one member of the Upper House hoped Jews would diverge from cosmopolitanism, be faithful and grateful sons of Hungary, and support the common weal and happiness.[55] The bill to emancipate the Jews was passed quietly and without any fanfare or public debate. The Act of 1867: XVII stated: "The Israelite inhabitants of the country are declared equally entitled to the practice of all civil and political rights as the Christian inhabitants;" "All laws, customs, or decrees contrary to this are herewith invalidated."

****

During the emancipation debates between 1839 and 1848, even the staunchest supporters of emancipation, Eotvos and Kossuth, had both concluded that there was no room for the Jew as Jew: Kossuth demanded that the peoplehood aspect of Jewishness be eliminated, and Eotvos foresaw a time when they would cease to be Jews. While the Hungarian Revolution of 1848 recalls the French Revolution in many respects, there was a significant difference in that in Hungary, legislation to improve the condition of the Jews had been seriously considered for some time; thus, the revolution provided the opportunity for the populace to fully express their hostility to this prospect. The Austrian government's assessment that the revolution would not have reached the dimensions it did without the help of the Jews accents not only the image of the Jew as very powerful and influential but also recalls the age-old theme of incivism.

Once a new format for Austro-Hungarian relations had been established in 1860, discussions on emancipation proceeded along liberal lines, in keeping with the dictates of the age. "So let's emancipate the Jews," said Trefort. At the same time, he articulated very strongly the demand that Jews "give up their old views." However, contrary to popular feeling, countless debates, and a century of prescriptive literature, Hungary's Jews (as Jews elsewhere) were emancipated without having to display their reform credentials, which in the case of newly arrived Eastern European Jews were nonexistent, and in the case of native-born Jews, indeterminate. The expectation (sometimes reduced in force to a hope) to reform remained. However, by eliminating the waiting period that many of the Enlightenment thinkers had favored until Jews had made reforms or, alternatively, incorporating reforms into the bills of emancipation, these expectations were unenforceable. The criteria of the *philosophes* having been bypassed, it was the 'Tolerated Jew' and not the 'Enlightened Jew' who was catapulted into the midst of society as the 'Emancipated Jew' via the bill of emancipation that had been promoted by liberalism.

Notes

1. The works of two Jewish historians stand out: Abraham Geiger's *Urschrift und Übersetzungen der Bibel* (1857) and *Das Judentum und seine Geschichte* (1864), and Heinrich Graetz's eleven-volume *Geschichte der Juden* (written between 1853 and 1876).

2. Heinrich Graetz, quoted in Susannah Heschel, "Abraham Geiger on the Origins of Christianity: The Political Strategies of Wissenschaft des Judentums in an Era of Acculturation," in *Jewish Assimilation, Acculturation and Accommodation: Past Traditions, Current Issues and Future Prospects*, ed. Menachem Mor (Lanham, Md.: University Press of America, Inc., 1992), 114-15, 121-22. Some of these comments may have been an updated version of Jewish argumentation against Christianity, which made its appearance in every historical era.

3. Adolf von Harnack, quoted in Heschel, "Abraham Geiger," 119-21. Heinrich von Treitschke referred to Graetz's work as a "fanatical fury against the 'arch enemy' Christianity, what deadly hatred of the purest and most powerful exponents of German character, from Luther to Goethe and Fichte." Quoted in Mendes-Flohr and Reinharz, *Jew in the Modern World*, 344.

4. Mosse, *Toward the Final Solution*, 129-130.

5. Justin Moser, quoted in Gerhard Kaiser, *Pietismus und Patriotismus im literarischen Deutschland* (Wiesbaden, 1961), 43.

6. In later years, Heine would express this view even more poignantly. "We do not have the courage to wear the traditional beard, to fast, to protest. . . . I, too, lack the courage to let my beard grow and risk the taunts of children crying 'Hep! Hep' or 'dirty Jew' after me." " Formerly I had little affection for Moses, probably because the Hellenic spirit was dominant within me, and I could not pardon the Jewish lawgiver for his intolerance of images, and every sort of plastic representation. . . . Now I understand that the Greeks were only beautiful youths, while the Jews have always been men, powerful, inflexible men." Quoted in Sachar, *Course of Modern Jewish History*, 153-56.

7. Baron, "Impact of the Revolution of 1848," 157-58.

8. First Minister Lamey, quoted in Werner E. Mosse, "From 'Schutzjuden' to 'Deutsche Staatbürger jüdischen Glaubens:' The Long and Bumpy Road of Jewish Emancipation in Germany," in *Paths of Emancipation: Jews, States, and Citizenship*, ed. Pierre Birnbaum and Ira Katznelson (Princeton: Princeton University Press, 1995), 85.

9. Between 1783 and 1825, little changed for the Jews, the *Toleranzpatent* of Joseph II notwithstanding, which was applied to Hungary as well with small changes in 1783, and fought all the way by the Hungarians. With the virtual rescinding of the *Toleranzpatent* in 1790, all the Hungarian municipalities demanded the annulment of the Jews' rights of residence and conducting business. The vice-regent prevaricated, stating, "The expulsion of Jews from cities is a matter of general economic concern to the country and should be decided by the General Assembly." Quoted in Aron Moskovits, *Jewish Education in Hungary (1848–1948)* (New York: Bloch Publishing Company, 1964), 4-5. Therefore, it was determined that for the time being, the *Toleranzpatent* should be restored. Still, in 1794, the vice-regent acceded to the demand made by the city council of Pest to expel all Jews who did not possess a permit prior to 1790. Discontent was expressed by the cities at both the 1802 and 1807 Diets. The 1802 Diet was flooded with complaints. The guilds of Pressburg compared Jewish merchants and shopkeepers to leeches which were flourishing on the very life blood of the populace and thus demanded that Jews be prohibited from the manufacture and retail sale of goods. The Commercial Association of Pest argued that neither peddling or selling wine and tobacco nor becoming property owners should be allowed. While the recommendation by the deputies of the 1807 Diet (as well as subsequent ones) that the Toleration Tax no longer be collected seems like a magnanimous

gesture on their part, Patai's interpretation is that rather than being a sign of goodwill towards the Jews, it was an act of defiance against the Austrians. Applying the concept of ownership, the levying of taxes on the Jews and the benefits to be derived therefrom properly belonged within Hungarian, not Austrian jurisdiction. In 1828, the deputy's suggestion was finally taken up, and the Toleration Tax was not collected. In 1846, it was abolished, at which time the government collected all the back taxes. Patai, *Jews of Hungary*, 202; Moscovits, *Jewish Education in Hungary*, 4-6, 8.

10. Handler, *Early Blueprint for Zionism*, 9.

11. For over thirty years, there had been a few Jews in rural areas who had owned both land and property in defiance of the law. Moskovits, *Jewish Education in Hungary*, 7.

12. *Hitel* [Credit], by Count Istvan Szechenyi, quoted in Nathaniel Katzburg, *Fejezetek az ujkori zsido tortenelembol Magyarorszagon* [Chapters from the New Age Jewish History in Hungary] (Budapest: MTA Judaisztikai Kutatocsoport—Osiris Kiado, 1999), 42.

13. Nathaniel Katzburg, *Hungary and the Jews: Policy and Legislation 1920–1943* (Jerusalem: Bar-Ilan University Press, 1981), 12-16.

14. Steven Bela Vardy, "The Origins of Jewish Emancipation in Hungary: The Role of Baron Jozsef Eotvos," *Ungarn-Jahrbuch* Band 7 (Jahrgang 1976. Munchen): 146; Patai, *Jews of Hungary*, 232.

15. Kalman Benda, at al. *One Thousand Years: A Concise History of Hungary*, ed. Peter Hanak, trans. Zsuzsa Beres, trans. revised Christopher Sullivan (Budapest: Corvina, 1988), 104.

16. Count Aurel Dessewffy, quoted in Patai, *Jews of Hungary*, 233.

17. Vardy, "Jewish Emancipation," 153.

18. Lajos Kossuth, quoted in Patai, *Jews of Hungary*, 233.

19. Benedek Virag, quoted in Mihaly Kolosvary-Borcsa, *A zsidokerdes magyarorszagi irodalma* [The Literature of the Jewish Question in Hungary] (Budapest: Stadium, 1943), 16.

20. Mahler, "Austrian Government and the Hasidim," 202-5; Katzburg, *Fejezetek*, 44. The word *maskilim* refers to proponents of the *Haskalah*, which is usually translated as the Jewish Enlightenment.

21. Quoted in Mahler, "Austrian Government and the Hasidim," 198.

22. Quoted in Mahler, "Austrian Government and the Hasidim," 205, 202, 207-9, 45. 3, 215, 221, 223-4. Joseph Perl and other fierce proponents of the *Haskalah* concurred with all these assessments; deeming the Hasids' conduct to be deleterious to the 'assimilated' image the *maskilim* were fighting so hard to cultivate, a virtual war against these 'intransigent' Jews was launched.

23. Moscovits, *Jewish Education*, 9-10; Vardy, "Origins of Jewish Emancipation," 154.

24. Quoted in Veghazi, "Role of Jewry," 57-58. Jews seeking to bypass this obstacle organized the Society for the Promotion of the Difficult Crafts and Agriculture Amongst the Israelites in Pest in 1842, with affiliated organizations in several towns where, overall, thousands of tradesmen were trained.

25. Vardy, "Origins of Jewish Emancipation," 146-61.

26. Jozsef Eotvos, *A zsidok emancipacioja* [The Emancipation of the Jews] (1840; repr., Budapest: Magyar Helikon, Szepirodalmi Konyvkiado, 1978), 207.

27. Eotvos, *A zsidok emancipacioja*, 215.

28. Eotvos, *A zsidok emancipacioja*, 215.

29. Eotvos, *A zsidok emancipacioja*, 213.

30. Eotvos, *A zsidok emancipacioja*, 227.

31. Jozsef Eotvos, Naplojegyzetek-Gondolat 1864–1868 [Diary Notes—Ideas 1864-1868], quoted in Katzburg, *Fejezetek*, 41. This conviction was not confined to the pages of Eotvos's diary. Also in *Fejezetek* is a comment by Geza Petrassevich, indicating that this view of Eotvos on the subject was common knowledge.

32. This negative outcome prompted the founding of the Association for the Promotion of the Magyar Language among Native Israelites (*A honi izraelitak kozott magyar nyelvet terjeszto egyulet*). Bela Bernstein, *Az 1848/49-iki magyar szabadsagharc es a zsidok* [The Hungarian War of Liberation of 1848–1849 and the Jews] (Budapest, 1898), 18-19, 20-21.

33. Patai, *Jews of Hungary*, 236.

34. *Pesti Hirlap*, 5 May 1844.

35. The subject of Jewish peoplehood was also addressed in another article published the same day. Gabor Fabian, a member of the Academy of Sciences, argued thusly: "The Jews are called, not only by us but by themselves as well, the Jewish people. We do not customarily call others as papist people, Calvinist people, Lutheran people or Unitarian people. This shows that under the word Jew lies more than just a difference in religion. The Jews therefore cannot be emancipated, because their religion is a political institution theocratically based, that cannot be brought into accord with the prevailing political system of the country." Despite this author's conviction, at the very least, "an indispensable condition of emancipation is the liberation of marriages between Christian and Jews." Quoted in *Pesti Hirlap*, 5 May 1844. Similarly, a pamphlet published by a 'Dr. J. G.' on *Some Modest Views from the Religious Perspective Concerning the Naturalization and Amalgamation of the Jews* expressed the view that "the emancipation of the Jews not only is not favored but is opposed by common sense" because they are a separate nation who are turned toward Palestine and whose messianic beliefs include a return to the Holy Land. Quoted in Patai, *Jews of Hungary*, 236.

36. Lajos Kossuth, quoted in Patai, *Jews of Hungary*, 235.

37. Jonas Kunewalder et al., quoted in Michael K. Silber, *The Historical Experience of German Jewry and Its Impact on Haskalah and Reform in Hungary* (New Brunswick, N.J. and Oxford: Transaction Books, 1987), 138.

38. Speech by Count Istvan Szechenyi in the Lower House, 24 April 1844.

39. Quoted in Bernstein, *Az 1848–49-iki magyar szabadsagharc*, 29-30.

40. *Pesti Hirlap*, 24 February 1848.

41. *Pesti Hirlap*, 2 March 1848.

42. Marton Vida, *ITELJETEK! Nehany kiragadott lap a magyar-zsido eletkozosseg konyvebol* [JUDGE FOR YOURSELVES! A few randomly chosen pages from the Book of Hungarian-Jewish Coexistence] (Budapest, 1939), unpaginated.

43. *Pesti Hirlap*, 7 April 1848.

44. Bela Bernstein wrote about the riots fifty years later. Beginning in Pozsony, 19 March 1848, there were demonstrations, the breaking of windows, and theft. The citizens demanded the dismissal of both the Jewish paper's editor and the Jewish keeper of the City Hall tavern, the expulsion of all Jews, and the prohibition of door-to-door sales. The first two demands were complied with immediately, and the latter two a month later when, on 6 April, mobs numbering in the thousands caused the Jews to seek refuge in the walled ghetto on a mountain. At the end of March, the town of Sopron ordered the expulsion of its Jews, as did the city of Pecs, but the City Council of the latter town agreed to a compromise and only Jews without residency status had to move out. On 5 April, the townspeople of Szekesfehervar and Szombathely attacked the Jews, but in the former town where they wanted to expel the Jews, they were convinced otherwise. In Pest, on 19 April, the mob beat up and robbed Jews and destroyed the Jewish quarter. The Jews of Bazin, Nadas, Szered, Nagyszombat, Modor and Szent-Gyorgy all fell victim to the same fate, but

in Vagujhely and a number of the surrounding villages, six hundred families were tortured, beaten, and pauperized. In Szakolca, Tura, Postyen, Hrus, Bosac, and Nagy-Tapolcsany, the story was the same. *A negyvennyolcas magyar szabadsagharc es a zsidok* [The 1848 Hungarian Freedom Fight and the Jews] (1898; repr., Budapest: Mult es Jovo Konyvek, 2000), 31-50. See also Salo W. Baron, "The Revolution of 1848 and Jewish Scholarship," *Jewish Social Studies* 9 (1949).

45. Katzburg, *Fejezetek*, 49; Baron, "Revolution of 1848," 169.

46. Nathaniel Katzburg, *Anti-Semitism in Hungary, 1867–1914* (Tel Aviv: Dvir Co. Ltd., 1969), 49.

47. Lajos Kossuth, quoted in Istvan Barta, *Kossuth Lajos az utolso rendi orszaggyulesen* [Lajos Kossuth in the Last Estate Parliament] (Budapest: Akademiai Kiado, 1951), 496.

48. Baron, "Impact of the Revolution of 1848," 198.

49. Baron, "Impact of the Revolution of 1848," 169; Bernstein, *A negyvennyolcas magyar szabadsagharc*, 31-50.

50. Two of the measures were directed against the Christian denominations. The revolutionary government had filled many of its positions with members of the Roman Catholic Church in an effort to bind the Church to the 1848 Revolution. These former deputies now found themselves purged from the ecclesiastical ranks by the Austrian government. Bela K. Kiraly, "Protestantism in Hungary Between the Revolution and the Ausgleich," in *Tolerance and Movements of Religious Dissent in Eastern Europe*, ed. Bela K. Kiraly (New York and London: East European Quarterly, Boulder, Colo. / Columbia University Press, 1975), 66-79. A dearth of clerical leadership, far from causing a withering of religious expression, simply redirected it from the church-based formality that was the hallmark of ecclesiastical centers to personally initiated signs of religiosity: pilgrimages, processions, rosary campaigns, and indulgences. Freifeld, *Nationalism and the Crowd*, 141. As for the Protestants, their participation in the Hungarian Revolution resulted in the enactment of 'Orders against the Protestants,' followed by The Protestant Patent of 1859 (which was supposedly meant to restore their legal status—but it did not). Protestants objected through petitions, meetings, articles, and outright refusal to implement the Patent. Church leaders were arrested and jailed by the score; nationwide defiance soon followed. While political overtones were evident, the intensity of the feeling surrounding this issue arose in large measure from religious commitment. Kiraly, "Protestantism in Hungary," 66-79. Both Catholic and Protestant reactions illustrate that religion was still a vital force in Hungary, again underscoring the need to questions assertions of mass secularization in the nineteenth century.

51. Quoted in Patai, *Jews of Hungary*, 276. After several rounds of pleading their inability to pay such an amount, the authorities agreed to a lesser sum to be used for a Jewish school fund. Moskovits, *Jewish Education in Hungary*, 18.

52. Patai, *Jews of Hungary*, 289-93, 302; Veghazi, "Role of Jewry," 59.

53. Katzburg, *Hungary and the Jews*, 17-18.

54. Trefort, "Riehl sociologiaja es munkassaga," [Sociology and the Works of Riehl] *Budapesti Szemle* 16, no. 53 (1862): 302-4.

55. Gyurgyak, *A zsidokerdes Magyarorszagon*, 61-62.

Chapter 5
Assessing Assimilation after 1867

Only a few months after emancipation in 1867, Jozsef Kiss, Jewish poet and future editor of a major journal extolled his newly legitimized homeland with such phrases as "Look up to the sky and then to the ground:/ This is where the Promised Land is found."[1] Within seven years, cogent arguments criticizing the Jews' progress in assimilation had appeared, occasioning a second poem by Kiss. Writing of a "new Ahasuerus": "You may build cottages, You may accumulate wealth, You will still not have a home in this country."[2] Lajos Csernatony's five-part series on the Jews in his journal, *Ellenor* (1874) pointed out that the real proof of assimilation was missing: as in the ghetto, Jews still focused on work, thrift, and social cohesion rather than adopting the outlook and behaviors of their Christian countrymen. Moreover, through the Jews' persistent attachment to German culture and language,* their ever-increasing involvement in the cultural sphere was actually obstructing the process of Magyarization in Hungary while simultaneously promoting Germanization.[3] Csernatony wrote this series as a liberal; his liberal credentials are impeccable. A former secretary to Lajos Kossuth, after the 1848 Revolution he went into exile for twenty years. Upon his return, he embarked on a career in journalism while also serving as an MP in Kalman Tisza's Liberal Party (*Szabadelvu Part*), although the public expression of such views put him into a minority position within his party. His series was an early but almost complete expression of the poor progress in assimilation. The same complaints would be registered by an increasing number of people and with increasing frequency as the perception spread that Jews were failing to reform.

An 1877 editorial in the popular daily *Magyar Hirlap* pointed out other problems, which were woven together in a series of tautologies. The people are ignorant and so those who are thrifty like the Jews succeed. Due to hatred, the Jew stays aloof and heartless and so they become rich. Jews and Christians don't understand each other and hence the hatred between them. A sense of solidarity

---

* In 1880, one-third of Hungarian Jews declared German to be their mother tongue, and just under two-thirds said that it was Hungarian. Yet, by 1900, only twenty-five per cent said they knew no other language than Hungarian. Clearly, then, bilingualism was the dominant trend among Hungarian Jews. Silber, "Historical Experience of German Jewry," 127. Open letters on the Jewish Question expressed the view that if only Jews would stop speaking German all would be well. *Fuggetlenseg*, 23 December 1880.355. The death of Rabbi Neuhasz was noted because he preached in Hungarian. *Fuggetlenseg*, 24 January 1881.23.

exists amongst the Jews.[4] This last trait, Jewish solidarity, was the third member of a family of traits which also included social cohesiveness and social exclusivism. While solidarity had been noticed during the era of Toleration, it was an indifferent trait. With emancipation, the other two traits made their appearance, signs of the limited degree to which Jews were willing to associate with non-Jews.[5] These three traits were immediately perceived as an obvious impediment to assimilation.

Kiss's sense of new realities also coincided with the government's stated wish to regulate the immigration and settlement of Eastern European Jews (often called the Eastern Question) in 1875.[6] Articulation of this position was prompted by MP Gyozo Istoczy's speech in Parliament on this subject.* It was a recurring theme whether, and to what degree, to restrict the immigration of Eastern European Jews.

> They were seeking a new homeland for themselves. Who are these people? They are the same rubbish that was filtered out of the Moscovite sieve and escaped to Galicia. There they were filtered out once again. The good ones remained, and the scrap material continued to wander. . . . They arrived here without anyone asking them. . . . They continued to arrive, bundles on their backs, deceitful scales in their hands, and a poisoned drink in their barrels. They came here with their fierce hatred of Christianity.[7]

Generally speaking, all Jews were considered unassimilated; however, in discussions about the Galizianers, using a measuring stick marked with relative increments, 'our Jews' were at least relatively assimilated but 'those Jews'— who came mostly from Galicia—were not and could not become so.

At the same time Istoczy raised the issue of the Eastern Question, he also asked if it was conjoined to the Jewish Question. There were a number of components to the Jewish Question. A fundamental component was the "caste-like, racially pure" aspect of the Jews, maintained by their resistance to intermarriage. Another was the fact that their numbers were rapidly increasing, both in absolute terms and due to immigration.[8] Having "bold plans of world domination,"[9] Jews already held a monopoly in the upper echelons of finance and commerce; at the lower level, they were parasitic as usurious moneylenders, innkeepers, and land leasers. They were committed to pan-Jewish expansion, facilitated by the *Alliance Israelite Universelle* in Paris. Furthermore, they were unassimilable on cultural and religious grounds. As such, Jews were a threat to Christian morality and Hungarian nationalism.[10] In response to Istoczy, Baron Bela Wenckheim, speaking for the government, answered, "The Government doesn't know about any Jewish Question, consequently it cannot take any position on it."[11] The gov-

---

* MP Gyozo Istoczy's name is synonymous with issues related to Jews in the political forum. Profoundly disturbed by the Jews' economic and social monopolization of Hungary, he was instrumental in the formation of the Anti-Semitic League (1880); the founding of the *12 Ropirat*, a journal through which he propagated his views (1880); and the formation of the National Anti-Semitic Party (1883). Throughout his many years in Parliament, he sought to bring about measures that would resolve the Jewish Question.

ernment was either unable or unwilling to acknowledge its existence, but a letter (20 April 1875) by Edmund Monson, British Chief Consul in Hungary, rather confirms it: "The truth is, Istoczy only expresses the secret, publicly-unspoken convictions of many."[12]

Perhaps "publicly-unspoken," but definitely not unwritten about. Looking at the *Judische Delikatessen* for the months July-September 1880, one can see that the comments about the Jews' failure to fit into the social and political systems in Hungary (that is, complying with the Enlightenment ideals specific to the Jews) were already escalating to a serious degree. The *Delikatessen's* 'editor' had collected six German pamphlets that were being circulated in Hungary and two pamphlets printed in German but of Hungarian origin (expressing their opposition to the Jews mostly in terms of the hold Jews had on the economy); a booklet of recent Hungarian dance music called *New Songs* that included in its repertoire some that criticized and ridiculed Jews; a satirical paper fond of publishing similar satires and cartoons; a small pamphlet issued as a series which featured anti-Jewish poems; and a pamphlet by a Jew entitled *What Can We Do Against Attacks?*[13] There was a long article by a Jewish man lamenting the current state of affairs and how they had worsened since emancipation. Articles on Jewish crime and immorality and Jews mistreating each other, interspersed with anti-Jewish jokes, were in abundance. In addition, one finds that Istoczy had formed the Anti-Semitic League and that its journal, *The Jewish Question*, would be launched in the fall of 1880, as well as Istoczy's *12 Ropirat* [12 Pamphlets].[14] MP Miklos stated in Parliament that the anti-Semitic movement was significant and inquired whether the Government was going to permit the League's formation; he then expressed the hope that the interreligious peace would not be harmed by it. During these months, a notice was posted advocating the emigration of Jews to Palestine. Some Christian inhabitants of a village burned down a house that had been recently purchased by a Jew, and there were reports about Jews being murdered in Ade. There were also several articles bridling at business closures on the Jewish festivals and an open letter to Orthodox Jews asking, "Why don't you use Hungarian?"[15]

These complaints were funneled into a productive venue. By 1880, we see the formation of organizations lobbying for the implementation of controls over the historical secular nexus between Jew and Christian: the economy. Protection for non-Jewish merchants and craftsmen against Jewish competition was one of the main points in the platform of the Association of the Non-Jews of Hungary. Beyond the erection of economic barricades, the mandate of such organizations was to establish social separation from the Jews, lobby the government, and serve as an informal political voice.[16] Istoczy's *12 Ropirat* served the same purpose. The first journal to be devoted to the Jewish Question, it was to remain in publication for twelve years, becoming the official organ of the anti-Semitic movement.[17]

As early as 1878, Istoczy could envision a solution to the Jewish Question, one that he outlined in his "Restoration of the Jewish State in Palestine" speech to Parliament.[18] Resituated in Palestine—their 'natural element'—Jews would revitalize that region, while their presence in Europe had had the opposite effect: it had "retarded the progress of European nations and threatened Christian civilization."[19] Importantly, he left the option open to Jews to remain if they assimilated completely; but those who "do not want to assimilate to us, become one people with us, must part with us."[20] Istoczy was not the only one who supported the relocation of Jews to Palestine. Others were running out of patience and had given up on the feasibility of Jewish assimilation. Hence, merchants of Zala, who were supporters of Mor Jokai, a Liberal MP, received this notice which announced: "The members of this city's electoral district who are [Jewish] wholesale merchants have arrived at the lucky moment of their lives, when they can emigrate to Palestine—and they can also take the city with them."[21]

Simultaneously, through Hungarianization offices set up by the state, the Magyarization of names was being promoted among both the ethnic minorities and the Jews.* While this tactic as a means of assimilation may be viewed as superficial, it was considered a vital part of the process by the government, although a bare majority of Hungarians supported this policy. At issue were the motives of Jews for changing their names and their choice of name. Expediency was deemed the most common reason for name changing. Taken to extremes, an anecdote related how one Mozes Lowy converted to Protestantism and at the same time changed his name to Martin Luther to save the monogram on his linen.[22] Expediency took on sinister overtones when a Jew who had changed his name to 'Dory' after a renowned family passed as one of the family members and obtained a substantial amount of credit from a Viennese firm. Eventually, he was caught. Commented the editor of the *Fuggetlenseg:* "Now the firm is cursing the national Hungarian chauvinists because they look for patriotism not in the heart and blood but in the name and are happily giving the biggest oldest names to these dirty Jewish individuals."[23]

"Some pretend to like traditional names; in reality, they want to hide in the nimbus of these names" in order to seem reputable and established.[24] And the "glaring fact" must be mentioned, stated the *Tolna Bulletin,* that Jews chose only well-known names and avoided unknown ones.[25] An anonymous letter to the editor considered it a "political crime" to adopt ancient names; "it has a communistic flavor."[26] An article published late in this debate (1885) stated that Jews abuse Christian names: they should be given numbers; it would be best to burn it into them.[27] Yet the Hungarianization Society defended the adoption of old Hungarian names, otherwise strange names would persist, but letters to the editor show that there was not a consensus on this. One editorial did not object to the adoption of names previously used by the nobility, but suggested that nobles should signal their nobility with "Esquire" for example, to distinguish their position as they did in Britain.[28] As for the Budapest Israelite Women's Society, they

---

* The government's policy to Magyarize names was not terribly successful among the ethnic minorities. As of May 1881, they composed fifty per cent of the population of Hungary, and Jews five per cent, yet four-sevenths of those changing their names were Jews. *Pesti Naplo,* 26 May 1881.144. In the 28 August 1881.235 issue, the paper again pointed out how many Jews were changing their names, saying there had been a five-fold growth; fifty-eight per cent of Jews were Hungarianizing their names. Therefore, when this matter was discussed, it was usually the Jews people had in mind.

would not even demonstrate their intention to assimilate: their bulletin was printed in German—and all Hungarian Jews still read German newspapers.[29]

****

The optimism of Jozsef Kiss was quickly dashed. Kiss had failed to grasp that emancipation had not opened the door to acceptance of the Jews but had only made it easier for them to reform. The popular consensus was that 'Jews are not reforming themselves,' also expressed as 'Jews are still behaving in the old pre-emancipated way,' and most succinctly, Jews are not assimilating. It was also phrased in a way that was *sui generis* to the post-emancipation period: Jews are making the wrong changes. The Jews' socially cohesive and "caste-like" nature was inhibiting conversion as well as intermarriage. Their 'work ethic' was at odds with Hungarian mores and furthermore, was triggering a monopoly in finance and commerce. This monopoly, in turn, was a stepping-stone to "world domination." Moneylending, innkeeping, and land leasing created ongoing sources of conflict with the Jews on a day-to-day level and highlighted unsavory Jewish characteristics. By 1880, organizations were added to popularly voiced complaints.

The government attempted to deal with the problem in two ways. It wanted to keep out Eastern European Jews whom they regarded as unassimilable and Magyarize 'homegrown' Jews by having them change their names, learn to speak Hungarian, and educate their children in Hungarian schools (below). These measures did not address the fundamental issue of wholesale reform and were therefore ineffective. Little provocation was needed to escalate matters: the imminent charge of Jews committing ritual murder—which had never been an issue during the emancipation debates, even among Catholics—showed the depth of the hostility to the expanded Jewish presence in Hungarian society.

NOTES

1. Jozsef Kiss, "December huszadikan," [On the Twentieth of December] in *Zsido dalok* [Jewish Songs] (n.p., 1868).

2. Jozsef Kiss, quoted in Aladar Komlos, "A szazadveg koltoi," [Poets of the fin-de-siecle] in *Tegnap es ma* [Yesterday and Today] (Budapest, 1956), 151. There are statistics on Jewish emigration for the period between 1870 and 1910, precisely the period under discussion in this chapter. While it is sometimes difficult to pin down the reasons for emigration when there is not some immediate catastrophe to attribute it to, it is reasonable to assume that the figure of 110,000 Jews over this forty-year period was due, at least in part, to strong anti-Jewish sentiment. This figure represents somewhere between ten and twenty per cent of the Jewish population, according to C. A. Macartney, in *A History of Hungary 1929–1945* (New York, 1956), 1:192. However, this statistic should be viewed with some skepticism. The Jewish population in Hungary swelled during this period, primarily due to the ongoing influx of Jews from Galicia. Since some of them eventually became part of the massive migration of European Jews to America, it seems more reasonable to consider them simply as temporary residents and not *bona fide* Hungarian emigrants.

3. Csernatony considered that some blame for the slow progress in Hungarianiz-ation should be laid at the foot of the government: both the lack of a comprehensive

naturalization bill and the prohibition of civil marriage retarded the desired assimilation. Andrew Handler, *Blood Libel at Tiszaeszlar* (Boulder, Colo.: East European Monographs / New York: Columbia University Press, 1980), 26-27. A Mr. Mor Hoffmann issued a pamphlet as a rebuttal to Csernatony. One of his comments reveals that he shared with Kiss the feeling that the public's perception of the Jew was a negative one: "Though he is tolerated, he is not a welcome guest. . . . the emancipation was given grudgingly." *Zsidoinkrol! Igaza van-e Csernatony Lajos urnak vagy nem?* [About our Jews: Is Mr. Lajos Csernatony Correct or Not?] (Nagy-Kanizsa: Fischel Fulop, 1874).

4. *Magyar Hirlap*, 2 January 1877.

5. It should be noted that, beginning in the Enlightenment and extending into the post-emancipation era, references were occasionally made to what were later called social cohesiveness and social exclusivism. To extract from these comments that these traits had been perpetual issues would be a mistake; before the Enlightenment, the notion of assimilation as a means through which Jews could join society was unimaginable. The *Spectator*, for example, in its Saturday, 27 September 1753 (no. 495, page 84) issue, wrote, "For they live all in a body, and generally within the same inclosure [sic]; to marry among themselves. . . . This shuts them out from all table conversation. . ." During the civil marriage debate in Hungary in 1883, MP Janos Janossy spoke of the "resistance of the Jewish race to racial assimilation. . . . A thousand ties of the coexistence bind them to us . . ." Speech in Parliament, quoted in *Pesti Naplo*, 21 January 1883.

6. In 1882, the government did issue a ruling halting immigration; it coincided with the Austrian government's evacuation of the large population of Hasidic Jews living in Brody, Galicia, many of whom tried to find their way into Hungary. *Fuggetlenseg*, 12 June 1882.161. The government's ruling, by the way, was unsuccessful. With the Jewish population of Galicia standing at 811,371 in 1900, 624,639 were concentrated in eastern Galicia, close to the Hungarian border. Robert S. Wistrich, "Austrian Social Democracy and the Problem of Galician Jewry 1890-1914," *LBIYB* 26 (1981): 91. No ruling was strong enough to prevent these Jews, who saw Hungary as a land of opportunity, from entering illegally.

7. Gyozo Istoczy, *Istoczy Gyoso orszaggyulesi beszedei inditvanai es torveny-javaslatai, 1872-1896* [Gyozo Istoczy's Speeches, Resolutions, and Bills in Parliament, 1872-1896] (Budapest: Buschmann F. Konyvnyomdaja, 1904), 77-78.

8. Istoczy stated that between 1785 and 1870 the Hungarian Jewish population had increased eight fold, and if this rate were sustained, there would be 1,100,000 Jews in 1900 (he was not far off), 4,400,000 in 1960, and so on. These figures are corroborated by Katzburg, *Anti-Semitism in Hungary*, 253. This rapid rate of reproduction among Jews was a pan-European phenomenon. According to Dr. Arthur Ruppin, Jews had the highest rate of reproduction of any group in Europe in the nineteenth century. In absolute numbers, he estimated the Jewish population to be 2,500,000 in 1800; 3,281,000 in 1825; 4,764,500 in 1850; 7,673,500 in 1880; and 10,602,500 in 1900. Population statistician Jacob Lestchinsky wrote that the quadruple increase was an "unprecedented phenomenon in the history of Jewish and non-Jewish demography." Ruppin and Lestchinsky, quoted in Uriah Zevi Engelman, *The Rise of the Jew in the Western World: A Social and Economic History of the Jewish People of Europe* (1944; repr., New York: Arno Press Inc., 1973), 102-3.

9. Istoczy, *Istoczy Gyozo orszaggyulesi*, 77-78.

10. Istoczy, *Istoczy Gyozo orszaggyulesi*, 1-14.

11. Baron Bela Wenckheim, quoted in Katzburg, *Fejezetek*, 122.

12. Edmund Monson, quoted in Katzburg, *Fejezetek*, 23. About the memoranda produced by the British Foreign Office, the *Fuggetlenseg* wrote: "The reports of English consuls are all reliable. They are not trying to varnish; they try to give a clear picture." 10 July 1887.180.

13. The author enjoined Jews to become peasants who do manual work, not only leasers and managers. *Judische Delikatessen*, Book 5.
14. *Judische Delikatessen*, Books 4, 5.
15. *Judische Delikatessen*, Book 10, item no. 11.
16. *Egyetertes*, 29 January 1880.50.
17. The first issue of *12 Ropirat* sold out in ten days. *Magyarorszag*, 28 October 1880.299. A second edition came out 30 October. *Pecsi Figyelo*, 30 October 1880. By the November 10th issue, Istoczy's portrait could be purchased. *Fuggetlenseg*, 10 November 1880.312.
18. Handler, *Early Blueprint for Zionism*, 45-46.
19. Istoczy, *Istoczy Gyozo orszaggyulesi*, 42.
20. Istoczy, *Istoczy Gyozo orszaggyulesi*, 59.
21. *Ellenor*, 16 August 1880.390.
22. *Fuggetlenseg*, 5 September 1881.244.
23. *Fuggetlenseg*, 20 October 1884.290.
24. *Pesti Naplo*, 1 March 1881.59.
25. *Tolna Bulletin*, 21 August 1881.34; *Magyarorszag*, 26 August 1881.193.
26. *Pesti Naplo*, 1 March 1881.59.
27. *Fuggetlenseg*, 11 February 1885.41.
28. *Pesti Naplo*, 3 March, 1881.61, 4 March 1881.62, 12 March, 1881.70, 19 August 1881.227, open letter, 1 March 1881.59.
29. *Tolna Bulletin*, 21 August 1881.34.

Chapter 6
A Case of Ritual Murder

The ongoing discussion of Jewish exceptionalism took a dramatic turn late in May 1882. The following incident was brought to the attention of the public by a local Catholic priest, Jozsef Adamovics, in the clerical paper *Magyar Allam*.

> This river of ours, this Tisza of ours, pure, unsullied and miserable? No one doubts that you are blameless of the innocent blood spilled in vain. No one assumes that you have sinned. On the contrary, everyone here knows with absolute certainty who the guilty parties are. A girl of fourteen [Eszter Solymosi], going shopping in the village, vanished in the vicinity of the synagogue. That is a fact! Who is guilty? It cannot be that you suspect this to be a case of a despicable, fanatic Jewish assassination. Are the Jews guilty of this mysterious event, taking place just before their Passover festival? Is it their fault that by chance a few strange slaughterers appeared in Tiszaeszlar[1] [Several Jews were in the town that weekend applying for the position of *shochet*.] and spent the night in the synagogue?
>
> For they are decent citizens, expressing their thanks for their emancipation by sacrificing Christian blood to their god. And the Jewish population is already at work; they have already begun their noble campaign to have this matter put to rest in a speedy and desirable fashion.*

The possibility that there were Jews in their midst committing acts of ritual murder stunned Christian Hungary, and this case, commonly referred to simply as "Tiszaeszlar", monopolized the attention of the nation. The press tended to shy away from the claim of ritual murder, viewing Eszter's death as a "special crime" or a "religious murder"[2] committed by "crazy fanatics;"[3] hence, this "*shakhter's* barbarous crime should not become a 'Jewish Question.'"[4] In this case, Jews were guilty of obfuscation of justice, not ritual murder, as this typical editorial pointed out.

---

* Father Jozsef Adamovics, quoted in Sandor Hegedus, *A tiszaeszlari vervad* [The Tiszaeszlar Blood Libel] (Budapest: 1966), 60. Attention should be drawn to the fact that along with their clerical duties, it was not uncommon for both Roman Catholic and Protestant clergy to assume political, academic, and journalistic positions, and via these channels, they regularly stated their views towards Jews. Even some village clergy participated in the public forum. Accordingly, many of their comments will find their way into this section.

> This [case] is so concrete that there probably was some terrible crime. We don't want to believe what the people say, that Jews need Christian blood for ritual sacrifices, but it seems most probable that a special crime has been committed. It is in the particular interest of the Jews to solve the mystery, because if people don't get an answer where the girl has disappeared to, it will be difficult to kick out from them the belief that Jews need blood for Passover. So a rational mind would propose that the Jews themselves would be the busiest in resolving the case. And what do we see? That they want to cheat the public and stop the inquiry. . . .
>
> . . . And yesterday, they wanted to pay the mother some money because they are nervous and want to use every tool to cover up the case. And of course, this extreme solidarity of the Jews in this case proves the terrible superstition, and if it gets stronger, there will be some horrible problems.[5]

While another editorial did use the term "ritual murder," its point was, "Christians tortured innocents based on ritual fanaticism, nobody denies that; only Jews don't have ritual killing?"[6]

The interim between the arrests and the trial was tumultuous. Within weeks of the arrests of thirteen Jews, multiple disturbances broke out: in Pozsony; in Nagyszombat, where the Jews had been frightened by threats, pamphlets, physical attacks, and stones thrown at the rabbi's windows—as a result of which they requested that soldiers be in attendance on Market Day.[7] Many of these disturbances had been instigated by the clergy, which Prime Minister Kalman Tisza in his capacity as Minister of the Interior attempted to address in a letter to the Bishop of Veszprem, June 1882.

> Your Grace is no doubt familiar with the regrettable misdemeanors committed in the seat of Zala County and other communities, under the guise of anti-Semitism. The other cause of these breaches of the peace is that the Roman Catholic clergy of County Zala also support the anti-Semitic ideas. . . .
>
> . . . I respectfully ask that the clergy under your ecclesiastic jurisdiction be warned, and those clergymen be directed to desist preaching to the adherents, not in the spirit of, but contrary to neighborly and Christian love . . .[8]

Tisza described the Catholic clergy as being supportive of anti-Semitism, but from the Church's point of view, Tisza was incorrect. The emancipation of the Jews could not possibly have occasioned a reassessment of its theologically based position of keeping the Jews at a considerable remove from the Christian population. The Church maintained, as always, that the influence of Jews upon Christians was profoundly deleterious, and that it was only through conversion Jews could become members of society. However, the Church's position was also to uphold the law of the land. Once the emancipation bill was passed, the Church had "no remark against this."[9] But as it witnessed what it regarded as increasing evidence of the insinuation of the Jews into the entire fabric of society, its ire escalated to the point of outrage and it became an active participant in movements to overturn emancipation.[10] It is impossible to calculate the influence of the Church's views, which it publicized in all of its organs, from the most official pronouncements from Rome to the smallest of local Church papers read weekly by Hungarians. What can be said is that they were widely circulated among the Catholic population and gained reinforcement from weekly sermons. Apart from Budapest and a few cities of modest size, the vast majority of Hungarians lived in isolated rural conditions where the Church was the predominant influence. Every time the opportunity was afforded by a public policy debate, the Catholic Church in Hungary firmly stated its stand that Jews should be removed from the mainstream of society.

Shortly after these disturbances, committed "under the guise of anti-Semitism," further episodes of violence broke out in the summer in western Hungary; at the end of September, they erupted again in Pozsony, and shortly thereafter spread to some twenty neighboring towns. Government correspondence recorded that "the disturbances lately happening in Pozsony according to general local opinion, are caused by the newspaper [*Westungarischer*] *Grenzbote*, with its anti-Semitic articles and especially its activities to collect money for anti-Semitic purposes," but that the outbreaks had gotten out of hand was due to the lack of any effort by the mayor and the city council of Pozsony to contain them.[11] They were severe enough to necessitate the presence of a Royal Commissioner and the declaration of martial law for a month.[12]

While the Ministry was advising that steps be taken for the prevention of "supposed anti-Jewish agitations,"[13] its greater concern was "those agitating anti-Semitic press products that have been flooding the country for some time, which threaten to upset the internal peace."[14] An official from the British Foreign Office noted that "the only newspaper professing anti-Jewish sentiments has during the last three months trebled the number of its subscribers."[15] The police were at war with the pamphleteers; daily, pamphlets were torn down only to be put up the next morning.[16] One pamphlet about which the authorities were particularly worried was *The Martyr Girl of Tiszaeszlar* whose "confiscation and annihilation" was ordered.[17] An article by 'Titus Aemilius' (a lieutenant in the Hungarian army whose real name was Emil Szemnecz) appeared in the July 1882 edition of Istoczy's *12 Ropirat*. Entitled the "Judaization of Hungary," it was typical of the literature in the journal. However, in light of the proliferation of such material, the chief state prosecutor decided to initiate action against Istoczy who, in the interim, had claimed authorship of the article in order to protect Szemnecz. While the Committee on Parliamentary Immunity was fully aware of this subterfuge, as the party responsible for the publication of the article, they suspended Istoczy's parliamentary immunity so that he could be tried for violating Section 172 of the Hungarian penal code, which stated that outright incitement to religious hatred was punishable under the law. The jury of twelve deemed otherwise and proclaimed Istoczy 'not guilty.'[18]

Concurrently, one of the first issues Istoczy had raised, the immigration of Eastern European Jews, was being pursued by the public through petitions. A petition submitted in March 1882 by the county of Szatmar was discussed in Parliament in June. Cosigned by five other counties and to which fourteen more later appended their names, it was entitled "Concerning the Curtailment of the Inundation of Jewish Immigrants from Russia through Galicia to the Regions Adjacent to Szatmar County." "Settling with the intention of enriching themselves but without making the slightest sacrifice to acquire Hungarian citizenship,"[19] even nominally, Galizianers were not taking steps to assimilate. At the end of July 1882, several Hungarian Reformed Church (Calvinist/Presbyterian) priests, landed estate owners, and various public figures from Tapolca, in Zala County drew up the Tapolca Petition. That those attending the convention already considered Jewish assimilation a failed venture is clear from the petition's recommendations:

> 1. 'The Jews set themselves off from Christianity, especially by means of their observance of the laws of *Kashrut* [keeping kosher] and ritual purity, which debase Christians and insult them;' therefore, the emancipation Law of 1867 should be abrogated.
> 2. Jewish education should be prohibited.
> 3. Members of the Jewish race must be forbidden to acquire real estate in Hungary.[20]

The Tapolca Petition was presented to Parliament 22 January 1883, bearing the signatures of 2,174 Hungarians.[21] By this time, thirty more petitions had accumulated. The repetition of certain themes in these petitions highlights them as key issues. The restriction against discussing the Jewish Question, due "to the curtailment of the freedom of the press," should be overturned. The Jewish faith did "not have a theology or morality that would make it suitable for state supervision." Jewish schools perpetuated a "mentality [that] is contrary to Hungarian educational interests." Due to "unconscionable practices," Jews were taking over "indigenous industry . . . squeezing out honest decent work and causing the loss of our foreign markets." In order to avoid serving in the military, "the Jews are keeping sloppy *matricula* [registration of births, marriages, deaths]; to evade paying taxes, they are "cheating intentionally in the keeping of records." "The tried and true owners of the land, those carriers of patriotism, are forcefully supplanted by this alien race that has never been tried as to its loyalty and chooses to live in religious and social isolation and Jewish emancipation." How to resolve this calamity? By curtailing "Eastern immigration" and revoking Jewish emancipation.[22]

The petitions provoked enormous debate in the country and provided ample fuel for further deliberation on the subject of the Jews. In the parliamentary discussions, those MPs who were sympathetic to the aims of the petitions further expounded on the points raised in them. But what should not escape our attention is the thrust of the Liberal parliamentarians who, while defending emancipation, made it clear that their expectation was complete assimilation; that this task was the responsibility of the Jews; and that Jews had not yet completed this process. MP Mor Jokai acknowledged the Jews' predominance in usury, which was "destructive", and their heavy involvement in the alcohol trade, which was "immoral", but he was confident that shortly, complete assimilation would occur.

> The Hungarian nation has assimilated two Semitic races. If I would not name them, nobody would remember them. One Semitic race is the Kuns, and the second race is the Armenians, who are also Semites and nobody can differentiate them from Hungarians. And the third one will be the Jews, who in the next century no one will recognize from Hungarians.[23]

MP Otto Herman's proposition was not to disturb the 1867 XVII Legislation concerning emancipation but to expect from the Jews that "since we demolished the walls built between man and man, now they should demolish the walls built between Jew and Christian."[24] Mimicking the bad habits of Hungarians such as the casino and horseracing was not social assimilation. Fiercely attacking Orthodox Jews who believed emancipation was harmful because it weakened religious belief, he concurred with "the Jewish voice Dr. Szigeti who has called upon his coreligionists to convene and clarify their religious customs and bring them up to date [a ban against the purity laws and the interdiction concerning intermarriage were mentioned]" in order to facilitate social assimilation.[25] MP Daniel Iranyi, who the editor of the *Fuggetlenseg* described as "the warmest sponsor of Jews," stated that Jewish immigration from the east would pose a permanent obstacle to the desired assimilation.

> In the last two or three decades, very many Jews have arrived from Galicia who live as innkeepers and other indirect businesses and expropriate the illiterate peoples' naïveté and are not favorable to the Hungarian Christian society. Consequently, it is not even in the interest of Hungarian Jews who are progressing in Hungarianization to let their numbers grow.[26]

The editor of the *Pesti Naplo* summarized the views of Parliament: "We did not give emancipation to the Jews as a gift, but it results from the freedom-loving Hungarian nation's duty. We do not expect as a gift from the Jews their complete melding with the Hungarian national interests, but as their duty."[27] This emphatic statement, coming from a staunchly liberal newspaper, not only underscored the expectation that Jews assimilate, but how incomplete their efforts at "complete melding with the Hungarian national interests" had been to date.

Although the petitions were fundamentally a parliamentary matter, they stimulated comment from a variety of sources. In the newspaper *Abauj-Kassai Kozlony*, which described itself as a "humble organ of liberalism in relation to the Jewish Question," we read that the Jewish Question had been provoked by a lack of assimilation. Jews had persisted in displaying "intolerance" and their "interpretation of Jewish religious and racial solidarity [had] set up the Jew in the state as a goal for itself." In this Jewish state, it was the practice "to slander judges, put legislation up to the pillory, hire false witnesses, bury the living, dig up the dead, possibly for the innocent, possibly for the guilty, against whom equally with Christians the procedure is progressing."[28]

General Gyorgy Klapka, hero of Komarom during the Revolution of 1848, involved himself in the debate, specifically addressing the issue of Jewish loyalty. He said that while he had not wanted to enter the anti-Semitic debate, he did desire to protect Hungary's reputation in the foreign press. So, it was his duty to defend the honor of the state by declaring that amongst the fighters of 1848-49, there was no difference between the Jews who are now condemned as cowards and the non-Jews. The *Fuggetlenseg* had its own response to this claim. Klapka had financial problems that everybody knew about, and so his statement looked more like an attempt to appease his Jewish creditors. Before speaking out, he should have considered the fact that some of his witnesses were still alive. Jews participated on both sides as spies and suppliers; both sides were forced to hang some of them. The general should not consider this letter as interference in his private financial matters, but rather a punishment for interfering in the business of the Jews.[29] The matter finally died down: in the words of the *Pesti Naplo*, "Luckily the Jew debate came to an end and the House of Commons can be happy with the decision."[30]

Organizing against the Jews continued. Just two days before the Tapolca Petition was presented, the Hungarian Defense Union was founded in Kecskemet.[31] On a much larger scale, and presumably in the works before Tiszaeszlar, Istoczy's attempt to unite those of similar views resulted in the convening of the First International Anti-Jewish Congress (sometimes known as the Dresden Congress) in Dresden, Germany, early in September 1882.[32]

The overlapping of the Tiszaeszlar case with the government's presentation of the Civil Marriage Bill[33] was not auspicious for its passage. One of the primary objections to the bill was its futility as a method to bring about the assimilation of the Jews: Jews were opposed to marriage to Christians.

> The resistance of the Jewish race to racial assimilation has nowhere proved as tenacious as in Hungary. They failed to be tamed through a long row of centuries. A thousand ties of the coexistence bind them to us since the beginning, and yet we experience that by and large they represent the focus of Germanization and in their morals and customs have remained alienated from Hungarian customs and morals.[34]

A British Foreign Office dispatch observed the general reason for the failure of the bill to pass.

> The one party ['all the Church Dignitaries, the gilded youth of Hungary, and the principal members of the most influential magnate families'] felt they were giving expression to the feeling, which I believe is very general in Hungary, of determination to resist all encroachment on the part of the Jews, that they were resisting an attempt to place that class on an equal footing with the rest of the population.[35]

Public opposition to the bill was expressed in the form of the defeat of "a strong Government candidate" by "an unknown man who had presented himself at the last moment as a declared anti-Semitic." About the Liberals' motives for supporting the bill, the official at the Foreign Office was most cynical: rather than being a sincere support of Jewish equality, the Liberals "felt they were promoting a concession which was demanded by liberalism and progress and which after the events of the last year [the agitations provoked by Tiszaeszlar] they considered to be indispensable as a proof that Anti-Semitism had no real power in Hungary."[36]

Finally, the Tiszaeszlar trial commenced in July 1883.

> A trial which has been going on in Hungary for the last few weeks deserves some notice on account of the lamentable picture it affords both of the

religious animosity prevailing, and of the manner in which criminal investigations are conducted and justice administered in this kingdom. . . .

. . . The chief and indeed only direct witness against the accused is a Jew boy, the son of one of the implicated who states that through the keyhole of the Synagogue he saw the girl bled to death and her blood caught in one of the vessels of the temple, and he still adheres firmly to his statement. . . .

The belief that the Jews were in the habit of slaughtering Christians for their blood has at all times prevailed in Eastern Europe, and this trial has shown that it is by no means confined to the ignorant portion of the population, but is equally shared in by persons of a much higher position.

Members of the Hungarian Parliament, Landed Proprietors, Judicial and other officials, and lastly also, unfortunately, the Clergy, have made themselves prominent in this prosecution, which must intensify the religious hatred already existing.[37]

On 3 August 1883, the following judgment was rendered: "The fact that the charge of murder against Salamon Schwarcz and his companions could not be proved precludes the concealment of the act of murder." There was an intrinsic ambiguity to this statement, one that was reflected in the press—"Where is Eszter Solymosi? Who killed Eszter Solymosi?"[38] and the reaction of the public. In front of a Jewish-owned inn in Budapest, where Jozsef Scharf, one of the accused, and his son Moritz, the principal witness, subsequently took up lodgings, a crowd of between four and five thousand gathered, but they were dispersed by the rain and belatedly by the police. The second night even more assembled, and within three-quarters of an hour, they had plundered and sacked the inn and four neighboring shops owned by Jews. On this occasion, the police did not intervene, despite the proximity of the police station.[39] The British Foreign Office interpreted these acts as "evidence of the bitter religious animosity now prevailing throughout Hungary, which is likely to exhibit itself in a similar manner in other places."[40]

Outside Budapest,

newspapers announced the occurrence of a serious Anti-Jewish riot at Zalaegerszeg in Hungary, in which a considerable number of persons are stated to have been killed and wounded both among the military and the mob . . . the Antisemitic party having as usual shown their zeal for the Christian religion by destroying or appropriating as much as they could of the property of the Jews.[41]

We may be led to a less skeptical interpretation of the looting by relying on this comment by MP Dr. Karoly Nedtvich: "Here in Hungary they don't let the people organize themselves to unite and stop the Jewish cheaters and robbers. But the people see that the government doesn't defend them—so of course they started riots and tried to free themselves from these vampires by illegal means."[42] Nedtvich's comment illuminates the link between the charge of ritual murder and the extensive looting of Jewish homes. Literally and figuratively, Jews were seen to be sucking the life-blood of the Hungarian people. It seems that the British Foreign Office concurred with Nedtvich's assessment, as seen in the above (albeit cynical) memorandum and the one below.

> Unfortunately, the great mass of the Hungarian Jews have only too well earned the execration in which they are held by the rest of the population in which they are established in any numbers, so that even those persons, who certainly disapprove of the persecutions of which they are now objects, feel but little sympathy for them.[43]

The decision of government officials to minimize the crimes committed against the Jewish population may be reasonably attributed to the enormity of the task with which they were faced. The cleanup from the 1883 riots went on for a year, involving many cases and thousands of witnesses.[44] However, not only would severe prosecution probably have been objected to, one must presume that the officials who minimized the crimes must have been among the "population" referred to by the British Foreign Office official.

"Did they acquit the accused?" Istoczy asked in Parliament. "This proves nothing concerning their innocence. The only thing to be learned from the acquittal is that once again Jewish money did its job. . . . Everyone is convinced in the depths of his heart that the poor girl from Tiszaeszlar came to a sorry end there in the synagogue of her village."[45] "Sad to say," concluded Ignac Acsady, "but since emancipation, the wall raised by the old hatred, instead of crumbling, recently became even sturdier."[46]

****

The Enlightenment thinkers' emphasis on religious reform had dissipated under the protective halo of liberalism. To quote Prime Minister Tisza: "Let the honest man be embraced by all honest men, and I do not ask where he adores his God."[47] When the subject had come under discussion, it was primarily directed at the Galizianers, the Jewish population having been bifurcated into 'our' Jews and 'those' Jews.[48] In the wake of Tiszaeszlar, the religious distinctiveness of all Jews became an issue once again, ironically through the heretofore ignored subject of ritual murder.[49] Also brought to the fore was the trait of solidarity, and many believed that the Jews, in the name of solidarity, had obfuscated the process of justice and directed the case towards an outcome favorable to the Jewish community.[50]

Prime Minister Tisza, speaking for liberals and liberalism in his post-Tiszaeszlar speech (September 1883), denied the existence of indigenous Jew hatred in Hungary, blaming the incursion of anti-Semitism into Hungary on "enemies": "If the racial and denominational hatred would want to insert itself here, let them just throw it out from their midst like any healthy body would a boil."[51] In making this statement, Tisza denied the perceptions and feelings of a significant segment of Hungarian society and drove a large wedge between them and his Liberal government. Until now, "Many people were restrained by pseudo-liberalism to make its program the solution of the Jewish Question. But now this hypocritical pseudo-liberalism is disappearing."[52] Amongst the "many people" who had restrained themselves until this point, what proportion of them truly believed that Jews had committed the act of ritual murder? It is almost impossible to assess this. One of the few indicators we have is the government's response throughout the Tiszaeszlar period; and the government considered the case a substantial threat to the stability of the country. Prime Minister Tisza spoke of anti-Semitism as "an enormous social danger that can divide the entire society."[53] For those who believed that the Jews were guilty of such a crime, this created more than sufficient grounds for them to demand the remarginalization of the Jews and the revoking of emancipation. Many Hungarians were, of course, assured of the Jews' innocence, but amongst them was a contingency roused to anger by the Jews' resistance to reform. For them, Tiszaeszlar served as a catalyst.

Together with those who believed in the Jews' guilt, these Hungarians intensified their struggle against the invasive Jewish presence in a variety of ways, such as the popularization of *zikzene-zakzene* music[54] and the decision of several prominent aristocrats—Csekonics, Festetics, Esterhazy, and Orczy among them—to cease leasing their lands to Jews.[55] The Hungarian Christian Society Union was formed,[56] and the first anti-Semitic political party, Istoczy's National Anti-Semitic Party, came into being in October 1883.[57] The anti-Jewish newspaper *Paksi-Kozlony* was revived and a new one founded in Pozsony; and the *Riado*, a conversionist newspaper, appeared in Budapest.[58] The tone of the non-liberal press became markedly sharper, and the theme of Jewish domination was central. Acerbic to the point of savagery, articles such as "The Rats of our Society" and "The Mob," and pamphlets like *The Jewish Money's Rule of Terror* proliferated.[59] Jewish domination was revealed in an article that prophesied life in the future. It is 1st December 1983, and the place is Budapest-Jerusalem. The Budapest rabbi is about to be appointed Cardinal of Esztergom. All the magnates, now Jews, are dressing up in velvet and silk caftans with fur. The government is Jewish, the Parliament is Jewish, and the Jewish calendar is observed.[60] Prime Minister Tisza they got back at personally. Of the two candidates for the honored post of chief guardian of the Reformed Church in Transtisza, Tisza was the favored choice, but under the circumstances, they elected the other candidate, and "The Calvinist masses celebrated the election of the new chief guardian with a torchlight procession voicing anti-Semitic slogans."[61]

Most importantly, Tiszaeszlar fundamentally changed the nature of the Jewish Question from one that was framed as a social issue and hence a matter of assimilation to one that was political, reflecting the notion of Jewish domination. Istoczy articulated this clearly: "The Jewish Question is not a social but a political question. The question is whether the Jews or the Hungarians should be rulers."[62] Framing the Jewish Question as a political question made assimilation irrelevant. In two varying historical reconstructions that were forged by Ignac Acsady and Prime Minister Tisza after Tiszaeszlar, the subject of assimilation was conspicuously absent. Both referred to the time before emancipation, Acsady alluding to the "wall raised by the old hatred" and Tisza describing it as tolerant towards the Jews. Acsady reconstructed the process of emancipation, comparing it to an invitation; the Jews had been invited to a "richly laid table." Tisza engaged in a similar reconstruction, saying, "In Hungary, the nation itself and society wiped away the laws of intolerance decades before the legislation." Both also addressed the Jewish Question, but neither made any reference to assimilation.[63]

The entire structure for the emancipation of the Jews had relied on their reform, which would culminate in assimilation and potentially allow Christians and Jews to coexist together. Now, Jews and Christians were perceived as adversaries locked in a struggle for hegemony. While the imperative to assimilate did not disappear, increasingly, complaints of Jewish dominance crowded it out. It is not the intention here to paint a picture of universal animosity towards the Jews. Tiszaeszlar also provided the occasion for editorials such as the one that urged the "preaching [of] harmony among the chaos that is in the life around us." A public letter by a minister of the Reformed Church stated, "I am proud that we don't join this disgusting movement [anti-Semitism] because we are the light of the Enlightenment and progress against the Inquisition. . . . We have to do everything to halt the agitators."[64] But, overall, in spite of government efforts to contain the matter and deny the existence of the Jewish Question, some of the public had drawn the conclusion that the Jewish religion was one which sanctioned the heinous act of murdering Christians for ritual purposes. And many Hungarians had become further agitated about the Jews' failure to reform; that far from assimilating, Jews had embarked on a voracious conquest of Hungary.

NOTES

1. Tiszaeszlar is a small village in northeastern Hungary, which at the time had 2,700 Christian inhabitants and some twenty-five Jewish families. For a detailed summary of the Tiszaeszlar trial, one may refer to Andrew Handler's *Blood Libel at Tiszaeszlar*.
2. *Fuggetlenseg*, 18 June 1882.167.
3. *Fuggetlenseg*, 18 June 1882.167.
4. *Egyetertes*, 6 June 1882.154; *Fuggetlenseg*, 31 May 1882.149, 23 June 1882.172; *Budapest*, 25 June 1882.173. Several *shochets* (ritual slaughters) were in Tiszaeszlar at the time Eszter disappeared. They had come to apply for the position of ritual butcher which had fallen vacant in the Jewish community. Not only the *shochets* but also several Jews of Tiszaeszlar were arrested.
5. *Fuggetlenseg*, 31 May 1882.149.
6. *Fuggetlenseg*, 8 September 1882.248.
7. *Fuggetlenseg*, 22 June 1882.171, 23 June 1882.172. Jozsef Bary, *Vizsgalobrio Emlekiratai-A Tiszaeszlari bunper* [Memoirs of the Magistrate: The Criminal Case of Tiszaeszlar [Budapest: 1993], 16.
8. Orszagos Leveltar [Hungarian National Archives], K149, 6 June 1882. In future references abbreviated as OL. The call number beginning with K represents the documents of the Prime Ministerial Council.
9. Katzburg, *Fejezetek*, 110.
10. Kertzer, *Popes Against the Jews*, 134, 137-38, 142-46.
11. OL, K149. 1882. 1362.
12. *Fuggetlenseg*, 22 June 1882.171, 11 July 1882.190, 16 July 1882.195; *Pesti Naplo*, 17 July 1882.195, 22 August 1882.230. Andrew Handler has noted an event held in Pozsony 8 September 1882 on the eve of the First International Anti-Jewish Congress in which Istoczy, Ivan Simonyi, and Geza Onody were enthusiastically received. *Early Blueprint for Zionism*, 85-86. It is possible that it played a role in these September agitations. Simonyi (publisher of the newspaper *Westungarischer Grenzbote* in Pozsony) and Onody (Independence Party deputy) were closely associated with Istoczy. Kubinszky,

Politikai antiszemitizmus, 61-62, 92. Rioting continued into the late autumn. *Pesti Naplo*, 10 November 1882.310, 10 December 1882.340, 11 December 1882.341.

13. OL, K149. 27 June 1882. 851.
14. OL, K149, 28 June 1882. 26/MT. See *Judische Delikatessen*, Books 21-26, for pamphlets.
15. British F.O. memorandum (30 September 1882), quoted in Katzburg, *Anti-Semitism in Hungary*, 233.
16. *Fuggetlenseg*, 26 June 1882.174, 29 June 1882.177, 30 June 1882.178, 1 July 1882.180, 18 July 1882.197; *Judische Delikatessen*, Book 23, 148-50.
17. OL, K149, 23 July 1882. 1024. Report #5835.
18. Hungarian penal code, quoted in Handler, *Early Blueprint for Zionism*, 94-96. The Tiszaeszlar case also stimulated a variety of personal responses that were published. Imre Tatay, for example, a priest from Szekesfehervar, sought to prove the guilt of the Jews by drawing on a childhood experience. He related that Jews had attempted to kidnap him in order to fulfill their ritual needs and only a miracle had saved him. Lajos Marschalko, *Tiszaeszlar: a magyar fajvedelem hoskora* [Tiszaeszlar: The Heroic Age of Hungarian Race Defense] (Debrecen, 1943), 246, 224, 235-36.
19. Excerpt from the Szatmar Petition, quoted in Handler, *Early Blueprint for Zionism*, 77.
20. Tapolca Petition, quoted in Bary, *Vizsgalobiro emlekiratai*, 434; Katzburg, *Fejezetek*, 127, e.n. 202.
21. Katzburg, *Antisemitism in Hungary*, 160.
22. *Pesti Naplo*, 24 January 1883.23; Kubinszky, *Politikai antiszemitizmus*, 246.
23. *Pesti Naplo*, 23 January 1883.22, 1.
24. *Fuggetlenseg*, 25 January 1883.25, 27 January 1883.27.
25. *Pesti Naplo*, 23 January 1883.22, 1.
26. *Pesti Naplo*, 23 January 1883.22, 1.
27. *Pesti Naplo*, 23 January 1883.22, 1.
28. *Abauj-Kassai Kozlony*, quoted in *Fuggetlenseg*, 27 January 1883.27.
29. *Fuggetlenseg*, 27 January 1883.27, 31 January 1883.31.
30. *Pesti Naplo*, 29 January 1883.28.
31. The declaration of the Hungarian Defense Union may be found in the *Egyetertes*, 22 January 1883, 1.
32. Handler, *Early Blueprint for Zionism*, 86-87.
33. *Fuggetlenseg*, 23 March 1881.81.
34. Speech in Parliament delivered by MP Janos Janossy, quoted in *Pesti Naplo*, 21 January 1883.
35. British F.O. memorandum, quoted in Katzburg, *Anti-Semitism in Hungary*, 243-44. A debate on civil marriage was also held in 1881. At that time, newspaper comments included the following: mixed marriages are only needed for promiscuous people; it heightens the Protestant-Catholic conflict; it is not mixed marriage we want—it is conversion; and, "We do not attack the anti-Christian proposition of Jew-marriage because we hate our Jewish fellow citizens—we do love them as the Savior orders it and we do hope that their expulsion should end quietly and they should unite to us in Christendom." *Magyarorszag*, 20 October 1881.239, 21 October 1881.240, 22 October 1881.241.
36. British F.O. memorandum, quoted in Katzburg, *Anti-Semitism in Hungary*, 243-44.
37. British F.O. memorandum, quoted in Nathaniel Katzburg, "Political Antisemitism in Hungary in the 1880s and the 1890s" (PhD. diss., Hebrew University, 1963), 110-11. In addition to the state prosecution, a private prosecutor representing Eszter's mother appeared at the trial. In his summation, he asked the court to render a just verdict

in this affair. The essence of the case was the "Jewish purse, which has been recruited in support of the slaughterer's knife, [which] is here challenging Christianity and the culture of love of all creation. The slaughterer's knife is here in confrontation with the Cross." Quoted in Marschalko, *Tiszaeszlar*, 206.

38. Handler, *Early Blueprint for Zionism*, 98.
39. British F.O. memorandum, Katzburg, *Anti-Semitism in Hungary*, 240-41. As to the eventual outcome of the Scharf family, in Scharf's own words, "Due to the movements during the summer of 1883, I was forced to leave Hungary. Since, however, under my own name my presence even abroad was dangerous, and likely to have caused upset, your Grace 1883 September 13th under No.28511 issued the attached travel document, under my wife's family name, Jozsef Muller." OL, K149-1886-6. 669.
40. British F.O. memorandum, quoted in Katzburg, *Fejezetek*, 136. Teachers played a leading role in instigating the many riots that occurred after Tiszaeszlar in Budapest and Pozsony and its neighboring counties.
41. British F.O. memorandum, quoted in Katzburg, *Anti-Semitism in Hungary*, 242.
42. *Fuggetlenseg*, 27 September 1883.266.
43. British F.O. memorandum, quoted in Katzburg, *Anti-Semitism in Hungary*, 242.
44. *Fuggetlenseg*, 21 June 1884.170.
45. Gyozo Istoczy, quoted in Hegedus, *A tiszaeszlari vervad*, 193.
46. Ignac Acsady, *Zsido es nemzsido magyarok az emancipacio utan* [Jewish and Non-Jewish Hungarians after the Emancipation] (Budapest: Weiszmann testverek, 1883), 36. Acsady was a noted historian, author, publicist, and member of the Academy of Sciences.
47. Lajos Szabolcsi, *Ket emberolto 1881–1931* [Two Generations 1881–1931] (Budapest: MTA Judaisztikai Csoport, 1993), 38.
48. *Magyarorszag*, 11 September 1880.257; *Egyetertes*, 19 February 1882.50; *Fuggetlenseg*, 2 October 1884.272. MP Denes Pazmandy said that Orthodox synagogues should be closed because they were bad for national progress. *Fuggetlenseg*, 24 September 1883.263.
49. Ritual murder had never been brought up as an issue either by the Enlightenment thinkers or those debating emancipation during the liberal era.
50. *Fuggetlenseg*, 31 May 1882.149, 14 June 1882.163.
51. Prime Minister Kalman Tisza, quoted in Szabolcsi, *Ket emberolto*, 38.
52. *Fuggetlenseg*, 15 August 1884.225.
53. Prime Minister Kalman Tisza, quoted in Szabolcsi, *Ket emberolto*, 38.
54. Commonly called *zik-zak* music, this was a style of music whose lyrics were explicitly anti-Jewish. Posters put up in the morning announcing the publication of *zik-zak* music were quickly taken down, but attempts to ban it were not very effective. *Fuggetlenseg*, 9 October 1883.278, 1 December 1883.331; *Riado*, 14 October 1883.1.
55. *Fuggetlenseg*, 28 January 1884.28, 30 January 1884.30, 10 February 1884.40.
56. The Hungarian Christian Society Union's mandate was to defend the interests of the Christian public. An office was to be set up which would facilitate contacts between honest businessmen and Christian small traders and merchants, and small holders and farmers who were in need of cheap credit. *Fuggetlenseg*, 19 August 1884.229.
57. In March 1883, Istoczy had published a manifesto urging the formation of an anti-Semitic party, which had the support of several members of Parliament. Kubinszky, *Politikai antiszemitizmus*, 156-57.
58. *Judische Delikatessen*, Books 37, 50; *Fuggetlenseg*, 2 October 1883.271; *Riado*, 14 October 1883.
59. *Fuggetlenseg*, 4 December 1883.334, 8 May 1884.127, 10 May 1884.129, 11 May 1884.130, 13 May 1884.132, 26 July 1884.205, 29 September 1884.269. See

Judische Delikatessen, Books 61-63.

60. *Fuggetlenseg*, 1 December 1883.331. The theme of domination was also conveyed in articles such as the "Chronicle of Jewish Sins," written by a priest who had once felt sympathetic towards a Jewish shopkeeper and occasionally helped him out during the 1850s but then discovered that "his shop had become a nest of sin. Openly they [people] began to talk of this homeowner or that one who was in the pocket of the Jew because he was drunk." Eventually their property and fields were seized by the bailiff and given to Jews. *Fuggetlenseg*, 3 August 1884.213.

61. Quoted in Marschalko, *Tiszaeszlar*, 227; Bary, *Vizsgalobiro emlekiratai*, 603.

62. Gyozo Istoczy, quoted in *Pesti Naplo*, 23 January 1883.22. Generally, historians have overlooked or disagreed with this statement of Istoczy's. George Schopflin, for example, dates the politicization of the Jewish Question from 1919. "Jewish Assimilation," 75.

63. Acsady, *Zsido es nemzsido*, 36; Prime Minister Tisza, quoted in Szabolcsi, *Ket emberolto*, 38.

64. *Fuggetlenseg*, 24 September 1883.263.

Chapter 7
The Politics of Assimilation after Tiszaeszlar

The Elections of 1884 and 1887

The 1884 election followed quickly on the heels of Tiszaeszlar, and the electoral passions were high. The prospects for the newly formed National Anti-Semitic Party were promising: the previous year, an anti-Semitic candidate had successfully run in the by-election in Szakcs; in this election, anti-Semitic candidates were nominated in fifty-five ridings;[1] and, helping to underwrite campaign expenses was a donation of 30,000 forints from the Anti-Semitic Congress in Dresden and another in the amount of 10,000 forints sent to Simonyi from Kiev.[2] All this worked in Istoczy's favor, but it was a challenge to the government in power. Therefore, Prime Minister Tisza was exercising prudence when he sent a circular order[3] to all the county chief executives and court officials to prevent any kind of agitation and to preserve the peace during the election campaign. However, its effectiveness—similar to the other threats by the government to curtail incitement against the Jews, "agitating anti-Semitic press products," and outbursts in Parliament—was extremely limited.

The first challenge to Tisza's circular order came only a few days later when, on 29 February 1884, it was reported that a pamphlet called *Zsido Indulo* (Jewish March) was being distributed by printer and bookseller Gyorgy Sogor in large quantities at fairs, amusement parks, and grocery stores.[4] Also published in time for his own election campaign was *Antiszemita Kate* [Anti-Semitic Catechism], which cleric Ignacz Zimandy had co-authored with a former employee in the Ministry of Finance. Articulating first a program for reversing emancipation, establishing Catholicism as a state religion, and removing Jews from public life, the book continued with a question and answer format.

Question 5. Why do Jews hate those who are not Jews?

Answer: Because they mistakenly believe other nations and races are inferior to them; compared to them, they are just animals towards whom it is allowed, indeed mandatory to behave inhumanely.

Question 10. How can such evil people be God's Chosen?

Answer: Long ago, the insatiable thirst for treasures in this race was not so dangerous as later. Its persistent nature, exclusivity, and other excellent attributes were exactly suitable for the purpose God wanted to accomplish.

Question 31. How do Jews get lots of money and wealth?
Answer: They have innumerable ways, which, for the sake of brevity, only the most conspicuous are mentioned here as fountainheads of the others: such as cheating, usury, and fencing.

Last Question: What is it, then, that a Hungarian person must know and believe?
Answer: He must know and believe that in Hungary there is a Jewish question .... the solution to this cannot be delayed any longer ... that he who is with the Jews is not a patriot ... that there is no redemption but in anti-Semitism. Whoever believes will go to heaven, and he who does not, will be condemned.[5]

Zimandy's book was also being distributed at fairs and grocery shops and had been translated into several languages as well, according to Count Istvan Esterhazy, chief executive of Pozsony County. "Does he [the Bishop of Veszprem] know that in the counties of Zala and Somogy, the strongest anti-Semites are the priests?" asked the *Pesti Hirlap* during the election.[6] Some maintained a high profile like Zimandy, several were candidates running under the banner of the Anti-Semitic Party, but many others, like a priest in the ecclesiastical jurisdiction of Vac, simply spoke out: "I can only recommend to Hungarian priests that they urge their fellow citizens to elect anti-Semitic deputies, and no one should care if the anti-Semitic candidate the priest recommends is from the government party or the opposition."* This trend was worrisome to Lajos Pongracz, vice-chief executive (*alispan*) of Hont County.

> Without naming names, I can report to your Excellency that the greatest part of the cantors and teachers of Roman Catholicism took political stands that are completely irreconcilable with their faith and profession and which exploit their ecclesiastical character, but at the same time, neglecting their profession and duties, they interfered with party struggles. The harmful consequences of this will not be long in coming and the harm suffered by the public good is regrettable.[7]

Highlights of the election campaign include the speech of candidate Dr. Geza Racz in Kalocsa: "The industrial law that is about to be introduced will sooner or later take bread out of the mouths of craftspeople, and the beggar's bag will hang on his neck." Racz then cut into his own train of thought and added: "We are not going to say 'Beat the Jew'—God forbid. We don't want that. We want to regulate matters in a tight legal framework."[8] In the village of Tamasi, where the Jewish merchant Mr. Frank objected to speeches by a number of MPs

---

* Quoted in Kubinszky, *Politikai Antiszemitizmus*, 197. Note that the priest also spoke of anti-Semitic candidates within the Liberal Party, further reinforcing my claim that nineteenth-century liberals were not a homogeneous group.

who were criticizing the Jews and calling on the residents to chase them out, he was beaten up by some of the villagers. Once he was removed from the scene, things calmed down and the speeches continued.[9] On another occasion, Odon Gajary, a Jewish candidate for the governing party arrived in Vadkert only to be greeted by an excited mob that had been stirred up by four agitators. The local authorities arrested the leader of the mob, whereupon the mob broke down the gates of the city hall and forced the judge to release him. He then goaded the mob to the point where they grabbed sticks and pitchforks and attacked Gajary and his entourage, driving them to the edge of town. As they stood tending their wounds, Jews arrived with the news that their stores had been broken into and other Jews robbed. The local sheriff of the district, having also been forced to flee with his bodyguard, telegraphed for military help, which did come, and they restored order.[10] The *Fuggetlenseg* summarized "the election battles, the massive violence," as "manifestations of the underlying bitterness; through them the general dissatisfaction comes to the surface. Misery makes its voice heard; the exploited are testing their strength."[11]

Even the prominent liberal Agoston Trefort seemed somewhat pessimistic about the situation.

> And now I want to speak about the Jews. They are one of the most significant world-historical phenomena.
>
> When the modern state was reorganized on the basis of equality, of course we had to give them all the rights Christians had. But the question is whether it was good for the country.
>
> I don't doubt that it is, but a law does not change hundreds of years of relations. The law changes at once, but the human being's drives and habits are slow to change; however, the process of assimilation has been started and it could have progressed swiftly except for anti-Semitism's arrival. . . . Jews should engage in agrarian activities and become handiworkers so that they will not look as if they are competing with the middle class, and common schools and the army are the best antidotes for this.[12]

Trefort could only suggest a healthy dose of 'Dr.' C. W. von Dohm's Enlightenment ideals specific to the Jews to remedy the situation.

When Parliament convened on 27 September 1884, Tisza's opening speech condemned the new National Anti-Semitic Party which had garnered seventeen seats in the election.[13]

> Do you know, gentlemen, what are the fruits of your work? Do you know what is the balance of your anti-Jewish agitation: they are the breaking of windows, persecution of peaceful citizens, robberies, and fights. I have had enough of your speechifying. Henceforth, those who mislead people will be punished and I thank the Jewish MPs for not speaking in the debate, but rather held themselves back.[14]

Unperturbed, one of the newly elected members, Count Gabor Andreanszky, addressed Parliament with the following words: the goal of the Jews is "undermining the foundations of Christian society, the moral and economic destruction of Christian peoples, and [politically] the overthrowing of Christian dynasties and thrones." Therefore, it is not only the task of the King but "apostolic avocation to defend the Christian people against the Jews."[15] And defiant, a bill was presented which stated, "Anti-Semitism merely means Christian peoples adopting a stance of self-defense against Jewish Semitism."[16]

In Tisza's New Year speech for 1885, he warned that he was willing to ask the legislature for stronger measures against those fomenting agitation against the Jews if it were necessary. The *Fuggetlenseg* responded with a warning of its own: if the Jewish Question was "not peacefully solved, the nation will have to burn out these wounds on its moral body with fire and iron."[17] While Tisza did not carry out his threat, he did decide to issue a circular order on the subject of "Scandals and Intimidations against the Free Constitutional Elections."[18] If the circular deterred agitators on the home front, it did not inhibit them from participating as delegates of the Universal Anti-Semitic Congress at the meeting of the Universal Anti-Jewish Alliance held in Bucharest, September 1886. Bylaws were agreed upon, which, once translated into French, were sent out to every country in Europe.[19]

In the event, the 1887 election was a nonviolent one, and opposition to the Jews was confined to print. Considering "the legal solution to the Jewish Question a matter of life and death,"[20] the press was active throughout the election campaign.

> If we slap a Jew on the face for his arrogance, Jewry takes that as the dishonoring of all Jews, and they consider the slapped a martyr of the Jews. To such distorted thinking, we can only answer, as our forefathers did, declare the newcomers as a foreign race that is allowed to stay in the homeland but cannot share in the nation's liberty and rights because he is not of this nation, and not even Christian. As determined as the Jew insists on the undisciplined rags of Jewishness, just as fast we insist on the glorious banner of Christianity [that] we can thank for our one thousand-year past.[21]

Jakab Engel, a resident of Nagy Kosztolany, brought the "Declaration of the Moderate Oppositional Anti-Semitic Party" to the attention of the authorities. Circulating among the Slovak-speaking population of the Highlands, its preamble noted that this was a new party which was a fusion of two other anti-Semitic parties (unnamed) that had now united in order to be more effective. The Declaration was an appeal to unite all those who opposed the government because they not only gave the Jews a free hand, but promoted them by creating laws that favored them, such as a reduced tax burden because Jews did not pay their share, and causing the national debt by letting them appropriate the national wealth. They further allowed Christians' lands to fall into Jewish hands; and in addition, permitted the Jews to obtain monopoly in education, various offices, and the professions.*

---

* Jakab Engel would be dissatisfied with the legal opinion offered. Wanting this Declaration to be prosecuted under the legislation forbidding incitement to hatred, the government ruled in favor of the liberal value of freedom of thought. OL, K149 1887-6-106; OL, K149 1887-6.313. April 19, 1887.

****

'Muted' describes the mood in Hungary in the years following the election. The battle against the Jews continued to be waged in print, but Tisza had successfully wrestled to the ground those who would agitate overtly against the Jews. Instead of agitations, a number of Hungarians practiced a policy of social exclusion. While Magyars on holiday gathered at Balatonfured on Lake Balaton, Jews stayed at Siofok. Christian Hungarians frequented the Pannonia Café while the New York Café drew a Jewish clientele. While hardly a social affair, the practice of dueling was deeply ingrained in the fabric of Hungarian society, and at times, Christians refused to enter into duels with Jews.[22] Similarly, Hungary's ruling class did not fraternize with the Jewish elite. Any suggestion that Christian Hungary had become reconciled to the Jews should be laid to rest by such events as the ball sponsored by the city of Kecskemet in 1887, to which only Christians were invited and which had the added feature of using the invitations to express their sentiments about the Jews. On the reverse side of each invitation was a song named after an MP from the Anti-Semitic Party.

Istoczy Csardas

Ergenberger, Schoszberger/ All the Jews are bad in there/ Be he a peddler, or most anything/ He lives after, lives after just cheating . . .

Zimandy Csardas

The national banner is out in the open/ On to its handle a wreath is taken. Come on comrade, swear to it you might/ You be the homeland's Anti-Semite.

Onody Csardas

Sad place is that Tiszaeszlar/ Solymosi girl killed by the Jew Shakter [butcher]/ Took off his coat, the old rascal there/ Thus he killed Mrs. Solymosi's daughter.

The Anti-Semitic Csardas

The thousand bank note, a nice piece of paper/ Red Viennese rags on the Jewish daughter/ Zikmusic zakmusic, so the Jew is humming/ Tatale, mamale, yellow knickers bulging . . .[23]

'Just Like Us'

The Recepcio

Fifteen years after the initial discussions, civil marriage was accepted into law in 1895. It was part of a package which also included the acceptance of Judaism as one of the 'received religions'[24] and the endorsement of the free practice of religion. Taken together, these changes in civil society were called the *Recepcio*. Before its passage, the civil marriage clause provoked acrimonious debate. The Catholic Church wrote a Memorandum to the government asking for clarification of the impending *Recepcio*, but it was equally an opportunity to express its objections.

> If it meant legal protection for the free exercise of religion within their own circle, we have no remark against this, since the 1867 XVII Article already declared Israelite citizens of the country to be equal with Christians in the exercise of civic and political rights.
> But if the high government in this proposition wishes to declare the Israelite religion as a legally accepted religion, so that between the Christian and Jew religion we shall have reciprocity, as presently exists between the accepted religions . . . that would mean something completely different than the emancipation of the Jews with other citizens of the country. . . .
> The difference between the Jewish and Christian religion is so great and deep that it is impossible to construct a legislation that could speak about conversion from Judaism to Christianity and vice versa. The Christian religion is not restricted to one nation, but is followed by all the peoples of the whole world due to its universal nature. . . . But to convert to the Jewish religion, the conversion in its substance would only be possible if the person, divesting himself of his nationality, would meld into the Jewish nation, because in Jewry, religion and nationality are indivisibly connected; the Jewish religion is a national religion. Therefore, while a Hungarian man can be Catholic or Protestant without losing his nationality, he cannot be a follower of Mosaism without sacrificing his nationality.25

Through the Church's understanding of Judaism, the Jewish religion was a national religion, and the Jews were a separate nation. Hungarian Christians therefore could not become Jews without sacrificing their national identity. This was why the *Recepcio* should not be passed. Emphasizing Jewry's designation as a nationality, the Church moved the Jewish Question further along the path of politicization and away from its social dimension—assimilation.

The tone and content of the statements directed at the laity were reflected in a "Shepherd's Epistle" read by priests to their congregations, warning them of the danger threatening the Catholic religion should the proposed reforms pass into law.26 The Catholic popular press forwarded the *Recepcio* as a Jewish plot: "The unadmitted goal of Jewish Reception [is] to make Christian Hungarians into members of the Jewish nation; this is how the Jews want to increase their numbers."27 Jews could not be good citizens because they were thought to be after world power, fomenting corruption and destruction everywhere, and wherever they were emancipated, "They attain power with the help of the Golden Calf."28

The *Recepcio* was also assessed from the viewpoints of science and morality. Based on the results of a scientific examination of current Judaism, Viktor Kereszty concluded in his article "The Jew Reception from a Scientific-Theological Point of View" that the idea of Reception was not a favorable one.29 In an examination of "The Jewish Reception from a Moral Point of View," cleric Ottokar Prohaszka condemned Jewry, whose "business morals in the business world lowers the level of morality." He went on to write that their lack of moral self-respect is evident every time a Jew commits some flagrant crime. . . . The press, high finance, science, the *Alliance Israelite*, all these honest noble factors are practically hyperventilating at the effort to put a stop to justice and law; and they make the threatening blow into a Tiszaeszlarian justice with the help of a good independence party and national flag-waving lawyers.[30]

Bishop Ottokar Prohaszka's name appears here for the first time. An eminent figure in late nineteenth- and early twentieth-century Hungary,* Prohaszka is considered an archetypal anti-Semite: bigoted and maliciously hateful, a man who was blinded by an irrational hatred that conjured up a completely distorted image of the Jew. Admittedly, he possessed certain other attributes, but not the quality of objectivity. It is difficult to accuse a person of Prohaszka's stature of being narrow-minded, illogical, and irrational only when it comes to the Jews, while in every other respect considering him an outstanding member of society. Therefore, an explanation must be sought that does not malign his overall integrity. What becomes apparent through an examination of his works is that the reference point for Prohaszka (and others) lay in the Enlightenment ideals specific to the Jews. One after the other, we see that the complaints compiled against the Jews after emancipation correspond to the demands once placed upon them by the Enlightenment thinkers. Now no longer theoretical, the injunction that Jews should "become just like us," should "become one with us in body and soul," was meant to be implemented. In a myriad of ways, individuals such as Prohaszka thought that Jews were failing to live up to this demand, provoking outbursts aimed against them. These outbursts came from all strata of society.

While the *Recepcio* passed with ease in the Lower House, it required the

---

* Bishop Ottokar Prohaszka obtained two doctorates, one in theology and one in philosophy, following which he spent seven years at the Collegium Germanico-Hungaricum. A passionate Christian Socialist, he was one of the founders of the Catholic Peoples' Party in 1894. From 1904, he was professor of Dogmatica at the Budapest University and in 1905, he became a bishop. His journalistic activities included editing *Magyar Sion* and the *Esztergom,* and later, he was a staff member at the weekly *A Cel.* He became a corresponding member of the Academy of Sciences in 1909 and a regular member after 1920. From 1920-22, he was a member of the Cabinet and leader of the Christian National Unity Party. Regarded by many as the outstanding figure and symbol of the Hungarian cultural and intellectual renaissance that took place in the late nineteenth and early twentieth centuries, Prohaszka was a determined advocate of religious modernism in Hungary, which was aimed at secular urban intellectuals, on the one hand, and designed to raise the intellectual sophistication of the faith of the peasants, on the other. His affect on Hungarian intellectuals was considerable: many converted from Protestantism to Catholicism, and others returned to the Church. The centerpiece of this modernism was perhaps his treatment of modern science and the theory of evolution, in particular. As a result, three of his books were put on the *Index Librorum Prohibitorum* in 1911. His collected works are contained in twenty-five volumes. Karoly Meizler, ed., *Prohaszka, a napbaoltozott forradalmar* [The Revolutionary Dressed in the Sun] (Buenos Aires: Editorial Pannonia, 1964), 1:125, 182, 388.

decisive vote of the Speaker of the Upper House to gain final approval in November 1895. Before the ink had time to dry, the *Alkotmany* was demanding its revision: "The civilization of society rests on Christian marriage.... All this, the Hungarian State denied us. The pagans threaten the Hungarian race with death. The laws that ruin Christianity force us under the lordship of aliens."[31] Jewish politician Vilmos Vazsonyi issued a rebuttal to this article in the *Pesti Hirlap*, pinpointing the great problem that legal measures such as the *Recepcio* could not overcome: "It would have been in vain to create liberal reforms if the spirit of society will not follow them."[32]

The Era of the Millennium

"The decade of the millennium and the *Recepcio*," wrote Lajos Szabolcsi, "were the years of sweet drunkenness, the shining era of assimilation."[33] 1896, the year of Hungary's millennium, was one of those 'Golden Years of Hungarian Jewry.' Vazsonyi's comment notwithstanding, the *Recepcio* had passed; perhaps the uproar around its passing was but a flash in the pan, having been preceded by ten years of relative calm. Wishing to join in the millennial celebrations, the Magyar Israelite Literary Society

> could not remain silent in this memorable year.... After all, its name is adorned by two words, Israelite and Magyar, which have been fused in our consciousness. We know that in our nation the former is as old as the latter, that of all the religions in our nation ours is the oldest. Thus, it is the only one that could celebrate with the Magyar nation the 1000th anniversary of its existence.[34]

An example of patriotism gone awry, the society's president not only privileged "Israelite" over "Magyar" in his speech but also disqualified the Christian religion as a celebrant in the momentous festivities—this, only a year after the bitter debate over the *Recepcio*.

Carnival season, the prelude to Lent, was a popular time in Hungary and was ushered in annually in January; the year 1896 was no exception. In this particular year, an article appeared in the local newspaper in Arad announcing that the Israelite Women's Association would start the carnival season with their ball to be held at the *Feher Kereszt Kavehaz* [White Cross Coffeehouse] on the 11th of January.[35] In considering this pre-Lenten event, the name of the venue only adds emphasis to a faultily constructed syllogism: 'Everyone goes to a pre-Lenten ball in Hungarian society. I (the Jew) am part of society. Therefore, I, too, will go to a ball.' Missing in this syllogism is that crucial piece of information that Hungarian society was a Christian society, a fact that Lajos Hatvany, a prominent publisher and 'man of letters,' and baptized Jew, was keenly aware of. He, too, wrote about Jews attending balls, twenty-five years after this announcement appeared. "My dear Jews," he wrote, "you must put on frock coats if you want to go to the ball." (In the context of Hatvany's comments, "frock coats" stood for conversion.)[36] In sponsoring this ball which was, after all, only the social aspect of a profoundly religious period, Christian society might easily have understood that in religious matters, these Jewish women's apprehension of the dictum that the Jews should 'become just like us' extended as far as, but no further than participating in the customs that appertained to the Christian religion. Perhaps this is the reason that these Jewish women could not have approached their female Christian neighbors to co-sponsor a ball . . . or, perhaps these women were practicing social exclusivism . . . or, did they feel that the idea of a shared event would not have been well-received?

There were numerous examples of Jews performing their pre-emancipated roles—as 'silent partners' or paying for the privilege of doing business, or a combination of the two. According to a deposition to the House of Representatives submitted in 1896,[37] fifty-five parliamentary members of the Liberal Party held seventy-seven positions with railroads and transportation companies, while another eighty-six held positions with banks and various industries. The railroads, transportation companies, banks, and various industries in question were all heavily under Jewish ownership.[38] The *Budapesti Hirlap* reported further that thirty-five members of the Liberal Party were paid two million crowns annually for services rendered and that some of the political elite additionally collected pecuniary rewards as legal advisors, lobbyists, and board members of these enterprises.[39]

The *Alkotmany* took note of the following event that occurred on New Year's Day of 1896 in Gyor.

> Amongst sales clerks, profit comes before honor. This is what we must conclude based on what happened between Christian and Jewish sales clerks in Gyor on New Year's Day. The salesmen had agreed, on their word of honor, to keep their stores closed on New Year's Day. Great though, was the surprise of the Christian salesmen when they noticed that all the Jewish stores are busy, making sales. The fooled traders of course could do no more than wish their Jewish colleagues back to Egypt, who once again kept in mind the instruction of the Talmud, that the word of honor given to a Christian is not binding.[40]

1896 was also the year the *Alkotmany* noted that the president of the Jewish community had spoken to MP Gyula Rosenberg about the need for the Jewish community to have autonomy, but Rosenberg had responded that it was not an auspicious moment to advance such a petition because there were "denominational incitements" everywhere in the country.[41] And, "In spite of Liberals declaiming against anti-Semitism," reported the *Alkotmany*, "it's getting stronger at the university, as seen by the new student presidential elections."[42]

1896 was also an election year. And a new party, the *Katolikus Neppart* [Catholic People's Party], commonly known as the Neppart, was participating in elections for the first time. Not only did it step into the breach left by the National Anti-Semitic Party's demise,[43] its formation should not be disconnected from the passing of the *Recepcio* only a year earlier. Controversy dominated its formation in 1895; one faction had wanted to create a distinctly Catholic anti-Semitic party while another group had maintained that a single-issue party could not succeed. The outcome was a party that considered Jewish issues, but was foremost staunchly Christian nationalist.[44]

An important part of the Neppart's activities revolved around the founding of consumers unions (companies for purchasing and marketing) and credit companies. These consumers unions were a component part of the Christian Socialist movement which the Vatican had launched to save nations from revolutionary socialism—and specifically to defeat Marxist trade unions. Quasi-political in nature, in Hungary, they were more concerned with issues revolving around the Jews, and primarily their economic hegemony. Organized under clerical patronage, with Prohaszka in the vanguard and the high clergy assuming spiritual leadership over them,[45] by 1904, some two hundred such companies had been established. In concert with the tactic of boycotting Jewish shopkeepers, these measures had the express purpose of protecting modest farmers from the Jews who employed such tactics as charging exorbitant interest and acting deceitfully in matters of trade, as a Parliamentary member of Neppart stated.[46]

> The Jewish cancer has eaten at the Christian Hungarian nation until it has worn it down and presented it as a naked skeleton. It has turned most of the Hungarian people into beggars. . . . it lowers the moral level and transforms corruption into an accepted way of life. No one has ever stolen and robbed as much as the modern liberal Jewish economic regime.
>
> Their religious outlook requires them to amass property, and to accomplish their goal they have to resort to all kinds of tricks, cunning, and misrepresentation—limitless and shameless. No one can aid Hungary; nothing can save her, other than a popular uprising against oppressive usury. Consumer societies are the concrete expression of such an uprising.[47]

From a historical distance, one could conclude that the Church stepped in to act on behalf of its flock, whose voice was not being heard by the government.

In 1896, Jews were not measuring assimilation in terms of social, religious, and occupational reform, but in terms of professional successes and participation in the cultural life of the nation. Jewish writer Jozsef Patai later described it as an "assimilatory rage [which] increased to the point of being nauseating."

> 'How much did we, Magyars of the Israelite faith, do for the nation. . . . The first national poet, the first linguist, the first factory owner, etc., etc., were all Jews.' This constant self-praise and big talk not only did not heal, it created resentment. For the 'second' national poet, the 'second' linguist, and the 'second' factory owner were not at all happy about the national treasure contained in Jewry; they rather thought, 'If that Jew were not here, I would be the first.'[48]

1896 was also the year Emil Reich, a Hungarian now living in England wrote into the eminently respectable journal, *The Nineteenth Century*. Due to the fact that the Jew had been a stranger for the last one and a half millennia,

> . . . he has the energy, aggressiveness, shrewdness, and frequently the recklessness of the stranger, but with threefold intensity. Being constantly on the alert either against danger or for rapid advance in fortune, he must needs be sober and temperate, and particularly keen in judging men and events. Being severed from broader interests of large aggregates of men, such as town, county, or nation, his emotions feed chiefly on family sentiments, and he becomes the most feeling of fathers as he is the most devoted of sons. . . . And finally,

whenever he is received into society, he is practically an upstart, a *parvenu*; and hence he manifests all the objectionable qualities of that class of strangers. Upstarts, whether individuals or nations ... are ostentatious, self-centred, vain, and boastful. These qualities are inevitable in upstarts. It is equally inevitable that good society resents these qualities very keenly. Good society ... *le monde*, as the French rightly say ... is in reality a state of its own; the laws, officers, and procedure of which are even more finely developed than in states proper.... No man can conform to them unless he has been in the habit of so doing from childhood on....

... In countries like Hungary, for instance, where the liberal professions were, up to 1867, exclusively in the hands of the nobility, the sudden influx of Jewish lawyers, teachers, judges, and writers could not but be most injurious to the interests of the hitherto privileged class. For a nobleman to be obliged to treat as his peer the son of the Jew whom his father kept as 'village-Jew' was a most tantalizing proposition. What made it absolutely unbearable was the lack of all social tact on the part of the *novi homines*. In the ball-room, in the 'casino,' or club of the town, in the street, the newly-emancipated Jew displayed a familiarity and forwardness with the men and women of the old Hungarian society, that, as it was in the worst taste, so it was bitterly resented.... And here is the heavy and unanswerable indictment against the emancipated and reformed Jew; he is profoundly immodest. The old Orthodox Jew is perverse and uncouth, if you please, but he is a character.... There is a grandeur in his stintedness, and fascination in his self-inflicted isolation.... But the reformed Jew [the 'modern or New Jew'], he who abandons the ritual of his father without adopting the creed of the Christians ... he is downright absurd and worthy of the lash of society.[49]

****

Not long after its millennium, Hungary entered a period of national crisis which led to a complete government breakdown by 1905. With the spirit of nationalism growing among both the Magyars and the ethnic minorities, the government set itself in opposition to Vienna while suppressing this same desire among its minorities. Independence from Austria and control over the independence-minded minorities were issues that consumed Hungary from the mid-1890s until the outbreak of the First World War. Being sensitive to this age-old struggle of Hungarians to liberate themselves from all control by Austria—a struggle which cannot be framed in relation to the Jews—helps to understand the lull in anti-Jewish activity between 1895 and, let us say, 1913. Simultaneously, the country was confronted by a number of other crises. There were lasting affects from the passage of the *Recepcio*; conflict between the landowning ruling classes (who united to put forward an agrarian program meant to fundamentally undermine liberal economic policy) and 'mercantilists'; the emergence of Peasants Parties; bourgeois radicalism; the Socialist Workers' movement and its politicization; ever-increasing labor unrest among both agrarian and industrial workers; and the breakdown of Parliament itself.[50]

Even so, by 1909, Szabolcsi noted that "unfriendly winds were blowing."[51] The formation of a coalition government partly accounts for Szabolcsi's impression, as the views of the opposition now became incorporated into the government's stance. Bela Barkoczy, Undersecretary of State, publicly stated that the Jewish religion was a doctrinal distortion.[52] Pressure was exerted upon Jewish teachers to convert, and students at the Budapest University continued to take exception to the Jewishness of their colleagues: contrary to a university ruling, they affixed crosses in every classroom (for which they were subsequently punished).[53] During Bela Makay's tenure as head of the Jewish section of the Ministry of Culture, he used all kinds of bureaucratic devices to handicap the Jewish community until he was finally removed.[54] MP Antal Mocsy referred to "that pagan, or at least neutral liberalism toward faith," and specifically the Jewish-oriented press, which not only spawned socialism but paradoxically resulted in "free usury, free industry, which are all in the service of moving capital that exploits and sucks dry the poor uneducated people."[55]

"So far from blaming the Jews for the dominant position which they have secured in Hungary," wrote Robert Seton-Watson from abroad in 1908, "I merely wish to draw attention to the very large grain of truth which underlies the odious nicknames 'Judaeo-Magyar' and 'Judapest' invented by Dr. Lueger, the mayor of Vienna."[56] "It is not the Magyars who are assimilating the Jews," remarked Romanian politician Alexandru Marghiloman, "it is the Jews who are assimilating the Magyars. *C'est un état israélite.*"[57]

NOTES

1. Kubinszky, *Politikai Antiszemitizmus*, 205-8.
2. *Fuggetlenseg,* 28 May 1884.
3. Months before the circular order came into effect, Tisza had publicly announced that he was contemplating such a measure to bring about a cease to "racial and denominational hatred." At that time, the *Fuggetlenseg* had had this to say: "The Prime Minister and the Public Prosecutor want to make a law against instigators, but it is the people themselves who are led by their instinct to anti-Semitism, because the people are losing their fields and their jobs and they have to emigrate. And who is the cause of this destruction? It is the Jews. Because the Jews sell alcohol and issue usury and destroy morals by their Talmudic morality." 29 September 1883.268, 26 September 1883.205.
4. Another popular pamphlet was the *Cry to the Christian Citizens of Hungary for the Education of Hungarian Christian People.* Published by Imre Nagy, the editor of a Kecskemet weekly devoted to articles concerning the Jews, the pamphlet advocated overturning emancipation. Kubinszky, *Politikai Antiszemitizmus*, 182.
5. Ignacz Zimandy, ed., "Antiszemita Kate," [Anti-Semitic Catechism] in *Ebreszto hangok: a muveltebb kath. korok szamara* [Awakening Voices: For the more Educated Catholic Circles] (Budapest, 1884), 4, 6, 12, 52. This was an ongoing series of essay collections concerning issues relevant to Catholics, many of which were about the Jews. Zimandy was editor of a Catholic journal and a member of the clergy and he was successful in his bid for election as an MP representing the National Anti-Semitic Party.
6. *Pesti Hirlap*, 3 June 1884.
7. The impetus for Pongracz's report was a complaint laid by the villagers of Kemence against Roman Catholic cantorial teacher Janos Stiblo who was exerting pressure on voters. *Az Orszagos Leveltarbol a Belugyminiszterium Altalanos, Elnoksegi es Rezervalt anyaga, valamint az Igazsagugy-miniszterium anyaga 1880-1884 kozott* [From the National Archives Ministry of the Interior General Presidential Reserve Materials as well as the Materials of the Ministry of Justice 1880-1884] 1587: 2 April 1884.

8. *Fuggetlenseg*, 28 May 1884.147.
9. Kubinszky, *Politikai antiszemitizmus*, 199-200.
10. Kubinszky, *Politikai antiszemitizmus*, 200-201.
11. *Fuggetlenseg*, 13 June 1884.162.
12. Agoston Trefort, quoted in *Nemzet*, 23 June 1884.172.
13. Kubinszky, *Politikai antiszemitizmus*, 212.
14. Szabolcsi, *Ket emberolto*, 45.
15. Appeal to the throne speech, quoted in Kubinszky, *Politikai antiszemitizmus*, 214.
16. Quoted in Katzburg, *Antisemitism in Hungary*, 19.
17. *Fuggetlenseg*, 1 January 1885.001.
18. Kubinszky, *Politikai antiszemitizmus*, 184, 200.
19. *Fuggetlenseg*, 11 July 1887.187. Presumably, the belated date noting the meeting is due to the fact that a translation was not available until the summer of 1887.
20. *Fuggetlenseg*, 28 June 1887.175.
21. *Fuggetlenseg*, 27 April 1887.114.
22. Patai, *Jews of Hungary*, 365.
23. *Fuggetlenseg*, 28 January 1887.27.
24. One of the public implications of not being a recognized religion is illustrated in the experience of the Jews of Arad. Wishing to pay their respects to the King at a reception, they fell in line after the fire brigade. Szabolcsi, *Ket Emberolto*, 43.
25. Quoted in Katzburg, *Fejezetek*, 110.
26. Nathaniel Katzburg, "The Struggle of Hungarian Jewry for Equal Rights in the Nineties of the Nineteenth Century," [in Hebrew] *Zion: A Quarterly for the Study of Jewish History* 22 (1957): 119-21.
27. Quoted in Tamas Dersi, *A szazadveg katholikus sajtoja* [The Catholic Press at the turn of the Century] (Budapest: Akademiai Kiado, 1973), 139; *Magyar Allam*, 27 March 1895, 1.
28. *Magyar Allam*, 20 January 1895, 5.
29. Viktor Kereszty, "*A zsdidorecepcio a tudomany szempontjabol*," [The Jew Reception from a Scientific Viewpoint] *Magyar Sion* 7 (1893): 164. Kereszty was editor of this Catholic journal at the time.
30. Bishop Ottokar Prohaszka [Dr. Petho, pseud.], "*A zsido recepcio a moralis szempontbol*," [The Jew Reception from a Moral Viewpoint] *Magyar Sion* (1893): 415.
31. *Alkotmany*, 24 December 1895: 2.
32. Vilmos Vazsonyi, *Vazsonyi Vilmos beszedei es irasai* [The Speeches and Writings of Vilmos Vazsonyi] (Budapest: Az Orszagos Vazsonyi-Emlekbizottsag Kiadasa, 1927), 62.
33. Szabolcsi, *Ket emberolto*, 103. Lajos Szabolcsi took over the *Egyenloseg*, a Jewish weekly, after his father died in 1915. The influence of this newspaper went far beyond its circulation, which was never more than 4,000 copies. Highly respected, in close contact with government circles, Szabolcsi was a relentless crusader against what he perceived as injustices against the Jewish people.
34. Excerpt from the speech by the society's president Dr. Samuel Kohn, quoted in Handler, *Blood Libel*, 8.
35. *Alfold*, 3 January 1896.
36. "A zsidokerdes Magyarorszagon," [The Jewish Question in Hungary] *Huszadik Szazad* 2 (1917).
37. Peter Hanak, "The Dual Monarchy (1867-1918)," in *A History of Hungary*, ed. Ervin Pamlenyi (Budapest: Corvina, 1973), 361-62.
38. Kepviselohazi naplo [Minutes of the House of Representatives]. 1896, XXI, 305.

39. *Budapesti Hirlap*, 25 November 1900.
40. *Alkotmany*, 8 January 1896.
41. *Alkotmany*, 7 January 1896.
42. *Alkotmany*, 10 January 1896.
43. There are no facts with which to construct an argument that the Anti-Semitic Party's demise was due to a lack of receptivity of the party's aims. What is known is that following their participation in the 1884 election, there was sharp dissension among the party members, one faction being committed to independence from Austria and the other satisfied with Hungary's role in the Dual Monarchy. This was followed by a disagreement about starting a daily newspaper, to which Istoczy was opposed. Those in favor of it went ahead, but it quickly foundered, at which time relations between party members worsened. In August 1885, a fissure in the party caused it to split into two, with Istoczy leading one of the factions. Furthermore, the lack of professionalism among his MPs distressed Istoczy, which in his view adversely affected the possibility of bringing about changes. He became increasingly withdrawn. By the 1890s, the party was no longer viable. Kubinszky, *Politikai Antiszemitizmus*, 219; Katzburg, *Fejezetek*, 138.
44. *Uj magyar lexicon* [New Hungarian Encyclopedia] (Budapest: 1961) 4:102.
45. *Uj magyar lexicon*, 4:102.
46. Parliamentary member of the Neppart party, Katzburg, *Antisemitism in Hungary*, 191-92.
47. Bishop Ottokar Prohaszka, quoted in Bosnyak, *Prohaszka*, 7-9.
48. Jozsef Patai, quoted in Patai, *Jews of Hungary*, 453-55.
49. Emil Reich, "The Jew-Baiting on the Continent," *Nineteenth Century* 40 (1896): 431-34. Reich (1854-1910), a Hungarian, first studied law and then became a historian and essayist. Spending years in the United States and France, he finally settled in England. There, he frequently lectured at Cambridge, London, and Oxford universities about the philosophy of history, ethics, and social questions.
50. Hanak, "Dual Monarchy," 373-404.
51. Szabolcsi, *Ket emberolto*, 113.
52. Katzburg, *Fejezetek*, 144-45.
53. Kovacs, *Liberal Professions*, 21-22.
54. Szabolcsi, *Ket emberolto*, 113, 115-127.
55. Katzburg, *Fejezetek*, 144-45.
56. Robert W. Seton-Watson, *Racial Problems in Hungary* (London: Archibald Constable & Co Ltd, 1908), 252-53. Seton-Watson was a well-known British historian who specialized in Hungarian and Romanian history and frequently acted as a consultant to the British government.
57. Alexandru Marghiloman, quoted in Hugh Seton-Watson and Christopher Seton-Watson, *The Making of a New Europe: R. W. Seton-Watson and the Last Years of Austria-Hungary* (Seattle: University of Washington Press, 1981), 2-3.

Chapter 8
Issues of Assimilation

Loyalty

From the time of the Enlightenment, Jews were given to copious and often dramatic efforts to proclaim their loyalty in order to dispel the legacy of alienage. They continued to do so after emancipation. In one such gesture, Jozsef Kuhn, a wholesaler in Miskolc, requested permission to name the synagogue he had built after Franz Jozsef, in order to commemorate the King's visit there. In Budapest, a special decoration of lights was mounted on the Dohany Street Synagogue, with the Hebrew inscription "*Yichje hamelech*" (long live the King); and money was collected for the erection of a statue of St. Stephen (who had introduced Christianity to Hungary).[1] These efforts were often mocked.

> ... [Rabbi Jakab Elfer of Heves] who gives newer and newer signs of his patriotism, every opportunity he can find. Recently, on the occasion of the Easter celebrations, he gave a Hungarian oration which, as our correspondent attests, was dripping with patriotic feelings. He emphasized that every Jew of good will must reconcile his religion with their patriotism, and he recalled the words of Lajos Kossuth, the embodiment of liberty, fraternity, and equality, that Jews must be faithful to their religion and their homeland, their Hungarian homeland, equally. At the mention of Lajos Kossuth's name, the synagogue was filled with enthusiastic cheering. But first of all, cheers went up for the good Hungarian Jewish rabbi.[2]

Beneath the mocking tones was an implicit criticism of Jewish loyalty, which went far beyond the way Jews were displaying their loyalty to the question of Jewish loyalty itself. Fear was expressed that in case of war, Jews would unite with Hungary's enemies or choose sides according to which offered them material gain.[3] Military service was also scrutinized under the lens of patriotism and its alleged evasion (which one newspaper contributor attributed to the Talmud, adding that it should be banished or "researched"[4]) aroused considerable wrath. Conscription lists were falsified; recently, this had occurred in Zemplen County and in Tolna.[5] Another strategy was to be judged incapable of army service due to physical handicaps. This was the approach used by three sons of wealthy parents in Tokaj. In fact, it seemed that these youths had not even shown up at the conscription office, the implication being that it had collaborated in the exemption. An inquiry was underway by the appropriate Ministry.[6] According to one newspaper article, birth registrations had often been made in German and

Hebrew rather than Hungarian as a way to 'hide' the birth of a son and so avoid his eventual conscription. As a result, only one-third of male births had been recorded, and with no proof of age, young Jewish males were able to exempt themselves from military duty.[7] The government tried to put a stop to this practice by passing a regulation to reform the *matricula* (birth, marriage, and death records) kept by Jews.

While no war was on the horizon in 1887, the *Fuggetlenseg* reflected on the Jews' likely response, should one come to pass.

> Spring is the time for wars. The sons of all languages and religions will be represented in the necessary statistical proportions in the ranks. They will defend the homeland that bore and sustained them. They will die if they must for every inch of the land. And where will the Jews be? Hiding in the corner. They don't consider valor a virtue. They can only suck the homeland, but die for it they can't.[8]

Even those Jewish youths who served in the army were seen to be of diminished stature: "*Oi vey*. He's a real hero. He doesn't dare to look in the direction of his weapon."[9]

When Jews described themselves as nationalists, they really meant Jewish nationalism, wrote Geza Petrassevich; therefore, they could never be described as patriotic.[10] (This was distinct from Zionism which was not well received by Jews in Hungary, and so it was not a substantial issue. However, the *Alkotmany* targeted the Jewish journal *Mult es Jovo* in 1913 for its overt preaching of Zionism, and more subtly, by its appealing presentation of Jewish literature and art which was promoting Jewish awareness and national feeling.[11]) The age-old identification of Jews as a nation was further reinforced by the newly displayed Jewish traits of solidarity, social cohesiveness, and social exclusivism. In any discussion then, which coupled Jews and nationhood, there was a distinct possibility that the loyalty of the Jews would be questioned.

The Jews' tendency to vote *en bloc* can also be understood in terms of loyalty. Around 1900, with the Jewish population of Budapest hovering around twenty-five per cent, fully half of those who qualified for the vote in the city were Jewish and they consistently elected Liberal deputies, contrary to the trends in other districts.[12] The most obvious conclusion is that they voted for the Liberal Party because it staunchly defended Hungarian Jewry, and if so, such a pattern belies assimilation: as Gyurgyak has made clear, assimilation means indifference to one's origins. But two other conclusions may be drawn from this voting pattern. One is that the Jews, having identified themselves as a distinct group, in the name of group solidarity, acted to further communal interests by voting *en bloc*; Jews were therefore loyal only to themselves. The other is that it was the manifestation of a cozy club where the Jews supported the Liberals and vice versa, displaying loyalty of a subversive nature.

The generous bestowal of nobility upon many Jews from the end of the nineteenth century poses a different problem. In contradistinction to the above-mentioned examples, ennoblement presumes an illustriousness and loyalty of at least some Jews. However, far too many of these ennoblements were only ostensibly an acknowledgment of accomplishment and high standing. More than anything, they reflected the Jew in his old role of being of economic utility to the ruling power, where loyalty had a very narrow range, extending only to those upon whom one depended for subsistence. As part of this process, there was a long tradition of rewarding the Jew for exceptional efforts, although during this period, the Jewishness of these new noblemen was rather gray: almost all of them converted, many before their title was bestowed. For the purposes of statistics, these noblemen were no longer Jews, but the public admission by one of the organs of the Jewish community that conversion was now being practiced for reasons of advancement only (below), coupled with the conviction among much of the Hungarian population that baptism did not remove Jewishness from the Jew, means that we can still speak of these men as Jews.

William McCagg postulates that the government had issued a 'standing invitation' to Budapest businessmen—most of whom were Jewish, whose wealth was on a par with the aristocracy, and whose exercise of economic power was enormous—to collaborate, in exchange for nobility. As of 1903, when the political crisis intensified, the government appealed to them from a position of need and in effect sold patents of nobility in return for financial support during these troubled times. McCagg's research into the archival material shows that the government was looking as far afield as Vienna to garner support. On the eve of his fall in September 1903, Prime Minister Geza Fejervary had been preparing a large-scale distribution of Hungarian ennoblements to Viennese Jewish businessmen. Beyond the disproportionate number of ennoblements and an unusually large number of baronages, there were innovations in the process of granting them. Rather than adhering to the traditional rigorous, complex, and time-consuming format to determine the qualifications of potential nobles, McCagg discovered that this process was being bypassed and further, that it was now in the hands of the Party. Nor was the tradition of bestowing ennoblements upon the great capitalists being kept; instead, they were going to second-level Budapest bankers, industrial managers, and provincial bankers—most of whom were Jewish—who were willing to bolster Prime Minister Istvan Tisza's regime.[13]

Istvan Tisza's reliance on Jews continued and, following a lull between 1906 and 1910, there were an unprecedented number of ennoblements. This suggests to McCagg that Tisza, with great intent, forged a political alliance with the Hungarian business community—which was primarily Jewish—and so, along with ennoblements came a number of appointments as Cabinet Ministers, State Secretaries, and Deputy State Secretaries, a process that went on until 1917.[14] McCagg does not consider it a coincidence that Ferenc Heltai, a Jew and one of the "Budapest lesser capitalists," was made Mayor of Budapest in 1913 and at the same time advanced from the Lower to the Upper House of Parliament.[15] To put this data into perspective, until 1876, thirty-one Jews had been ennobled. Between 1878 and 1899, ninety-five Jews were ennobled; and between 1900 and 1914, 195 Jews were similarly advanced in stature.[16]

We can look at this phenomenon in several ways, any one of which could account for this dramatic rise in ennoblements. Captains of industry and financiers were making headway by the latter third of the nineteenth century, even among underdeveloped countries, and ennoblement was a frequent reward for these magnates. There was the effect of emancipation itself, which allowed Jews to participate in the economy in formerly unimaginable ways, and again, to be rewarded for their efforts. And there was the old Jewish reflex of serving and being rewarded for supporting those in power. While the first two explanations undoubtedly have merit, McCagg's findings do seem to support the conclusion that aiding the government financially garnered not just special privileges, as of old, but the far greater reward of nobility.

On the occasion of the Jews' emancipation in Prussia (1812), David Friedlander, one of the foremost campaigners for the reform of Judaism, described the efforts he had to make in order to become assimilated. Before itemizing these requirements, he first affirmed his loyalty to the state, underscoring just how crucial this facet of assimilation was.* Yet, the typical displays of Jewish loyalty were often distrusted, and the apparent dodging of military service left protestations of Jewish loyalty marooned. By voting *en bloc*, Jews provoked the accusation that they were acting in the name of group solidarity, which not only meant that loyalty beyond their own community was an undeveloped quality, but also, in acting on behalf of their own interests, they had not become assimilated. To the degree that loyalty is presumed in the bestowal of nobility, the research done by McCagg and Andrew Janos shows that this was not a factor in its acquisition. Rather, by ennobling the Jew, the government was simply paying for services rendered. Jews were still behaving in the old pre-emancipated way, and that is why Petrassevich wrote that Jews always aligned themselves with the ruling power.[17]

The Role of Jews in the Economy

Land

Early in the debates among the Enlightenment thinkers, Jews were made to understand that a large part of 'economic integration' was making the change from their traditional occupations to agrarian-based ones. Now, Jews did take to the land in Hungary, but primarily as owners and lessees. This was problematic, for neither of these positions would bring much "improvement of the nation" because, as Dohm had argued, each was "too similar to commerce" and "nourishes the spirit of speculation and profit-seeking."[18] Only agrarian activity performed with one's own hands could bring about the desired moral reform of the Jews. This issue was fundamental to one Sandor Almassy who wrote that, so far from the present emancipation being the last level of emancipation—"In fact we have been thrown back a minimum of one century because this is a curved road"—yet, if two conditions had been met, emancipation might already have reached its apogee: "if the Jews had abjured commerce and begun to work with their

---

* "I am a Prussian citizen," declared Friedlander. "I have sworn solemnly to promote and support the weal of my Fatherland. Both duty and gratitude demand that I with my fellow citizens achieve this with all my might." Quoted in Katz, *Jewish Emancipation and Self-Emancipation*, 69-70.

hands;" or, if they had not stopped engaging in commerce, then stopped "buying belief," "putting individuals they sponsor into good positions," and "paying the judge and falsifying public opinion"—in a word, "stopped corrupting all institutions."[19]

While Hungarian society agreed with Dohm's perspective on land ownership and how it would help put the Jew on the path of moral reform, there was another consideration of equal importance: the nation's economic stability and prosperity, which was largely tied up in land. As Count Sandor Karolyi had written, "What is good for agriculture is good for the country. We must judge all policies by this standard, for three-quarters of the population derive their livelihood from agricultural production."[20] Upon the announcement of the purchase of Count Geza Batthyany's estate by Izsak Stern, the *Fuggetlenseg* lamented, "We are destroyed."[21] "This proves how much anti-Semitism is necessary," commented the same editor when yet another estate was bought up only a few days later.[22] By 1910, Jews owned 19 per cent of all estates between 200 and 1,000 cadastral yokes (one cadastral yoke equals 1.45 American acres); 19.9 per cent of those exceeding 1,000 cadastral yokes; and a further 14.6 per cent may be added to this tally when the largest estates are taken into consideration. The Popper family, for example, owned 47,000+ cadastral yokes; Albert Wodianer, 30,700+ cadastral yokes; and Sigismund Schossberger, 20,000+ cadastral yokes.[23]

Having purchased the land, the capitalist realities of such an endeavor were exhibited: if the land did not yield a profit, Jews at times sold it (thereby adding another dimension to Dohm's argument that land ownership in itself was too similar to commerce). Those more unfortunate saw their land auctioned off. Whether this was due to poor management skills as new landowners or a lack of commitment to being proprietors, the official data of 1883 shows that in fact, more Jews than Christians lost their estates this way.[24] Thus, in buying, selling, or through auction, the perception was that Jews had not only taken the land out of the possession of those who had a traditional right to it, but were abusing this sacred trust.

Although it was frequently acknowledged that the nobility who had formerly owned these estates were at fault because their priorities were reversed—pursuing a life of leisure while eschewing any sort of work ethic—still, Petrassevich and others were convinced that the economy would have developed slowly, methodically, and organically in Christian hands. In conjunction with the restoration of the old idyllic economy based on decentralization, cooperatives, and state-owned lending institutions, the exclusion of Jews could rectify what had been reduced to a stock market trading floor, annihilating both the peasants and the landed classes.[25]

> This whole liberalism that we have here is only aiming to ensure the rule of patented capitalists in Hungary, where exactly the opposite, the agrarian interests should come to the fore. We are an agrarian state; only on the basis of healthy agrarianism can we survive and develop. The land can be destroyed; the people of the earth miserable—the main thing is to save the capitalistic liberalism which wants no religion, only to dance around the Golden Calf.[26]

A memorandum from the British Foreign Office in 1883 noted that while the Hungarian Parliament rejected "any attempt at reactionary legislation or curtailment of the equal rights enjoyed by the Jews," nevertheless,

> it is impossible however not to be struck by the very strong feeling against the Jews which is gaining ground in Hungary among the Upper and Lower classes and especially among Landed Proprietors. The excesses of the leading Anti-Semites and the ridicule which they have brought upon themselves by their unpractical proposals are sufficient to prevent many prominent Hungarians from openly professing the views which they do not scruple to express in private as to the disastrous effects produced on the economic progress of the country by the growing influence of the Jews and by the gradual concentration of landed property into their hands.[27]

Another memorandum pointed out that "most of the large properties [which had not been bought up by Jews] are heavily mortgaged and largely indebted to the 'Sparkasses' [a forerunner of credit unions] and local banks which are mainly directed or influenced by Jews."[28] This symbiosis provoked much antagonism towards the Jews, adding yet another dimension to the topic of Jews and land ownership. Still, though the land-owning aristocracy and gentry found the incursions into land ownership intolerable, at least for the time being, the benefits outweighed the disadvantages. As the grand seigneur of the Karolyi family admitted, "Just as we keep the gypsies so that they play, we keep the Jews so that they work instead of us."[29] Furthermore, noted Endre Ady, "Towards beautiful Jewish women they are not anti-Semitic, for the rich Jews with daughters marry them to impoverished debt-ridden gamblers."[30]

Many Jews, rather than purchasing land, leased it. Of these, a rather large number chose to be absentee landlords, indicating that Jews lacked that essential ingredient: a natural feeling of attachment to the land. This constituted yet another area of contention. Moreover, the *General Pachtung*, whereby "individuals from the same family or families organized themselves into tenant partnerships, or financial consortiums and rented 40-60,000 hold (a hold is equal to two acres) . . . establishing connected chains of maintained subsidiary tenants," proved to be a most provocative innovation in land leasing and a very attractive proposition.[31] As early as 1858, the journal *Falusi Gazda* noted that Jews were becoming the foremost land leaseholders: "What kind of leasing system is now in vogue in Hungary? None in the legal sense—all there is any more is the Jewish lease."[32] The statistics for 1913 show that Jews were lessees of 62 per cent of those estates between 200 and 1,000 holds; lessees of 73.2 per cent of estates approximately 1,000 holds in size; and lessees of 42 per cent of estates between 1,000 and 2,000 holds.[33] In one respect, Jewish lease-holders were favorably looked upon. The parliamentary records of 1890 contain this comment by a conservative deputy: "The truth is, gentlemen, that if you have a Gentile for a tenant, he will come at the end of the year and appeal to your Christian brotherhood and mercy. On the other hand, you can be sure that your Jewish tenant will pay the rent even if his wife and children will freeze or go without eating."[34]

Not only were the landed classes considered victims of mercenary Jews, but the peasants were as well. Their situation was considered very serious in the sub-Carpathian region, and Minister of Agriculture Ignac Daranyi was approached to help alleviate the poverty of the Ruthenian peasants living there. Turning to Ede Egan,[35] Egan produced an official report filled with agrarian reforms that were widely debated in 1900. Apart from these suggestions, he also mentioned a number of issues that were adversely affecting the peasants, all of which involved Jews. Mortgages were never offered in the countryside, only personal credit, and those extending it were overwhelmingly Jews who charged a minimum interest of one forint per week for every ten forints borrowed. This credit arrangement, combined with the peasants' persistent drunkenness, frequently resulted in the loss of their properties. Their loss was exacerbated by the conditions under which land auctions were held: Jewish innkeepers, in the absence of other bidders, formed cartels and artificially forced the price down. Egan's attempt to implement credit cooperatives was sharply opposed by the local merchants, who were almost all Jews and made much of their living by lending money. He reported that they tried to scuttle the establishment of these cooperatives by any and every means possible. When his consumer co-ops applied for and received a license to sell alcohol,* it raised a furor among the Jewish merchants who until that point had held a monopoly over the sale of this staple in the peasants' diet.

Complementary to his public report, Egan also published his private notes. In them, he wrote that no Jewish Question had existed in his mind until he encountered these Jews in the sub-Carpathian region. Unless three things happened, Jewry (both Khazars and homegrown Jews) would ruin Hungary. First, assimilationist efforts had to be strengthened. The historical separation between Christians and Jews was understandable, but now, when Jews experienced the greatest of liberty, it was completely unacceptable.

> They are welcome among us as a very healthy factor of our people by whom those attributes missing in Hungarians will be rounded out. Those Jews who are real Hungarians, who are not only emulating appearances but are inwardly in their character and their morals into the Hungarian state and into the Hungarian type that is sanctified by the traditions of a thousand years, will meld; who don't wish to form a state within a state but without any afterthought and without any intention either openly or covertly join a clique and confront us, those who sincerely and truly wish to be on our side.[36]

Second, he wanted limits put on immigration, well as the screening of illegal immigrants, because the Jews who had arrived in Hungary from Russia via Galicia were the "leftovers of the leftovers." Third, any economic and social conditions that might be the outcome of the agricultural measures he initiated must not be inviting to those "suspicious and dangerous elements."[37] Egan also made a point of saying that broaching the Jewish Question was contrary to the prevailing winds and could cost him his job; nevertheless, he felt compelled to speak up.[38]

---

* Egan had reached the conclusion that in these parts of the world alcohol was not a luxury but an important grocery item and that the only control he could exert was over its quality, which he sought to do by offering an alternative to liquor that was typically diluted with water and mixed with vitriol or some other caustic ingredient to retain its bite.

Occupations

The business of finance was largely in the hands of Jews in Hungary.[39] The truth of this statement has been repeatedly confirmed, and so there is little point in either challenging this fact or providing countless examples of how outraged many Hungarians were about it. Suffice to say, that in the eyes of the non-Jew, monopolization was soon transmogrified into domination: "No one would have anything against Jewish emancipation . . . if the Jews would not provoke hatred with their unlimited drive to power. . . . . The rule of capital is poisoning all the spirit."[40] Writ large, it was the arrival of Albert Rothschild in Paris on 8 March 1881 to assist in the conversion of the Hungarian gold debt; milliards were given as credit through the French banks[41] (about which Istoczy commented in Parliament: "The deficit can only be covered by Jewish kings."[42]). On 31 March 1882, we find that the Finance Minister had again signed a contract with the Rothschild credit institution. This time, unable to meet the full interest payment by twelve million forints, the government offered up 5.85 per cent of the railway shares to cover the shortfall.[43]

This process was begun after 1867, at which time Jews spearheaded the founding of most of the large banks. Once a financial infrastructure was in place, these bankers stimulated the development of whole sectors of the economy, particularly industry and natural resources, over which they ultimately had control. By 1880, certain industries had already become identified as 'Jewish' industries: sugar beets, textiles, textile dyeing, the food industry (especially canning), shipbuilding, railways, and heavy industry.[44] By 1895, an official from the British Foreign Office would report:

> There is in fact probably no country where the Jews exert so much influence as in Hungary. In the Capital alone with a population of some 500,000 souls, there are over a hundred thousand Jews belonging to the situated, intellectual and wealthy; and although, as has been seen during the recent debates in the upper House on the Bill providing for the recognition of the Jewish religion [*Recepcio*], there is still a great feeling against them among the aristocracy and landed gentry, yet they have succeeded in establishing themselves so firmly throughout the provinces as well as in the capital that an anti-Semitic crusade such as that which is now to be observed in Vienna has hitherto been found to be impossible in this half of the Empire.[45]

By the first decade of the twentieth century, almost half of those engaged in trading or credit-related enterprises were Jewish: some 110,000 out of a total of 225,000.[46] However, at the highest level of these enterprises, as owners and directors of financial institutions, Jews occupied eighty-five per cent of the positions nationally, and this percentage rose to over ninety per cent in Budapest.[47]

Exactly why this pronounced Jewish involvement in finance and commerce occurred, and why it was viewed with such hostility, being perceived first as monopolization and then as domination, has been the subject of some discussion among historians. Various causes have been mentioned, but a common thread running through most of them is that Hungarians brought this situation on themselves. Therefore, historians tend to label the hostile reactions to the Jews as anti-Semitic. A different approach to this phenomenon would take into account the historical secular nexus between Jews and Christians: the Jews' economic utility, on which their very presence in the state had often been predicated and which was carefully measured. While emphatic that Jews turn away from finance, trade, and commerce and become agriculturists in order to improve their morality, the Enlightenment thinkers had with ease exchanged their 'Enlightenment ideals specific to the Jews' hats for their 'secular' hats and lauded the Jews' contributions to the expansion of the economy. This old secular basis for toleration never became obsolete: Jewish contributions to the economy continued to be welcomed provided Jews did not become an economic liability through overperformance—that is, being overly competitive with the Christians. (We have no contemporary examples of underperformance in Hungary.) Even after emancipation, overperformance continued to result in a reduced level of tolerance.

The large influx of Jews into the legal and medical professions raises another issue that the Enlightenment thinkers had discussed a good deal (although mostly in the context of commerce and usury, those being the main professions of Jews at the time). Dohm and others had been persuaded that "when no occupation will be closed to Jews, then they should, in all fairness, not have a monopoly on any occupation in preference to other citizens."[48] However, in the legal profession, the percentage of Jews had already risen to 30 per cent by 1900, and to 45.2 per cent by 1910 (to which may be added an unspecified number who had converted).[49] In the field of medicine, out of a total number of doctors engaged in private practice, 62 per cent were Jews; of those practicing medicine as government doctors, 40 per cent; of those employed in clinics and hospitals, more than 33 per cent.[50] This large entry of Jews into medicine and law began in the 1870s and coincided with a plummeting in the reputation of both professions; many saw a direct correlation between the two. Formerly, lawyers were those in whom the highest ideals rested and who acted as guarantors of political freedom. Now, it was said, they had been downgraded to little more than economic entities in the service of capitalism, asserting a heartless individualism. Doctors were seen to be under the same influence, discrediting their profession by closing the professional guilds and emphasizing the growth of medical care, transforming the medical profession into one of the free trades.[51] A number of doctors reflected upon these trends at the turn of the century, and according to Maria Kovacs became—depending on their perspective—neo-conservatives or leftist radicals; in either case, they rejected liberal values, seeing them as the cause of this turn of events.[52] Long before this, however, in a related field, the *Pharmaceutical Bulletin* had written, "No one should employ a Jew because this is a race that is interwoven and if you only have one hundred druggists in a generation, Christian druggists will disappear. Since we cannot expect the government to defend us, we have to decide not to ever employ a Jewish boy as an assistant."[53]

This leaves the activities of many Jews in the economy as yet unaccounted for. And overwhelmingly, they were perceived to be engaging in most unprofessional professions or occupations that were actually illicit. How do we know that it was Jewish individuals who committed these infractions? By the regular use of the terms 'Jew', 'Israelite', or 'Hebrew'; by the information that the person hailed from Galicia or Poland; or by the inclusion of a very Jewish-sounding name in the newspaper reports.[54]

The practice of usury was brought up time and again. In public debates: Istoczy declared that Jews were parasitic as usurious moneylenders, innkeepers, and land leasers.[55] In articles: Csernatony viewed this practice as one of the causes of destitution so prevalent among the Magyar population.[56] And in the press: reported cases of usury frequently had criminal overtones. In the month of July 1880, for example, the newspapers told of two usurers who had been attacked by their customers because they could not pay;[57] a German-speaking rabbi who nobody could understand and was a usurer;[58] the murder of a usurer;[59] and in the most prominent case that month, the plight of twenty-two young army officers (one of whom committed suicide) whose debts to a usurer had been increased through trickery. In the court case that ensued, Izidor Selinger pleaded Jewishness (although he had converted, which, as he told the court, he had been forced to do in Poland in order to obtain a job with the Lemberg railway) and therefore usury was not a crime for him.[60] When the debate about limiting the interest rate was still not resolved by the Parliamentary recess in 1883, the *Fuggetlenseg* bemoaned: "The innkeeper takes away the poor peasants' crop, the poor peasants are no longer sowing and harvesting and are only kept in the useful service of the fat, selfish Jew, and the Parliament has left them to their fates."[61] Once a decision had been reached, the paper railed against it: "[Parliament] is dominated by the sickly Jewish rule that dominates everything. It turned out that the interest rate limit *ex principiis* is a Jewish Question, in which their overwhelming power won again today. The interest rate will not be limited."[62]

In the same month, we are apprised of other Jews involved in nefarious activities: a merchant who had used false weights; a woman trying to sell tobacco (a state privilege) illegally in a restaurant; a life insurance scam where the man faked his own death; a gang of linen thieves (which also included non-Jews); a Jew claiming to be a deaf-mute, collecting money for wounded Turks; a man accused of writing fake documents; four family members accused of false bankruptcy; several cases of issuing false promissory notes (one of which was passed by a Jew who converted and became a monk, and then a Jew again); cheating; counterfeiting; a scam for cripples to stand in for able-bodied men who had been conscripted and did not want to serve; the absconding of funds; the absconding of 500,000 forints by an employee of the Rothschild Bank; and a lottery started in a newspaper owned by a Jew, but there were no winners. (This same person also accepted payment for printing false accusations about others.)[63]

It seems that there were also a large number of Jews on the police force in 1884. Reporting a particular case of police corruption, the *Fuggetlenseg* was "surprised that in the inquiry about the shady dealings of the police so many of the accused are Jewish." (In fact, the paper stated, all eleven of the accused were Jews, amongst them the brother-in-law of Police Chief Elek Thaisz, his wife having been born a Jew.) The paper then alluded to the fragility of Jewish morality: great care should be given when choosing those who are to defend the people from crime, for the Jews have nested themselves into offices where there is so much temptation.[64] Tax evasion also became a frequently noted crime around 1884;[65] and "Everybody knows the Jewish race makes a business out of highly insuring bad buildings and bad wheat, for which the insurance company pays a lot." Another alleged tactic was to set fire to the homes of Christian neighbors in the expectation that it would spread to their own house, which was insured. The paper then stated that Schon Salomon's house had burned down four times in four years. The last time, the villagers caught him and threatened to throw him into the fire.[66] And, according to the Declaration of the Slovak Moderate Oppositional Party, Jews were also heavily involved in making counterfeit foods and wine as well as selling poisoned spirits.[67]

Perhaps the greatest outrage of all was the number of Jews involved in the white slave trade.

> We have positive evidence that Yiddish speaking Jews are maintaining a regular flow of Jewesses to almost all parts of North and South Africa, India, China, Japan, Philippine Islands, North and South America, and also to many of the countries in Europe, trafficked solely for the purpose of prostitution. We know that they were taken to brothels owned by Yiddish speaking Jews. We fear unfortunately this horrible blot on the reputation of our race exists in most places of the world where there is the chance of these unscrupulous men and women making money by the sacrifice of young Jewish women.[68]

The problem was seen to be so serious that leagues were established throughout Europe to try and stamp out this trade. Between 1899 and 1914, national anti-white slavery committees were created in a dozen countries; Hungary's Prime Minister was in fact a patron. The traffickers originated primarily from Galicia, but also from the Habsburg province of Bukovina, the Russian Pale of Settlement, and Hungary. The extent of Jewish involvement was pegged at approximately thirty-eight per cent, based on lists compiled in Hamburg in 1905 and in Berlin in 1908. However, this figure was arrived at by counting the number of Jewish-sounding names, and as a number of Jews had changed their names, historian Edward Bristow thinks this figure is too low. Seen as the epitome of immorality, the frequent reports of missing Christian girls allowed for the suspicion that if not being 'pressed into service' as prostitutes, then perhaps they were being used for ritual purposes.[69]

With the accent on unprofessional rather than illicit, the ancillary profession of a Jewish teacher caught the attention of the *Fuggetlenseg*. The paper reported how, early in the morning, the teacher went to the market to buy up the goose liver, which he then packaged and shipped to Paris and Amsterdam for a good price. The editor commented that this strange method of accumulating an income did not fit his social position, nor did he belong to the Chamber of Commerce or pay taxes.[70] The selling of Christmas trees as a Jewish business was discussed. "Many of the young pines were not sold and it's simply destroying the woods;" and furthermore, many Jews brought pine trees from Galicia in order to force down the price.[71] "This is Jewish morality," read one headline: "A Jewish man leases a bathing house which he leaves filthy and disorderly; he even uses the same water twice."[72] The reader of these news items was informed of the Jews' complete disregard for social norms, fair business practices, and social responsibility; only making money interested them.

Immorality and Other Jewish Traits

"Do you think that the Jew will stop at Temes etc.? No, he will continue to Ung and then on to Bihar. They will be enriched, and it is not a pais-wearing Jew that will arrive in the Hungarian lowland, but his Excellency, the noble Jew. He changes his clothes, but not his morals."[73] And the morals of the Jews, which had been a foremost concern of the Enlightenment thinkers, continued to preoccupy the public. Thus, Augustus Rohling's *Talmudjude* (1871)[74] was widely read throughout Germany and the Austro-Hungarian Empire. Like many of the *philosophes*, Rohling held the view that the Talmud contained very negative attitudes towards Christians and that it sanctioned all kinds of immoral acts against them. According to his investigation of the Talmud, Christians were referred to as swine, dogs, and donkeys; there was no limit to the amount of interest Jews could charge Christians; ritual murder was a commandment, a sacrifice to God; sodomy and the violation of Christian women were permitted; and Jews were the servants of Baal.[75] Hence, Judaism was actually immoral, and adherence to its precepts made its followers immoral, the implication being that Jews could not reform their character without converting.

Petrassevich also agreed that the Jewish character was morally depraved, but he felt that the roots of this flaw lay not only in the Talmud but also in pagan materialism. Together, these influences produced the fundamental Jewish characteristic of hate, as opposed to the cornerstone of Christianity, love: a hatefulness that expressed itself by taking revenge, underhandedness, cunning, craftiness, hypocrisy, cheating, stealing, blackmail, and usury.[76] The very idea of emancipation for idealists such as Eotvos had been to draw Jews closer to Christianity, eventually become Christian, and join the body of the nation and throw away the Talmud.[77] Instead,

> The lemonade he [the Jew] offers us is our own making, only he adds a drop of venom from his fang; unnoticed, the first dose does not harm. At first. In our glass, day by day will be more and more poison of the Talmud; gradually our souls become addicted, as our body would be to absinthe or opium, and cannot escape; it must choose between death or the poison.[78]

The *Fuggetlenseg* also produced a list of Jewish character traits. "What is the cause of their being hated by all the nations?" it asked rhetorically. "Not jealousy. In their racial character, their refined ruse, their base tendencies, their cowardice and dishonesty, and if they are pressed, they display false humility, and if they are wealthy, they are provocatively haughty."[79]

Prime Minister Kalman Tisza also made a dry reference to Jewish morality in the context of a demand made by the noted Calvinist minister, Aron Szilady,[80] who argued for a "common morality" to be taught to all Hungarian youth and its content determined by the state. Tisza replied: "In a philosophical sense there is indeed one morality—but not in real life; I am used to distinguishing between Christian and non-Christian morality."[81]

There is no end to the examples through which Jews' negative character traits were given prominence. To avoid paying their rent, Polish Jews told their landlady they had left, but hid in the room.[82] A printing press used in the production of immoral postcards was found on a Jew's premises.[83] A newspaper campaign was conducted against the converted Jew, Karoly Csemegi, a member of the Supreme Court and author of the *Csemegi Codex*. The *Codex* was a summary of forty years of court cases, and it seems there was no record of any punishment meted out for the abortion advice and services offered by one Dr. Fux.[84]

The press also had a penchant for reporting incidents that occurred between Jews, revealing that, even towards each other, Jews had no sense of morality.[85] A husband accused his wife of stealing money from him, whereupon he sold their house and disappeared;[86] a son cruelly confined his sick seventy-year old father;[87] a pseudo-rabbi posing as a government agent cheated passport-less Jews who wanted to immigrate to the United States;[88] and ex-convict Mr. Rosenfeld entered a village synagogue claiming that the Torah scroll was his, and started beating up congregants.[89] In the early 1880s, Jewish high school teachers were often treated scurrilously by the Jewish community, prompting the *Magyarorszag* to trenchantly note: "If the law of education comes into effect and wants to protect those who enterprise to propagate the Hungarian spirit, you can be sure that the people of *'Geld für Alles'* will find a way around it."* Suicides and acts of bigamy frequently caught the attention of the press.

> The daughter of a local merchant married a merchant from Vienna a few months ago, and the young couple lived through the honeymoon with happy satisfaction. The letters of the young wife were gushing with heavenly happiness. . . .

---

* *Magyarorszag,* 29 June 1880.178, 9 July 1880.188, 29 December 1880.358. From the broad and protracted coverage that this issue received in both the Jewish and non-Jewish press, there can be no doubt that many Orthodox educational institutions fought secularization and Hungarianization tooth and nail, employing every means at their disposal. Additionally, it appears that the conditions in many of these schools were far below government standards. One article written by a Jewish teacher protested the poor working conditions among teachers, while another told of the economy measure of issuing only yearly contracts. Yet another Jewish writer to the *Magyarorszag* related the expulsion of eighty-nine teachers in Szekesfehervar, although his main point was that similar German-speaking replacements were found and this was damaging to the patriotic Magyar trend. Jews who complained about this state of affairs were subject to censure: in one locale, some members who supported their pro-Magyar teacher found themselves cut off from the services of the Jewish community: rabbi, cantor, and *shochet. Judische Delikatessen,* Book 4, July 1880. See also *Budapest,* 7 August 1880.218; *Pesti Naplo,* 11 September 1881.249, 19 September 1881.257.

But suddenly, unexpectedly, a dark cloud came over the sunshiny life of the young couple. From Pest, a poor and abandoned widow visited the quiet nest stating that she has rights to that nest, because she is the unhappy wife of the happy husband he abandoned miserably, leaving four children to the whims of uncertain fate. . . . The local Israelite community has already received official notification . . .[90]

The case of Laszlo Bauer was cited as another example of Jewish immorality. Bauer converted to Judaism and married a Jewish woman, but he subsequently reconverted to Catholicism. However, before he did, he stole money five times, thus revealing the influence of Jewishness, because he only became a thief while he was a Jew.[91]

Observance of the Jewish Sabbath and the festivals inserted itself in a number of ways into complaints about Jewish morality. Keeping Saturday as a day of rest meant that Jews worked on Sunday, and this created a number of problems for Christians. "It is to be expected that they honor their holidays, but they should also honor the law of the land;" that most of the peasants work on Sunday stems from the "Moses-believing land-leasing caste that I honor otherwise," but they work on Sunday and accordingly, so do the peasants.[92] This situation was exacerbated by choosing to pay their Christian workmen on Sunday.[93] Some people were fighting to make Sunday a legal holiday, but Jews were opposed to this proposition. On the one hand, they already had Saturday as a day of rest and on the other hand, "they want to raise their profits. . . . In one generation, Jews can become very rich and they don't care if others are oppressed. So should there not be Sunday as a holiday until the Jews get rich?"[94] This 'double standard' provoked a demand from the *Fuggetlenseg* that "Christians should have equal rights with Jews," and a warning from the *Magyar Allam* that "the Jews themselves should see that it is dangerous for them if they are identified as the caste of easy money."[95] Self-serving, money-grabbing, and socially exclusive are only some of the character traits to be distilled from these complaints.

While Sabbath observance and holiday closings would seem to contradict Goethe's belief that "to grab the purse of non-Jews" was the essential impulse in the formation of the Jewish character, it is another character trait that is at issue here—what Fichte described as the unassimilability of the Jew. Several other examples highlight this trait. Orthodox Jewish prisoners were not eating in jail because there was no kosher food and as a result, a certain Jewish prisoner, if he continued to fast, would have to be removed to a special facility.[96] A court case was underway against a Jewish doctor in Apatin because he refused to let the priest perform the rite of extreme unction on a dying Catholic.[97] And in a letter to the newspaper, a writer complained that he could only get kosher food at the railway station.[98]

Little time elapsed from the initial mandate to change, to the observation that Jews are not changing, to the belief that Jews cannot change and are therefore unassimilable. This sequential overlapping was due to the expectation that assimilation should occur in tandem with emancipation in order to prevent the impinging of negative Jewish values on the general society and the imposition of Jewish practices upon it. Only twenty years after emancipation, the *Fuggetlenseg* was claiming that "Hungary is losing its Hungarian character and becoming a Jewish country, and the Liberals don't care."[99]

Education

As much as all the reforms were stressed, the *philosophes* had considered education to be the best corrective for the faults of the Jews, while serving as the primary vehicle through which to inculcate all those values necessary to make of them good citizens and moral individuals. At once the most concrete and seemingly feasible, in the years subsequent to emancipation, the success of this process was jeopardized as both a number of Jews and Christians attempted to thwart it: Jews, by not being responsive to the assimilative thrust of education; Christians, by advocating separate schools for Jewish children.[100] As little as they themselves wanted to mingle with Jews, just as little did they want their children to; and schools, more than any other environment, were a source of ongoing, intimate contact between Christian and Jew.

There was no possibility of the government acceding to such a demand, and so Jewish students found themselves attending schools where many of their teachers naturally shared the same views as the Christian students' parents. These teachers exhibited enough hostility towards the young Jewish students to make their lives, if not a "misery", then at least uncomfortable. Minister of Public Education Trefort's written communications that school was not the place for anti-Semitism went unheeded.[101]

School attendance on Saturday, the Sabbath—for those Jewish children who were placed in the public school system, and by no means all of them were— along with the concomitant (forbidden) tasks such as writing, which were a necessary part of this attendance, was a provocative issue. Our interest here is not the dilemma Jewish children and their parents were faced with. Rather, it is what this issue signified to the general public when, for example, the Jewish students at the Nyitra Middle School challenged the principal's ruling to write on the Sabbath. The editor of the *Fuggetlenseg* erupted: "Should this be changed, then shall all the laws against cheating, thieving, and killing be changed?"[102] This rejection of the principle of assimilation was exhibited elsewhere. Trefort repeatedly tried to put Jewish high school students on the path of assimilation by advising them to follow any pursuit or vocation, but they should not enter culture-related professions, to which they were overwhelmingly and disproportionately drawn.[103] Jewish educators rejected his message of assimilation and advised students not to heed the minister's directive, as it was meant to derail intellectual pursuits among the Jews.[104]

At the university level, Christian students had their own complaints. There were too many Jewish students: "Suitable proportions should be taken into account" during enrolment,[105] they said, when they were called to meet with the rector of the University of Budapest following an incident where Christian students insulted Jewish youth, provoking such exciting scenes that the police were called in (February 1881). The admonishments of the rector and promises of reprimand seemingly had little effect, for the students immediately set out to organize a public meeting, which was banned by the Ministry of the Interior.[106] Apart from this prominent incident, an Anti-Semitic Committee had been formed at the university (whose president received a strong letter to stop agitating).[107] Jewish students also found it increasingly difficult to be accepted in the numerous student bodies.[108] From 1890 onward, demonstrations against the Jewish students occurred with mounting frequency. As the rector complained in his 1898 report, "I have had many problems with the *antiszemita* [old form of 'anti-Semitic'] party which fought with the reform party—but it's a minority." He also noted that within the student unions there was a contingent opposed to their Jewish counterparts, and that the unions had become the scene of student fights and attacks.[109]

Another issue at the university was the behavior of certain Jewish students, which was considered offensive—and unassimilated. Dr. Lipot Szorengi was among those Jews who admitted to the existence of this problem in universities, and one of the very few who spoke out about it.

> A professor wants to light a cigar, and who is the one jumping like a waiter to light it? The Jew. Who is the one who should stay quiet if he doesn't know the answer? The Jewish student; instead, he's talking like a swindler. The richer Jewish students are behaving proudly, as if they belong to the Magnates' circles, partying until dawn, and glad when their friends don't think they're Jewish. And that's how they think to meld into Christian society. But such pretence fits Jewish children badly. In one word, we lack this fine Christian-like sense of honor. . . . So nobody should wonder why university students have anti-Semitic feelings. And what I have said about students goes for all Jews.[110]

Finally, one may observe two sustained differences between Christians and Jews in the matter of approach to education. The first is the contrast between those in the middle stream of society: Christian youth of the gentry and Jewish youth who had a capitalist merchant background. In Hungary, many gentry families became increasingly impoverished over the nineteenth century, but its youth, unwilling to give up the lifestyle associated with their position, preferred to suffer in silence. Eventually, their circumstances became so dire that they chose employment and flooded to the bureaucracy—but not to the universities until after the war, when administrative posts were no longer available.[111] Jewish youth also had a choice to make: stay in the traditional occupations of their fathers or take the leap towards an intellectually oriented education that would lead to a career in the arts or one of the professions.[112] (This choice would take into account the fact that an official or academic career was by and large out of the question without conversion.) In droves, they chose to attend university. Both sets of parents applied their respective traditional approaches to education. Christian parents saw to it that their children were educated to a level that would enable them to perform in accordance with their position in society. Jewish parents promoted higher education, viewing it as the best mechanism to catapult their children into a higher level in society.[113]

The second difference emerges from an examination of statistics on Jewish enrolment patterns. The liberal paper *Pesti Naplo* published the following statistics on 21 April 1881. It noted that the number of Jewish students attending *gimnazium* had risen significantly: out of a total student body of 33,908 in 1867, Jewish students numbered 2,995; out of a total student body of 34,947 in 1880, Jewish students numbered 6,559.[114] Thus, the proportion of Jewish students in the student population rose from almost ten per cent to almost twenty per cent in thirteen years. The statistics of sociologist Viktor Karady on Jewish enrolment patterns present a more extreme picture. His calculations give a 3:2 ratio of school attendance in favor of the Jewish students.[115] And in certain institutions, their presence was even more dominant. Written up in the *Fuggetlenseg* in 1884 were the following statistics: attending the Commercial Academy, there were 105 Christian students and 378 Jewish students; at the Girls School, 120 Christian students and 226 Jewish students; and at the IV District High School, 112 Christian students and 228 Jewish students. These figures caused one teacher to fear for the "ancestral morality."[116] But most glaring of all was the discrepancy between Jewish and Christian female students by 1918. In that year, out of 160,000 women who qualified for the vote in 1918 because they had the necessary school certificate, 124,000 were Jewish.[117]

No matter which angle we examine this topic from, Jews were not making use of the educational process for the purpose intended by the Enlightenment thinkers: to put them on the path to assimilation.

Acculturation

It is estimated that by the turn of the century, twenty per cent of those in the arts were Jews.[118] Their activities were criticized not only on the basis of talent but also on its distinctive Jewishness, which was palpable. One of the frequent complaints that cropped up was the absence of a sense of aesthetics among Jews. Whereas the non-Jewish approach to art was through beauty, the Jewish approach was to apprehend it through the intellect.[119] Further affecting their artistic sensibility was a lack of attachment to the national traditions. This was compounded by their inability to understand the Christian soul. Figures in books were dressed up as Gentiles, but their characters were really Jewish, and the average Christian could not identify with them.[120] Their artwork was little more than copying; and while they showed a lot of talent in the theater, they were just playing roles. "Jews are unable to create," wrote Franz Liszt; rather, they exhibited *"utanerzes"*—vicariously or inauthentically participating in the sentiments of the source without the slightest personal experience.

> In the theatre, painting, and music, they are following Christian schemes and they don't even try to get rid of our systems: Meyerbeer only melded the German and Italian schools. It was a new combination, but it was a combination. And Mendelssohn copied Handel. Jews are constantly attacking the oldest

institutions—the Church, the throne, and the kingdom. They have to be sent back to their real homeland, Palestine.[121]

Bertalan Szterenyi, the son of a rabbi and a ferocious critic of his coreligionists (who eventually converted), wrote that Ferenc Pulszky's "high level literary articles are filled with such Jewish spirit, from all his words a *tallis* and *tzitzit* hang out. So, his articles are not wearing a leopard [such as Hungarian aristocrats wore] but a torn caftan."[122] Writer Janos Horvath went further:

> The linguistic vagrancy that settles into others' property with the unabashed cold blood of a usurper, the insolent consistency in the way this strange element goes from nest to nest to drop its cuckoo eggs, and the meek tolerance with which the Hungarian audience watches its language being defiled day by day— what is more, they even applaud it—all the above boils your blood and calls for the whip![123]

To Petrassevich, the current literature was "rife with some indeterminate old, melancholic pain," coupled with a "limitless uppityness, false superiority, sarcasm, and evil mockery" for which journalism was the only suitable endeavor.[124] Even this, Horvath opposed. "The *Nyugat*," he wrote, "is a gathering of Jewish and definitely philo-Semitic writers, representing the Hungarian nation with its assimilated Jews. Assimilation [of the Hungarians] completed."[125] This perception, that Jews were assimilating the Hungarians rather than the other way around, gains some support from an article on the contributions Jews made to Hungarian culture, written by Erzsebet Balla. Incidentally, she notes that a large number of Jews who were directly involved in cultural activities were also journalists and, to a lesser degree, politicians.[126] The implication of this should not be overlooked. In this double capacity, the influence of 'Jewish' sensibilities on society could be profound. This notion may also help to account for the undeniable popularity of culture produced by Jews.

Far from seeing culture as the spiritual wealth of the nation and helping to build up its resources, it was said that Jews saw it as a commodity. They were embarking on a voracious conquest of the arts in order to make money from it and, according to Horvath: "Their situation is so favorable and the road to their prosperity and success is so unobstructed; something that has never happened for a Hungarian writer."[127]

Just as explosive was the monopolization of the press. As of 1880, 516 out of 1,214 newspaper editors were Jews, according to the count done by the *Magyarorszag* newspaper.[128] And all papers were employing Jewish journalists: "Jewish *schlemiels*"—"not at all Hungarians"—were replacing the earlier great journalists because it was in the Jewish interest to do so. The increasing power of the Jewish press was dramatically revealed by their coverage of the Tiszaeszlar trial which, many claimed, had consistently denied the 'truth'.[129] In 1895, a British foreign official noted:

> In answer to an interpellation addressed to the Prime Minister at yesterday's sitting of the Chamber of Deputies His Excellency stated that the Hungarian Government had exercised no influence whatsoever in regard to the decision

taken by the Crown and the Austrian cabinet.... But however correct the action of the government may have been, it can hardly be said that the same discretion was observed by the majority of the leading Hungarian journals which are entirely in the hands of the Jews and which made no secret of the bad impression which would be produced in Hungary if Count Badeni should venture to recommend to the Crown to sanction the election of the great anti-semitic leader [Karl Lueger].[130]

Further proof that "the most influential portion of the Press being however Semitic"—as another memorandum from the British Foreign Office put it[131]—were the press monopolies, such as those held by Miklos Lendvai, who was the editor of several provincial newspapers, and Kornel Oszi, under whose direction sports magazines were consolidated.[132] In one case, it seems the Jewish press was determined to exercise its monopoly even if it meant the use of subterfuge. A correspondent of the Jewish paper *Fonfeirchass Zeitung* had received a speech by the King with the understanding that he share it with other members of the press, but he reneged on the agreement. The *Pecsi Figyelo* publicized this devious act; therefore, "We are reporting the King's speech only in short version."[133]

Monopolization of the press meant influence: "Jewish journalism usurps the highest post and as jury it criticizes every literary product that is not written by a Jew," wrote the pamphleteer Saulus.[134] It was Istoczy's conviction that the Jewish-controlled press was directing the capitalist transformation.[135] This influence had an iconoclastic bent to it. Under the guise of enlightenment, wrote the *Fuggetlenseg*, the 'Jewish press' imbued the public morality with the most unusual ideas and did so most cynically: "Just yesterday, one Jewish paper stated openly that history, the past, is nothing. Let's forget it; we should concentrate only on the present."[136] The *Huszadik Szazad*, a periodical which began publishing in 1900, spearheaded the bourgeois radical movement, with converted Jew Oszkar Jaszi at the helm and many other Jews among its retinue.[137] The journal condemned both the liberalism and chauvinistic and romantic nationalism of the previous decades.[138]

Andor Miklos, the press magnate, was considered the Jewish mentality incarnate. Coming from a family of modest means, Miklos was forced to leave school at a young age. Finding employment at the *Pesti Hirlap* in 1903, he was first a gofer, then an ad agent, and finally rose to the post of editor of the economics section, and in that capacity, he established his social connections. In 1910, he was fired, under suspicion for taking more than his fifteen per cent share of the regular monthly payments received from banks and large companies. Striking out on his own, he started the newspaper *Az Est*, which became the most widely read paper of the time.[139] Journalist Gabor Andor described it as "this boil on the Hungarian press, *Az Est*, this tricolor toilet paper, that is after use in relation to every regime."[140] During the war, Miklos insisted that the publishing house Athenaeum deliver the paper according to the original contract amount of 1.85 fillers, while he was selling it for 20 fillers, due to galloping inflation. 1.85 fillers was not even enough to pay for the newsprint; the Athenaeum went bankrupt, and Andor bought it for a song in 1917. In 1919, he bought the *Magyarorszag*, which had also gone bankrupt, for pennies. Then, when Lajos Hatvany was forced to emigrate, Miklos acquired the major liberal paper *Pesti Naplo* from him. In its heyday, his newspaper empire had 6,500 employees, 354 of them journalists.[141]

Little more needs to be said here. For those persuaded of the existence of a 'Jewish mentality,' thirty years after emancipation, with Jewish monopolization of the press standing at eighty per cent, with Jewish participation in the arts standing at twenty per cent—a number of whom also occupied prominent positions in journalism and politics—the Jewish influence on society was overwhelming. While not universal, the view was widely held that having monopolized many aspects of Hungarian culture, Jews then proceeded with the 'Jewification' of Hungarian culture.

Ethnic Minorities

Unfortunately, the stand of the 'nationalities'[142] towards the Jews is a very understudied subject, but given their majority status in Hungary if we exclude the Jews,* it definitely warrants investigation. Particularly in the countryside and smaller towns, the nationalities were the immediate neighbors of the Jews. In 1871, the priest Peter Sasinek, an advocate of the pan-Slavic movement known for delivering sermons against the Jews that had a theological underpinning, turned his attention to their patriotic support of Hungary and their embrace of the policy of Magyarization. In his estimation, Jews were as much of an ethnic minority as the Slavs, and their decision to abandon their social and political dimensions and become Magyars was nothing short of a sell-out.[143] In the name of ethnic solidarity, Jews should be part of the fight to claim the rights they had been promised under the *Ausgleich*. If they did not, it could only provoke enmity between the Slavs and the Jews.[144]

The comments of a Russian Orthodox priest make an interesting juxtaposition to Sasinek's views. He contrasted the so-called Russian priest's home in which one finds the clearest of Hungarian conversation with the emancipated and protected caftan-wearing so-called Hungarians who speak a "rotten" (distorted) form of the German language, which they effect only when they must, and even then, the Hungarian cannot but smile at that. He then expressed the fear that "our homeland" was being sucked into a whirlpool, in part due to the prac-

---

* In no European country that emancipated its Jews over the nineteenth century were Jews classified as a nationality or separate ethnic group, although from the outset of the emancipation debates, the peoplehood aspect of Jewry was regularly cited as an obstacle to emancipation. But in Hungary, this aspect was often overlooked for strategic reasons. Since the nationalities composed 49.6 per cent of Hungary's population, one of the advantages of Jewish emancipation would be to incorporate the Jews as part of the Magyar element. Augmenting the Magyar population so that it stood at 50.4 per cent, they thus acquired a technical majority over the nationalities. Jews were never considered one of the nationalities, but in a classification of their own.

tice of usury, and, without the help of providence, the Hungarian word and Hungarian statehood would be swallowed up.[145]

Before long, Sasinek's threats were translated into action when, in the spring of 1881, Slavs in the localities of Pazsto and Losonc beat up Jews, broke into their houses, and stole from their shops. Both the law introducing civil marriage (1883)[146] and the 1884 election campaign prompted letters to the editor from Slovakian electors. These writers expressed the feeling that they had no rights anywhere, and that while both the Hungarians and the Jews were oppressing and expropriating them, the real representatives of Hungary were the Jews. Hence the call to anti-Semitism from Pan-Slav circles: they should embrace the cause of the liberation of Slovaks and Ruthenians who had become slaves of the Jews.[147] But it was Tiszaeszlar which prompted the strongest reaction. As a memorandum from the British foreign Office reported, "More fear is felt as to the possible recurrence of the Pressburg [Pozsony] disorders among the Slovak population in the north of Hungary."[148]

This memorandum also made a reference to the Germans who were even more "animated by fanaticism against the Jews" than the Slovaks. In fact, the *Alfold* pointed a finger at the aristocracy, most of whom were German in origin, as the party largely responsible for the 1882 riots against the Jews in Pozsony.[149] Andrew Handler has stated that both the Jews and the Germans were disliked.[150] That may be so, but the nature of this dislike needs to be examined before concluding that this common ground somehow establishes a similarity between Jews who had experienced hundreds of years of marginalization and Germans who were frequently substantial citizens and occupied positions of authority in Hungarian society. Handler might also have added that the Germans were united with the Magyars in their sentiments towards the Jews.

Social Assimilation

So far, one layer of social assimilation has been looked at, that which devolved on the individual and was conducted at the personal level. Assimilation into the institutional structures of society was also a facet of social assimilation. Jews as members of a social class, and marriage between Jews and Christians, fall within this category.

Jews and Class

Prior to the nineteenth century, the organization of society was ordered by, in the words of Samuel Johnson, "the fixed, invariable external rules of distinction of rank, which create no jealousy, since they are held to be accidental."[151] Each rank could be distinguished by "manner, speech, deportment, dress, liveried equipage, size of house and household, the kind and quantity of food they ate," and, most importantly, "gentlemen"—unlike the "common people"—"maintain themselves without manual labour."[152] This system of ranks was succeeded by the class ideal, whose essence historian Harold Perkin describes as one of conflict: struggle for income and a "conscious image of the class in its relation to rival classes."[153] While the birth of the class system in England may be pegged around 1820, the seeds were generously sown elsewhere, and in time took root.

The earliest date of emancipation is, of course, tied to the French Revolution; therefore, Jews had never been members of any rank. As the notion of class was taking hold, almost all Jews were still in an unemancipated state, and contemporaries continued to refer to them as a caste, or race, or people, not as members of a class. If, occasionally, Jews were described as 'middle class' at this time, as Peter Sugar has pointed out, it should not be confused with being a member of the middle class; it meant no more than engaging in an occupation usually engaged in by members of the middle class.[154] Therefore, the most that can be said of Jews was that they possessed certain attributes of the different classes.* Hannah Arendt's comment about the *Hofjuden* equally applies to all Jews: they "stood outside all social connections;" "their economic rise remained independent of contemporary economic conditions, and their social contacts remained outside the laws of society. Friendships between princes and *Hofjuden* were not at all rare, but they never created a social atmosphere."[155]

Having never belonged to the historical social system, there was no common ground between the Hungarian serfs' struggles against the aristocracy to achieve self-determination and the position of the newly emancipated, impoverished, Eastern European Jewish immigrants in Hungary. Nor can a parallel be drawn between Jews who were in occupations regarded as 'middle class' and middle-class Hungarians who primarily belonged to the gentry, were greatly indebted, and increasingly dependent on jobs in the bureaucracy. As far as the upper class is concerned, nobility was carried in one's blood and in the possession of the *pergamen*,[156] neither of which the Jews could acquire. No title could transform them into true members of the elite. Since entry into one of the social classes was an impossibility, the mandate of the Jew—to assimilate—was out of the question in this context. Not fitting naturally into one of the newly created classes, Jews were simply slotted into one of them: Eastern European Jews into the lower class; industrialists, financiers, and comfortably positioned merchants into the middle class; and those whose business acumen had parachuted them into the arena of the wealthy were loosely considered upper class. But these were arbitrary and artificial designations and could not forward the goal of social assimilation in any way.

Some historians have drawn an analogy between the Jews and the serfs based on a similar lack of rights. They have argued that if a nation had not

---

* Within their own community as well, Jews were not organized along class lines. As Katz has made clear, no rigid class structure existed within the Jewish community. Jewish society before emancipation can only be described as stratified. Its criteria were wealth and Talmudic learning; both of these attributes were theoretically within the grasp of many Jews. Mobility both upward and downward was quite frequent. Katz, *Out of the Ghetto*, 21-22.

'emancipated' its serfs one could hardly have expected it to have emancipated its Jews. However, the proceedings at the Congress of Berlin (1878) belie the viability of such an argument. At the Congress, the Western powers made it a condition of Romania's impending sovereignty that it grant political emancipation to its Jewish inhabitants,[157] but no one entertained the notion of making sovereignty contingent on the dismantling of the Romanian class structure which still had feudal overtones. In the case of Romania, the order was in fact reversed: the position of the Jews (theoretically and theoretically only, as it turns out) was enhanced while that of the peasant population remained the same. It may also be argued that because adjustments had to be made by everyone as society was transformed into a class-based one, Jews should not be excluded from the class schematic; however, this argument at attempted homogenization fails to take into consideration the fact that Jews were outside the polity for much of this period.

What are some of the implications of this classless status for Jews? First and foremost, it left Jews in the same condition as they were before emancipation—outside the social structure. Furthermore, in an era of class consciousness, being classless severely disadvantaged Jews in any attempt to assimilate. This means that the primary relationship of Jews to society remained an economic one. Rather than gravitating to national movements such as universal enfranchisement, Jews tended to become involved in supranational movements such as socialism, Marxism, and anarchism. Finally, it may account for the pronounced revolutionary tendencies among Jews.[158] Beyond the usual observation that fomenting revolutions is an activity engaged in by those who feel oppressed (and as an oppressed people it was therefore a natural thing for Jews to pursue), the broad swath that the Jews cut in revolutionary movements seems to suggest something more at work. While revolution—either in the sense of revolutionary thought or actually advocating revolution—is one of the hallmarks of the nineteenth century, the idea of promoting revolution on a worldwide scale, to which a number of Jews subscribed, may be viewed as a phenomenon that is a natural outgrowth of a people that is not rooted at any level: not to any class, not to one country.

Intermarriage

The greatest obstacle to the assertion that social assimilation was not being accomplished is the phenomenon of intermarriage. Involving between eight per cent and forty per cent of Jews (depending on the county*) after intermarriage was lawful following the *Recepcio* in 1895, the higher figure argues strongly in favor of successful assimilation. The subject of intermarriage between Jews and Christians is a very understudied one, as Hungarian sociologist Viktor Karady has pointed out. While enumerating a number of areas that need investigation,

---

* The higher figure reflects intermarriage patterns in Budapest. Twenty per cent of Hungary's Jews lived there and altogether they accounted for over two-thirds of the intermarriages in Hungary. Yehuda Don and George Magos, "The Demographic Development of Hungarian Jewry," *Jewish Social Studies* 45, nos. 3-4. (Summer/Fall 1983): 195.

he has made two general observations that help circumscribe discussion of this topic. First, the definition of intermarriage is not standardized. While the law in some countries defines intermarriage as the union between a Jew and a Christian, the law in other countries allows for either the union between a Jew and a Christian or between a baptized Jew and a Christian to be defined as intermarriage. In Hungary, only those marriages between Christians and Jews were recorded as mixed marriages. Second, not even the anti-Semitic pressures during the 1930s reduced the occurrence of intermarriage; rather, it continued to increase until the enactment of the Jewish Laws of 1938.

Concerning the details of these mixed marriages, Karady has been able to ascertain that many were "typical second choice or belated matches." Other intermarriages were often informed by the drive to improve one's status: the Jewish male gained an "entry ticket" into non-Jewish society; the Christian female gained financial security and often chose a Jewish partner higher up on the social ladder. Karady further observed a distinct "instability" in these marriages, and a "statistically well observed low fertility."[159]

In a similar study, Yehuda Don and George Magos discovered that opportunities to assimilate—presumably "mixed" working environments, living in large urban centers, and mixed neighborhoods—affected the intermarriage rate. Another factor governing the choice to intermarry was the Jews' attitude toward assimilation. Like Karady, Don and Magos noted that the fertility of mixed marriages between Jews and Gentiles was considerably lower than any other subsection of the population. Several reasons for this last observation were suggested by the authors: mixed marriages tended to occur within upper middle-class circles, which always had a lower birth rate than the other classes; the durability of these marriages was generally low; and also, childlessness would avoid the problem of which religion to bring the child up in.[160]

The recent findings of Karady, Don, and Magos corroborate Uriah Zevi Engelman's analysis of intermarriage in Germany, Russia, and Switzerland, published in 1940. Engelman's data showed that intermarriage was constantly on the rise and that the rate of divorce was higher amongst intermarried couples than amongst couples of the same faith. Among his observations, one is of particular interest: the number of marriages entered into by Jewish couples plummeted during the First World War, but those between Jews and non-Jews remained steady.[161] By drawing on Karady's research, a reasonable explanation may be provided for this seemingly odd phenomenon. During wartime, both Jewish males and Christian females had ever more reasons to contemplate intermarriage: Jewish males because of sustained or increasing anti-Jewish sentiment; Christian females, because of severe economic hardship and the reduced number of marriage partners due to the high casualty rate among soldiers at the front. (Why these Jewish men were not at the front and were therefore available as marriage partners is addressed in a later chapter.)

Marian Kaplan is one of the few historians who have made an in-depth examination of Jewish marriage patterns, which also falls within the dates of this study. She found that certain conditions governed the contemplation of intermarriage in Imperial Germany (1871-1918) and that with one exception, they affected Jewish females. A shortage of Jewish men caused some women to conclude that an intermarriage was better than no marriage at all. (There was a pronounced tendency for Jewish males to move from small towns to larger urban centers, or even outside Europe, where both their marital and professional options were brighter.) Another 'shortage'—the ability of a family of modest means to offer only a tiny dowry—had the same ramifications. These conditions may be subsumed under Karady's observation that many intermarriages on the part of females were "second choice or belated matches." The last condition identified by Kaplan, the deliberate choice to marry out of the faith as the ticket into Christian society, applied mostly to Jewish men. It corresponds to Karady's identification of improved status as a motive for intermarrying.[162]

As I stated at the outset, an intermarriage rate of up to forty per cent has been considered a strong indicator of assimilation. But assimilation, when considered in the context of marriage, is a particularly two-sided affair. In examining intermarriage from the Jewish perspective, this figure of up to forty per cent of Jews marrying Christians argues strongly in favor of successful assimilation (although among those Jews who wished to perpetuate the Jewish identity, this intermarriage rate was a calamity). From the perspective of the Christian host society, forty per cent of Jews marrying Christians augured well for the complete assimilation of the Jewish people in the not too distant future. But the actual affect on the Christian population was not significant, for the number of Christians actually marrying Jews was quite low: just over eight per cent. This means that few of those who were opposed to such an intimate Jewish presence in their families were really confronted by this prospect. Even in the city of Budapest, with its exceptional concentration of Jews, only a modest number of Christians were intermarrying with Jews.

In examining intermarriage from the perspective of those individuals who actually entered into this type of union, the explanations given by historians and sociologists account for why Jews intermarried, and to some extent, why Christian women married Jewish men. However, they have not accounted for why Christians as a whole (although their actual numbers were fairly low) were receptive to the idea of marrying Jews. This receptivity, I would suggest, grew out of the fact that by the time it became legal to intermarry in 1895, it had become a social norm to view intermarriage as the best vehicle for complete assimilation. In the emancipation debates, intermarriage and its merit as a vehicle of assimilation, had regularly been mentioned. After emancipation, this was one of the main arguments for advocating a civil marriage law in Hungary. It follows that, if intermarriage was deemed the primary mechanism for achieving assimilation (short of conversion), a Jew who was willing to intermarry was already less of a Jew and on his way to becoming a Christian, and therefore a reasonable prospective marriage partner for a Christian. That the children of these marriages were almost always raised in the Christian faith[163] supports this assertion.

A number of Jews and Christians agreed with artist Anna Lesznai (the product of converted parents) who was convinced that "one of the healing effects" of the many manifestations of the Jewish condition (The Jew is one who "does not have a social circle. To be a Jew means an unusual, sickly, excited state of the nerves. The possession of money is a substitute for socialization for the Jew . . .")

"is mixed marriage; that will eliminate the Jewish Question as it eliminates the Jew."[164]

However, as it turned out, the intimate setting of marriage rather exposed the gulf between the two parties. Hence, the low rate of reproduction among these couples and their high divorce rate. Each partner had brought to the marriage his/her own set of misconceptions: the Jewish partner assuming that he was assimilated, the Christian partner being under the impression that the marriage itself would complete the process of assimilation.

NOTES

1. OL, K148, 1881, VII/4556; *Pesti Naplo*, 3 May 1881.121, 22 November 1881.321.
2. *Fuggetlenseg*, 25 April 1883.114.
3. *Fuggetlenseg*, 14 August 1884.224.
4. *Magyarorszag*, 30 September 1881.222.
5. *Fuggetlenseg*, 25 April 1882.113, 1 May 1882.119.
6. *Fuggetlenseg*, 25 April 1882.113, 1 May 1882.119.
7. *Fuggetlenseg*, 29 August 1882.238.
8. *Fuggetlenseg*, 9 January 1887.8.
9. *Uj-Jeruzsalem es nepe*, [New Jerusalem and its People] *Judische Delikatessen*, Book 5.
10. Geza Petrassevich, *Magyarorszag es a zsidosag* [Hungary and the Jews] (Budapest: Szent Gellert Konyvnyomda, 1900), 64-73. Petrassevich worked for a variety of Catholic newspapers including *Magyar Allam, Alkotmany*, and *Uj Lap*, where he was editor. He also translated Russian literature.
11. Patai, *Jews of Hungary*, 446-47.
12. Andrew C. Janos, *The Politics of Backwardness in Hungary, 1825-1945* (Princeton: Princeton University Press, 1982), 117.
13. William O. McCagg, Jr., *Jewish Nobles and Geniuses in Modern Hungary* (Boulder, Colo.; East European Monographs, 1972), 172, 178. Istvan Tisza was the son of former Prime Minister Kalman Tisza.
14. McCagg, *Jewish Nobles*, 177-79. Jewish members of the government: Members of Cabinet, Baron Samu Hazai, Minister for Defence (1910); Janos Teleszky, Minister of Finance (1912); Baron Janos Harkanyi, Minister of Trade (1913). State Secretaries: Lipot Vadasz, State Secretary (Deputy Minister) in the Justice Department (1913); Elemer Hantos, State Secretary in the Trade Ministry (1916); Imre Nemenyi, State Secretary in the Cultural Ministry and Lajos Beck, State Secretary for Justice and Laszlo Fejer, State Secretary attached to the Prime Minister (1917). Deputy State Secretaries, all of whom seem to have attained this position before the end of the monarchy, largely because of services rendered during the Tisza period: Samu Fejer, Artur Gaspar, Bertalan Kallos, Dezso Pap, and Geza Pap.
15. McCagg, *Jewish Nobles*, 179.
16. Janos, *Politics of Backwardness*, 179.
17. Petrassevich, *Magyarorszag*, 64-73. See also *Fuggetlenseg*, 26 July 1884.205.
18. Dohm, *Concerning the Amelioration*, 63.
19. *Fuggetlenseg*, 25 May 1884.144.
20. Count Sandor Karolyi, quoted in the Naplo (1895), in Janos, *Politics of Backwardness*, 143; Petrassevich, *Magyarorszag*, 93-95.
21. *Fuggetlenseg*, 24 September 1883.263.

22. *Fuggetlenseg*, 28 September 1883.267.
23. Alajos Kovacs, *A zsidosag terfoglalasa Magyarorszagon* [The Ascendancy of Jewry in Hungary] (1923; repr., Budapest: Kellner, 1935), 40. Of the 10.8 million cadastral yokes of land in Hungary, Jews owned 1.5 million by 1916. Katzburg, *Hungary and the Jews*, 254.
24. Acsady cited the auction appendix of the 1883 Official Gazette. *Zsido es nemzsido*, 26.
25. Petrassevich, *Magyarorszag*, 93-95, 97-98, 110, 115-16, 124, 128-29.
26. Ignacz Zimandy, *Kossuth Lajos* (Budapest: Marton Bago, 1898), xiii.
27. British F.O. memorandum (1883), quoted in Katzburg, *Antisemitism in Hungary*, 109-10.
28. British F.O. memorandum (1883), quoted in Katzburg, *Anti-Semitism in Hungary*, 245.
29. Count Sandor Karolyi, quoted in Patai, *Jews in Hungary*, 360.
30. Endre Ady, a lyric poet and one of the most talented representatives of the modern spirit in Hungary, "Lazban eg a vilag," [The World Burns in Fever] in *A zsidosagrol* [About Jewry] (Nagyvarad, 1919). This book was a collection of articles written between 27 August 1901 and 12 April 1903.
31. Lease-holder Ferenc Schorbel modified the *General Pachtung* by establishing his own land renting venture as a joint stock company in 1848. Juliana Puskas, "Jewish Leaseholders in the Course of Agricultural Development in Hungary, 1850-1930," in *Jews in the Hungarian Economy 1760-1945: Studies Dedicated to Moshe Carmilly-Weinberger on his Eightieth Birthday*, ed. Michael K. Silber (Jerusalem: The Magnes Press, Hebrew University, 1992), 107-110.
32. *Falusi Gazda*, quoted in Puskas, "Jewish Leaseholders," 108-9.
33. Alajos Kovacs, *A Csonka-Magyarorszagi zsidosag a statisztika tukreben* [Rump Hungary's Jewry in the Mirror of Statistics] (Budapest, 1935), 13-14.
34. Quoted in Janos, *Politics of Backwardness*, 115.
35. Early in his career, Egan was employed as a manager of various estates. In 1883, he organized the department of milk production and shortly thereafter played a major role in starting the cheese industry. In 1897, he became the Royal Commissioner of the mountain area, and two years later, he was awarded the third class of the Iron Crown Order.
36. Ede Egan, quoted in Gyurgyak, *A zsidokerdes Magyarorszagon*, 355.
37. Ede Egan, quoted in Gyurgyak, *A zsidokerdes Magyarorszagon*, 350-59.
38. Before Egan could carry out his entire program, he died under mysterious circumstances that have variously been described as an accident or murder at the hand of the Jews.
39. Nathaniel Katzburg, "Hungarian Jewry in Modern Times," in *Hungarian Jewish Studies*, ed. Randolph L. Braham (New York: Harry Gantt Publishers Printing Representative, 1966), 144. The fact that half of Budapest's Jewish population qualified for the vote in an era of extremely limited enfranchisement was yet one more indication of the wealth of Jews—wealth being a decisive factor in gaining the franchise—and their correspondingly lopsided power in Hungary at the time. Janos, *Politics of Backwardness*, 117.
40. *Fuggetlenseg*, 13 May 1884.132.
41. *Pesti Naplo*, 8 March 1881.66, 19 March, 1881.72.
42. *Pesti Naplo*, 3 March 1881.61.
43. *Pesti Naplo*, 31 March 1882.89.
44. Katzburg, "Hungarian Jewry in Modern Times," 144-46.
45. British F.O. memorandum, quoted in Katzburg, *Antisemitism in Hungary*, 246-47.

46. Katzburg, *Anti-Semitism in Hungary*, 16-17.
47. Kovacs, *Liberal Professions*, 21.
48. Dohm, *Concerning the Amelioration*, 60.
49. Kovacs, *Liberal Professions*, 17, 21.
50. Katzburg, *Anti-Semitism in Hungary*, 16-17.
51. Kovacs, *Liberal Professions*, 30.
52. Kovacs, *Liberal Professions*, 31-32.
53. Quoted in the *Fuggetlenseg*, 30 October 1884.300.
54. *Pecsi Figyelo*, 19 June 1880.25 (two articles), 3 July 1880.27; *Magyarorszag*, 24 June 1880.173, 25 June 1880.174, 27 June 1880.176, 7 July 1880.186, 8 July 1880.187 (two articles), 11 July 1880.190, 14 July 1880.193, 25 July 1880.204, 28 July 1880.207 (two articles), 30 July 1880.209; *Egyetertes*, 25 June 1880.174, 16 July 1880.195, 17 July 1880.196, 19 July 1880.198.
55. Istoczy, *Istoczy Gyozo orszaggyulesi*, 1-14; *Pesti Naplo*, 23 January 1883.22.
56. Handler, *Blood Libel*, 26-27.
57. *Pecsi Figyelo*, 3 July 1880.27.
58. *Egyetertes*, 19 July 1880.198.
59. *Egyetertes*, 17 July 1880.196.
60. *Egyetertes*, 16 July 1880.195, 17 July 1880.196; *Magyarorszag*, 17 July 1880.190.
61. *Fuggetlenseg*, February 1883; *Judische Delikatessen*, Book 37, 22.
62. *Fuggetlenseg*, 1 February 1883.32. Taking advantage of the entrenched belief that Jews exploit honest Christians, a Roman count by the name of Langrand-Dumonceau created a financial system for Christians. With capital in Christian hands, he said, the recession caused by Jews since the mid-1860s could be alleviated. Through this ploy, this confidence man managed to extract enormous sums from vulnerable Hungarian widows and orphans, clergymen, and peasants before being caught and tried (although he escaped to America). Lajos Venetianer, *A magyar zsidosag tortenete—kulonos tekintettel gazdasagi es muvelodesi fejlodesere a XIX, szazadban* [The History of Hungarian Jewry: With Special Emphasis on Its Economic and Cultural Development in the 19th Century] (Budapest: Fovarosi Nyomda, 1922), 338-39.
63. *Judische Delikatessen*, Books 4, 5, July 1880.
64. *Fuggetlenseg*, 17 October 1884.287.
65. *Fuggetlenseg*, 21 June 1884.170. See also *Judische Delikatessen*, Books 58, 59.
66. *Fuggetlenseg*, 30 September 1884.270.
67. OL, K149 1887-6-106.
68. Arthur Moro, an officer in London's Jewish Association for the Protection of Girls and Women, quoted in Edward Bristow, "The German-Jewish Fight Against White Slavery," *LBIYB* 28 (1983): 301. For a comprehensive treatment of this subject, see Edward J. Bristow's *Prostitution and Prejudice: The Jewish Fight Against White Slavery, 1870-1939* (New York: Schocken Books, 1983).
69. Bristow, "German-Jewish Fight Against White Slavery," 304, 309-11, 313; *Fuggetlenseg*, 29 March 1884.58, 30 March 1884.59, 2 April 1884.93.
70. *Fuggetlenseg*, 5 October 1883.274.
71. *Magyar Allam*, 25 December 1881.294.
72. *Fuggetlenseg*, 4 October 1883.273. It will be recalled that Michaelis asserted that Jewish villains outnumbered Christians by a ratio of 25:1.
73. *Fuggetlenseg*, 3 May 1884.122.
74. According to most accounts, Rohling's *Talmudjude* drew heavily on Johann Andreas Eisenmenger's work, *Entdeckes Judentum* [Judaism Discovered] (1700). Parkes, *Enemy of the People*, 18-19. *Talmudjude* was first translated into Hungarian in 1881, and

Istoczy repeatedly quoted from it. See Gyozo Istoczy, *Istoczy Gyozo orszaggyulesi beszedei inditvanyai es torvenyjavaslatai, 1872-1896*. In 1905, Rohling's book was published under the title *Jewish Poison*, and in 1920, *A Cel* published it in installments.

75. Mosse, *Toward the Final Solution*, 138-40.
76. Petrassevich, *Magyarorszag*, 56-58, 62-63.
77. Petrassevich, *Magyarorszag*, 68.
78. Petrassevich, *Magyarorszag*, 147-48.
79. *Fuggetlenseg*, 27 May 1884.146.
80. In addition to being a priest, Aron Szilady was a Hungarian historian and linguist, and a member of both the Kisfaludy Association and the Academy of Sciences.
81. Venetianer, *A magyar zsidosag tortenete*, 322-23.
82. *Magyarorszag*, 19 June 1880.168.
83. *Magyarorszag*, 13 August 1880.223.
84. *Judische Delikatessen*, Book 37, February 1883, 21-22, 27.
85. *Egyetertes*, 1 September 1880.242; *Magyarorszag*, 20 October 1880, 5 November 1880, 7 December 1880, 22 December 1880; *Pecsi Figyelo*, 23 July 1881.30; *A Hon*, 20 July 1881.198, 22 July 1881.200; *Pesti Naplo*, 10 January 1881.9, 11 November 1881.310, 15 November 1881.314, 7 January 1882.7, 12 January 1882.12, 21 January 1882.21, 6 February 1882.37.
86. *Pesti Naplo*, 8 September 1881.246.
87. *Magyarorszag*, 14 July 1880.193.
88. *Magyarorszag*, 8 August 1880.218.
89. *Egyetertes*, 1 September 1880.242.
90. *Magyarorszag*, 8 July 1880.187, 22 July 1880.201.
91. *Magyarorszag*, 1 August 1880.216.
92. *Tolna Bulletin*, 21 August 1881.34.
93. *Fuggetlenseg*, 23 June 1882.172.
94. *Fuggetlenseg*, 4 October 1883.273.
95. *Fuggetlenseg*, 23 June 1882.172; *Magyar Allam*, 5 October 1881.220.6502.
96. *Magyarorszag*, 12 October 1880.283; *Ellenor*, 16 August 1880.390.
97. *Pesti Naplo*, 12 October 1881.280; *Magyarorszag*, 12 October 1881.232; *Magyar Allam*, 12 October 1881.232.6508.
98. *Magyar Lap*, 21 April 1885.37.
99. *Fuggetlenseg*, 6 March 1887.63.
100. Moscovits, *Jewish Education in Hungary*, 110.
101. "In some schools, the teacher asks on the first day, how many Jews are there? Such and such they answer. 'Very sorry to hear,' says the teacher. If a Jew is answering a question, he does not get any positive feedback, and no mistake is accepted—but when a Christian makes some mistake, the teacher smiles and is encouraging." "*Antiszemitizmus a gimnaziumban*," [Anti-Semitism in the High School] *Egyenloseg* 6 (1883): 5. One may refer to other issues of the *Egyenloseg*, including numbers 35, 41, 45 written in 1884. High school entrance examinations were made especially difficult and once this hurdle was overcome, there were financial barriers. Because many of the high schools were operated by various Christian denominations, they were free to set the tuition: it was generally higher for Jewish students (One *gimnazium* in Budapest with an excellent reputation charged Jewish students six times more than the set tuition.). On the other hand, they were excluded from scholarships and discounts. Viktor Karady, *Zsidosag Europaban a modern korban: tarsadalomtorteneti vazlat*, [Jewry in Europe in the Modern Age: Sociohistorical Sketch] trans. from French into Hungarian by Laszlo Toth (Budapest: Uj Mandatum Konyvkiado, 2000), 234-35; Moscovits, *Jewish Education in Hungary*, 108-9, 113.
102. *Fuggetlenseg*, 27 October 1884.297.

103. Lest Trefort's urgings be construed as anti-Semitic, it may be pointed out that the *Fuggetlenseg* was assured that Trefort leaned in the direction of philo-Semitism: "This jolly Trefi-ort, with his cosmopolitan chimeras and spiritual St. Vitus dance, wants to reform the Upper House so that the newly made Talmud barons and big landowners and high rabbis may enter." 17 July 1884.196.
104. Moskovits, *Jewish Education in Hungary*, 109.
105. *Egyetertes*, 23 February 1881.53; Venetianer, *A magyar zsidosag tortenete*, 342-43.
106. *Pesti Naplo*, 23 February 1881.53, 11 February 1881.41, 3 March 1881.61; *12 Ropirat*, February 1881.
107. *Fuggetlenseg*, 24 February 1881.54.
108. Karady, *Zsidosag Europaban*, 235.
109. Katalin Szegvari, *Numerus Clausus* (Budapest: Akademiai Kiado, 1988), 93; Karady, *Zsidosag Europaban*, 235.
110. *Fuggetlenseg*, 20 June 1882.169.
111. Janos, *Politics of Backwardness*, 204.
112. Karady, *Zsidosag Europaban*, 232-36.
113. Katz, *Out of the Ghetto*, 21-22; Beller, *Vienna and the Jews*, 66-68. This was the case in Vienna; from my own reading, the situation was the same in Hungary.
114. *Pesti Naplo*, 21 April 1881.108. The figures from Alajos Kovacs's book of statistical compilations are similar: between 1864 and 1914, the percentage of Jewish students attending high school rose from 9.6 per cent to 22.5 per cent of the total student body; and, over the same period, the percentage of Jewish students attending university rose from 10.3 per cent to 28.6 per cent of the total student body. Kovacs, *A zsidosag terfoglalasa Magyarorszagon*, 32-35.
115. Victor Karady, "Jewish Enrolment Patterns in Classical Secondary Education in Old Regime and Inter-War Hungary," in *Studies in Contemporary Jewry*, ed. J. Frankel (Bloomington, Ind., 1984), 1:232-34.
116. *Fuggetlenseg*, 7 September 1884.248.
117. *A Cel*, 9, no. 3 (1 March 1918): 162. Although Aron Moscovits states that the number of Jewish students in the middle schools decreased by seven per cent in the 1880s, it is difficult to give credence to this statistic because of the substantial increase in high school and university attendance. On the other hand, it is possible that the marked hostility towards Jewish students did prompt a number of parents to take their middle-level children out of the public school system. However, during this same period, a number of children, due to the government's efforts to promote Magyarization, were being rerouted into the public schools: traffic went both ways. In any case, even if one accepts Moscovits's figure, it does not offset the trend among Jewish youth to attend high school, and often university, or disturb the ratio of Jewish students to Christian students. *Jewish Education in Hungary*, 108-9.
118. Katzburg, *Anti-Semitism in Hungary*, 16-17.
119. Beller, *Vienna and the Jews*, 213-14.
120. Petrassevich, *Magyarorszag*, 141-57.
121. Franz Liszt, quoted in the *Pesti Naplo*, 23 November 1881.322. A pamphlet which outlined Liszt's views was also published and may be found in the *Judische Delikatessen*, Book 17.
122. Bertalan Szterenyi, quoted in the *Fuggetlenseg*, 20 July 1884.199. Like many others, Pulszky was still considered a Jew even though he came from a converted family.
123. Janos Horvath, "Szomoryzmusok a Nemzeti szinpadjan," [Szomoryisms on the Stage of the National Theater] in *Magyar Nyelv* [Hungarian Language] (Budapest, 1914), 2:88-89.

124. Petrassevich, *Magyarorszag*, 141-57.
125. Janos Horvath, *Aranytol Adyig* [From Arany to Ady] (Budapest, 1921), 45. The *Nyugat* was a monthly literary magazine.
126. Erzsebet Balla, "The Jews of Hungary: A Cultural Overview," *Hungarian Jewish Studies* 2 (1969): 92-100.
127. Horvath, "Szomoryzmusok a Nemzeti szinpadjan," 88-89.
128. Katzburg, *Anti-Semitism in Hungary*, 16-17. Somewhat related to the issue of the monopolization of the press was the 1919 statistic that out of 919 independent printers in Hungary, 534, or 58.7 per cent were Jewish. Patai, *Jews of Hungary*, 366.
129. Zoltan Bosnyak, *Harc a zsido sajto ellen* [Struggle Against the Jewish Press] (Budapest: Held Janos Konyvnyomdaja, 1938), unpaginated.
130. British F.O. memorandum, quoted in Katzburg, *Antisemitism in Hungary*, 248.
131. British F.O. memorandum, quoted in Katzburg, *Antisemitism in Hungary*, 237.
132. Balla, "Jews of Hungary," 124, 94.
133. *Pecsi Figyelo*, 26 September 1880.
134. Saulus, "The Jewish Money's Rule of Terror," *Fuggetlenseg*, 13 May 1884.132.
135. Bosnyak, *Harc a zsido*, unpaginated.
136. *Fuggetlenseg*, 5 July 1885.182.
137. These Jews correspond to the "endless stream of middle-range individuals" that Herzl wrote about. Theodor Herzl, *Der Judenstaat*, trans. Henk Overberg (Northvale, N.J.: Jason Aronson Inc., 1997), 141.
138. Patai, *Jews of Hungary*, 447-48.
139. Balla, "Jews of Hungary," 92.
140. Erno Pesti, foreword to *Az Est-lapok 1920-1939* [The Evening Papers 1920-1939] (Budapest: Repertorium, Petofi Irodalmi Muzeum, 1982).
141. Pesti, foreword, *Az Est-lapok*.
142. The term 'nationalities' was taken from the Nationality Law of 1868, which applied to the ethnic minorities. Hugh and Christopher Seton-Watson, *Making of a New Europe*, 25.
143. Jews did more than embrace the policy of Magyarization for themselves, according to this statement made by a Jewish MP in 1895: "Statistics prove that the Jews of the districts inhabited by nationalities carry on regular missionary work [Magyarization]." An MP, quoted in Seton-Watson, *Racial Problems in Hungary*, 188.
144. Venetianer, *A magyar zsidosag tortenete*, 323-24, 342.
145. *Fuggetlenseg*, 24 February 1883.55.
146. Seton-Watson, *Racial Problems in Hungary*, 185.
147. *Fuggetlenseg*, 14 May 1884.133.
148. British F.O. memorandum, quoted in Katzburg, *Anti-Semitism in Hungary*, 233.
149. *Alfold*, 10 October 1882, 1.
150. Handler, *Blood Libel*, 4.
151. Samuel Johnson, quoted in Harold Perkin, *Origins of Modern English Society* (1969; repr., London: Routledge, 1991), 25. The terms 'orders' and 'degrees' were also used.
152. Extract from what Perkin describes as "the most popular eighteenth-century handbook on Britain," in *Origins of Modern English Society*, 24-25.
153. Perkin, *Origins of Modern English Society*, 219, 209.
154. Peter F. Sugar, "Governments and Minorities in Austria-Hungary—Different Policies with the same Result IV," in *Eastern European Nationalism, Politics, and Religion* (Aldershot, UK and Brookfield, Vt.: Ashgate, 1999), 6 [11-12].
155. Arendt, "Privileged Jews," 64.
156. The *pergamen* was the parchment upon which the royal patent was written.

157. Sachar, *Course of Modern Jewish History*, 297-300.

158. Amongst those labeled as revolutionaries in Hungary, a designation which included social democrats, socialists, reformers, Marxists, and anarchists, the proportion of Jews ranged from forty to sixty per cent. Janos, *Politics of Backwardness*, 177.

159. Victor Karady, "Demography and Social Mobility: Historical Problem Areas in the Study of Contemporary Jewry in Central Europe," in *A Social Economic History of Central European Jewry*, ed. Yehuda Don and Victor Karady (New Brunswick, N.J. and London: Transaction Publishers, 1990), 103-9.

160. Don and Magos, "Demographic Development," 195-96.

161. Uriah Zevi Engelman, "Intermarriage Among Jews in Germany, U.S.S.R., and Switzerland," *Jewish Social Studies* 2, no. 2 (April 1940): 157-76.

162. Marian A. Kaplan, "For Love or Money: The Marriage Strategies of Jews in Imperial Germany," *LBIYB* 28 (1983): 275-80.

163. Engelman, "Intermarriage Among Jews," 166-67.

164. Anna Lesznai, "A zsidokerdes Mgyarorszagon," [The Jewish Question in Hungary] *Huszadik Szazad* 2 (1917).

Chapter 9
1914-1920

Considering the Jewish Question

The same issues that were raised by the Enlightenment thinkers were part of the public discourse in wartime Hungary. Stimulating this discourse was a book by Peter Agoston entitled *A zsidok utja* [The Way of the Jews] (1917), about the Jewish Question. So much interest was aroused by the timeliness of the problems it discussed that it prompted converted Jew Oszkar Jaszi, the editor of the noted journal *Huszadik Szazad*, to invite responses from 150 Jews and non-Jews—members of the intelligentsia, politicians, artists, writers, teachers, church leaders, and other observers of the Hungarian social scene—to these three questions:

1. Is there a Jewish Question in Hungary, and if yes, wherein do you see its substance?

2. What are the reasons for the Jewish Question in Hungary? What phenomena of Hungarian society, what social relations, institutions, characteristics, and customs of the Hungarian Jews, as opposed to the non-Jews, play a role in giving rise to the Jewish Question?

3. What do you see as the solution of the Hungarian Jewish Question? What social or legislative reforms do you consider necessary?[1]

"When two to three people get together nowadays, first they look around to see if there is anyone nearby, and if not, they freely discuss the Jewish Question."[2] Many of them considered Jews a race—or a caste.[3] Jews themselves struggled to define their status: "Just as I reject to the last that the Jew is not Hungarian," wrote novelist Tamas Kobor, "so I recognize without reservation the separate raciality of Jewry. It is impossible to deny and just as superfluous. Over the centuries, the Jewish community has maintained its raciality together with its religion. . . . the racial difference in body and in soul equally can be seen and experienced."[4]

About the Jew and his character, "There is a complete and impenetrable, that is eternal, foreignness. . . . in the foreign light of Hanukkah candles, which they probably cannot help and which is probably unconscious since it is stitched into their flesh and bones with the thread of millenia."[5] "Jews are selfish, unable to be altruistic; Jews are exclusive."[6] "The Jew is always a ridiculous, asymmetric, alien figure that at the same time pretends he isn't alien," wrote Prohaszka. "I must call the Jewish spirit witless, because it is the denial of the Ideal, grinning down upon the majestic. It reduces everything to zero that is not profit, gain, or interest. Witless, because it is lowly, dirty, works with numbers, and sees nothing else."[7] Their negativity, a character trait that only Jews have, "manifests itself in our national life."[8] Jews display a "moral of utility and love of publicity. They lack good taste and manners. . . . their lack of self respect, bothersome extroversion . . ."[9]

"In culture, Jews do not create, but only convey diverse foreign ideas," wrote Aladar Korosfoi-Kriesch.[10] "The language of Jews is un-Hungarian, and they write about characters that have nothing in common with Hungarians,"[11] stated Emma Ritook. This view was echoed by Istvan Lendvai and in his assessment of Erno Szep's *Patika* (Pharmacy) he described the book as an example of the "intellectual megalomania of the Jews:" "The Caesarian madness of the intellectual ghetto, which entertains that he is the only *civis europaeus* and everybody else is a stupid barbarian." No Jew could possibly know the rural Hungarian; "This is something that should be terminated and its bones ought to be cracked."[12]

> Time and again, the Jewish blood seeps through the Hungarian skin. . . . There is Jewish blood circulating behind Ferenc Molnar's heroes' skin. . . . Ignotus stands on a Hungarian nationalist basis but in his extreme liberalism, he involuntarily fights for Jewish interests. And the way he fights, his dialectics and rhythm of thoughts, are singularly Jewish . . . Erno Szep always feels that he is from a different world and not from the Hungarian people's world. And as a Jew, he would consider it a little false if he dedicated himself to the folkish ethos without restriction.[13]

This same influence was perceived by the president of the Hungarian Zionists in the following way: "In all peoples within which Jewry is active, the Jewish genius leaves its mark on literature and art."[14]

It has caused disappointment within Christian society that "the willingness of Jews to apply themselves has proven to be so superficial. Behind their national and patriotic phrases, undesirable atavistic Jewish proclivities have appeared so many times."[15] Whether it was because Jews adhered to their religion, or became irreligious and thus forfeited the morality associated with religion, either way, they had not taken advantage of "the civilizing force of Christianity."[16] True assimilation had never taken place: "The ridicule accorded to [so-called 'assimilated'] Jews when they demonstrate their Hungarianness; they are received with derision,"[17] while "the lower social strata," which had no such aspirations, "keep to their religious practices, and these separate them from others. The customs and rituals are constant reminders of their standing apart."[18]

As to the possibility of assimilation—"Given peaceful times [it] provides some relief, but it is not the solution." Rather, "The mixing of the two races [through intermarriage] would be beneficial."[19] However, the harm done to this process by the constant influx of Galizianers was brought up by many contributors. As soon as a certain number were assimilated, their place was taken by new Galizianers; thus, "The work is never done."[20] "Hungarian Jews," according to distinguished writer Cecile Tormay, were an endless stream of Jewish immigrants, who have "scooped our soul out of things, and put his own face in its place" in the city and in the countryside. Once a secret, this process of Judaization was now out in the open.

> For decades, the Polish and Russian Jews have come to us; they cut off their *payes*, sidelocks, in Kassa, throw off their gabardines in Miskolcz and become barons and millionaires in Budapest. There he [Oscar Jaszi] stands in the midst of a poisoned town, the son of Russo-Polish Jews, declaiming, with all the destructive vigour of his race, separatist theories against associations made by nature itself.[21]

The Jewish Question as it related to economic matters "is caused by the appearance that everything is getting worse except the progress of the Jews,"[22] and therefore, "The limit of equality is reached when some members of society claim an advantage at the expense of others, and which does not benefit the commonwealth at the same time."[23]

In the Jew's choice of occupation, Agoston wrote that even the Jew who has converted has not given up the idea of the Jews as a chosen people who should not perform menial work or earn his living through physical labor. Jews may be suitable for intellectual work, but why would the convert support this intention in the Jew? The outcome has been the creation of a modern Jewish nobility.[24]

In their relationship to the polity, "The Jews gave up on assimilating as Hungarians and on their inclination to join the nation and the state. . . . and became a state within a state."[25]

> As a state within a state, they have imperialistic ambitions on capital and the press, and these ambitions are in stark opposition to the desires of the patriotic and Christian majority. There is a conspiracy of destructive Jewry to annihilate Christian and national Hungary. Class hatred and moral turpitude in Christian countries are a result of intellectual Jewish processes.[26]

Considering the Jews and the war, Agoston wrote that it had given the Jews many opportunities to get closer spiritually to the host nation. The Jew, however, is so egocentric in his thoughts and feelings that he does not even notice how unjust his loud complaints of suffering are in time of war. The sacrifice for one's own people should not be decried so much. It hurts the host nations (Austria and Hungary) that military authorities were forced to conclude that many of the eligible Jews from Galicia and the eastern part of the country did not report on time to the military commands but hid out instead. On 4 October 1915, the military command addressed the municipal authorities regarding this and called special attention to the draftees of the Jewish religion. Every reasonable person knows that the charge of desertion does not include every Jew, but even the military authorities were forced to write 'Jews' just as everybody is forced to say 'Jews'. The Jew feels the same way as he did in the Middle Ages; wars then were no affair of his because he did not belong to any party. Jews do feel that they are expected to support national ideals and they do. But unwilling to give up their own, they are serving two masters.[27] The first prerequisite "of taking in and without worrying about using the Jews in moral and patriotic assimilation— 'moral taming'—is their extrication from the international Jewish community which considers the homeland only an opportunity and is destructive."[28]

Dr. Jeno Cholnoky, like many others, found the trait of Jewish solidarity (variously described as clannishness, unity, cohesiveness, coherence) very disturbing. Even the assimilated Jews "adhere to each other more than any other nationality" and "insist on a different morality and eastern customs."[29] Agoston pointed out that even in someone like Sandor Brody, the feeling of Jewishness and solidarity could be reawakened at the sight of a refugee from Galicia. This feeling of Jewishness was what Heine wrote about, that when a Jew falls, ten Jews run to pick him up; but when a Christian falls, they do not care. Jews had entered many fields beyond their proportion because the Jewish community was organized in such a way that it helps its members. The war rekindled the sense of clannishness among some Jews: mutual support is reinvigorated in the trenches as more than once Jews sensed that they are Jews. Even in the heat of battle the sword raised for the deathly blow fell because the intended victim cried out *"Shema Yisrael!"* This cohesiveness, which typically exists only among members of the same class, is so strong that even the long-emancipated Jew—this potential convert entering the middle class—unconditionally supports his brethren. This coherence prevents Jews from being judged as individuals and furthermore, is unpleasant to others. In their political shortsightedness, Jews did not understand Clermont-Tonnerre when he said: "To the individual Jew, every right; but to the Jews as a Nation, nothing."[30]

As soon as one asks the question, why do Jews only help other Jews, the Jew is immediately separated and unassimilated, declared Agoston, for assimilation implies that the Jew would pick and choose from the whole population. Jews have not assimilated, as their increasing numbers show. Even amongst those who had assimilated in some way into society, the Jewish Question was still present. Jews, it seems, did not understand the meaning and goal of emancipation, which was a device of equalization. It did not mean the continuation of differences: the preservation of memories of different origins; the practice of customs that separate; and keeping together and supporting each other against others.[31]

Conversion of the Jews continued to be discussed. Some felt that "Conversions did not mark Jews or Jewry."[32] Many felt that although it was theoretically a good option, it was generally unsuccessful.[33] Others, among them some Jews, concluded that it was a good idea and should be undertaken.[34] Author and newspaper owner Lajos Hatvany made an impassioned plea to his coreligionists.

> Those who suffered for their race half a lifetime, can't help it; they must bear the cross, the 'cross of the Jews.' But! Every enlightened father must raise Christian children. 'My dear Jews, you must put on frock coats, if you want to go to the ball.' More than enough hardship awaits your children; at least they should be relieved of the burden of Jewishness. . . . Getting rid of Jewish characteristics must be the main goal of the new Jewish generation.[35]

In his book, Agoston discussed the abandonment of a Jewish identity and the undertaking of national, religious, and economic assimilation. He wrote that Jews must be determined to do something about the situation and understand "that amongst the host nation those who treated them liberally, who gave them equal rights, is the expectation that the Jews who enjoy these equal rights become equal in their souls, spirits, and disappear within them."[36]

The First World War

Only weeks after the First World War broke out, the loyalty of Jews as Hungarian citizens was challenged. Jews were thought to be reluctant to serve in the military, and at the front in particular.* As early as 1 October 1914, a weekly in Szeged asked why there were not more Jews on the battlefields, while a small weekly paper in Beszterce and the official gazette of the Peasants Alliance were discussing the Jewish Question. Jews were further accused of being less than loyal to their country of residence because their fellow brethren were counted among the 'enemy' (see Agoston, above). Scores of articles criticizing the Jews were written within the first four months of the war.[37] So intense was this barrage that the military leadership launched a defense on behalf of the Jews. It was unconvincing, and the Jewish community felt compelled to set up a Hungarian Military Jewish Archive that would document Jewish participation in the war effort.[38]

"Let's count those who form all age groups, from all professions, who went to the front line and fought their fight," wrote Prohaszka in 1918.

> . . . those drafted to the front and not left behind on supply carriages; who are standing in front of barbed wire fences and not in the offices of military supply companies and not wasting their days behind desks in banks; let's go along the wrinkled jagged front lines and experience that the closer we are coming to the fire, there we find more Christian people; and the further back we go, there we find more Jews. That is dying; this is saving his skin—for the future benefit of Hungarian culture.[39]

---

* Actually, a rather large number of Jews served in the military; however, many of them did not serve at the front. With the *Ausgleich* (the Compromise between Austria and Hungary) in 1867 came compulsory military service, but a one-year volunteer program (as opposed to the average length of three years) was available to those who had completed secondary school. Many Jewish males qualified for this program which, in addition, made them eligible for officers' training school. A disproportionate number of Jewish reserve officers was the outcome. Somewhat related to this was the overrepresentation of Jews in non-combative units due to particular skills acquired in the course of obtaining a higher education. Istvan Deak, "Homeless Defenders of the Homeland: The officers of the Habsburg Monarchy," in *Hungarians and Their Neighbors in Modern Times, 1867-1950*, ed. Ferenc Glatz (New York: Columbia University Press, 1995), 48.

In September 1918, Vazsonyi published an article[40] which stimulated further comment by Prohaszka. Prohaszka accused the Jews of hiding out in offices and storage houses; most of them retreated at the sound of bullets and grenades. He was also concerned about university students who were ignoring their studies in order to help with the defense of their homeland while others stayed home because they were degenerates.[41]

It was also unpatriotic to profiteer, to hide and hoard merchandise, and to buy and sell on the black market; especially after 1915, Jews were accused of engaging in all these activities. In Parliament, MP Janos Frey attacked the Jews as loafers and war profiteers.[42] In particular, they were held to be the chief abusers of war contracts. One major scandal erupted over the supply of inferior cloth for army uniforms by a Jewish manufacturer, concerning which Jewish writer Jozsef Patai defensively argued that "the indispensable prerequisite of the delivery of that false cloth was its acceptance, which was not done by Jews."[43]

Absolutely convinced that the Jewish citizenry were unreliable, government-sanctioned raids became commonplace. Szabolcsi termed these raids *oblava*—Jew raids—because no citizens from other religions were subjected to such a procedure.[44] In order to put a stop to hoarding, one police raid in Budapest netted sixty kilograms of lard, nine kilograms of paprika, eighteen kilograms of flour, and over two thousand Galizianers. In Szatmar, 150 Jews were escorted in rows to the police, although no charges were laid. In Nyiregyhaza, the commandos shepherded seventy Jews in front of the Hotel Royal; they were publicly searched, and their money, coats, and pants confiscated before they were released. Searching for deserters in Munkacs, a unit of the military surrounded the synagogue. For the same purpose, a protracted and violent raid was carried out in Satoraljaujhely 16-20 July 1918. Together, the gendarmerie and the police broke into the Sephardi temple, beat up the people at prayer, and then walked them through the streets, bleeding. Similar raids occurred over the next five days in many locations. Jews were stopped at the railroad station, arrested, their money confiscated, and a tax imposed on them that was to be collected on the spot. In Ermihalyfalva, the entire Jewish population was captured and escorted through the streets in a search for profiteers and deserters. In Szerencs, the raid lasted three days, and a tax was imposed on Jewish storeowners. In Kisvarda, Jews were allowed to keep only three sets of underwear and two pairs of socks, by order of the gendarmerie. The most spectacular incident occurred on Yom Kippur, 1918, when two thousand soldiers armed with bayonets entered all the synagogues in Maramarossziget. In a check for documents—which, because of the holiday, nobody had—hundreds were arrested and taken away.[45]

If raids were the primary method used by the government to eliminate antipatriotic behavior among Jews, members of the Church, having no such means at their disposal, concentrated on increasing the circulation of relevant reading material. Under the sponsorship of Bishop Gyula Zichy, a book by Sandor Martinovics entitled *The Jewish Question* was published and sent free of charge to the front. Focusing on the theme of patriotism, the Jew was "unpatriotic and selfish," "a cynical lowly soul" who was "hiding" in order "to save his skin."[46] The newly founded Catholic Central Press Company [*Kozponti Sajtovallalat*—KSV] distributed one million copies of Prohaszka's article (above) decrying the lack of patriotism among Jews.[47] Cleric Bela Bangha floated a war bond for the purpose of establishing an anti-Semitic press. In a countrywide door-to-door campaign, he succeeded in collecting tens of millions of crowns[48] with which to found the Anti-Semitic Press Company. Headed by several university professors, the company contributed to the proliferation of condemnatory books and articles that were already flooding the market.[49]

Members of the intelligentsia like Istvan Milotay wrote of "[Jewish] bankers sitting in huge cars looking like English tanks in the rotting city streets, where Hungarian bureaucrats are faint with hunger, while their face is fat with satisfaction. . . . eating grapes in hotel bars and theatrical foyers with gold-ringed hands."[50] Cecile Tormay described a wartime incident. The scene was a lineup at a Jewish-owned grocery store in Budapest. Noting a Jew at the end of the line who was complaining loudly, Tormay pointed at him.

> The crowd approved, but failed to notice that the Semitic race was only to be found at the *two ends* of the queue, and that not a single representative of it could be seen as a buyer amongst the crowding, the poor and the starving. . . . This was symbolical, a condensed picture of Budapest. The sellers, the agitators were Jews. The buyers and the misguided were the people of the capital.[51]

The war, so it seemed to many Hungarians, had failed to touch the Jews: they had avoided serving on the front and they had withheld (by hoarding) necessary supplies for their own benefit and thus maintained their prewar standard of living . . . unless one spoke of the war as having improved their condition, as they lined their pockets through profiteering.

There were exceptions to this monolithic portrayal. Some Hungarians such as the Calvinist Bishop Dezso Baltazar of Debrecen spoke out against the mistreatment of the Jews: "Anti-Semitism is the creed of a declining society. The talent, diligence, tenacity, and selflessness of Hungarian Jewry are extraordinarily valuable to society. Those who turn against them are envious, hateful, and do it out of impotence."[52] Expressing his thoughts in terms of the value of the Jews, typically, there is no mention of genial feelings toward them; citing the Jews' "selflessness" is the closest Bishop Baltazar comes.

The litmus test of Jewish loyalty—how they would conduct themselves in war—Jews were accused of failing miserably. However, the Jews' perceived poor behavior in war was only the occasion for the accounting Hungarians were about to make with the Jews, not the chief provocation. Jews, as stated above, had failed to take advantage of the "civilizing force of Christianity" (a more eloquent, and by Christian lights, a more accurate way of saying that the Jews had failed to reform). Whether this meant outright conversion or something short of this depended on who was expressing this sentiment. In any event, Jews *qua* Jews had infiltrated every dimension of society, to its detriment. A race, a caste, a nation, Jews were a state within a state; and by favoring their coreligionists they had furthered their own economic interests rather than the nation's.

If postwar legislation would try to pull the Jews back from their positions of dominance, the lawless atmosphere under which a lost war was coming to a close allowed Hungarians to proceed in an unrestricted fashion to vent their hatred towards the Jews.

Red Terror and White Terror

With the end of the war imminent, the government disintegrated, and the vacuum was filled by a short-lived liberal-socialist coalition under Sandor Wekerle, which gave way, on 31 October 1918, to the October Revolution. Count Mihaly Karolyi became Prime Minister, and a month later, Hungary was declared an independent republic. When Tormay expressed her outrage at the large numbers of Jews who participated in the October Revolution, she spoke of "eleven Jews and eight bad Hungarians,"[53] thus making it clear, that in her view, Jews had never been Hungarians, and also, by not describing them as "bad", one could not have expected anything different from them.

Karolyi called this takeover a bloodless revolution, which may have been true in Budapest, but in the countryside, pent-up feelings towards the Jews were released over the next two weeks. In Totkomlos, 1 November 1918, the mob set upon the rabbi's house and then killed the cantor and looted his house. Engineer Sandor Erdos, his wife, and child all disappeared without a trace. Illes W. Schwarz, a seventy-five year old Jew, was killed in front of his home. The remaining eight families were given written orders to leave within twenty-four hours. All the Jewish homes were looted, down to the pillows. The Jews of Nagyszombat and neighboring area suffered damages exceeding one hundred million crowns. In the surrounding villages, houses of Jewish landowners were burned down, cattle taken away and killed, and Jewish stores plundered. In Kisracs, stolen goods were immediately sold at the village market, and in Nagykallo, not only were all the stores looted but all the Jews' money taken as well. Altogether, 6,206 families were said to have been affected, and the Ministry of the Interior estimated damages at one billion crowns.[54]

Karolyi's government felt unable to accede to the Peace Conference's repeated demands to evacuate further territories and to establish a neutral zone between the Hungarian and the Romanian forces, and so it, too, fell. This crisis provoked a hasty agreement between the Socialists and the Communists who stepped into the breach and established a coalition government, with the Communists as the dominating force. Almost immediately, the leader of the Communists, Bela Kun, declared Hungary a Soviet Republic (Dictatorship of the Proletariat). Much to Tormay's surprise, this declaration was actually quite popular among Hungarians, for in the last year of the war, "embittered soldiers at the front talked of pogroms [against the Jews] 'when the war was over;'" "The people were preparing for the final reckoning and the fist of the people slowly horrifyingly rose over the guilty ones." But instead of striking out at "the Galician immigrants, profiteers, usurers," they had turned against "the Hungarian manors and castles, against the Hungarian authorities." This change in targets could only have come about because of the Jews, wrote Tormay.[55]

However, this support was short-lived. The radical nature of the Communist program quickly caused an uproar throughout the country. Spearheading the Republic was Bela Kun, a Jew (the effective leader of the government, his official title was the People's Commissar [Minister] for Foreign Affairs), as were eighteen out of the twenty-nine members of the Revolutionary Ruling Council, and thirty-two out of the forty-five Commissars (who were either Jewish or of Jewish extraction). In addition to this executive group must be added Jews in positions of authority at the county level and members of allied political groups.[56] Therefore, to someone like Endre Bajcsy-Zsilinszky, the term 'communist' would not have captured the essence of this new government. Rather, it was a 'Jewish' government: with the dissolution of the Hungarian State, "power falls into the lap of the Jews."[57]

The reproach by the Synod of Bishops was emblematic of the feeling throughout the country: "The terrible rampaging of Bolshevism has shocked the public conscience and aroused recognition of Christian self-value."[58] As it appeared to many Hungarians in 1919, Jews

> steal over the Russian border into the heart of Europe and join with those whose features resemble theirs. And there are such in Paris, in London, and in New York too. . . . In Russia, Trotski-Bronstein, Krassin-Goldgelb, Litvinoff-Finkelstein, Radek, and Joffe are all-powerful. In Munich, Kurt Eisner is the master and president of the Republic. In Berlin, Beerfeld is at the head of the Soldiers' Council and Hirsch at the Workmens'. In Vienna, the power is in the hands of Renner, Adler, Deutsch, and Bauer. And in Budapest. . . .
> . . . Is this all accidental?[59]

Time and again the Jewish community countered these accusations in a defense framed by proclamations of allegiance to the Hungarian homeland on the one hand, and protestations that Judaism was a religion, not a nationality, on the other, as if the source for the hatred of the Jews lay in the misunderstanding that Jews were a nation; if this point could be cleared up, the hatred would recede.[60]

> Jewry for 2,000 years is only a religion, not a nation or a nationality. This ancient religious stand was the stand of the National Rabbinical Seminary, and is still so today. We profess, and do profess, that Hungarian Jewry is an organic part of the Hungarian nation; it has been and shall remain. The Hungarian Jews, besides preserving their religion, are the sons of the Hungarian nation. We shall continue our work in this spirit, to the betterment of our denomination and of our country.[61]

Such protestations had no affect on most Hungarians who held the Jews in large measure responsible for bringing about a reign of Red Terror: an extreme and brutal regime that was in the process of overturning every institution held dear to one segment or another of the population. However, anti-Jewish sentiment was not only aroused by the 'Jewish' Communist regime; it was rife, as a comment by Kun makes clear: "How can the Red Army fight, how can the Red Army have morale, when here, in the Congress of Councils and in the Congress of the Party, incitement to anti-Semitism and agitation for pogroms is going on?"[62]

After only four months in power, Bela Kun fled to Vienna on 1 August 1919. An unsuccessful military campaign against the Romanians which was followed by the Romanians' march into Budapest was only the immediate cause for the demise of the Soviet Republic of Hungary, not the overarching one. The next few months were chaotic, characterized by governance that was ephemeral, negotiations with the Allies, and the onset of the White Terror.[63] Immediately after the end of Communist rule, military units attached to the command of officers of the Hungarian National Army organized and carried out a purge of Communists and Communist sympathizers and performed acts of retaliation against those who had committed crimes in the name of the Dictatorship of the Proletariat. Jews, having played the dominant role in the Communist revolution, were targeted in the purges.

"It is believed that he [Prime Minister Istvan Friedrich] proposes to start a reign of white terror which will make Bela Kun's red terror look like a billy goat by the side of an elephant,"[64] wrote Major General H. H. Bandholtz, the American member of the inter-allied military mission to Hungary. So fearful was Bandholtz about the animosity towards Jews in Hungary that he sent a communique to forestall the arrival of a Jewish officer, Colonel Nathan Horowitz.

> In writing to General Bliss about the matter, I explained to him that although all Bolshevists were not Jews nor were all Jews Bolshevists, nevertheless Bela Kun, the Hungarian Bolshevist leader, practically all his lieutenants, and most of his followers were Jews, and as a result the people of Hungary were simply furious and determined to rid themselves of the Semitic influence.[65]

The unprecedented degree of the antagonism towards the Jewish population was reflected in the uncharacteristic ways Jews reacted. Jewish youth formed a self-defense commando unit against street attacks in the Jewish quarter.[66] Under financier Jeno Polnai, the National League of Hungarian Jews was formed to seek intercession from the western military missions and work with the government to reduce hostilities.[67] One hundred thousand Jews—forty per cent of Budapest's Jewish population—reached out directly to the Peace Conference with a petition; so unbearable had their lives become, they would prefer occupation under the Romanian troops.[68] Those Jews who believed that the situation had irretrievably deteriorated set out on a fourth course: "An epidemic of conversions started;" "*Echt judisch* [truly Jewish]," exclaimed Bishop Prohaszka, at the sight of the long lineups for conversion. From the twenty-seven baronial Jewish families, twenty-three people converted in just a few days. And not only the ennobled felt the need to take this step: in Budapest alone, more than 10,000 Jews converted.[69]

"Reports from western Hungary indicate all kinds of atrocities on the part of the Hungarians who are torturing and butchering the Jews, and having their will on the population," wrote Bandholtz.[70] While they were not committed by clergymen, there were chaplains with the murder detachments,[71] and it was reported that they often gave their blessings to these acts.[72] Aggression—or retribution—was on the whole much more severe in the countryside: executions, hangings, quarterings, and the rounding-up of Jews occurred almost without exception in every town.[73]

But the cities were by no means exempt. In carrying out Regent Admiral Horthy's promise to punish the 'sinful city,' there were organized pogroms, special courts ordering imprisonment or execution, and specially constructed internment camps in Budapest.[74] Randomly organized groups attacked Jewish students and professors in the city; four hundred Jews were hospitalized in the first week.[75] The Entente delegate, Sir George Russel Clerk expressed his surprise at the anti-Semitic posters (issued under the direction of Istvan Haller, then

Minister of Propaganda) displayed everywhere in the city, portraying Jewish caricatures that could easily incite pogroms.[76] The newspaper *Uj Nemzedek* concurred with Prohaszka that Hungary must get rid of its Jews and wished that the White Terrorists would come to Budapest to continue their murders there.[77]

> Budapest, this culturally nouveau riche city has a patch of shame. . . . In the center of the city winds many streets drowning in dirt . . . Those foreign diplomatic missions who believe that the wild, uncultured, and uncouth Hungary and the artificially resuscitated intolerance that manifests itself in the upset against the Galicianers . . . should be led to these streets to see what kind of life is going on here . . . [The article then goes on to say that although the streets are very busy, it is not real traffic, because the "dirty Orthodox" are simply doing 'chain' deals, gradually making profit on all kind of commodities, making large profits as the commodity makes its way along the chain and thus artificially driving up the price of everything.] . . . There are no workshops here, only coffeehouses, where everything is bought and sold. It is easy to see that people live much better here than in a working class district, where the traffic is the milling of the unemployed . . . They spend an awful lot on expensive food, but do no intellectual or physical work; so they must make their money on deals.[78]

In an earlier article, the newspaper *Nemzeti ujsag* had explained that the atrocities were in retaliation for "the revolution of the assassins [that] was born from the marriage of war neurosis with Galician Jewish blood."[79] To future Prime Minister Count Pal Teleki, the basis for the terror lay in the Jewish Question itself.

> I believe, along with the many strata of Hungarians who contend that those Jews who feel with us, whose family has lived on this land for a long time, who recognize that this Hungary can only stand on the basis of the Hungarian national ideal and Hungarian Christian morality, and are pursuing their happiness within this framework, and want to cooperate with us conscientiously in the flourishing of this country, to those, the Jewish Question does not pertain. They cannot receive aggression from us—but only them—because those who do not make these principles unconditionally their own cannot be a true Hungarian, cannot be a sincere citizen of Hungary.[80]

Those instrumental in orchestrating the White Terror were known as the 'Men of Szeged'[81] and included the military—specifically Imperial and Royal officers who were still active (*Kaiserlich und Koniglich—K und K*); members of the bureaucracy and administration; refugees from the newly-formed successor states who had formerly been public servants; university graduates; and the clergy.[82] Their leitmotif, the "Thought of Szeged" [*Szegedi Gondolat*], crystallized as the Christian National Course,* which Prohaszka described as a

---

* Nicholas M. Nagy-Talavera, *The Green Shirts and the Others: A History of Fascism in Hungary and Rumania* (Stanford, Calif.: Hoover Institution Press / Stanford University, 1970), 96. Nationalism also had strong overtones of revanchism after the war. Hungary's defeat meant a loss of two-thirds of its territory, and reconstituting the original borders of the country was a primary goal of virtually all Hungarians.

protest against that economic and intellectual order that wanted to strip the nation of its Christianity as well as its racial feelings; that falsified and suppressed the national genius in the age of dumb liberalism and sleights of hand; that wanted to give a deathly blow to Christian national culture, and after it exploded the military and broke the Hungarians' sword, the national emblem — it ruined Hungary and under the knives of *schochets* wanted to drown Hungarians in blood. . . . This truth must not be forgotten . . . this is not hatred but love, love for oneself and love for one's race.[83]

Prohaszka summarized what he and others wanted in three points: to prevent the breakdown of Christian society, to prevent the Judaization of Hungary, and to help the well-intentioned and nationalist Jews to unite with the national Christian society. He then asked, "Why does this make us anti-Semites? How else can the Hungarian Christian nation preserve its hegemony? This is Hungarism—national self-defense—not denominational strife, and legality is of lesser importance than saving Christian Hungary."[84]

The coordinating body of the 'Men of Szeged' was the Hungarian Social Alliance *[Tarsadalmi Egyesuletek Szovetsege—T.E.Sz.]*, comprised of both public sections and covert subdivisions that swelled to some 10,000 associations of every description after the counterrevolution. They were formed as a response to the lack of government action in the defense of Hungary—within its borders and internationally. Beyond this, historian C. A. Macartney calculates that between 1919 and 1922, 212 'public' patriotic organizations were founded.[85] One of these was The Association of Hungarian Defense [*Magyar Orszagos Vedero Egyesulet—M.O.V.E.*], founded and led by Gyula Gombos, who would be elected Prime Minister in 1932.[86]

The most popular group within *M.O.V.E.* was the Association of Awakening Hungarians [*Ebredo Magyarok Egyesulete—E.M.E.*]. In the earliest days of the Counterrevolution, its leadership was mostly composed of key military figures and representatives of the National Assembly.[87] Its membership was drawn from the middle class, students, and former army officers and swelled to an estimated 80,000 in only a matter of months.[88] The stated goal of the Awakening Hungarians was the reinstitution of "the reign of pure Christian morals and national feeling throughout the country and the extermination of those destructive doctrines spread by the Jews."[89] Running counter to the Church's view that baptism removed Jewishness, they proclaimed:

> The Jew may be christened a thousand times; he can never strip off his Semite race. If he remains a good Jew, he may be respected for not having left the faith of his ancestors, but we do not see why we should regard him as our equal and brother from the moment he changes his Israelite confession for the Christian Church.[90]

Domestically, the policy of the Awakening Hungarians sought to curtail Jewish involvement in the supply of consumer necessities and to regulate the Jewish population numerically and occupationally "in accordance with their relative weight" in an attempt to minimize their cosmopolitanism which was destroying all sense of nationality and was a result of their "destructive and immoral heritage."[91] It also claimed all of Christendom in their mandate: "Anti-Semitism in Hungary means the protection of Christianity against progressing Judaism and does not aim only at local circumstances, sad as they may be—but embraces the interests of all Christendom in every part of Europe and of the world, where Christian civilization is, or should be established!"[92]

Seesawing between general outrage and specific demands, thousands upon thousands of Hungarians funneled their dissatisfaction into membership in one of the countless associations that sprang up in the immediate postwar, post-Kun period. The speed with which these associations were established is striking, given the general chaos at the end of the war and the politically divided state of the country for a year after. They were far from being extremist in the sense of being marginal: many parliamentarians were members of these organizations, making the Government to some degree an armchair participant in the outpouring against the Jews. In fact, government members suspected of being less than 'one hundred per cent Hungarian' found themselves unable to secure or maintain posts. Contributing to the defeat of Count Istvan Bethlen in a 1920 by-election were accusations made by the *E.M.E.* candidate that Bethlen was un-Hungarian, un-Christian, a friend of the Jews, and of Jewish origin—Bethlen being an abbreviation of the Jewish name Bettelheim. Prime Minister Sandor Simonyi-Semadam (15 March 1920-19 July 1920) received a letter from Count Albert Apponyi, the chief Hungarian negotiator at the Paris Peace Conference, calling the Prime Minister's attention to the fact that persecution of the Jews was not in the interest of the country and that if it continued, he could not be held responsible for the possible failure of the negotiations. Conveying Apponyi's warning to the National Assembly was sufficient to compromise Simonyi-Semadam's status as a patriotic Hungarian. The object of catcalls, he lost the confidence of the House shortly thereafter and had to resign.[93]

Culling the literature for statements made by MPs, one finds MP Father Gyula Zakany attacking the Jews at a mass meeting of the Awakening Hungarians.[94] Corroboration and expansion of this event come from Bandholtz's diary.

> A Mrs. French, from California, who is over here on some sort of suffrage proposition, was in to tell me about a meeting that took place in Budapest, and, if all her statements are true, there is still a wild-eyed bunch of fanatics who will have to be skinned alive before much progress is made in Hungary. She said that a Catholic priest, at a public meeting on the thirtieth of November [1919] said: 'The Bible tells us we must forgive our enemies as Christians, but not as Hungarians. Hungarian people must never forget and the Jews must be punished. They say it is shameful to have pogroms, but we say it is just as shameful to have communism in the twentieth century, and we had it.' [sic] The second speaker, a professor by the name of Zakany said: 'The Jewish Question is a national one for the Hungarian people to settle and we will settle it.'[95]

MP Count Gyula Andrassy published a book in which he suggested the Jews' exclusion from the economy, while in the National Assembly he said the Jewish race must be limited and reduced.[96] Addressing the same body, MP Laszlo

Budavary made an all-encompassing speech against the "Christian-murdering liberal freemason Bolshevik Jewry:" they had not participated in the war sacrifices; they had forced the emigration of several hundred thousand Hungarians to America; it was their fault that there was no land for distribution; and those in the successor states had repudiated their Hungarianness.[97]

As had been done forty years before by the *Fuggetlenseg*, MP Bela Daner took the converted Jew, Karoly Csemegi (prominent member of the Supreme Court in the nineteenth century) to task. In his book, he argued that Csemegi had been overly harsh when prescribing sentences for physical assault and conversely, too lenient in cases related to cheating; since Jews are not violent, the exaggerated punishment for physical assault was a burden on the strong and *volkish* Hungarians. Daner also launched a concerted attack on MP Vilmos Vazsonyi: he was not a "Hungarian type," had not "even one Hungarian trait," and "not one drop of Hungarian blood in his veins."[98] Daner was eventually tried for his statements. In his defense, his lawyer presented data about the increasing progress of the 'Jewish conquest' that ultimately led to Daner's acquittal.

There was no perceptible difference in the position held by most MPs and those at the top level of government. Pal Teleki, when he assumed the prime ministership in July 1920, described Jews as "untrustworthy" in his first speech to the National Assembly; he then excluded them from the military.[99] When Istvan Bethlen assumed power in April 1921, he stated in his program that he wanted to make the country great—without Jews.[100] Minister of Defense, Istvan Friedrich, declared: "We cannot tolerate an alien race, under the disguise of various slogans, in foreign alliance, wanting to rule us. A Jewish International is facing us; we must set a Christian International against it. It is stunning that when a couple of Jews are hanged for their communist prejudices, the entire 'abroad' wants to save them."[101]

"The political union of Christians" (Catholics together with Protestants) which resulted in the creation of the Christian Socialist Party was viewed as an important step by the Catholic Church.[102] Bandholtz, judging by the great number of telegrams he had received "from the so-called Christian Socialists" thought they should more "properly [be] called Anti-Jews, because most of their petitions are devoted to a tirade against their Semitic fellow countrymen."[103] In conjunction with this party, a professional organization called the United Christian League was established (as the Catholic People's Party had also done twenty-five years before), electing as its first president, Pal Teleki.[104] It should be clear by now that the moniker 'Christian' attached to political parties—Christian National Party, Christian National Unity Party, Christian Socialist Party—as well as organizations and ideologies, had become a primary form of denotation. Hungarians tended to privilege Christianness over other factors when considering aspects of Hungarianness. The purpose of this moniker was twofold: to distinguish themselves from Jews and, by doing so, to show their opposition to Jews.

While not compromising its position towards the Jews, the newly appointed Teleki government[105] announced its intention on 19 July 1920 to curb the excesses being perpetrated against them. Its efforts—dissolving the Association of Awakening Hungarians with the help of the armed forces; breaking up the special commandos stationed in Budapest; and the decision to strike a parliamentary committee to resolve the Jewish Question—slowly brought an end to the depredations. A return to the rule of law replaced aggression with legislation.

Law 1920. XXV – The *Numerus Clausus*

If Prime Minister Teleki had been able only with difficulty to control the perpetration of violence against the Jews, he proved much more successful in curbing the perceived excesses of the Jews. This came in the form of Law 1920. XXV, known as the *Numerus Clausus* (22 September 1920). Its purpose was to establish proportional representation according to race and nationality in institutions of higher learning. And it was considered necessary because, as Endre Bajcsy-Zsilinszky stated, "even if Jews were completely melding into Hungarians," "it is disproportionate to have five per cent of the population rule over the most important institutions."[106]

The National Assembly started to discuss this proposition in the fall of 1919 due to a report generated by professors at the Medical University and endorsed by the faculties of law and philosophy shortly thereafter.[107] The report called for a ceiling on the number of students attending university and, within that, the establishment of quotas. However, Jews were not specifically referred to in this report.[108] Simultaneously, a file entitled "How to Prevent the Israelites from Applying for Writing Examinations" (a prerequisite before registration) was lodged with the Ministry of Culture; two student organizations, the *Turul* [Student Union] and the *MEFHOSZ* [Hungarian University and High School Students Countrywide Union][109] were lobbying for a change in admission standards; and spontaneous fights were breaking out in all the universities as Christian students tried to prevent Jewish students from enrolling.[110] (They were, in fact, successful: Jewish students were kept out during the 1919-20 academic year.[111])

These agitations were not only tolerated by the leadership of Pazmany Peter University in Budapest but also explicitly supported on occasion, despite the fact that several Jewish students lost their hearing or eyesight during these incidents. The dean of the medical school, Janos Barsony, exhorted his students not to give up on the *Numerus Clausus*.[112] "Wherever the priests are exterminated, the intelligentsia slaughtered, there you find the Jew," Jozsef Trikal, a Catholic priest and philosophy professor at the divinity school of Pazmany Peter University informed his students. The speech by divinity school dean Mihaly Kmosko against the Jewish press was so inflammatory that it led to a student riot, following which the students rushed over to the *Az Est* newspaper building and demolished it.[113]

"Does the Hungarian government know that every social class of the Christian Hungarian homeland desires with enormous force the regulation of the Jewish Question via legislation? Is the government going to table the legislation in this year?" demanded MP Balazs Szabo in an interpellation.[114] The debates did progress, and in the effort to resolve the Jewish Question, the Jews were subjected to the same scrutiny the Enlightenment thinkers had placed them under—with one obvious difference. Rather than scrutinizing Jews with a view to emancipating them, the postwar critique was made with a view to curtailing their influence in society. In both cases though, the current condition of the Jews informed the next step to be taken.

There were also some who demanded *numerus nullus*: complete exclusion in certain spheres. MP Karoly Ereky demanded its introduction for the distributors of restricted commodities (flour and copper sulfate[115]) because, he said, they were being administered for the most part by non-Christian officials.[116] Friedrich, Minister of Defense, demanded that distribution of newsprint among newspapers be "in accordance with numerical proportions of nationalities living in the country."[117] (The estimates of Jewish control of the press ranged from fifty to eighty-five per cent, depending on the region.) MP Rezso Rupert suggested turning movie theater licenses into a state monopoly and using the proceeds to support war victims; Prime Minister Teleki favored direct redistribution instead. Intended to "Change the Guard," his order #8454/1920 M.E. withdrew all movie house licenses and granted them to Christians who appeared to be reliable entrepreneurs.[118] (The vast majority of these licenses had been held by Jews.) All wine-selling licenses were revoked and distributed to those who had been handicapped in the war. (This was another occupation in which Jews were heavily involved.) Permits to open small shops such as those that sold tobacco were now reserved for ministerial and military bureaucrats. There was also a ruling concerning other shops: proof first had to be given that one's father had been born in Hungary.[119] The decision to exclude Jews from the Ludovika Military Academy actually was in line with Teleki's desire to eliminate Jews from the military. The remaining 1.6 per cent still attached to the military were, according to Erno Laszlo, working in the general accounting and general economic departments within the army, gendarmerie, revenue, customs guards, and the police, and only remained until suitable replacements could be found.[120] Finally, MP Budavary submitted a ten-point proposition which met enough of the demands concerning the Jews but which he felt would avoid pogroms. His ten-point proposition did not progress very far in the Assembly. However, it closely resembled the Hungarian (and German) Jewish Laws that would be passed in the 1930s.[121]

Only the method to implement proportional representation at universities was in question. While MP Ereky said he personally condemned violence, he was sure that if there was any protest against the bill it would be "followed not only by a slap in the face, but the Jews will be murdered in Hungary."[122] However, MP Gyorgy Szmrecsanyi, along with the *Turul* (which demanded "numerus clausus in the banks, factories, even the streetcar conductors, as well as in academe"[123]), wanted to achieve *numerus clausus* through institutional legislation, not clubs and pogroms.[124]

When Minister of Religion and Education Istvan Haller first presented the *Numerus Clausus* bill on 22 July 1920, he coupled the end of liberalism with the passing of measures against the Jews.

With the *Numerus Clausus* bill, the spirit of liberalism ceases to exist. It is certain that we have not been preceded by anyone else in such legislation. But it is also certain that if any nation in the world would fall into the situation into which we have fallen, that a high percentage of the intelligentsia raised in the institutions of the Hungarian state attempted to strip the nation of its noble character, then other nations will follow us.[125]

"If we limit the overall enrolment, then it is very natural that it will affect the strongest coefficient of overproduction—the Jews."[126]

MPs Gombos, Milotay, and Prohaszka took issue with Haller's formulation and suggested an amendment, which was seconded by seventy-five other MPs (over one-third of the parliamentarians). It recommended that enrolment be circumscribed by proportional representation according to *race and religion*. However, at the suggestion of Nandor Bernolak and several other MPs, the final bill was formulated as follows: enrolment was to be based on proportional representation according to *race and nationality*.[127] According to Maria M. Kovacs, the most satisfactory explanation for the final version in which "nationality" was substituted for "religion" is to be found in a government submission to the League of Nations in 1925, at the time the *Numerus Clausus* was being challenged.

In the case of the Jews, race, religion, and nationality are mixed and take a different form in every country . . . this law discussed here intentionally avoids any reference to a religious minority, because religion is such a thing that is under the influence of the person, since the person can change religion any time. Therefore, religion is not suitable to define a minority in such a way as to exclude the possibility of abuse.[128]

Two-thirds of the MPs were absent from the House when the *Numerus Clausus* was voted upon, 22 September 1920. Of the sixty-two members present, seven opposed it.[129] The enacting clause applied proportionality to university enrolment and stipulated the rates of each race and nationality based on statistical calculations: Jews were limited to six per cent. Two other clauses demanded loyalty of a national and moral nature; however, those who were already enrolled were exempt from this provision.[130]

Not only are the reasons for implementing the *Numerus Clausus* relevant to this discussion—which are best summed up by Bajcsy-Zsilinszky, that "even if Jews were completely melding into Hungarians," "it is disproportionate to have five per cent of the population rule over the most important institutions"—but also the grounds on which some objected to the law. These are to be found in Pal Bethlen's book, *Numerus Clausus* (1925) that assembled the views of prestigious Hungarians who had been opposed to it. Most frequently mentioned were religious reasons and the feeling that the *Numerus Clausus* was unpatriotic. Often the two were conjoined: "As a Christian and a patriot it is un-Hungarian and inhuman and un-Christian."[131] Beyond this, a major theme was that this law was detrimental to the image of the country: "Politically, the question is whether we pay attention to public opinion abroad."[132] And more specifically, "We have to be accepted as the leaders in Eastern Europe, therefore we should stick to the strict legality."[133] The theme of competitiveness also preoccupied many contributors. Arguing for the importance of competition, many felt that it would be eliminated through the *Numerus Clausus*: "I would be ashamed as a lawyer and politician if I attained a high level only because other races more talented have been banned." Another argued that the state did have the right to diminish rights, but that the issue of competition would not be resolved through such a measure. This contributor pointed out, as did others, that if rich Jews were sent away to study they would be even "more valuable," having received a foreign education.[134] As for the poor Jews, this situation of adversity would strengthen their resolve to attain a higher level of education: "Jews have in their cells a desire to learn," and they will conquer.[135] Only one expressed the view that while he was against exclusion on a denominational basis, it would be an economic catastrophe to have "an overproduction of intellectuals;" however, he did not want to deal with this issue now, but later.[136] The argument that advancement gained through rioting and joining paramilitary organizations set a bad example for youth was put forward by Karoly Peyer, leader of the Social Democrats, for in the end, "People will choose an architect not according to how he wears his military cap, but the expert trained in Zurich."[137]

Among the contributors to Bethlen's book, some voted for the *Numerus Clausus* contrary to their personal convictions. One of them admitted that he "voted for the *Numerus Clausus* because I wanted to satisfy the demands of an enthusiastic outcry."[138] As Peyer noted, "Even within the Christian community, then, being on the politically correct side promotes their rank" and was of more importance.[139] Another contributor was not so much opposed to the law as he was philosophical about it: it was the "outgrowth of the chaos of the war, and is one among many superstitions, so it will disappear."[140]

In this book, which collected the views of those who were opposed to the *Numerus Clausus*, should one also have expected to find evidence of the acceptance of Jews or mention of their successful assimilation? In any case, none of their objections was informed by such sentiments. Rather, it was the moral high ground and pragmatism that shared first place in their considerations.

****

A story was circulating among Jews in the Budapest coffeehouses sometime after the war. In a lawsuit brought by a Jew against a Gentile, the Jew was asked by the judge if he had anything to say when the hearing was over. "Yes, your Honor," answered the plaintiff. "I beg your Honor to pass a prewar sentence instead of a postwar one." "What do you mean?" asked the judge. "Well," replied the plaintiff, "before the war, the judge used to say that though the plaintiff was a Jew, he was right. Now the judge says, 'Maybe the plaintiff is right, but he's a Jew.'" In liberal Hungary, in spite of the dislike of Jews, Rustem Vambery explains, when liberalism was dominant, Jews enjoyed equal rights.[141]

Not all historians agree with Vambery's assessment that liberalism played the key role in sustaining Jewish rights. Some, like Mendelsohn (above), see the change in any one of a number of conditions as the possible source for the deterioration in the relations between Christians and Jews. Others have made use of the scapegoat theory, viewing the tumultuous period in Hungary between 1914 and 1920 as the catalyst for the souring of relations. However, it would be a mistake to underestimate the prophylactic quality of liberalism, which stressed the ethos of universal equality over and above the special obligations upon the Jews to reform. Although, all the while, liberals did hope, and even believed that Jews living in a liberal environment would naturally assimilate and become Hungarians. But this had not happened, as long-time liberal, scholar, writer, and politician Count Gyula Andrassy pointed out. Consequently, according to Andrassy, the Jewish Question had yet to be solved.[142] It was Andrassy's father who, as Prime Minister in 1867, had signed the bill of emancipation. Andrassy himself had been a mainstay of the Liberal Party for decades, then proceeded to modify some of his views early in the 1900s, and by 1921, had not only accepted the presidency of the Christian National Unity Party but also joined former Prime Minister Istvan Friedrich's Christian National Party. "Of slogans such as liberalism, culture, the west, and civilization—we are by now horribly disillusioned," pronounced writer Ferenc Herczeg in his toast at the banquet of the Hungarian Authors' Association, 4 February 1920. To which the association's president, eminent author Dezso Szabo, added: "An honest Hungarian cannot be liberal; we are going to teach every Hungarian to hate."[143] Far from being ironic, this shows the historic progression of liberalism in Hungary, both in general and *vis a vis* the Jews. For some, as in Andrassy's case, this took them right out of the liberal camp.

Since, as Dr. Geza Lencz had written, "The link tying Protestants and Jews together is liberalism" (equally applicable to a certain number of Catholics),[144] it was axiomatic that the abandonment of liberalism would have implications for the Jews. Because their relationship had been based on the sharing of liberal values and *not* on the assimilation of the Jews into the Hungarian nation, this meant, of course, that when the liberal era was over, there was nothing tying these two groups together.

NOTES

1. "A zsidokerdes Magyarorszagon," *Huszadik Szazad*, 2 (1917). The entire issue was devoted to the responses to the questionnaire.
2. Appeal Court Justice Ede Alfoldi, "A zsidokerdes Magyarorszagon."
3. These included legal scholar Dr. Gyozo Concha, journalist and author Laszlo Lakatos, Hungarian Reformed minister (and later Bishop of the Calvinist Church as well as professor of theology) Dr. Laszlo Ravasz, Catholic priest and Christian Socialist MP Dr. Sandor Giesswein, former cabinet minister Endre Gyorgy, author Lajos Hatvany and Agoston himself. "A zsidokerdes Magyarorszagon."
4. Tamas Kobor, "A zsido kerdesrol," [On the Jewish Question] *Mult es Jovo* (Budapest, April 23, 1920): 7-8. Kobor was a journalist, political commentator, and novelist.
5. Istvan Lendvai, *A harmadik Magyarorszag—joslatok es tanulsagok* [The Third Hungary—Predictions and Conclusions] (Budapest: Pallas, 1921), 151. Lendvai was a prominent journalist, publicist, and poet who later joined the Christian National Party.
6. Author Zoltan Bosnyak, "A zsidokerdes Magyarorszagon."
7. Ottokar Prohaszka, quoted in Bosnyak, *Prohaszka*, 23-25.

8. Gyozo Concha, "A zsidokerdes Magyarorszagon."
9. Author Emma Ritook, "A zsidokerdes Magyarorszagon."
10. Painter Aladar Korosfoi-Kriesch, "A zsidokerdes Magyarorszagon."
11. Emma Ritook, "A zsidokerdes Magyarorszagon."
12. Istvan Lendvai, "Szep Erno, Patika es egyebek," [Erno Szep, Pharmacy, and Others] *Uj Nemzedek,* 21 March 1920; Lendvai, *A harmadik Magyarorszag,* 145-53.
13. Aladar Komlos [Almos Koral, pseud.], *Zsidok valaszuton* [Jews at Crossroads] (Eperjes, 1921), 12-13. Komlos was a literary historian, critic, journalist, and teacher.
14. President of the Hungarian Zionists Armin Beregi, "A zsidokerdes Magyarorszagon."
15. Bela Bangha S.J., "A zsidokerdes," [The Jewish Question] in *Magyarorszag ujjaepitese es a keresztenyseg* [The Rebuilding of Hungary and Christianity] (Budapest: Szent-Istvan Tarsulat, 1920), 160. Bangha was a Jesuit priest who frequently wrote in Catholic newspapers and journals, some of which he founded. He also edited significant religious works.
16. Editor of the *Alkotmany* Bela Turi, "A zsidokerdes Magyarorszagon."
17. Teacher and writer Marcell Benedek, "A zsidokerdes Magyarorszagon."
18. Secretary of the Steel Workers' Union Janos Vanczak, "A zsidokerdes Magyarorszagon."
19. Marcell Benedek, "A zsidokerdes Magyarorszagon."
20. Editor Gyorgy Boloni, editor of the *Alkotmany* Bela Turi, and Endre Gyorgy, "A zsidokerdes Magyarorszagon."
21. Cecile Tormay, *An Outlaw's Diary: Revolution* (Translator not named) (London: Philip Allan & Co., 1923), 1:229-30. Tormay was a founder of the Hungarian Women's Association and a well-known author.
22. Author Laszlo Boross, "A zsidokerdes Magyarorszagon."
23. Ede Alfoldi, "A zsidokerdes Magyarorszagon."
24. Agoston, *A zsidok utja,* 290-95.
25. MP Istvan Milotay, *Nemzetgyulesi beszed* [Speech in the National Assembly], 18 September 1920. Milotay was also a prominent writer and editor of the *Uj Nemzedek.*
26. Bangha, "A zsidokerdes," 158.
27. Agoston, *A zsidok utja,* 287-90, 309.
28. Bangha, "A zsidokerdes," 158.
29. Professor Dr. Jeno Cholnoky, "A zsidokerdes Magyarorszagon."
30. Agoston, *A zsidok utja,* 271, 279-80, 293-95, 278.
31. Agoston, *A zsidok utja,* 290-95.
32. Armin Beregi, "A zsidokerdes Magyarorszagon."
33. Founder of the National Statistical Office Elek Fenyes and Laszlo Lakatos, "A zsidokerdes Magyarorszagon."
34. Laszlo Boross and writer Gabor Olah, artist Anna Lesznai, Lajos Hatvany, and editor of the journal *Nyugat* 'Ignotus', "A zsidokerdes Magyarorszagon."
35. Lajos Hatvany, "A zsidokerdes Magyarorszagon."
36. Agoston, *A zsidok utja,* 290-92, 308.
37. Szabolcsi, *Ket emberolto,* 169, 172.
38. *Magyar-Zsido Szemle,* no. 32 (1915): 172.
39. Ottokar Prohaszka, "Pro juventate 'catholica,'" *Alkotmany,* 26 May 1918, 11.
40. Vilmos Vazsonyi's article protested against the use of Jews as scapegoats for the miseries of war and insisted on the maintenance of equal rights for the Jews. Implicating the government, he asked if it wanted "a Jewish Question along with all the other questions?" Quoted in Szabolcsi, *Ket emberolto,* 233.
41. Ottokar Prohaszka, "Pro juventate 'catholica,'" 11.

42. Szabolcsi, *Ket emberolto*, 191-93.
43. Jozsef Patai, quoted in Patai, *Jews of Hungary*, 450.
44. Szabolcsi, *Ket emberolto*, 227-29.
45. Szabolcsi, *Ket emberolto*, 227-38.
46. *The Jewish Question* by Sandor Martinovics, quoted in Szabolcsi, *Ket emberolto*, 231.
47. Szabolcsi, *Ket emberolto*, 233.
48. As of 1892, the currency in Hungary was stabilized: one American dollar was worth 4.935 crowns. Peter Hanak, *One Thousand Years: A Concise History of Hungary*, ed. Peter Hanak, trans. Zsuzsa Beres, trans. revised Christopher Sullivan (Budapest: Corvina, 1988), 147. Inflation during the war reduced the value of the crown, but this was still a great deal of money especially considering the extreme financial hardship most Hungarians on the home front were enduring.
49. Patai, *Jews of Hungary*, 456; Szabolcsi, *Ket emberolto*, 225.
50. Istvan Milotay, quoted in Mihaly Kolosvary-Borcsa, *A zsido kerdes magyarorszagi irodalma* [The Literature of the Jewish Question in Hungary] (Budapest: 1943), 59-60.
51. Tormay, *Outlaw's Diary*, 1:45.
52. Bishop Baltazar, quoted in Szabolcsi, *Ket emberolto*, 231.
53. Tormay, *Outlaw's Diary*, 1:7.
54. *100 eves a cionista mozgalom* [100 Years of the Zionist Movement] (Budapest, 1997), 65. The amount of one billion crowns was substantial. While inflation was ongoing throughout the war, hyperinflation only began in mid-1919. Laszlo Kontler, *A History of Hungary: Millennium in Central Europe* (Houndmills, Basingstoke, UK: Palgrave Macmillan, 2002), 350-51.
55. Tormay, *Outlaw's Diary*, 1:87-88.
56. Katzburg, *Hungary and the Jews*, 32, 34; Denis Sinor, *History of Hungary* (George Allen & Unwin Ltd, 1959), 284.
57. Endre Bajcsy-Zsilinszky, *Ujjaszuletes es sajto* [Rebirth and the Press] (Taltos, 1920), 71. Bajcsy-Zsilinszky was a writer, editor of *Szozat*, and a founder of *M.O.V.E.*
58. Jeno Gergely, ed., *A puspoki kar tanacskozasai: a magyar katolikus puspokok konferenciainak jegyzokonyveibol* [Debates of the Synod of Bishops: From the Protocols of the Conferences of Catholic Hungarian Bishops, 1919-1944], 74.
59. Tormay, *Outlaw's Diary*, 1:111.
60. Peter Ujvari, ed., *Magyar Zsido Lexicon* (Budapest, 1929), 200.
61. Declaration issued by the entire faculty of the National Rabbinical Seminary, 13 January 1919, quoted in Samu Stern, *A zsidokerdes Magyarorszagon* [The Jewish Question in Hungary] (Budapest: A Pesti Izraelite. Hitkoseg, 1938), 30.
62. Bela Kun, from the minutes of the National Session of Councils (21 June 1919), quoted in Gyurgyak, *A zsidokerdes Magyarorszagon*, 103.
63. Not until 16 November 1919 did the situation stabilize. On this date, the Counterrevolution under Commander Admiral Miklos Horthy succeeded in formally taking over.
64. Major General H. H. Bandholtz, *An Undiplomatic Diary by the American Member of the Inter-Allied Military Mission to Hungary, 1919-1920*, ed. Fritz-Konrad Kruger (New York: AMS Press, Inc., 1966), 49 (31st August 1919).
65. Bandholtz, *Undiplomatic Diary*, 86 (15 September 1919); 91 (17 September 1919).
66. Szabolcsi, *Ket emberolto*, 297.
67. Katzburg, *Hungary and the Jews*, 46-47.
68. Yehuda Don and Victor Karady, eds., *A Social and Economic History of Central*

European Jewry (New Brunswick, N.J.: Transaction Publishers, 1990), 148.

69. Prohaszka, quoted in Szabolcsi, *Ket emberolto*, 292. Katzburg's estimate of conversions is somewhat lower: 9,509 over the years 1919-1922. *Hungary and the Jews*, 26.

70. Bandholtz, *Undiplomatic Diary*, 102 (20 September 1919).

71. Bela Balazs, ed., *A klerikalis reakcio, a Horthy-fasizmus tamasza* [Clerical Reaction, the Pillar of Horthy Fascism] (Budapest, 1953), 37, 50.

72. Macartney, *History of Hungary*, 1:182.

73. Szabolcsi, *Ket emberolto*, 297.

74. Rothschild, *Central Europe*, 371; Gustav Gratz, *A forradalmak kora—Magyarorszag tortenete, 1918-1920* [The Age of Revolutions—The History of Hungary, 1918-1920] (1935; repr., Budapest: Magyar Szemle Tarsasag, 1992), 270; Bandholtz, *Undiplomatic Diary*, 49 (31 August 1919).

75. Gratz, *A forradalmak kora*, 270-71.

76. Szabolcsi, *Ket emberolto*, 294-95.

77. *Uj Nemzedek*, 12 October 1919, 18 December 1919.

78. "A Walk in the Ghetto of Pest," *Nemzeti Ujsag*, 9 December 1919, 7.

79. *Nemzeti Ujsag*, 28 November 1919.

80. Pal Teleki, *Grof Teleki Pal programbeszede* [Program Speech of Count Pal Teleki] (Szeged: Tevel Nyomda, 1919), 2. This was an excerpt from a speech delivered in the First Electoral District of Szeged on the occasion of the formation of the Christian National Unity Party. Teleki was a demographic and economic geographer, a member of the Academy of Sciences, and, by the way, Chief of the Boy Scouts of Hungary.

81. It was in Szeged that some politicians and the military had gathered to establish a counterrevolutionary force and overthrow the Communist government. They became known as the 'Men of Szeged.'

82. C. A. Macartney, *October Fifteenth: A History of Modern Hungary 1929-1945* (Edinburgh: Edinburgh University Press, 1961), 1:18, 50, 77.

83. Prohaszka, quoted in Bosnyak, *Prohaszka*, 18.

84. Prohaszka, quoted in Bosnyak, *Prohaszka*, 12, 13, 16.

85. Macartney, *October Fifteenth*, 1:30-31.

86. *M.O.V.E.* had both an official department and a secret division. It also maintained a military arm known as the Blood Alliance of the Double Cross [*Kettoskereszt Verszovetseg*]. Dezso Nemes, *Az ellenforradalom tortenete* [The History of Counterrevolution] (Budapest, 1962), 158.

87. After the war, a unicameral legislative body called the National Assembly replaced the former bicameral system. Katzburg, *Hungary and the Jews*, 45, 81.

88. Katzburg, *Hungary and the Jews*, 81, 45; Nagy-Talavera, *Green Shirts and the Others*, 50.

89. Ebredo Magyarok Egyesulese [Association of Awakening Hungarians], Preface to *Antiszemitizmus Magyarorszagon* [Antisemitism in Hungary] (Budapest, 1920). This booklet outlined the formal program of the Association.

90. Ebredo Magyarok Egyesulese, *Antiszemitizmus Magyarorszagon*, 15. In 1923, Gyula Gombos proposed that students who had converted to Christianity be reclassified as Jews, although this was not accepted. Peter Tibor Nagy, "A Numerus Clausus—hetvenot ev utan," [The Numerus Clausus—After Seventy-five Years] *Vilagossag* 36, no. 2 (1995): 72-80.

91. *Nemzeti Ujsag*, 12 December 1919.

92. Ebredo Magyarok Egyesulese, *Antiszemitizmus Magyarorszagon*, 20. Presenting the British and American representatives in Budapest with a copy of their pamphlet was a gesture in this direction as was the establishment of connections with right-wing movements in other countries. The Awakening Hungarians also took part in a conference in

Vienna (along with the Christian National League) that advocated anti-Semitic and Christian "world solidarity." In September 1925, they convened a World anti-Semitic Congress in Budapest. Katzburg, "Hungarian Antisemitism," 348, 342; Tibor Zinner, *Az ebredok fenykora 1919-1923* [The Golden Age of the Awakening Hungarians, 1919-1923] (Budapest: Akademiai Kiado, 1989), 114; Nagy-Talavera, *Green Shirts and the Others*, 72.

93. Szabolcsi, *Ket emberolto*, 300, 302.
94. *Nemzeti Ujsag*, 2 December 1919.
95. Bandholtz, *Undiplomatic Diary*, 257 (3 December 1919).
96. Szabolcsi, *Ket emberolto*, 335.
97. Nemzetgyulesi Naplo. IV. 7 August 1920, Session 80, 287. Orszaggyulesi iromanyok. III, 338-39. BFL Nb. 778/1945. Laszlo Budavary's case in the People's Court, 125; Laszlo Budavary, *Zold bolshevizmus* [Green Bolshevism] (Budapest, 1941), 39.
98. Bela Daner, *Penz es hatalom* [Money and Power] (Budapest: Pallas Reszvenytarsasag, 1921), 4-7; *Szozat*, 15 February 1925. Daner was a lawyer and then appointed a judge in 1913. An initiator and leader of the Awakening Hungarians, he later joined the Party of Race Protection. Between 1920 and 1922, he was a member of Parliament; afterwards, he opened his own law office.
99. Szabolcsi, *Ket emberolto*, 307. Regent Horthy instituted an action complementary to Teleki's. The *Vitez rend* [Order of Heroes] was an exclusively Christian paramilitary corps which pledged personal allegiance to Horthy. Nagy-Talavera, *Green Shirts and the Others*, 87.
100. Szabolcsi, *Ket emberolto*, 307.
101. Minister of Defense Istvan Friedrich, quoted in *Nemzeti Ujsag*, 3 January 1920, 3.
102. Gergely, *A puspoki*, 74.
103. Bandholtz, *Undiplomatic Diary*, 40 (27 August 1919).
104. Gergely, *A puspoki*, 74.
105. Pal Teleki was committed to a liberal democracy operating within a parliamentary system. But the current state of affairs rendered this commitment theoretical; practically speaking, a conservative democracy with 'liberal tendencies' was the path he pursued to achieve political consolidation and lawful rule. Kontler, *History of Hungary*, 345-46.
106. Bajcsy-Zsilinszky, *Ujjaszuletes*, 29-30, 48, 70-71, 75, 77.
107. Szegvari, *Numerus Clausus*, 95-96, 98, 100.
108. Maria M. Kovacs, "A numerus clausus es az orvosi antiszemitzmus a huszas evekben," [The Numerus Clausus and Medical Anti-Semitism in the Nineteen-Twenties] *Budapesti Negyed*, 8 (1995/2), http://www.bparchiv.hu/magyar/kiadvany/bpn/08/kovacs1.html
109. The basis of the *Turul* was the protection of Hungarian honor deemed innate in the Hungarian race; its goals were to propagate Christian morality, loyalty to the State, and the honor of camaraderie. The goals of the *MEFHOSZ* were similar but additionally they wanted to put the question, as it pertained to university students, on a scientific and practical basis. Szegvari, *Numerus Clausus*, 101, 94-95.
110. Katzburg, *Hungary and the Jews*, 60-61.
111. Szegvari, *Numerus Clausus*, 94. MP Gyula Zakany demanded a permanent state of *numerus nullus* with respects to certain university departments. Orszaggyulesi iromanyok I, no. 57, 381.
112. *Kereszteny magyar orvosbajttarsunk hiv a MONE* [Our Christian Hungarian Medical Comrade, the MONE is calling You] (Budapest, 1940), 4.
113. Jozsef Trikel, quoute in Robert Major, *25ev ellenforradalmi sajto 1919-1944* [Twenty-five Years of anti-Semitic Press 1919-1944] (Budapest: Cserepfalvil, 1945), 30.
114. Nemzetgyulesi Naplo. III, 212.
115. Since 1895, the grape crop, which was vital to the economy, had been sprayed

with copper sulphate in order to combat a fungus that was decimating it.

116. Orszaggyulesi iromanyok. I, no. 26, 281.

117. Orszaggyulesi iromanyok. I, no. 40, 264.

118. The examination folder of Roland Beszterczey-Jacobi, *TH V-79/932*, 63.

119. Pal Bethlen, ed., *Numerus Clausus* (Budapest: A Magyar Zsidosag Almanachja Konvykiadovallalata, 1925), 158-59.

120. Erno Laszlo, "A Demographic Overview, 1918-1945," *Hungarian Jewish Studies* 2 (1969): 137-82; Braham, *Politics of Genocide*, 30.

121. Budavary's Ten Points: 1) All lands in Jewish hands to be expropriated at the price paid for it originally, but not more than ten million crowns, including buildings, machinery, and equipment. All leases contracted with Jews are invalid. 2) Jews in Hungary are denied permission to settle; those who immigrated after 1914 to be expelled. 3) A Jew can maintain only one house. All other real estate is to be redeemed at the price paid at the time of construction. 4) In every school, office, public institution, factory, plant, and other enterprises, the *numerus clausus* must be introduced. There may be no Jewish schools. No Jew may be admitted to teacher's college. Movie theaters owned by Jews are to be expropriated. 5) Only Christians may be employed in state-run buildings and transportation. Sixty per cent of all shares to be given to Christian workers and other Christians. Neither Jewish craftsmen nor merchants may acquire raw materials. Jews cannot employ Christians for personal service. 6) No Jews may be among the three leading officers of a newspaper. 7) All state permits (tobacco, stamps, matches, alcohol etc.) to be revised and issued to Christians. 8) Jews cannot be leading civil servants. Jews cannot exercise civil rights. 9) All organizations not established on a nationalist platform are to be dissolved. 10) All those responsible for communism and the Treaty of Trianon, or who mock the Christian national feelings are to be punished by death. Nemzetgyulesi Naplo. IV. 7 August 1920, Session 80, 287. Orszaggyulesi iromanyok. III, 338-39. BFL Nb. 778/1945. Laszlo Budavary's case in the People's Court, 125.

122. Nemzetgyulesi Naplo. V, 463.

123. Quoted in Bela Zsolt, "A Zsido," [The Jew] in *A vegzetes toll* [The Fatal Pen], ed. Andras Bozoki (Budapest: 1992), 172.

124. Nemzetgyulesi Naplo III, 435.

125. Istvan Haller, quoted in Kovacs, "A numerus clausus."

126. Istvan Haller, quoted in Kovacs, "A numerus clausus;" Laszlo Gonda, *A zsidosag Magyarorszagon 1526-1945* [Jewry in Hungary 1526-1945] (Budapest: Szazadvega Kiado, 1992), 171-72.

127. Orszaggyulesi Jegyzokonyv. K2A XIV.1.61.

128. Government submission, quoted in Kovacs, "A numerus clausus."

129. Janos Pelle, *A gyulolet vetese: a zsidotorvenyek es a Magyar kozvelemeny 1938-1944* (Budapest: Europa Konyvkiado, 2001), 79.

130. Katzburg, *Hungary and the Jews*, 60-62. The reaction of the Hungarian Jews to the *Numerus Clausus* is effectively revealed through two communiques written by the *Alliance Israelite Universelle* during its efforts to challenge the legality of the *Numerus Clausus* at the League of Nations. "We note that the Hungarian Jews are courageously fighting for their rights and in their patriotic feelings protest against any foreign intervention. They expect remedies from their own government." After the trial's conclusion, another communique was issued by the *Alliance*: "Hungarian Jewry could have and possibly should have joined us in submitting a petition to the League of Nations about the *Numerus Clausus*. But no, Hungarian Jewry proved to be extremely proud and extremely patriotic in its behavior. They think the *Numerus Clausus* to be an internal matter, which they want to settle with their Christian compatriots and without any foreign intercession. . . . they expect to better enlighten Hungarian opinion in order to stop the injustice." Quoted in Szabolcsi, *Ket emberolto*, 365-66, 358.

131. MP Pal Hegymeghy-Kiss, MP Dr. Rezso Rupert, and Dr. Ivan Strauss, quoted in Bethlen, *Numerus Clausus*, 31, 40, 44.

132. MP Gyozo Drozdy, quoted in Bethlen, *Numerus Clausus*, 21-22.

133. MP Tivadar Batthyany, quoted in Bethlan, *Numerus Clausus*, 17-18, 32, 43, 15. Batthyany was a liberal in the Kossuth tradition. Others who concurred with him included Vice Minister Dr. Lajos Beck, Secretary of the Medical Association Humer Hultl, Baron Jozsef Szterenyi, and Count Albert Apponyi.

134. Dr. Marcel Baracs, Lutheran minister Lajos Duszik, and MP (and former minister) Dr. Vince Nagy, quoted in Bethlen, *Numerus Clausus*, 16-17, 23-25, 33.

135. Former minister Dr. Karoly Grecsak, Calvinist minister Beno Hay, and MP (and former minister) Karoly Ereky, quoted in Bethlen, *Numerus Clausus*, 29-30, 26.

136. Transdanubian Bishop of the Reformed Church Dr. Geza Antal, quoted in Bethlen, *Numerus Clausus*, 13-14.

137. Social Democrat leader Karoly Peyer, quoted in Bethlen, *Numerus Clausus*, 35-36.

138. Karoly Ereky and Karoly Peyer, quoted in Bethlen, *Numerus Clausus*, 26, 35-36.

139. Karoly Peyer, quoted in Bethlen, *Numerus Clausus*, 26.

140. Dr. Gyula Szavay, quoted in Bethlen, *Numerus Clausus*, 42.

141. Vambery, *Hungary—To Be or Not to Be*, 96.

142. Count Gyula Andrassy, "A zsidokerdesrol," [On the Jewish Question] *Uj Magyar Szemle* (Budapest, July 1920). "It is also the intelligentsia's task," he wrote, "that propaganda against the Jews be kept within the boundaries of fairness and wise foresight and not let hatred, which has undoubtedly spread, become the chief motif." Count Gyula Andrassy, *A magyar ertelmiseg feladatairol* [On the Hungarian Intellectuals' Tasks] (Budapest: Magyar Kultura, 1921), 3-13.

143. Ferenc Herczeg and Dezso Szabo quoted in Szabolcsi, *Ket emberolto*, 300.

144. Dr. Geza Lencz, "A zsidokerdes Magyarorszagon." Lencz was a Hungarian Reformed Church minister who taught theology at the Divinity School and was later rector of the University of Debrecen.

Conclusion

Circumscribing the life of the Jew both socially and politically during the era of Toleration had been a comprehensive set of laws regulating their relations with Christians. Laws of emancipation could alter only one aspect of these relations, a fact that the Enlightenment thinkers had been keenly aware of, leaving the 'real problem,' the fundamental and negative distinctiveness of the Jew unresolved. The reasonable solution, from the *philosophes*' point of view, had been for the Jews to carry out the Enlightenment ideals specific to the Jews, thereby eliminating this distinctiveness.

Kalman Mikszath was one of a small minority who considered Jewish efforts to assimilate successful only shortly after their emancipation, but even a cursory glance at this quote reveals how superficial his criteria were.

> There are no Jews in Szeged any more. There is only a separate traditional Hebrew religion and its followers. Jewish people speak and think of Jehovah's greatness in Hungarian. . . . Rabbis preach in the synagogue in Hungarian and quote Vorosmarty to support their points. Girls in love express their sorrow in Hungarian popular songs, and the portrait of the late rabbi in Jewish homes is covered with a cloth in the red, white, and green colors of the Hungarian flag. The younger generation in Szeged may even think of Jehovah as an old man wearing a Hungarian short coat with gold lace. (1879)[1]

By looking elsewhere, one may gain another impression of the Jews in Szeged. In Szeged, the Jews are assimilated, noted one paper, but few are altruistic or patriotic enough to participate in public affairs.[2] "Szeged has become a Jewish town," wrote the *Riado*. "All the cafes are full of Jews. The shopowners use tricky, catchy slogans like, 'You can get this watch free; you only have to pay for the gold.' Who owns the beautiful buildings? The Jews."[3]

Mikszath's 'assimilated' Jews had not carried out the prescribed reforms exhorted by Csernatony, Istoczy, Prohaszka, and others, and which they expected would 'emancipate' Jews from their inherited Jewishness. Instead, Jews practiced the art of 'self-definition', which allowed for the persistence of Jewish traits and practices. Under the rubric of reforming the Jewish religion, recommendations ran the gamut from changes in outward appearance to conversion. While carrying out some parts of this mandate, Jews also created their own version of 'religious assimilation.' In their application of such a concept, Jewish ladies planned a carnival ball before Lent, and Jewish men took time off from work for the Jewish holidays only to spend it at the museum rather than the synagogue.[4] Money was donated for the erection of a statue of St. Stephen.[5] Conversions were undertaken, but not out of sincerity; rather, they were for purposes of professional advancement. The *Evkonyv*, the yearbook of the Magyar Israelite Literary Society, pointed this out freely in 1908: "We can state boldly that today no Jew converts out of conviction any more." They are at times a necessity, the article continued, because "the emancipation law is incomplete. The State rewards converts. Anyone who seems perfectly unacceptable for a given office simply because he is a Jew is perfectly acceptable if he converts."[6] (This assertion was borne out in fact: of the new and substantial number of 'Jewish' MPs, an estimated three-quarters underwent baptism at some point. They then composed twenty-two per cent of parliamentarians in 1910, seventeen per cent beyond their proportion in the population.[7])

Neolog Jews* frequently determined that they were religiously assimilated by comparing themselves to the Galizianers; in comparison to them, they were religiously assimilated. In fact, many Jews arrived at a definition of assimilation through a series of contrasts between themselves and their Galizianer brethren. However, it was the opinion of the Christian public that these Jews also exhibited character traits that were sorely in need of reform and were manifested in their monopoly over the press and the economy; accumulation of great amounts of wealth; ownership of large tracts of land; disproportionate representation in the free professions; appropriation of the cultural arena—indeed, the Judaization of society. And, like their Galizianer brethren, these 'assimilated' Jews had a preference for endogamy and continued to exhibit that trilogy of clannishness: solidarity, social cohesion, and social exclusivism. Acsady wrote that the Neologs were deluding themselves: "The bashful anti-Semite . . . swears at the Orthodox but means the Neolog."[8]

An assessment of the role of Jews in the economy revolves around the dictum that Jews should be heavily involved in agricultural pursuits. Again, the art of self-definition is evident. This section has shown that they deviated from this expectation and instead participated in large numbers in the managing, leasing, and owning of land, which had little in common with working *on* the land. Whether the demand to work the land was reasonable or even feasible in the era of industrialization is irrelevant: even well along the path to modernization, some liberals like Trefort considered tilling the land an antidote to anti-Semitism. Furthermore, land ownership among Jews had a selfish slant to it: it was meant to give them status and to reflect their prosperity, as opposed to being a sacred trust and representing the primary source of the nation's prosperity.

In other endeavors, Jews practiced the art of self-definition more magnanimously. In business, they considered themselves to be playing a crucial role in the transformation of Hungary into a capitalist, industrialized, modern, and prosperous state. In the free professions, they were filling a void. In the arts and the intellectual realm, they were helping Hungary to reach great cultural heights. But these achievements, accompanied by "constant self-praise and big talk" as Jozsef Patai expressed it, relegated the non-Jew to a secondary position or even excluded him altogether.

---

* 'Neologs' were those Jews who had modified many of their religious practices. By and large, they constituted that contingent of Jews who were identified as being somewhat 'assimilated' and who identified themselves as 'assimilated'.

In becoming educated, it was not the criterion of the Enlightenment thinkers that was adhered to, to produce useful citizens, but the age-old traditional criteria: the intrinsic value of study and its ability to be parlayed into social and economic advancement.

Due to the writings of David Friedlander (1812), for example, which stated first his loyalty to the state and then articulated the program of assimilation that he was prepared to undertake, we know that some Jews, at least, perceived the link between assimilation and loyalty. Yet Hungarian Jews tended to dodge this requirement and instead, especially in the early years after emancipation, proclaimed their allegiance through excessive acts of loyalty, which were unconvincing and brought on ridicule. In later years, they mounted the podium and proclaimed, "Jewry for 2,000 years is only a religion, not a nation, nor a nationality," but this was a contradiction of fact, both with respect to the past and the present. Maintaining ties with their fellow Jews in the spirit of social exclusivism and social cohesion, solidarity was also at work as they continued to make special efforts to help their coreligionists at home and abroad, and worked closely together on commercial and financial projects. Employing further self-definition, while 'our' Jews, the homeland Jews, completely separated themselves from 'those' Jews, the Galizianers, yet, they protested that 'Jews' had contributed more than their share to the war effort.

To understand the ongoing charges of Jewish immorality and place them within the framework of this work, one must pull from the bag of Jewish traits the recurrent charge of hatefulness towards Christians. According to Eotvos, this hatefulness had served as a sanction for Jewish misdeeds, which ranged from sleazy business practices to outright criminality. However, as Eotvos pointed out, this paradigm had in fact been cultivated by Christians: hatefulness was only natural given the mistreatment Jews had been subjected to; and not only Jews, but all "nations under oppression tend to lose their [public] morality."[9] Nevertheless—and herein lay the problem, according to Hungarians—despite the elimination of oppression after emancipation, Jews still viewed Christians as their adversaries and treated them immorally.

The liberals' decision to codify the general values of the Enlightenment but not to incorporate the Enlightenment ideals specific to the Jews into law had been done in the naïve belief that emancipation would overcome the particularist traits of Jews and with that, society's entrenched attitudes towards Jews, the former being the springboard for the latter. But once emancipated, it was a matter of choice whether to become "useful citizens" in the way the Enlightenment thinkers had meant it and to comply with the Enlightenment ideals specific to the Jews. As early as 1883, many concluded that Jews had chosen not to comply or were incapable of doing so. And this failure to undertake reforms was leading to the Judaization of society.

Apprehending this notion was an almost impossible task for contemporary Jews. And so we have still one more example of the art of self-definition. When Moritz Goldstein wrote of Jews "administrating the spiritual property of a nation,"[10] he was describing the ceiling of possible assimilation permitted to the Jews. Yet, this phrase precisely describes the objection of many Hungarians—only from their perspective, it constituted the 'Judaization' or 'Jewification' of Hungarian society.

Failing to assimilate through reform but instead substituting self-defined methods of assimilation which allowed for ever greater monopolization of Hungarian institutions gave the impetus for the evolution of the Jewish Question as a social question to one that was political in nature. While Istoczy expressed politicization in terms of hegemony, there was more to it than that. The politicization of the Jewish Question also meant that the stimulus for change was taken out of the hands of the Jewish people and given to the Christian body politic. There were already signs of this evolution late in the First World War and it was complete by 1920.

While there were extended periods of calm, they had not been engendered either by the Jews' assimilation or by the acceptance of unassimilated Jews. On the one hand, the pervasiveness of the liberal ethos made most of those who publicly commented on the lack of assimilation appear disreputable. On the other hand, liberalism demanded behavior from its adherents that reflected liberal principles, and so that fairly sizeable portion of the population who wished to identify themselves as liberals had been restrained from openly expressing any reservations they may have felt towards Jews; instead, they had focused on ways to promote the Jews' assimilation. When Haller declared, "With the *Numerus Clausus* bill, the spirit of liberalism ceases to exist," he meant that liberalism would no longer act as a protective shield against the Jews' failure to assimilate along the prescriptive lines of the Enlightenment. The liberal conviction that assimilation was conjoined to emancipation was fallacious; the Jews' emancipation had not brought about their reform.

Since reform was no longer a possibility, the only option was controls. Struggling with how to neutralize the dominating presence of Jews in society, the path chosen was a tentative (at first) reversion to the Jews' status during the era of Toleration. Limiting (although not yet eliminating) their educational aspirations (and hence their future participation in the cultural and institutional life of the nation) but not curtailing their role in the economy was a first step towards reimposing the pre-emancipated status of the Jew. (The laws passed around 1920 had a real effect on the large number of small Jewish entrepreneurs, but none of them applied to the Jewish oligarchy which controlled the financial sector, industry and commerce, and mining—the real source of economic utility.) Expressed in contemporary terms by the radical converted Jew Oszkar Jaszi, "Landed estates allied themselves with big Jewish capital;" "the Bethlen Regime made peace with the capitalists."* No law of proportionality was yet applied to the economic utility of the Jews. Also expressed in contemporary terms with a sincerity that we cannot gainsay, Bajcsy-Zsilinszky and others like him argued that "it is disproportionate to have five per cent of the population rule over the most important institutions." And thus, the *Numerus Clausus* could also be

---

* Oscar (Oszkar) Jaszi, *Revolution and Counter-Revolution in Hungary* (London, 1924), 225. The general economic landscape in Hungary as of January 1937 looked somewhat like this according to the Budapest newspaper *Uj Magyarag*. Land ownership: of the largest estates, fifteen per cent were in Jewish hands; of large estates, thirteen

understood as an attempt to impose assimilation, insofar as assimilation, being 'just like us,' meant that the number of Jews engaging in any activity *should* be proportionate to their number in the general population. The grounds for such a suggestion rest on the fact that 'proportionality' was the operative word, and not 'restriction' or 'exclusion'.

Although it would be reasonable to assume that the *Numerus Clausus*, because it did not contain the word 'Jew,' was directed at all sub-groups in Hungarian society and therefore did not target the Jews, there are three points which refute this idea. First, the entire debate in the National Assembly about the need for *numerus clausus* in institutions of higher learning (or elsewhere) revolved around the Jews. Second, Haller's presentation speech of the bill in July 1920 made explicit reference to Jews. Third, the number of races and nationalities residing in rump Hungary after the Trianon Peace Treaty (4 June 1920) was minimal. From a prewar figure of 50.5 per cent of the total population, their percentage dropped to 10.5 per cent.[11]

In 1923, Vilmos Vazsonyi made an appeal to Prime Minister Bethlen in which he pointed out that "the *Numerus Clausus* does not speak of religious groups [confessions] but of race. This law therefore considers the Jews to be a race or a distinct nationality."[12] However, this reclassification did not occur only in Hungary. The Bolsheviks, by a single act, had recently emancipated several million Jews and classified them as an ethnic minority. The Balfour Declaration (subsequently affirmed by the other Allied Governments) had concretized the efforts of the Christian restoration movement and British interests in the Levant and established the framework for a Jewish state, a tacit admission of the Jews as a people. At the Paris peace talks, President Wilson's Fourteen Points (January 8, 1918) were being discussed. One of the points was concerned with the fair treatment of ethnic minorities and it was considered a basic principle for ensuring future peace. A series of Minorities Treaties were drafted, guaranteeing minorities the free exercise of cultural and educational rights along with a degree of autonomy, while assuring them of perfect equality before the law with all other citizens. Jews, according to these treaties, were counted among the ethnic minorities.[13]

Hungary's decision, therefore, cannot be judged as a singular or unilateral act. It was done in concert with many other nations at the time. The means by which Hungary accomplished this change were considered extreme and condemned by the international community. But the fact remains, Jews were broadly viewed as a separate ethnic group and not a confession by 1920.

---

per cent; as lessees of the very large estates, thirty-seven per cent. Industry: when averaged, Jews owned forty-six per cent of the largest industrial enterprises. They comprised seventy per cent of their board membership and in all but one industry, had a majority of Jewish directors. Concerning medium-size industrial enterprises, seventy-eight per cent were owned by Jews. Income: tax returns indicated that 83.2 per cent of those declaring income above one million pengo (excluding land owners) were Jews; of those earning 100,000 pengo, 84.3 per cent; and of those earning between 30,000 and 100,000 pengo, 85.6 per cent. The average per capita income of Jews was 2,506 pengo, compared to 427 pengo for non-Jews. *Uj Magyarsag*, 23 January 1937.

The import of this change as a trend cannot be overemphasized. For a hundred and fifty years, Jews had been told that true and successful emancipation rested on their assimilation into the country in which they were resident through the elimination of all particularist traits. With one stroke of the pen, the Balfour Declaration, the *Numerus Clausus*, and the Minorities Treaties erased the entire body of Enlightenment and liberal thought as it pertained to the Jews, along with their two-pronged program for the Jews' emancipation: reform, and the classification of Jews as citizens of the 'Mosaic' faith. In its place was a celebration of the linguistic, cultural, educational, and legal distinctiveness of the Jews who were to be dealt with (hopefully) on an equal footing with the majority population, coupled with the formal designation as a people with their own homeland. Redefined as a nationality or race in the case of Hungary, and an ethnic minority in the new nation states and Russia, these Jews were identified as a separate entity distinct from the majority society; while internationally, the Balfour Declaration had approved, in principle, the creation of a Jewish state, formally entrenching the Jews as a people or nation. There is no intention here to deliberately impute the same motives to the members of the Peace Conference as were operative in Hungary. Nevertheless, the conclusion cannot be avoided that, multilaterally, the status of the Jews was renegotiated.*

It is not surprising that this new status bore some resemblance to the status of the Jews during the era of Toleration, given that emancipation had been based on the expectation that Jews would successfully undertake reforms culminating in their assimilation. This expectation had not been fulfilled.

NOTES

1. Kalman Mikszath, quoted in Zsoldos, *Magyar iroldalom*, 84-85. Mikszath was an extremely well-known novelist, journalist, member of the Academy of Sciences, and a member of Parliament in the latter third of the nineteenth century.
2. *Judische Delikatessen*, Books 5, 26.
3. *Riado*, 6 January 1884.1.
4. *Pesti Naplo*, 4 October 1881.272; *Magyarorszag*, 12 September 1880.253.
5. *Pesti Naplo*, 22 November 1881.321.
6. *Evkonyv* 25 (1908): 310.
7. Janos, *Politics of Backwardness*, 180.

---

* The question of the position of the Jewish populations in these incipient nation states arose immediately in the minds of Jewish leaders. Opinion was divided into two camps: western-assimilated Jews, and eastern-nationalist Jews. The former was mainly interested in the Enlightenment form of emancipation: removal of all personal disabilities and the provision of guarantees for every individual Jew to enjoy such liberty as was the right of the rest of the population. The latter wished to secure recognition for the Jewish communities as separate cultural and political entities, in keeping with nineteenth-century ideas of ethnicity. The eastern-nationalist faction took a leading role in discussions at the peace table, since they alone constituted minorities in all the countries under consideration. Their view prevailed. James W. Parkes, *The Jewish Problem in the Modern World* (London: Thornton Butterworth Ltd, 1939), 132-37.

8. Acsady, *Zsido es nemzsido*, 3.
9. Baron Jozsef Eotvos, *Eotvos osszes munkai*, [Complete Works of Eotvos] ed. Geza Voinovich (Budapest, 1902-1904), 12:115, 117.
10. Moritz Goldstein, quoted in H. D. Schmidt, "German Jewry's Dilemma," *LBIYB* 2 (1957): 244.
11. Tibor Hajdu and Zsuzsa L. Nagy, "Revolution, Counterrevolution, Consolidation," in *A History of Hungary*, ed. Peter F. Sugar (Bloomington, Ind.: Indiana University Press, 1990), 314.
12. Vilmos Vazsonyi, quoted in Mendelsohn, *Jews of East Central Europe*, 105. As Vazsonyi noted, he and Gyula Andrassy had left for Switzerland together; "I left as a denomination and came back as a race."
13. Parkes, *Jewish Problem*, 132-37.

SECTION 3

THE BASIS FOR COMPARISON: BRITAIN 1830-1920

Introduction

Based on the understanding some British historians have of nineteenth-century British history and the position of Anglo-Jewry within it, Britain is ill-suited to serve as a comparison with Hungary. Historian David Itzkowitz, for example, has made the following comment:

> In England, Jews had not been bound by restrictive laws, and native-born Jews were full English subjects even before the ghetto walls began to crumble in Europe. As a result, the English pattern did not conform to that of other European countries. . . . [D]uring the Victorian period the leaders of the Anglo-Jewish community . . . worked towards enunciating a vision of the relationship between Jews and non-Jews that was unique in the European experience, a vision that contained within it elements of cultural pluralism. Nowhere else in European society was the majority community expected to accommodate itself to the cultural peculiarities of the minority populations in its midst. Indeed, it has been a major theme of recent historiography to stress the accommodations that Jews had to make in order to fit into European society rather than the reverse . . . . Anglicization . . . was not an effort to lessen Jewishness. . . . In fact, the opposite was the case.[1]

Itzkowitz's comment is typical of the "realist school" of scholarship which advocates contextualization as the way to analyze the presence of Jews in any given country: "looking at Anglo-Jewish history in its most obvious context," that of the host society, is the way Geoffrey Alderman expresses it.[2] Todd Endelman has concluded that since "the Anglo-Jewish experience was not indebted to German currents," then, "wherever Jews lived in conditions substantially different from those in Berlin and Frankfurt their entry into the majority society would have taken a course shaped by local conditions. The individuality of historical phenomena can too easily be sacrificed in the pursuit of a common pattern of Jewish modernization."[3] A similar reading has led Israel Finestein to cite the unity of Church and state to account for how emancipation differed in Britain.[4] In yet another claim to support Britain's singular status *vis a vis* emancipation, Abraham Gilam has stated, "For Anglo-Jewry, political emancipation [was] not as futile and worthless as it seemed to disillusioned European Jews, to Zionist ideologists and Socialist thinkers."[5] Overwhelmingly, these context-oriented examinations have concluded that the Anglo-Jewish experience was distinct.

If previous histories did a poor job of presenting and interpreting Anglo-Jewish history, the "realist school" is performing no better. A rendering of the emancipation period that not only sidesteps the emancipation debates but also presumes the existence of an expectation that the majority community accommodate the "cultural peculiarities" of the minority population bears no relation to the situation at the time. The goal of the Sephardi settlers and those primarily German-Jewish immigrants over the nineteenth century was to become the 'perfect English gentleman:' elevated to the status of a credo, they made every effort to achieve this goal, not the least of which was for some of them to wish their recently arrived Ashkenazi brethren back to Europe in the late 1700s and again in the late 1800s, because they were jeopardizing this effort. As for the British populace (with the fewest of exceptions), at no time did they describe the 'massive wave' of Russian-Jewish immigration as anything but 'alien'.

The "realist school" further contends that "accommodation" to "cultural peculiarities" was a phenomenon unique to Britain. Presumably, the inclusion of a Jewish religious program in London's East End elementary schools and permission for Jews to trade on Sunday are examples of this, as is Gilam's statement that there was "the tendency to allow English Jews to retain their traditional autonomy."[6] In fact, we know that similar kinds of accommodation were made in Hungary. Despite the mandate that Jewish children should receive a 'Magyar' education, statistics show that many Hasidic children continued to be educated along parochial lines. And in its dealings with the Jewish communal authorities, the government, contrary to its own policy (and particularly the intentions of Jozsef Eotvos), agreed to permit two organizations, one representing the Orthodox and one representing the Neolog. There is no basis for concluding that these accommodations, either in Hungary or England, were made to forward "cultural pluralism." Rather, it is more reasonable to presume that since liberals had demanded no reforms by Jews in the bills of emancipation—everything was reduced to an expectation or hope—they had forfeited the right to demand that Jews act in accordance with the norms and standards of the country they lived in. They also illustrate the divisiveness within the Jewish community on this issue in both Hungary and Britain—which the governments, in the name of liberalism, "accommodated".[7] Not only have these "realist" historians mistakenly claimed a unique status for Britain, they have misread events in their own country. Insular, and not just in the geographic sense, the reductivist use of context is as narrow as the "ghetto histories" which they decry.

Finally, there are aspects of the British context which seem to have been ignored in the course of examining Anglo-Jewish history but which would certainly bear examination. The first is the abridged Jewish presence in Britain. If we date the onset of the era of Toleration around 700 CE (admittedly an approximate date) and the end of the era around 1800, then Jews were only present in England some 375 years. And out of the eight and a half centuries when 'toleration' was most stringently applied, they were present a mere 250 years. England's good reputation has been earned at the expense of not having to cope with a Jewish presence during those centuries of the era of Toleration when it became increasingly disturbing to Christians. Furthermore, the first Jews who were actually readmitted to England were what may be called 'neutral' Jews: *conversos* and Marranos. In considering the perspective of the host society, perhaps a study of the willingness to accept these Jews not only in England but also in France, Holland, Spain, and Portugal would be illuminating.

Three other aspects that deserve consideration revolve around the process of emancipation. An essential part of the context of the emancipation debates was the contributions made by those who identified themselves as liberals, but there is a paucity of such sources in the literature. Secondly, what historian M. Salbstein refers to as "expectations of due conformity," and which he stated was one of the three questions surrounding Jewish emancipation, are only hinted at in his book and almost absent elsewhere. Also absent is a sufficient appreciation of the contribution made by millenarian Christians to the emancipation movement.

My last observation provides a starting point for yet one more area that might be addressed. 'Alien' is the key word in Britons' perception of the Jews, definitely before emancipation, but very much so thereafter. Without question, the term 'assimilation' was used, and all the issues that were raised in Hungary were raised in Britain as well. Being termed an alien may have presumed a state of nonassimilation, and alienage may be the British framework that denoted a lack of assimilation, but by privileging the alienage of the Jews, the rhetoric of assimilation that was front and center in continental Europe was less prominent in Britain. Thus, Jews in Britain were to some extent shut out from this trend. The practical outcome of this was that while assimilation—as continental Jews apprehended it—was being pursued through participation in the cultural life of the nation and high rates of university attendance with a professional career as the outcome, for example, such 'assimilatory thrusts' were decidedly lower among Anglo-Jewry.

****

The influences on the emancipation process in Britain mirrored those in France: the Enlightenment ideals and religious convictions—but significantly, in reverse proportions. The process itself was a protracted one, and hardly had Jews time to enjoy their new status when there was a marked decrease in the goodwill towards them, due to the reaction of the Jews to the 'Bulgarian atrocities' in 1878, followed by the onset of Russian-Jewish immigration in 1881. This sudden influx of Russian Jews to Britain posed many problems: in the areas of labor and housing; in the connection made between immigration and emigration; as a threat to political security; and as a source of criminality, so much so, that a Royal Commission was established. Its findings, supported by countless articles, speeches, and the formation of various organizations, reveal in detail how problematic the presence of these Jews was. Control of the 'alien problem' was hoped for through the passing of the Aliens Act of 1905.

The reaction to the other segment of Anglo-Jewry, the wealthy and ostensibly assimilated sector, was much less dramatic, but there were complaints about the original Sephardi settlers and a small coterie of immigrants, almost all of whom came from Germany, as well. By the prewar period, these complaints had increased substantially, and not coincidentally, they occurred at the same time as signs that liberalism was falling into disrepute. With the First World War, antipathy towards aliens reached new heights, and the grounds for distrusting the loyalty of all Jews who might be even loosely construed as 'alien' were abundant. In the anti-alien mood of the immediate postwar period, the trilogy that contributed to anti-Jewish feeling everywhere during the 1920s—Bolshevism, the establishment of a Jewish state, and the idea of a Jewish world conspiracy provoked it in Britain as well.

NOTES

1. D. C. Itzkowitz, "Cultural pluralism and the Board of Deputies of British Jews," in *Religion and Irreligion in Victorian Society: Essays in Honor of R.K. Webb*, ed. R. W. Davis and R. J. Helmstedter (New York: Routledge, 1992), 85-86.
2. Geoffrey Alderman, Review of David Feldman's *Englishmen and Jews: Social Relations and Political Culture, 1840-1914* and David Cesarani's *The Jewish Chronicle and Anglo-Jewry, 1841-1991*, English Historical Review 109 (September 1994): 970.
3. Todd Endelman, "The Englishness of Jewish Modernity in England," in *Toward Modernity: The European Jewish Model*, ed. Jacob Katz (New Brunswick, N.J.: Transaction Books, 1987), 242-43.
4. Israel Finestein, *Jewish Society in Victorian England: Collected Essays* (London: Valentine Mitchell, 1993), 165-66.
5. Gilam, *Emancipation of the Jews*, 151-53.
6. Gilam, *Emancipation of the Jews*, 151-53.
7. Patai, *Jews of Hungary*, 320-23; Charles H. L. Emanuel, *A Century and a Half of Jewish History* (London: George Routledge & Sons, Limited, 1910), 10-12. Countless articles in the *Jewish Chronicle* discuss both of these subjects, some of which are mentioned later.

Chapter 10
The Emancipation Process 1830-1858

No government member or faction initially came forward in Britain to advance the cause of Jewish emancipation in Parliament. It was logical, then, when it came to choosing someone to petition Parliament on the Jews' behalf following the introduction of the first bill for the removal of Jewish disabilities (5 April 1830), no more sympathetic prospect could be approached than someone with strong liberal convictions. Such a person was Lord Henry Holland. He championed the cause of Jewish emancipation with the same fervor as Catholic emancipation, the suspension of the *Habeas Corpus Act*, opposition of union with Ireland, and the abolition of slavery. A Whig to his fingertips, he was their social leader. He refused Sir Isaac Goldsmid's request, however: "I am not clear that the appreciation of such a Latitudinarian as I could help you with Church of England men or would be of much use," but Lord Bexley "would present your case most effectively."[1]

Holland's statement can be looked at as a reflection of the nascent state of liberalism in Britain, which had not yet developed to the point where it applied the principle of universal humanism, a fundamental characteristic of mature liberalism. Holland was certain that the successful prosecution of Jewish emancipation in Britain would be reliant on religious convictions and hence his choice of House of Lords member Lord Bexley, a millenarian Christian.[2] (As has been discussed above, millenarians believed that emancipating the Jews would hasten their conversion, a prerequisite to the Second Coming of Christ.) A fervent supporter of missionary societies, Bexley was in fact a founding member of the Philo-Judean Society whose express purpose was to promote the removal of civil disabilities so that Jews would look more favorably upon Christians—and hence Christianity—and convert.[3] Another fundamental aspect of millenarianism, the belief in the restoration of the Jews to Palestine, was also thought to be facilitated by the emancipation of the Jews.[4] Bexley was duly approached and agreed to take up the cause of Jewish emancipation. Robert Grant, whose background and commitments were identical to Bexley's, agreed to promote emancipation in the House of Commons.[5]

Many other supporters of Jewish emancipation proved to have similar profiles. Augustus Frederick, Duke of Sussex, and Secretary of War John Cam Hobhouse (1832) were both liberals, but the Duke was also a deeply pious Anglican with a consuming interest in Hebraic scholarship (and a vast collection of Hebrew manuscripts) and Hobhouse came from a strong Unitarian family.[6]

Colonel George Gawler was a millenarian Christian who "truly rejoiced to see the progress of civil emancipation. . . . every step towards emancipation is a movement towards Palestine."[7] By 1847, future Prime Minister William Gladstone had come to the conclusion that he could wear both his hats—as a man of deep religious convictions and as a parliamentarian—comfortably. Both Church and state would benefit from separation (short of disestablishment), as no compromise would be required on either side: the Church could maintain its principles, and the state would no longer be seen as a discriminating agent. Richard Whately, the Archbishop of Dublin and leader of the liberal wing of the Anglican Church, applied a principle of his own which underpinned his support of emancipation: "A law giving to Christians generally as such, or to Christians of any particular church, a monopoly of any civil rights, is to make Christ's kingdom, so far, a kingdom of this world and is a violation of the rule of 'rendering unto Caesar the things that are Caesar's.'"[8]

Within this religious grouping, there were Nonconformists such as the Welsh Calvinist Methodist minister John Mills, an active conversionist in London and Palestine who, on the basis of contrast, were not opposed to emancipating the Jews: "There is an essential difference between Judaism and Roman Catholicism. . . . Popery [is] aggressive . . . ready to subvert political and social order" for the purpose of aggrandizement of the Church. Judaism, on the other hand, "intermeddles not with the civil rights of other creeds . . . and nothing in it is inconsistent with loyalty."[9] Others, particularly Unitarians and Quakers (Joseph Priestly and William Hazlitt representing the former, and John Bright, Elizabeth Fry, and Joseph Pease, the latter), identified with the Jews because of their common history of suffering civil disabilities in England and supported Jewish emancipation on this account.[10] Hazlitt also articulated one of the classical arguments used to support emancipation in his tract, *Emancipation of the Jews* (1831): Jews were a product of their past, and political emancipation would inspire self-emancipation—a common euphemism for reform.[11] Abraham Gollomb has correctly observed that "if the possibilities of assimilation . . . are good"—in this case, the optimism of millenarians and other philo-Semites about the conversion of the Jew—then "'equality of right' movements arise."[12]

A substantial proportion of pro-emancipationists were, of course, secular. Interestingly, the Church played a prominent role in their rationale for favoring Jewish emancipation: it would help dismantle the hegemony of the Church. Politician Arthur James Roebuck was not opposed to Jewish emancipation so much as he was opposed to the stumbling block posed by Jewishness. He repeatedly wondered why the oath 'on the true faith of a Christian' was such an obstacle to Lionel de Rothschild's taking his place in Parliament. Pragmatism should be given pride of place as far as Roebuck was concerned; both one's own conscientious objections and the opinions of others should be ignored.[13] In spite of the support from non-religious quarters, had the cause to emancipate the Jews in England not been taken up by religious Christians of various stripes, it seems to be a real question at what point liberals would have galvanized themselves into action.

The primary arguments used against emancipating the Jews were less inflammatory than the medieval basis for their marginalization—deicide, ritual murder, and the Jews' enmity to Christianity—but their alien nature, which had arisen out of these allegations was still at issue. Some relied on this alien nature as determined by religion. Thomas Arnold, Oxford professor, Anglican minister, and eminent liberal was very explicit on this point.

> I want to take my stand on my favourite principle, that the world is made up of Christians and non-Christians; with all the former we should be one, with none of the latter. I would pray that distinctions be kept up between Christians and non-Christians. Then I think that the Jews have no claim whatever to political right. . . . the Jews are strangers in England, and have no claim to legislate for it than a lodger has to share with the landlord in the management of his house.[14]

Others, like the future Lord Shaftesbury, believed that, in general, citizenship could only be granted to those who were Christian.[15] MP Richard Cobbett proffered more traditional arguments: the title of one pamphlet he authored—*Good Friday; or the Murder of Jesus Christ by the Jews*—illustrates his theological foundations for opposing emancipation. And in a letter, he discussed his 'economic' objections: the term "Jew" was "synonymous with *sharper, cheat and rogue*," and this was "the case with *no other* race of mankind." "Living in all the filthiness of *usury and increase*," they were "extortioners by habit and almost by instinct."[16] MP Sir Robert Inglis articulated another classical, religious argument against Jewish emancipation: the essential requirement of preserving the Christian character of the state, for "admitting Jews to parliament would have the effect of "unchristianizing the Legislature."[17]

Opposition to emancipation was also expressed in purely secular terms. "You cannot call them English even though they are born among us. They are no more Englishmen than they are Romans, Poles, or Prussians, among whom we also find them," said Tory MP Viscount Belgrave in a speech he delivered to the House of Commons 17 May 1830.[18] Another issue revolved around loyalty: "So long as he [the Jew] looks forward to another Kingdom, his sympathies would be given more to a Jew in Paris or Warsaw, than to a person residing in the same, or the next county to him."[19] Although the tasks of administration (such as municipal positions) were acceptable, the most serious threat to the nation would exist if Jews were permitted to participate in the making of laws.[20]

The first emancipation bill, submitted in 1830, was defeated, as were twelve more, until 1858. That year, two bills were passed by the House of Commons and the House of Lords: the "Act To Substitute One Oath For The Oaths of Allegiance, Supremacy And Abjuration," commonly referred to as the 'Emancipation Bill,' and "An Act To Provide For The Relief Of Her Majesty's Subjects Professing The Jewish Religion." The latter bill, which was subject to annual renewal, required that prospective Jewish MPs be approved by "resolution," either by the Upper or Lower House. So, if emancipation is to be defined as having full political rights, the year 1858 is premature. This bill was supplanted by another, the "Parliamentary Oaths Act of 1866," which stipulated only that the prospective member believe in God.[21] Ecumenism may have taken hold, but not secularism. Only in 1871, via the "Promissory Oaths Act," were Jews able to hold most offices of state.

This protracted process of emancipation reflects the gradual acceptance of the liberal ethos as the prevailing ethos over these decades, and with it, the corresponding withdrawal of support for what was becoming an anachronistic position. The sense of inevitability that Thomas Macaulay had alluded to in 1831 had by now become pronounced. At that time he had written, "In fact the Jews are not excluded from political power. They possess it; and as long as they are allowed to accumulate property, they must possess it. The distinction which is sometimes made between civil privileges and political power, is a distinction without a difference. Privileges are power."[22] Mr. Croker was in receipt of this letter from Lord George Bentinck, in which one may detect a sense of resignation.

> Disraeli, of course, will warmly support the Jews, first from hereditary prepossession in their favour, and next because the Rothschilds are great allies. . . . The Rothschilds all stand high in private character, and the City of London having elected Lionel Rothschild as one of her representatives, it is such a pronouncement of public opinion that I do not think the party, as a party, would do themselves any good by taking up the question against the Jews. It is like Clare electing O'Connell, Yorkshire, Wilberforce. Clare settled the Catholic Question, Yorkshire the Slave Trade, and now the City of London has settled the Jew Question.[23]

As for Macaulay's personal feelings towards Jews, these may be gleaned from a letter he wrote to his sister about a costume ball at the home of eminent financier Isaac Goldsmid: it had a "little too much of St. Mary Axe [a Jewish neighborhood in London] about it—Jewesses by dozens, and Jews by scores. . . . the sound of fiddles was in mine ears, and gaudy dresses, and black hair, and Jewish noses were fluctuating up and down before mine eyes," which prevented him from falling asleep.[24] Like Macaulay, the Chartists were considered very progressive. In the 1830s and 1840s, they had taken a strong stand against the persecution of Jews. Yet they characterized Jews as jobbers, oppressors, and murderers in their publications.[25] Its organ, *The Poor Man's Guardian* declared, "We do not live in a Christian country—we live in a country of Jews, and usurers . . . and hangmen."[26] Chartist leader Thomas Attwood bemoaned that England was in the "thraldom of Jews and jobbers."[27] While espousing the values of liberalism, Macaulay and the Chartists were typical of the many for whom the promotion of an improvement in the condition of Jews did not coincide with any sentiment that one might describe as acceptance of the Jew. Favoring liberal values did not mean that one favored the Jews.

NOTES

1. Lord Holland, quoted in Gilam, *Emancipation of the Jews*, 76.
2. Katz, *Jews in the History of England*, 71; Scult, "Conversion of the Jews," 167-69, 239. William Wilberforce, the Duke of Kent, Sir George Leith, and Lord Shaftesbury were some of the prominent members of these societies. Millenarianism had a long history in England, dating back to the end of the Elizabethan era. It was reinvigorated during the French Revolution, which generated a good deal of apocalyptic fervor. Kobler, *Napoleon and the Jews*, 25-30.

3. Scult, "Conversion of the Jews," 243-44.
4. Kobler, *Napoleon and the Jews*, 84-87. Joseph Priestley spoke for many millenarians: "[Your] restoration [to Palestine] cannot fail to convince the world of the truth of your religion; and in whose circumstances your conversion to Christianity cannot fail to draw after it that of the whole world." Quoted in J. van den Berg, "Priestley, the Jews and the Millennium," in *Sceptics, Millenarians, and Jews*, ed. David S. Katz and Jonathan I. Israel (Leiden, N.Y.: E. J. Brill, 1990), 273. Napoleon's effort to reconstitute the Jewish state (not, one may note, out of any religious belief) was seen by many to be the beginning of this process. "When I was a boy," wrote Thomas Macaulay, "no human being doubted that Buonaparte was the principal subject of the prophecies of the Old Testament. . . . I heard my father [Zachary Macaulay, London merchant and prominent Evangelical] say that the prophets were then wilder than ever he remembered them. They fully expected the battle in the valley of Jehosaphat and the restoration of the Jews within a year." Reverend Henry Highton, a member of the Evangelical arm of the Anglican Church and a master at Rugby School, saw "many signs" that restoration was imminent: "in the political events of the world . . . in the movements of the Jewish mind . . . in the feelings towards your nation awakened far and wide among the Gentiles." E. L. Mitford's *An Appeal on Behalf of the Jewish Nation in Connection with British Policy in the Levant* (1845) reveals a two-pronged interest in Palestine. In this tract, Mitford, a staunch British imperialist who had spent his career as a colonial civil servant, expressed the increasingly popular view that the establishment of Palestine as a "protected State" under British control was a way of building British power in the Levant and securing a corridor to "her Eastern possessions." Drawing on his millenarian beliefs, he found additional support for the establishment of an "independent State" (eventually) as a way to redress the "unprotected and wronged" status of the Jews, of which Britain might "have the privilege of being the instrument." Thomas Macaulay, Rev. H. Highton, and E. L. Mitford, quoted in Finestein, *Anglo-Jewry*, 140-41, 152-54.
5. Scult, "Conversion of the Jews," 247.
6. Gilam, *Emancipation of the Jews*, 27-29, 24.
7. Colonel George Gawler, quoted in Gilam, *Emancipation of the Jews*, 27-30.
8. Richard Whately, quoted in Gilam, *Emancipation of the Jews*, 26; Finestein, *Anglo-Jewry*, 141.
9. John Mills, quoted in Finestein, *Anglo-Jewry*, 19-20.
10. Gilam, *Emancipation of the Jews*, 17-19.
11. Salbstein, *Emancipation of the Jews*, 33.
12. Abraham Gollomb, "Jewish Self-Hatred," *YIVO Annual of Jewish Social Science* 1 (New York: Yiddish Institute, 1946): 259. Gollomb's idea corresponds to the concept presented in this work that tolerance was more expansive when hopes for the Jews' conversion were high.
13. Gilam, *Emancipation of the Jews*, 78.
14. Thomas Arnold, quoted in Gilam, *Emancipation of the Jews*, 24.
15. Roth, *History of the Jews*, 258.
16. Salbstein, *Emancipation of the Jews*, 68-69.
17. Sir Robert Inglis, quoted in Lucien Wolf, *Essays in Jewish History*, published posthumously, ed. Cecil Roth (London: Jewish Historical Society of England, 1934), 329-30; Roth, *History of the Jews*, 258.
18. Viscount Belgrave, quoted in Endelman, *Jews of Georgian England*, 93-94.
19. Sir Robert Inglis, quoted in Endelman, *Jews of Georgian England*, 94.
20. Wolf, "Introduction", *Essays*, 329-30.
21. Feldman, *Englishmen and Jews*, 46-47; Lipman, *History of the Jews in Britain*, 3-4, 30; Lipman, "The Age of Emancipation, 1815-1880," 82.

22. Thomas Macaulay, quoted in the *Edinburgh Review*, in Mendes-Flohr and Reinharz, *Jew in the Modern World*, 150.
23. Lord George Bentinck, quoted in Wolf, "Introduction", *Essays*, 330-33.
24. Thomas Macaulay, quoted in Endelman, *Jews of Georgian England*, 108.
25. Alderman, *Jewish Community*, 107.
26. *Poor Man's Guardian*, quoted in Rubinstein, *History of the Jews*, 54.
27. Thomas Attwood, quoted in Rubinstein, *History of the Jews*, 54.

Chapter 11
Alienage after Emancipation

The Evaporation of Goodwill

The theme of alienage dominated many of the issues relating to Jews in Britain following their emancipation, but in addition, the word 'alien' became shorthand for many of their faults. While it had been commonly understood by everyone—including the Jew himself—that the Jew was an alien, however, to apply noted historian Cecil Roth's assertion that legal change in England never outstripped the pace of change in public sentiment, what could have happened to invalidate his assertion? For, a "remarkable change has during the past few years come over the outer world in relation to Judaism," as the *Jewish Chronicle* noted in 1882. "Where previously all was good-will towards Jews and all that was Jewish, one finds in many quarters a tendency to criticize every point that can by any means be regarded as open to criticism."[2] It seems that the stand taken by the established Jewish community at the time of the Balkan insurrection (1876-78) made it evident to many Britons that one of the expected and natural outcomes of emancipation—that Jews would now be loyal citizens—had definitely not occurred.

Between April and August 1876, there was an insurrection by Christian Bulgarian nationalists against Turkish rule. In the process of suppressing it, Turkish irregular troops massacred some fifteen thousand Christian civilians—men, women, and children.* While there was a groundswell of public outrage in which several prominent clergymen, politicos, and intellectuals participated, it is William Gladstone's name that is usually associated with spearheading what soon became known as the Bulgarian atrocities agitation, and more generally, the Eastern Question. Distilling this issue to its most basic element, Britain, through the Government's continued support of Turkey, was helping the Turks to oppress the Christians. And so, it appeared, was Prime Minister Benjamin Disraeli as well as most of Anglo-Jewry who both took the unpopular stand of supporting Turkey. In Disraeli's estimation, British interests were "not affected by the question whether it was 10,000 or 20,000 persons who perished in the suppression."†

---

* The reasons are not germane to this work. For a full explication, see R. T. Shannon, *Gladstone and the Bulgarian Agitation 1876* (Edinburgh, 1963).

† Prime Minister Benjamin Disraeli, quoted in Shannon, *Gladstone*, 23. In R. T. Shannon's opinion, "more than any other single statement . . . [this] made the debate on the Eastern Question from 1876 to 1880 the most clearly defined public conflict in English history on the fundamental problem of the moral nature of the State."

On two counts, the Jewish community did not support retribution against Turkey: a number of them held substantial investments there and, as expressed by the rabbi of the Central Synagogue in London, "The Christian populations of the Turkish provinces have held, and continue with an iron hand to hold, my coreligionists under every form of political and social degradation."[3] Consequently, the Jews *en bloc* proceeded to withdraw their long-time support of the Liberals.

This act of solidarity was denounced as ingratitude and an act of defection, and some even hinted at a Jewish conspiracy between Disraeli, built on his ancestral Jewishness, and Anglo-Jewry.[4] MP John Bright spoke of Disraeli as "not having a drop of English blood in his veins;" Goldwin Smith, professor at Oxford and chief spokesperson for the Liberal Party, publicly accused Jews of "subordinating their patriotism to Judaism," and others such as Professor Edward Freeman and the Duke of Argyll spoke out about the Jewish peril.[5] William Morris seconded his associates from the Pre-Raphaelite movement; together, they spent much energy on the Eastern Question, employing rhetoric that was frequently anti-Jewish.[6] Leopold Gluckstein's contemporary piece, *The Eastern Question and the Jews* was only one of numerous venues in which Gladstone pronounced his views: "I deeply deplore the manner in which, what I may call Judaic sympathizers . . . are now acting on the question of the East."[7]

It is timely, here, to comment on Benjamin Disraeli's prime ministership, a position he held between February and December 1868, and again from 1874 to 1880. Disraeli was, of course, of Jewish descent, having been baptized in 1817 at the age of thirteen. At the very least, his prime ministership seems a curiosity or an anomaly. From the Jewish perspective, Disraeli's conversion was the act of a disheartened father who believed that the prospects for Jews in England were permanently bleak. From the perspective of the host society, Disraeli's conversion could reasonably be attributed to assimilation. But, one should also consider the perspective of millenarians and philo-Semites who were so prominent in the emancipation movement in Britain. With their emphasis on the conversion of the Jews, might not the election of a baptized Jew to the highest office in the land serve as confirmation that conversion was the road to—successful—assimilation? And what greater incentive could there be?

From these great heights, Disraeli's popularity fell precipitously; in the election held proximate to the Bulgarian atrocities agitation, April 1880, he suffered a resounding defeat at the polls. One cannot presume a correlation between the numerous negative references to Disraeli's Jewish origins summoned by his stand on the Bulgarian atrocities and his defeat; the scholarship on the subject does not lend itself to such an interpretation. What can be said is that Gladstone was not only the acknowledged leader of the campaign against the Government stand taken towards Turkey but that he also came out of retirement to run against Disraeli and conducted an intense, one might say vicious election campaign to oust him. "Doctrines false, but the man more false than his doctrine," Gladstone spoke of how Disraeli "demoralized public opinion, bargained with diseased appetites, stimulated passions, prejudices and selfish desires, that they might maintain his influence."[8]

Shortly after emancipated Anglo-Jewry suffered this first attack on its political loyalty, Jews fleeing persecution in Russia began to arrive in 1881. Before commencing on an analysis of this definitive event in Britain's relationship to its Jews, the following should be pointed out. At the time of the 1871 census, the recorded number of persons of foreign birth was only 105,000.[9] Thirty years later, this figure had been greatly augmented. According to the 1901 census, there were now 339,000 people who had taken advantage of Britain's right of asylum policy[10] to claim refugee status and become officially registered as aliens. Other official estimates pegged the number somewhere between 90,000 and 150,000 calculated for the years 1880-1914 (an estimate generally accepted by historians). Both statistics are suspect in Jill Pellew's view. Before 1890, the arrival of aliens was hardly checked at all. Moreover, the Home Office, which was responsible for accumulating statistics on the arrival of aliens, did not even look at the figures, "let alone collate and report on them." Only in 1888, when a Select Committee composed of members of the House of Commons advised that alternative ways of collecting this data should be implemented and the task handed over to the Board of Trade's labor statistical bureau did matters improve.[11] But in any case, no distinction was made between Jews and non-Jews.[12]

While figures ranging from 90,000 to 150,000 should be discounted as unrealistically low, still, there is room to argue that the number of Jews who arrived was rather small. After all, Britain's population by 1901 was thirty-two million. From this we might conclude that there was extreme sensitivity to the Jewish presence. Alternatively, we can conclude that Jews, generally speaking, were unwelcome in Britain.

However, having greater impact on British society than this unquantified yet fairly small number of aliens, whose proportion we do not know, is the figure of almost three million Jews who actually landed on British soil over the course of these three decades.[13] These were Jews in transit. Britain was a primary stopover point in transmigration, and it is this fact that gives credence to the feeling of so many Britons that they were being swamped by alien Jews. As one councillor for London's East End stated, "I don't care for statistics. God has given me a pair of eyes in my head . . ."[14] Arranging passage to their ultimate destination, usually America, would have required time. If they did not have sufficient funds to make the trip across the Atlantic—and it is safe to say that many of them did not—they would have had to stay in Britain to work and accumulate the necessary passage, or earn money to return home, or adopt Britain as their homeland, however reluctantly and temporarily (and perhaps illegally). At any given time, Jews were present in Britain in numbers far greater than statistical records indicate and for an indefinite length of time. The 'immigration problem' the British felt they had was based on the combined and sustained presence of both immigrant and transient Jews.

Negative reaction to the arrival of these Russian Jews was initially muted, by virtue of the fact that the mass exodus from Russia into Britain was thought to be a temporary situation, to be reversed when affairs returned to normal. On the contrary, the British populace was horrified at the news of the atrocities, which they expressed by holding 'Indignation meetings,' first in London, then in all the major towns in England. In the meantime, Baron de Hirsch's munificent fund, which eventually reached £8,000,000, was meant to enable the resettlement of Russian Jews to agricultural colonies in North and South America (which it failed to do in any great measure).[15] The persecutions in Russia did not abate, however, and what was at first a temporary escape was transformed into a twenty-five-year trek westward, with Britain as one of the most sought-after destinations. Their presence soon exercised most of British society.[16]

The Alien Problem

The years following 1881 were ones of continual debate in Parliament: should the immigration of Jews from Russia be curtailed or not. Those opposed to any change in the current laws cited foremost their desire to protect the precious British institution of the right of asylum.* Those in favor of immigration restriction argued that the Jews from Russia were having a deleterious affect on numerous aspects of British society. These parliamentarians seemed aware that their comments would be perceived as anti-Semitic—a taboo in liberal England in the public forum—and therefore necessitated a disclaimer before they embarked on their objections to Jewish immigration.

> Before I deal further with this matter, I wish to say that, so far as I am personally concerned—and I think I am also speaking for all those who are cooperating with me in this matter—nothing could be further from our objects and sentiments than to cause pain to that injured race, many of whose members in this country are among the most loyal and charitable subjects of the Queen.[17]

> It is said that this agitation is aimed at the Jewish race. Sir, it hardly seems necessary for me to repudiate so monstrous and groundless a charge. . . . They [the aliens] are objected to not because they are Jews or Gentiles, but purely on social and economic grounds.[18]

By 1887, the debates in and out of Parliament had become sufficiently insistent for the Government to assure the House that it was considering an immigration bill that year. In fact, only an investigation was undertaken, the results of which included tables prepared by the Board of Trade and a report on conditions in London's East End. Two Select Committees were appointed in 1888: one composed of members of the House of Commons to investigate immigration, the other composed of members of the House of Lords to see into the problem of sweating. Both reports concluded that while immigration was indeterminate in number, it was not threatening, nor was it having a deleterious effect.[19] Those contesting the findings continued to object to the ongoing influx of aliens, and the new Liberal government of 1892 felt compelled to make further inquiry. Again, similar data was produced. For the next nine years, continual agitation

---

* Between 1823 and 1905, no one claiming to be a refugee was refused entry into Britain, nor were any of them expelled. During this period, the policy of asylum was considered a sacrosanct one. For a full discussion of this topic, see Bernard Porter, *The Refugee Question in Mid-Victorian Politics* (Cambridge: Cambridge University Press, 1979), chap. 1.

was countered by tentative responses on the part of the government, and then, in 1902, the debates in Parliament heated up in earnest, influencing the Government to set up the Royal Commission on Alien Immigration that year.[20] Lasting fourteen months, the Commission's mandate was to inquire about and report upon:

1. the character and extent of the evils which are attributed to the unrestricted immigration of aliens, especially in the Metropolis;

2. the measures which have been adopted for the restriction and control of Alien Immigration in Foreign Countries and in British Colonies and to advise what remedial or precautionary measures it is desirable to adopt in this country, having regard to the above matter and to the absence of a statutory power to exclude or expel any individual alien or class of aliens from its borders.[21]

One of the first steps taken by the Royal Commission was to send some of its members to Russia to see firsthand how severe the persecutions against the Jews were. Towards fulfillment of the first point, more than 23,000 statements were accumulated, particularly from residents of London's East End, where the vast majority of these immigrants congregated. With regard to the first part of the second point, inquiries were made; and with regard to the second part, the Commission members determined that a bill limiting immigration should be put in place.[22] "The feeling is rapidly becoming desperate," said one Mr. Brown of Stepney in his submission to the Commission, "and if something is not done very soon, I should not be surprised if the people took the matter into their own hands."[23] Like many witnesses to the Commission, Mr. Brown did not describe his own attitudes but spoke in the third person. This tendency should not detract from the reliability of their statements. It rather serves to underscore the disreputability of anti-Jewish expression in a public forum due to the constraints of liberalism. For two decades, Britons had been speaking out in the first person about the alien problem.

On arrival, the immigrants were described as dirty and spreading disease; they were "heavily pauperized" and moreover, included criminals, anarchists, and immoral persons amongst them.[24] It seems that many concurred with Professor W. Cunningham who argued in his book (which traced alien immigration since the time of the Normans) that most of the benefits to be gotten from immigration were past; "At all events, we have not much to gain from imitating the institutions of the Polish Jews."[25] Once they settled in, labor and housing became the major, but by no means the only issues said to be affecting British society.

The Labor Issue

Russian-Jewish aliens provided a cheap pool of labor for the sweated industries and they not only undercut the English laborer but in doing so, reflected the cultural differences between them.

> *Witness for the Royal Commission*: [The] aliens ... sold their lives, and do now, at the rate of 15 hours a day for a crust of black bread and a piece of garlic and a corner filled with filthy straw to lie upon. ... [This] is a competition between wants, between standards of subsistence. It is a struggle between rye and gluten bread, between common and cheap things and good ones. Since 1760 the English workers have maintained the wheaten bread standard, and they have rarely since reverted to the rye standard. They have maintained this standard in the face of famine and extreme poverty. ... All industrial struggles are struggles to maintain a standard of wants, and to improve that standard. Alien immigration, it seems to me, has to be looked at in that light.
> *Chairman:* What is the meaning of 'all industrial struggles are struggles to maintain a standard of wants?'
> *Witness*: A standard of wages.[26]

Their competitiveness, which Beatrice Potter saw as "unrestricted by personal dignity of a definite standard of life and unchecked by the social feeling of class loyalty and trade integrity,"[27] provoked a deterioration of labor standards and depressed the wages of British workers. J. A. Hobson wrote that even "a very small addition of low-living foreigners will cause a perceptible fall in the entire wages of the neighbourhood in the employments which their competition affects."[28] This connection was profound in the minds of those whose wages were already at the subsistence level: "If it keeps on, we shall be brought to the same condition that they are in, and it is not fit for a dog to live in the way they live."[29]

> They can live on about 2 d. a day, whereas an Englishman would not, or could not if he would. It is a fact that seven of these Jewish or Polish workmen will work in one room from 7 o'clock in the morning to about 10 o'clock at night with a half-a-quartern loaf. You will admit that an Englishman cannot compete with that.[30]

Even someone such as John Burnett, the first Labour Correspondent of the Board of Trade's statistical bureau, who had acknowledged the prior existence of sweating and the effect of economic trends on the London tailoring and shoe-making trades, was persuaded that the Russian-Jewish aliens had reduced "thousands of native workers" to the "verge of destitution."[31] "What is the use of talking to them [the poor] of their low standard of life if you insist on leaving them at the same time in competition with a class of foreign labour with a standard of life so low that the native born cannot live under it?" the Earl of Dunraven asked in despair.[32] "Should foreigners deprive our little ones of the oxygen which, disinherited as they are, is surely their inheritance and right?" demanded R. H. Sherard.[33]

Another issue was job displacement. The proof of job displacement was that "newcomers find employment, [which] infers of necessity the displacement of labor previously employed. It implies the denial of employment to natives anxious to obtain it."[34] Rarely did the workers become proactive, as they did in Leicester, when the shoe factory workers went on strike to force their demand that factories should stop hiring Jewish workers.[35]

As for conditions in the sweatshops, often run by Russian-Jewish aliens who had climbed one step up on the economic ladder, inspectors' reports unanimously condemned them as deplorable. Crammed into every conceivable space, from sheds to kitchens, inspectors found that they were damp, steamy, overheated, filled with toxic fiber particles, poorly lit and poorly ventilated, and in a general state of filth. Washroom facilities received much attention in their reports: human excrement and water leaking from the toilets (if there were any, and often there were not) frequently covered the floors, and in many of these workshops unenclosed urinals substituted for proper toilets.[36] The Jewish sweatshop owner, according to the submission to the Royal Commission made by Herbert Evans, an assistant inspector of factories, was as revolting as the premises he oversaw: "an unprincipled and loathsome individual whose tyrannical methods and disposition are only equaled by his complete ignorance and open defiance of everything that is normal and humane."[37] The commodities produced in these sweatshops were described by Charles Freak, Secretary of the National Union of Boot and Shoe Operatives as "a lot of cheap, nasty stuff that destroys the market and injures us," and even worse, "hundreds of our men have to walk about, particularly in the wintertime, who used to be employed on that class of work." In an attempt to improve their situation, some Jews persuaded Freak to establish a Jewish trade union (Jews only, due to what Gainer sees as a general mutual unwillingness—with some exceptions—on the part of both the English and the Jewish aliens, coupled with the immigrants' poor grasp of English that excluded and precluded Jewish membership in other unions). Over the course of four years, two unions were ultimately formed, but both were almost useless, which he attributed to their members being "Slaves . . . I can call them nothing else."[38]

Frequent charges of unfair business practices highlighted the Jews as an immoral people. Christian costermongers, for instance, accused Jewish costers of stealing their pitch (spot on the street). In their efforts to regain this valued piece of territory many fights ensued, so much so, that the police overturned the ancient custom of rights determined by common usage and consent, in favor of whoever got there first. It was said that Russian-Jewish costers had an advantage by going to both morning and evening markets; their ignorance of English enabled them to circumvent orders to leave; and they received permission from police to trade on Sundays and at certain forbidden locations. Shopkeepers, in turn, were aggravated by the lower prices charged by the alien costers and sought the help of the local authorities to remove them.[39] It was true that they were hardworking, but this attribute had unsavory overtones: behind it was "an excessive love of profit."[40] In an unprecedented act, alien Jewish shop owners claimed ownership of the road, which supposedly entitled them to charge a fee for its use. So severe was the animosity of the costers towards the Jewish competition that one of their union leaders pleaded with the Royal Commission to resolve the issue, for "If something isn't done before long, there will be some of our chaps doing murder or something of that, because it is getting so their wives and children can't get anything to eat."[41]

Many who urged immigration restriction "to protect British labour against foreign labour working here" extended their arguments to the issue of protectionism: "We must logically protect British labour against the products of foreign labour working abroad."[42] Free trade was identified with "Free Trade in destitution, with Free Trade in sweating, and with Free Trade in disease," as MP James Lowther put it.[43] "Free Trade in paupers" became a common epithet.[44]

The Housing Issue

Initially, labor issues were considered the most pressing problem brought on by the waves of Russian-Jewish immigration. By the time the Commission tabled its report, it was seen to be housing-related: rack-renting and uncaring alien Jewish landlords and alien Jewish renters whose habits, mores, and ethics were intolerable.

Charles Booth, in his monumental *Life and Labour of the People of London* wrote, "The whole district has been affected by the increase in the Jewish population. It has been like the slow rising of a flood. Street after street is occupied .... No Gentile could live in the same house with these poor foreign Jews."[45] The East End is "maddened to a frenzy by the filth, the insolence, and the depravity of this refuse of Europe," wrote the *Pall Mall Gazette*, not usually given to extreme commentary.[46] Suggestions that certain areas of London be prohibited to Jews were turned down by Secretary of State James Callaghan not on discriminatory grounds, but because they were not feasible.[47] Dockworkers, however—and among the very few who did so—actually pursued exclusionary tactics to keep alien Jews out of their neighborhoods: "They will not have them at any price," as one Jewish family discovered in November 1901. As they prepared to unload their belongings from a van, the local residents surrounded it, chased the family away, and "reduced [the house] to almost complete wreckage."[48] As East End Alderman Silver complained, "Charity was a virtue," but it "became a vice when a man offered shelter and bread to strangers when his own wife and family were starving."[49]

The longstanding scourge of Britain's industrialized cities—chronic housing shortages—was compounded by the excessive demands of the numerous Jewish profit-obsessed landlords and the immigrant Jews' willingness to pay exorbitant rents and key money and to live in overcrowded conditions. The effect on the East End residents, who were unable or unwilling to pay these monies, was to force many of them out, on the one hand, and to raise the proportion of Jews in the neighborhood, on the other.[50] The desperation of Jewish aliens to find accommodation at any price was so well-known that apparently some English landlords posted the following sign, "To let: No Christians need apply."[51]

The health hazards posed by living and working in the same environment, a common practice among Russian-Jewish aliens, was also a source of public concern. "No greater squalor in houses can be seen, no more unhealthy workshops can be found" in which "the stench and foul vapours about the place were very bad, and a more unhealthy condition of things it would be impossible to imagine," reported a factory inspector for East London.[52] "Of the foreign and alien Jewish community," wrote the *East London Observer*, their "manners and customs are a distinct menace to the public health not only of East London, but of the metropolis as a whole and the nation in general."[53] The conviction that the flood of Jewish aliens into formerly Christian neighborhoods forced them into a state of decline was unshakeable. It was during the worst years of the housing shortage, 1899-1903, that a Jewish trade unionist declared that the efforts of his union along with English trade unions had averted many violent episodes in the East End.[54]

The perceived takeover of the East End found expression in yet one more way. The concentration of Jews there resulted in the phenomenon of some sixteen Board schools operating on a 'Jewish format.' To the outrage of some, they closed early on Fridays, observed Jewish holidays, hired many Jewish teachers, and included between one and a half and seven hours of Jewish religious education weekly during and after school hours.[55]

Living cheek by jowl, the social cohesion of the Jews—they "will not conform to our ideas, and, above all, they have no sort of neighbourly feeling"[56]— increased the tensions brought on by the housing problems. Working on the "Christian Sunday," for example, embodied both of these complaints.[57] The invisible wall separating these Jews from the larger society was made higher by the trait of solidarity, about which Arnold White wrote: "There is not a synagogue or a Jewish congregation in Poland, Lithuania, or Galicia which does not in case of need justly exercise over humane Jews in Western Christendom a stronger influence than any of the social or religious forces of the country in which they are domiciled."[58] In fact, the Jews' strength lies in the trait of "corporate cohesion:" "Left entirely to himself the Jew would succumb to the Anglo-Saxon."[59] When we then consider social exclusivism, whose manifestations extended far beyond the strictly social, the wall separating many members of the Russian-Jewish community was so high that it precluded any real assimilation into the host society. Because these Jews insisted on dealing only amongst themselves, the local Christian merchants thereby suffered a loss of business.[60] White cited their refusal to intermarry, the maintenance of separation as a Chosen People, separate diet, different habits, the non-observance of Sunday as a day of rest, the claims of the *Cohanim* to evade civic duties, the Talmudic education given in both the *chedorim* (Jewish schools) and elementary schools, the religious claims of prisoners for synagogues at the public expense, the Jews' phenomenal success in business, a racial pride among the poorer class leading them to express contempt for their Gentile neighbors, and their pronounced Orientalism.[61] Oddness, strange habits, clannishness, refusal to deal with the local Gentile merchants, in all, it was "a compacy [sic] non-assimilating community."[62]

Crime

The issue of Jewish criminality was not too far behind the concerns of labor and housing and it certainly had the greatest impact on the population at large. Repeatedly, those making submissions to the Royal Commission complained about the number of Jews involved in acts of crime. A list of offenses that Jews were said to be involved in accumulated throughout the nineteenth century: fencing, fraud, swindles, arranging false bankruptcies, staging mock auctions (where a partner would drive up the price), crimping (where sailors were indebted virtually on debarking from ship and thereby forced to enlist once again), and,

"Few burglaries, robberies, and false coinages are committed in which some of them are not, in one shape or another, concerned."[63] This criminal image was fueled, in part, by notorious murders in which Jews were implicated or found guilty. The 'Jack the Ripper' murders stand out.[64] Only police intervention prevented "mass attacks on Jews in Stepney, since the locals considered that 'No Englishman' could commit such a crime,"[65] reported one paper. Even the head of the Criminal Investigation Department between 1888 and 1901 was convinced that it was "a definitely ascertainable fact" that the murderer was a Polish Jew."[66] The murder of fellow boarder Miriam Angel, six months pregnant, by Polish Jew Israel Lipski gained such notoriety that Lipski's name became used as a term of anti-Jewish abuse.[67] In 1910, three immigrant Russian Jews were identified as the murderers of three policemen in Hounsditch, one of whom had copies of *Arbiter Fraint* and other anarchist material in his home. This provoked a wave of anti-alien and anti-Jewish protest.[68] "I would like to protest against the Jews who shoot our policemen being described as Russian," wrote W. S. Shaw. "When a Jew gives to charity he is a Jew: when he shoots a policeman he is a Russian."[69] The journal, *The People*, published a verse that went: "But I think it's time to plead once more/ to get rid of the cursed breed/ Of alien Jews who seem to have been/ the authors of the deed."[70]

> One of the curious things about the regular criminal is the absence of any grudge against the police who are regarded as doing their duty and engaged in a fair match of wits and nimbleness. A savage delight in taking life is the mark of the modern Continental anarchist criminal. We have our ruffians but we do not breed that type here and we do not want them.[71]

Since many Britons believed that Jews came to compose the majority of "modern Continental anarchist criminals," it is not surprising that the *Times'* statement would have conjured up the image of a Russian-Jewish alien.

The burgeoning of Jewish crime after 1900, with the concomitant attention paid to it, caused MP for Stepney Major William Evans-Gordon to lament that it was overshadowing the greater issue of the "social and industrial results" of the immigration from Eastern Europe.[72] The judicial system was flooded with cases involving Jews. This caused complaints and resolutions to be registered by the juries at Middlesex and County of London Sessions as well as by the Chairman of the London Sessions. MP Akers-Douglas (MP for Whitechapel at the time of the 'Jack the Ripper' murders) sought resolution through the Aliens Bill of 1904, and MP Sir Howard Vincent formulated a bill to expel criminal aliens.[73]

As early as 1829, Jews were accused of being the chief brothel keepers in London.[74] Even the liberal newspaper, the *Daily News*, wrote about the Jews' involvement in prostitution in very harsh terms.

> The English working man has his faults, but he has never fallen so low as this. And I venture to think it is better to be even a healthy skull-cracking purse-snatching highwayman than to learn the kind of civilisation and acquire the moral and religious ideals taught by the daily lives of these unwashed, cringing, lying and wage-cutting aliens, who have elbowed thousands of Englishmen out of their homes and out of their employment.[75]

Later, Jewish immigrants were heavily implicated in the white slave trade, discussed in the previous section, supplying immigrant Jewish girls to London and all the major world centers. Articles in the *Jewish Chronicle* reinforce the assertion that the number of Jews involved in crime, particularly immigrants, was substantial.[76]

The Correlation between Emigration and Immigration

There were further reasons for advocating restriction of Jewish immigration. Many saw a correlation between English emigration and alien immigration. During the first years of Russian-Jewish immigration, 1881-85, 675,000 Britons emigrated from the United Kingdom, whereas in the previous twenty-seven years 2,250,000 had emigrated in total, indicating a doubling of the annual rate, according to J. H. Clapham.[77] The trade unions calculated that "for every man who is sent out, as is now the case, two foreigners come into this country."[78] Every country based on immigration such as Canada, Australia, and the United States, "which boasts of its hospitality to all the world, and which has opportunities of providing work," still had immigration policies—but not Britain.[79] Conversely, those who stayed were forced to accept lower wages, a lower standard of living, and were affected by the Russian-Jewish aliens' "customs [which] exert a most injurious effect upon the English community with whom they come in contact."[80]

The Connection between Alien Immigration and Political Stability

Some also suggested restriction of immigration as a means to keep revolution in check. Wages having been forced downward by the Jews, "that spirit of discontent and disorder on which the agitators live and batten, and which in time may pollute the ancient constitutional liberalism of England with the visionary violence of Continental Socialism" would be strengthened.[81] In an atmosphere where the "lowest passions are ever ready to burst out and avenge themselves by frightful methods,"[82] revolution was a real threat. Furthermore, anarchism, and to a lesser degree, socialism were considered primarily foreign imports. Once Jewish immigration had achieved a certain mass, Russian-Jewish aliens were indeed among the most prominent in the anarchist movement, posing a second threat to the stability of society.[83] Jews, then, were seen to be not only the incitement for potential revolutionary insurrection, but also the advocates of revolutionary activism.

Social Darwinism

Social Darwinism also played a role in the assessment of aliens. "They are sifted here by natural selection," wrote S. H. Jeyes, "and we keep the refuse:" only the best quality Jewish immigrants were able to gain entry into the United States; those in a poor condition settled in Britain.[84] Joseph Chamberlain expressed the popular belief that "imported foreign labour of the lowest class" could only exacerbate the "struggle for existence."[85] For his part, Alderman

Silver was reported to have said that he hoped never would "be grafted onto the English stock and diffused into English blood, the debilitated, the sickly and the vicious products of Europe."[86]

Eugenics promoter Karl Pearson advocated the restriction of "undesirable aliens" who, classified along with habitual criminals, mental defectives, paupers, and the insane, would endanger the race, for "you cannot get a strong and effective nation if many of its stomachs are half-fed and many of its brains untrained."[87] With respect to those "undesirable aliens" already present in Britain, the well-known physician Robert Reid Rentoul argued against their intermarrying with Britons, for "breeding an imperial race from degenerates must fail." As for the greater, numerically speaking, complaint against the Jews—the condition of being a pauper—this, Rentoul did not see as a transient state: "Heredity is the great cause" and largely responsible for criminality.[88] For many in this scientific age, the merit of immigration restriction was enhanced by giving it a biological foundation; for others, it added a third reason, beyond the social and the political, to advocate such a measure.

Towards a Solution of the Alien Problem

Throughout the immigration debate, associations were founded with the express purpose of controlling Jewish immigration. In 1886, the Society for the Suppression of the Immigration of Destitute Aliens was established, financed by White and the Earl of Dunraven. It held only a couple of meetings, and there is no record of any membership list, but supporters included a number of MPs as well as representatives from the Jewish community.[89] A few years later, the Association for Preventing the Immigration of Destitute Aliens was started. Not only MPs, but also a goodly number of peers appointed to higher offices supported the aim of "organizing and directing public opinion, as a preliminary to an attempt to obtain legislative enactment."[90] However, like its predecessor, it was short-lived.[91]

While the timing of a meeting of East End Conservative Associations in June 1901 which produced the Londoners' League (which wedded the housing and alien issues under one political mantle, for the "social amelioration of the people"[92]) was auspicious for its success, it was the British Brothers League, also founded in 1901, that became well-known. Backed by Tory MPs representing the East End constituencies and some liberals as well, its founder William Stanley Shaw emphasized that this group would be oriented towards the labor classes.[93] The League's agenda, largely formulated by MP Major Evans-Gordon, reflected the day-to-day concerns of East Enders: excessive rent, overcrowding and displacement, job competition, and immigrant crime;[94] it also attacked the broader issue of the lack of patriotism among the aliens.[95] Garnering a membership of 45,000 in only eighteen months, Evans-Gordon's strategy of simply acquiring a signature did not make these Londoners members 'in name only.' There were large turnouts at the mass rallies, as well as attendant support from

East End MPs and clergymen.[96] The League expanded its mandate through the formation of the Immigration Reform Association in 1903, which sought to inform the public and the government about recent alien immigration and disseminate pamphlets on their findings.[97]

Apart from the restriction of Jewish immigration, another solution to the unwelcome presence of Jews was proposed. This was the idea of a Jewish homeland. Evans-Gordon was a strong supporter of the Jewish Territorial Organization (JTO),[98] and Joseph Chamberlain pondered over a suitable location for this homeland in discussions with Theodor Herzl—preferably "under the aegis of the British flag" and "without interfering with the subsistence of others."[99] There was "no reason why a great Jewish State should not be rebuilt,"[100] wrote White, who eventually came to see this as the only solution. (The *Jewish Chronicle* was worried about this prospect. "Supposing that a Jewish State were re-established, what reason is there to anticipate that Jews would be tolerated in the lands where they now suffer ill-treatment? . . . Many are enamoured of the proposal, and hug it as a refuge from the present troubles." But this was illusory: "Nationalism, so far from offering an escape from anti-Semitism, is the avenue to it."[101])

Advocates of immigration restriction were vindicated to some degree by the Royal Commission's report. It emphatically recommended the institution of legislation.* The Aliens Act of 1905 put a cap on immigration thereafter, offered immigrants tickets back home, and broadened the grounds for deportation. In addition, the right of political asylum, which had been automatic prior to the Act, was now a matter of discretion.[102] While the Act included all aliens, it was clearly aimed at the Jews. These measures were to reduce the number of Jewish settlers by over fifty per cent: from 11,000 in 1906, to 4,000 by 1911.[103] Not satisfied with this decrease, in 1913, the *East London Observer* reprinted an article that had been published during the Jew Bill debate in 1753: "This is to inform the public that the good ship Rodrigue. . . . [is] ready to take on Christian families that may be inclined to transport themselves into any part of Turkey, as choosing to live under a Mohammedan rather than a Jewish government."[104]

It takes us until the very end of this discussion on the immigration restriction debate to arrive at another one of the reasons for advocating this measure. When the Aliens Act was before Parliament, Prime Minister Arthur Balfour articulated what he saw as a most compelling rationale for the Act: the Jews' failure to intermarry.

> A state of things could easily be imagined in which it would not be to the advantage of the civilization of the country that there should be an immense body of persons who, however patriotic, able and industrious—however much they threw themselves into the national life—still by their own action remained a people apart and not merely a religion differing from the vast majority of their countrymen, but only intermarried among themselves.[105]

---

* The conclusions drawn by the commissioners from the multitude of submissions they examined resulted in a bill—the Aliens Bill of 1904—that was more stringent than the one that was actually passed. It was scuttled by the Liberals. Lipman, *Social History*, 137.

Balfour does not complain about Jewish immorality or criminality, let alone the most prominent issues, the effect of Russian immigrant Jews on the lower-class workforce and housing. Rather, they may be "patriotic, able, and industrious," but they will not intermarry. That this issue was and continued to be an ongoing one is revealed in an analysis of an interview the *Jewish Chronicle* conducted with Arnold White. "Mr. White demands the intermarriage of Jews as a condition of tolerating the immigration of Jewish aliens at all, as did Mr. Balfour when the Alien Bill was before Parliament. No good purpose would be served by reopening the well-worn intermarriage theme."[106] As soon as it became clear that Russian Jews had by and large rejected intermarriage, assessed as the most effective way to achieve assimilation, it was added to the other reasons for advocating immigration restriction.

****

"If the Jews will consent to be absorbed and to mingle their blood with ours, all will be well,"[107] wrote Arnold White, "but if not, the unpopularity of the foreign Jews is likely to increase."[108] And it was White's personal opinion that this would be the case because the pattern of Jewish history was that Jews were either oppressed or they

> became predominant to an alarming extent, partly by their abilities and partly by the indifference of many of them to the ethical laws which govern the relations between man and man.... Since the numbers of the Jews are largely on the increase, and their wealth and power have enormously developed, the prospects for the future are not encouraging either for them or for Christendom. The comparatively small minority of Jews who are honestly absorbed in the various nationalities of their adoption are too few to do more than delay a crisis seemingly inevitable and now within the arena of practical politics. In the twenty years that succeeded the expulsion of the Jews from England in 1292, every country, with the exception of Poland, followed the British example. After the lapse of 600 years a new unrest is perceptible throughout the civilized world on the subject of the Jewish Question, while the problem in Russia is no longer soluble by mere administrative restrictions. The conclusion, therefore, seems obvious that either the situation must be dealt with—i.e., by Europe as a whole—or an alarming outbreak against the race, the members of which are always in exile and strangers in the land of their adoption, will result, and the clock of civilization thus be thrown back for a hundred years.... During the last century the Hebrew community have had every opportunity for exhibiting their capacity for complete and honest absorption.... Since the Hebrew race, after a century of trial, under fairly good conditions, at all events for sixty or seventy years of the time, have persistently refused to unite with other nationalities, no other alternative is possible than to discover some territory which should be Oriental, at no great distance from Europe, and associated, if possible, directly or indirectly with Palestine. [Armenia was White's choice.][109]

No easier on his fellow citizens, White argued that

> where the nations are being destroyed by the Jews they deserve to be destroyed; that weakness, self-indulgence, stupidity, want of proper education and of

common foresight, and indifference to the trust that each generation holds for its successor, are the real reasons why the Jews are victorious and the non-Jews are vanquished.[110]

Not only does this portion of White's work summarize the views of other British writers on the Jewish Question, his assessment dovetails so very closely with Gyozo Istoczy's.

If Jews were predominantly viewed as aliens in late nineteenth-century Britain, it was because they were not reforming and thus melding in with the rest of the population; it was not because they were alien as related to citizenship or birthplace. As the *East London Observer* had stated, "Of the *foreign* and *alien* Jewish community . . ."

NOTES

1. Roth, *History of the Jews*, 267.
2. *Jewish Chronicle*, 24 November 1882.
3. Rabbi of the Central Synagogue, quoted in Alderman, *Jewish Community*, 37.
4. Wolf, "Introduction," *Essays*, 355.
5. John Bright and Goldwin Smith, quoted in Wolf, "Introduction," *Essays*, 354.
6. Shannon, *Gladstone*, 199-200, 219.
7. William Gladstone, quoted in Alderman, *Jewish Community*, 39.
8. William Gladstone, quoted in George Earl Buckle, *The Life of Benjamin Disraeli, Earl of Beaconsfield* (London: John Murray, 1920), 59.
9. C. C. Aronsfeld, "German Jews in Victorian England," *LBIYB* 7 (1962): 312.
10. Bernard Gainer, *The Alien Invasion: Origins of the Aliens Act of 1905* (London: Heinemann Educational Books Ltd, 1972), 2.
11. Jill Pellew, "Communication: The Home Office and the Aliens Act, 1905," *Historical Journal* 32 (1989): 370-71.
12. Todd M. Endelman, *The Jews in the History of Britain, 1656 to 2000* (Berkeley, Los Angeles, and London: University of California Press, 2002), 127.
13. Rubinstein, *History of the Jews*, 95-96.
14. A city councillor, quoted in the *East London Observer* (1902), in C. Bermant, *Point of Arrival: A Study of London's East End* (London: Eyre Methuen Ltd, 1975), 122.
15. Wolf, "Introduction," *Essays*, 357-58.
16. In the issue of the *Jewish Chronicle* dated 25 October 1881, the editor wrote that the immigration of Russian and Polish Jews was causing the Jewish Question to surface. The accuracy of this forecast is seen in his lament fourteen years later: "The rehabilitating work of nigh upon a century of emancipation in the Occident is being clogged by the medievalist overflow of the Russian and Roumanian Ghettos." 18 October 1895, 11.
17. MP James Lowther, quoted in John A. Garrard, *The English and Immigration 1880-1910* (London: Oxford University Press, 1971), 63.
18. MP Major William Evans-Gordon, quoted in Garrard, *English and Immigration*, 63.
19. V. D. Lipman, *Social History of the Jews in England 1850-1950* (London: C. A. Watts & Co. Ltd., 1954), 135-36; Gainer, *Alien Invasion*, 168-69.
20. M. J. Landa, *The Alien Problem and Its Remedy* (London: P. S. King & Son, 1911), 9-30; Gainer, *Alien Invasion*, 166-83.
21. Quoted in Lipman, *Social History*, 137.
22. Lipman, *Social History*, 137.

23. Mr. Brown, quoted in Garrard, *English and Immigration*, 65.
24. Colin Holmes, *Anti-Semitism in British Society 1876-1939* (London: Edward Arnold [Publishers] Ltd, 1979), 18.
25. W. Cunningham D.D., *Alien Immigrants to England*, ed. Kenelm D. Cotes (Social England Series. London: Sonnenschein & Co., Limited, 1897), 266.
26. Parliament (Commons), Royal Commission on Alien Immigration, vol. 2, Interviews, par. 12209-12210: 413-14.
27. Beatrice Potter wrote a good deal on this topic at the time. Quoted in Holmes, *Anti-Semitism*, 18.
28. J. A. Hobson, *Problems of Poverty: An Inquiry into the Industrial Condition of the Poor* (1891; repr., New York: Augustus M. Kelley Publishers, 1971), 61.
29. Quoted in Gainer, *Alien Invasion*, 28-29. Gainer's book offers an exhaustive source of newspaper and commission reports on the perceptions held by the public on alien Jews.
30. Quoted in David Englander, *Landlord and Tenant in Urban Britain, 1838-1918* (Oxford: Clarendon Press, 1983), 271-72.
31. John Burnett, quoted in Gainer, *Alien Invasion*, 24.
32. Earl of Dunraven, *Parliamentary Debate*, 3rd ser., vol. 345 (1890), col. 296-97; Earl of Dunraven, "The Invasion of Destitute Aliens," *Nineteenth Century* 31, no. 184 (June 1892): 993-94.
33. R. H. Sherard, *The Child Slaves of Britain* (London, 1905), xii, xix, 61-76. Sherard was a prominent journalist and foreign correspondent who wrote a good deal on this topic. In a piece of research journalism, he traveled with Jews from Hamburg to see how they were received by the New York Immigration Board. His views were widely publicized in the *Daily Express*, the *Standard*, and later, in a book, *At the Closed Door*. Typical was this comment: "Long ages of hunger and suffering have brutalized a race which of all races is the most intelligent. The faces . . . under matted and verminous locks. . . . are scarcely human. They are the faces of imbeciles, of idiots, ape-faces, dog faces—all that is hideous and most profoundly pitiful. . . . Their half naked bodies are black with filth and red with sores." Quoted in the *Standard* (January 1905), in Holmes, *Anti-Semitism*, 38.
34. W. H. Wilkins, *The Alien Invasion* (London, 1892), 76.
35. *Fuggetlenseg*, 22 November 1883.322.
36. Endelman, *Jews of Britain*, 135-36.
37. Herbert Evans, quoted in Stephen Aris, *The Jews in Business* (1970; repr., London: Jonathan Cape Ltd, 1971), 101.
38. Charles Freak, quoted in Gainer, *Alien Invasion*, 24, 30-1.
39. Gainer, *Alien Invasion*, 33-35.
40. Beatrice Potter, quoted in Holmes, *Anti-Semitism*, 19. The contemporary historian Elie Halevy took issue with this assertion, but his alternative assessment is no more favorable to these Jews. In *History of the English People, 1895-1905*, in the chapter entitled "The Aliens Act," Halevy wrote, "It is very doubtful whether the commercial morality of the East End Jews was worse than that of their native rivals. . . . It was their insatiable appetite for work which made them formidable. For the Jew, no amount of wealth was so great that he would not seek to earn more, no wages so small that he was ashamed to work for it." Quoted in Israel Finestein, "The New Community, 1880-1918," in *Three Centuries of Anglo-Jewish History: A Volume of Essays*, ed. V. D. Lipman (Cambridge: Jewish Historical Society of England, 1961), 112.
41. Quoted in Gainer, *Alien Invasion*, 33-35.
42. Earl of Dunraven, "Invasion of Destitute Aliens," 996.
43. James Lowther, *Parliamentary Debate*, 4th ser., vol. 8 (1893-4), col 1165.
44. Gainer, *Alien Invasion*, 133.

45. Charles Booth, quoted in Aris, *Jews in Business*, 37-38.
46. *Pall Mall Gazette*, quoted in Bermant, *Point of Arrival*, 145.
47. Aris, *Jews in Business*, 35; Alderman, *Jewish Community*, 69. This topic made its way into the assessments of the Royal Commissioners; those in favor of prohibiting certain areas to Russian Jews outnumbered those against. Gainer, *Alien Invasion*, 184.
48. *Eastern Post*, 16 November 1901.
49. Alderman for Stepney, James Lawson Silver, quoted in *Eastern Post*, 23 November 1901. See also "The Invasion of Pauper Foreigners," *Nineteenth Century* 22, no. 133 (March 1888): 417-18; Arthur A. Baumann, MP, "Possible Remedies for the Sweating System," *National Review* 12, no. 69 (November 1888): 298-99; letters to the editor, *Evening News*, 22 May 1891; *Evening Post*, 11 May 1901; *East London Observer*, 18 January 1902.
50. Gainer, *Alien Invasion*, 43-44; Holmes, *Anti-Semitism*, 16. We may look forward a few years to "The Report of the Finance and Parliamentary Committee of the Stepney Borough Council," produced in 1908. In it, we find that the Stepney Borough Council had been questioned about the large number of empty properties in the borough. (Located within the East End, the Borough of Stepney had the largest concentration of Russian Jews.) They discovered the following reasons for this situation: an influx of foreigners which had caused many of the residents to relocate; "enormous removal" to the outer suburbs; high rentals; and slackness in riverside employment. *Jewish Chronicle*, 17 January 1908, 8; Hobson, *Problems of Poverty*, 58.
51. *Eastern Post*, 19 October 1901.
52. As a member of the Housing Committee of the Stepney Borough Council reported, "They dirt all over the floor. If you do not mind how you go you may slip down and find yourself covered with vermin, or something else.... It is worse than what it is in the main road when it has been a very wet day." Quoted in Gainer, *Alien Invasion*, 27, 46.
53. *East London Observer* (18 December 1900), quoted in Bermant, *Point of Arrival*, 148.
54. Gainer, *Alien Invasion*, 57.
55. Lloyd P. Gartner, *The Jewish Immigrant in England, 1870-1914* (London: Allen & Unwin Publishers Ltd., 1960), 221-31.
56. Alderman Silver, quoted in Gainer, *Alien Invasion*, 49.
57. Quoted in Lipman, *Social History*, 134-35.
58. White, *Modern Jew*, 144-64. In addition to being one of the foremost opponents of Russian-Jewish immigration and a member of the Royal Commission on Alien Immigration, White was perhaps the most well-known figure in Britain who addressed the Jewish Question.
59. *Truth* (1878), quoted in Feldman, *Englishmen and Jews*, 81.
60. Gainer, *Alien Invasion*, 33-35.
61. White, *Modern Jew*, 144-60.
62. Royal Commission, quoted in Lipman, *Social History*, 134-35.
63. G. F. A. Wendeborn, quoted in Katz, *Jews in the History of England*, 358-60.
64. Fearing negative publicity against the Jews, Metropolitan Chief Commissioner Sir Charles Warren rushed to have the message, "The Jews are the men that will not be blamed for nothing," erased immediately. Even without such an incitement, the *East London Observer* reported "Ripper riots" against the Jews. Quoted in Colin Holmes, "East End Crime and the Jewish Community, 1887-1911," in *The Jewish East End, 1840-1939*, ed. Colin Holmes (London: Jewish Historical Society, 1981), 114. Since a link had been made between the location of the murders and the likely identity of the murderer, the Vienna correspondent of the *Times* suggested that a recent case of ritual murder in Cracow could enlighten matters in Whitechapel. David Cesarani, *The Jewish Chronicle and Anglo-*

Jewry, 1841-1991 (Cambridge: Cambridge University Press, 1994), 81. The *Church Times* proposed that a *shochet* "steeped in Old Testament law might have felt some religious justification for killing prostitutes." Quoted in Holmes, "East End Crime," 115. So seriously was this idea taken that the editor of the *Jewish Chronicle* felt compelled to take a set of *shochet's* knives down to the city divisional surgeon and show him how they differed from the murder weapon. *Jewish Chronicle*, 12 October 1888, 4. After the third victim's body was discovered outside the Berner Street International Club where many Jewish anarchists congregated, an accusation was printed that the 'Ripper' was a Russian anarchist. William Fishman, *East End Jewish Radicals, 1875-1914* (Gerald Duckworth & Co., 1975), 73.

65. Quoted in Fishman, "Jewish Immigrant Anarchists," 241.

66. Head of the Criminal Investigation Department, quoted in Holmes, "East End Crime," 114-15.

67. Holmes, "East End Crime," 113.

68. Rudolf Rocker, *The London Years*, trans. Joseph Leftwich (London: Robert Anscombe & Co., 1956), 206.

69. W. S. Shaw, quoted in the *East London Observer*, in Holmes, *Anti-Semitism*, 37-38

70. *People*, quoted in Colin Rogers, *The Battle of Stepney* (London: Robert Hale, 1981), 70.

71. *Times*, 19 December 1910, 12.

72. *Parliamentary Debate,* 4th Series, vol. 101 (1902), col. 1278. See also the *Times*, 25 April 1904.

73. *Parliamentary Debates*: 4th Series, vol. 2 (1892), col. 681; vol. 21, (1893-4), col. 721; vol. 61 (1898), col. 315; vol. 114 (1902), col. 1357-8; vol. 118 (1903), col. 938, 954-5, 971; vol. 132 (1904), col. 987-9; vol. 133 (1904), col. 1139. See also Sir Robert Anderson, "The Problem of the Criminal Alien," *Nineteenth Century and After* 49, no. 408 (February 1911): 217-25; *Eastern Post*, 19 October 1901, 23 November 1901, 14 November 1903; the testimony of Sir Alfred Newton, Commissioner of the Central Criminal Court, Alderman, and Lord Mayor of London (1899) in Census of England and Wales, General Report, Cd 1742, Min. 10447-95.

74. From John Wade's *A Treatise on the Police and Crimes of the Metropolis*, quoted in Katz, *Jews in the History of England*, 359.

75. *Daily News*, 5 September 1904, quoted in Bermant, *Point of Arrival*, 145.

76. In 1909, the Jewish International Conference for the Suppression of the Traffic in Women and Girls would be hosted in London. Gartner, *Jewish Immigrant*, 184-86.

77. J. H. Clapham, *An Economic History of Modern Britain* (Cambridge, 1930-8), 2:441, 3:2, 49-50, 449.

78. Quoted in Gainer, *Alien Invasion*, 108.

79. Joseph Chamberlain, "The Labour Question," *Nineteenth Century* 32, no. 189 (November 1892): 705. See also A. A. Baumann, "Possible Remedies for the Sweating System," *National Review* 12, no. 69 (November 1888): 304-6; Alderman Silver, quoted in *Eastern Post*, 23 November 1901; Earl of Meath, quoted in the *Times*, 13 April 1887; Sir Howard Vincent, quoted in the *Eastern Post*, 28 September 1901; Montague Crackenthorpe, "Should Government Interfere?" in *The Destitute Alien in Great Britain*, ed. Arnold White (London, 1892), 3, 63, 67-70; S. H. Jeyes, "Foreign Pauper Immigration," in Arnold White ed., *The Destitute Alien in Great Britain* (London, 1892), 186-7; Wilkins, *Alien Invasion*, 127-35. *Parliamentary Debates*: Captain J. C. R. Colomb, 3rd ser., vol. 311 (1887), col. 1724; Louis Jennings, vol. 353 (1890-1), col.1190-1; James Lowther, 4th ser., vol. 8 (1893-4), col. 1159, 1166; Sir Carne Rasch, vol. 22 (1894), col. 83; Lord Salisbury, vol. 26, (1894), col. 1050-1; Evans-Gordon, vol. 101, (1902), col. 1278.

80. Wilkins, *Alien Invasion*, 4.

81. Jeyes, "Foreign Pauper Immigration," 189. Jeyes was at one time assistant editor

of the most reputable *St. James Gazette*. H. W. Massingham, *The London Daily Press* (London: Religious Tract Society, 1892), 167-68. See also Lord Charles Beresford's comment in the *Times*, 20 April 1887; "Jews as Anarchists," *Evening News*, 21 May 1891; *Eastern Post*, 21 September 1901 (reprint of article in the *Standard*); "Foreign Undesirables," *Blackwood's Magazine* 169, no. 1024 (February 1901): 287-88; Wilkins, *Alien Invasion*, 55.

82. Wilkins, *Alien Invasion*, 109.

83. Lloyd P. Gartner's *The Jewish Immigrant in England, 1870-1914*, chap. 4, provides a good summary of the Jewish involvement in the socialist and anarchist movements. (London: Allen & Unwin Publishers Ltd., 1960). See also W. J. Fishman, "Jewish Immigrant Anarchists in East London, 1870-1914," in *The Jewish East End 1840-1939*, ed. Kenneth Lunn (London: Jewish Historical Society, 1981); Rudolf Rocker, *The London Years*, trans. Joseph Leftwich (London: Robert Anscombe & Co., 1956).

84. Jeyes, "Foreign Pauper Immigration," 174-75; *Evening News*, 15 and 17 June 1891.

85. Chamberlain, "Labour Question," 705.

86. Alderman Silver, quoted in the *Eastern Post*, 2 November 1901.

87. Karl Pearson, *National Life from the Standpoint of Science* (London, 1905), 54, 104-5.

88. Robert Reid Rentoul, *Race Culture: Or Race Suicide* (1906; repr., New York: Garland Publishing, Inc., 1984), 4, 7, 26-27, xii.

89. *Times*, 20 April 1887.

90. *Evening News*, 11 June 1891.

91. Gainer, *Alien Invasion*, 63; Bermant, *Point of Arrival*, 145.

92. *Eastern Post*, 29 June 1901.

93. William Stanley Shaw, quoted in the *Eastern Post*, 23 November 1901.

94. *Times*, 14 December 1904.

95. Gainer, *Alien Invasion*, 71.

96. Gainer, *Alien Invasion*, 69-71.

97. *Times*, 8 August 1903.

98. A letter Evans-Gordon wrote to JTO president Israel Zangwill on this topic was published by the *Times*, 12 December 1905.

99. Joseph Chamberlain, "Tariff Reform and Unemployment," (1904) in *Mr. Chamberlain's Speeches*, ed. Charles W. Boyd (London, 1914), 2: 264-65.

100. Arnold White, "The Truth About the Russian Jew," *Contemporary Review* 61 (May 1892): 705.

101. *Jewish Chronicle*, 14 June 1901, 17.

102. Porter, *Refugee Question*, 218.

103. Alderman, *Jewish Community*, 77.

104. *East London Observer*, 1 March 1913, quoted in Bermant, *Point of Arrival*, 123. Alfonso Rodrigues's name is strongly associated with the readmission of Jews to England.

105. Prime Minister Arthur Balfour, quoted in Lipman, *Social History*, 141.

106. *Jewish Chronicle*, 17 January 1908, 8.

107. And amongst the Jews there were those "whose sympathy, exquisite refinement of mind, delicate perception, intellectual power, and social charm make them the most delightful of human beings" and whose numbers are increasing as "education spreads and the spirit of the Jewish religion is shed abroad." White, *Modern Jew*, 144-60.

108. White, *Modern Jew*, 208-9.

109. White, *Modern Jew*, 273-75.

110. White, *Modern Jew*, 161.

Chapter 12
Jews in Business

So far, only Russian Jews, invariably described as alien and indigent, have been discussed. The presence of these Jews was the source of one form of tension in Britain. Less in the public eye was the extraordinary success of certain Jews engaged in capitalist enterprise and finance. This created another form of tension, for, "What power in civilized society is so great as that of the creditor over the debtor? If we take this away from the Jew we take away the security of his property. If we leave it to him, we leave him a power more despotic than that of the king and all his cabinet."[1] There were thus two prongs to the belief that Jews were throwing the traditional structure of British society out of kilter.

This stratum of Anglo-Jewry was composed of long-time Sephardi inhabitants and recent immigrants, primarily from Germany. Rather little was written in the post-emancipation period in the way of assessing their efforts at social assimilation. The tendency was to write about these Jews in relation to their business activities. Charlotte Lea Klein discusses a number of novels of the time in which financial power was the theme, but indirectly, the degree of social assimilation may be ascertained.[2] Not only these novels but also the following extract from the correspondence of a "Jewish Lady"—while it is expressed from the Jewish perspective—indicate that the efforts of these Jews to socially assimilate had not been terribly successful. In fact, in this lady's opinion, the lack of social acceptance was to the degree that the only option was to convert Jewish children to Christianity.

> Should we expose them to the ridicule of their classmates and to the spiteful allusions of teachers who fancy themselves comic with their Jewish intonation? Should our sons be barked at in the army by some coarse sergeant or some insolent boor of a second lieutenant simply because they are Jews? Should they fulfill their military service conscientiously only to be discriminated against? Should our daughters who attend a public ball, even if graced with physical and spiritual charm and impeccably and modestly dressed, be scorned by geese with crosses on their breasts, avoided by men and forced into a gloomy corner?[3]

On the other hand, S. H. Jeyes exemplifies those who wrote in positive terms about this upper echelon of Anglo-Jewry, and, like a number of others, he juxtaposed 'our' Jews with 'those' Jews—immigrant Jews—as part of his construction of this favorable image. "We have our native English Jews . . . a better, sturdier stock, a more desirable body of fellow citizens, it would not be easy to find. They have their faults, but they are English to the core." But the immigrants "have all the vices which are generated by many centuries of systematic oppression."[4] Only after liberalism becomes somewhat discredited as the normative ethos do comments on the lack of assimilation within this group appear with more frequency.

Among those whose businesses flourished under their acumen were research chemist Ludwig Mond (1839-1909), who was behind the formation of the Imperial Chemical Industries; Hugo Hirst, founder of the General Electric Company; and Siegfried Bettmann, developer of the motorcycle industry. The linen and yarn trade in Northern Ireland was transformed by Sir Otto Jaffe when he incorporated new, saleable designs from abroad.[5] Beginning in 1892, the firm of Marcus Samuel & Co. began to carve out a corner of the oil business in the Middle East, eventually capturing a considerable part if it.[6] In many other industries, German Jews shared control with Christian entrepreneurs: Dundee's jute trade; Belfast's shipyards; Nottingham's lace trade; and Yorkshire's wool trade. In 1857, a historian of worsted manufacture in England wrote of the Jews' "salesmanship, languages and foreign contacts" which had bolstered the wool trade, and "in seasons of depression . . . [they] bought largely for the future and thus rendered efficient aid in times of difficulty and pressure."[7] Seventy-five years later, the *Yorkshire Observer's* retrospective on the wool trade confirmed the importance of Jews to this mainstay of the British economy: if the "merchant princes of Bradford" had not actually pioneered Bradford's export trade in wool, it had ripened under their direction.[8] Many of these Jews cast their nets abroad: the bankers Messrs. S. L. Behrens, for example, developed the South American railways; Alfred Beit and Barney Barnato amassed fortunes in South Africa's diamond fields and gold mines.[9]

In an 1888 issue of the *Banker's Magazine*, MP Samuel Montagu wrote, "The Jews have shown a marked excellence in what can be called the commerce of imperceptibles. They have no particular superiority in the ordinary branches of trade." However, they "excel on every Bourse in Europe; they have a preeminence out of all proportion to their numbers."[10] As proof of Montagu's observation, and bracketing the nineteenth century were the two most successful Anglo-Jewish financiers, Nathan Meyer Rothschild and Sir Ernst Cassel. Rothschild arrived in Manchester in 1804 and transformed the £20,000 his father had given him to start up as a textile dealer into a fortune of between £5 and £6 million. By 1815, he had become the dominant figure on the London Stock Exchange, with official status as the bullion broker to the Government of England.[11] For a hundred years, the firm of N. M. Rothschild and Sons would be the world's leading private bankers. Sir Ernst Cassel is often considered the last of the *Hofjuden*. To him goes the credit of underwriting King Edward VII's "monarchy as the most glittering constellation in the social galaxy."[12] His fortune was further used to establish the London School of Economics and provide London with a more viable transportation system.[13] Internationally, he developed the iron and steel industry in Sweden, railways in the United States and Mexico, central banks and agricultural banks in the Middle East,[14] and he was behind the construction of the Assouan Dam in Egypt. "The regeneration of Egypt during the last fifteen or twenty years has been largely the work of Cassel," read the Government's tribute to him upon his death in 1918. These larger-than-life figures were a minority;

more typical of those engaged in the "commerce of imperceptibles" were David Salomons and Moses Montefiore, founders of the Westminster Bank and the Provincial Bank of Ireland, respectively.[15]

This phenomenon increasingly provoked comment. The *Fortnightly Review*'s editor, T. H. S. Escott, wrote that "English society once ruled by an aristocracy is now dominated by a plutocracy. And this plutocracy is to a large extent Hebraic in its composition. There is no phenomenon more noticeable in society than the ascendancy of the Jews."[16] Just as in Germany, the *Daily News* reported, "There has been a tendency of late . . . to speak disparagingly, not to say resentfully, of Jewish enterprise and Jewish success."[17] It was a natural step to extend the Jews' perceived dominance to other realms: "With the sceptre of finance the Jew also dominates the politics of the world. . . . It is the Jewish mind that is guiding the religious and moral movements in society in our day, and in secret the Jew is forging the chains with which he is preparing to load those miserable Gentiles who are looking on in their folly."[18] Between 1877 and 1878, Baron Lionel de Rothschild, who in addition to his banking activities owned a silver refinery in England, and Gerson von Bleichroder, head of the Bleichroder Bank in Berlin, carried on an intense communication of political and commercial information which involved the manipulation of the world silver market.[19] This Rothschild was only one of the Anglo-Jewish representatives of what historian Howard Sachar, from the Jewish perspective, calls "The Frankfurt Tradition: Internationalization,"[20] but what some non-Jews at the time called cosmopolitanism, domination, or an international conspiracy.[21]

The extensive involvement of Jews in the press also provoked comment. A contributor to *The Contemporary Review* saw it as very natural, for "None understand[s] the public as the Jew does, for he stands apart from it . . . and surveys it pathologically. He dominates the Press on the Seine, the Spree, and the Danube. For he possesses the self-assurance, the suppleness and alertness of mind needful for success in journalism."[22] This writer might also have included the press in South Africa, which Hobson maintained was controlled by the Jews.[23] In fact, according to Hobson, the Boer War had been "press-made", coordinated by the South African press which was owned by Jewish financiers, "two important London daily papers," and "several considerable weekly papers" also owned by British Jewish financiers (who were rapidly gaining control of other organs of the press).[24] While the alliance between Jewish finance and newspaper ownership had not progressed as far as on the Continent (Paul von Reuter's telegraph news service is perhaps the most commonly cited example), it was increasing and "has notoriously exercised a subtle and abiding influence upon leading London newspapers."[25]

For some, the Boer War was one more example of Jews holding "the sceptre of finance" and hence the frequent reference to it as the "Jewish War."[26] Hobson covered the war for the *Manchester Guardian* and later summarized these reports in his book, *The War in South Africa*. He wrote of a "little ring of international financiers" that had cold-bloodedly provoked the war in order to consolidate their gold holdings in the Transvaal.[27] And who were they? Foreign Jews. While Hobson was apologetic to state the truth about our doings in South Africa without seeming to appeal to the ignominious passion of *Judenhetze* [hatred of the Jews]. . . . [nevertheless] recent developments of Transvaal gold-mining have thrown the economic resources more and more into the hands of a small group of international financiers, chiefly German in origin and Jewish in race.[28]

This war was the result of "modern forces which are world-wide in their scope and revolutionary in their operations,"[29] that is to say, the result of Jewish domination of international capitalism. The war enjoyed popularity among the people because they mistakenly supported imperialism;[30] the Conservatives had been duped by the fiction that "trade tends to follow the flag," but in truth, according to Hobson, a coterie of detached opportunists were creating a terrible national sickness for their own material benefit.[31]

Hobson's views were echoed elsewhere. The Liberal-dominated South African Conciliation Committee talked openly about a "capitalist conspiracy" in 1900: "cosmopolitan capitalists" was the expression reserved for its more formal publications; "Jewish financiers" was the expression used in the pamphlets meant for mass distribution. In both, it was implied that British soldiers were dying to fill the coffers of Jewish capitalists.[32] In Labour circles, the sentiment was the same. A resolution by the Trades Union Congress in 1900 stated that the purpose of the Boer War was to "secure the gold fields of South Africa for cosmopolitan Jews, most of whom had no patriotism and no country."[33] Labour MPs, when delivering anti-war speeches, almost invariably framed them in anti-capitalist and often anti-Jewish terms: "In the interest of gold and diamonds in South Africa," the "financial Jew [is] operating, directing, [and] inspiring the agencies that have led to this war," and "who if [he] got the vote would sell it."[34] Historian Bernard Porter found that organs of the Labour movement—*Reynold's Newspaper* was one—consistently had leader articles such as the "Anglo-Jewish Financial Party."[35]

For historians such as Colin Holmes and W. D. Rubinstein, it is puzzling and disturbing that Hobson and Goldwin Smith (above) were committed liberals while at the same time holding "anti-Jewish" views. Hobson was one of the architects of the New Liberalism, whose vision of social and economic affairs was one of the most "sophisticated" prior to the Second World War, according to Holmes. Goldwin Smith, who held the Regius Chair of Modern History at Oxford from 1858 to 1866 and later held a professorship at Cornell University, was a recognized defender of liberalism. In an effort to resolve this discrepancy between Smith's reputation as a liberal and his "extreme" and "illogical" intolerance, Holmes suggests a personal public quarrel Smith had with Disraeli years earlier as the only possible reason for his otherwise inexplicable attitudes. Hobson's intolerance is pushed to the side, while his conviction that Jews wielded untold power in the economic sphere, Holmes concedes, may have some merit. Rubinstein views this anti-Semitic streak in Smith and Hobson as a "gross inconsistency," a "gross contradiction." While Smith's quarrel with Disraeli makes his antipathy somewhat less "incomprehensible", still, it was "highly deviant from the mainstream of British liberal thought . . . which emphasized religious tolerance, minority rights and the merits of upwardly mobile capitalists and democracy." I would suggest that the conundrum they perceive is one of their own making. Nineteenth-century liberalism's ethos of tolerance, as I have discussed at length in the previous chapters, was no surety of positive feelings towards Jews or their activities. While most liberals were tight-lipped about any reservations they had, outspoken figures like Hobson and Smith did not share this inhibition. It is the misapprehension that the liberal ethos of tolerance precluded negativity towards Jews that has caused difficulties for Holmes and Rubinstein.[36]

****

Throughout the nineteenth century, a dichotomized view of both capitalist entrepreneurs and the working class existed. The former was portrayed as both a stimulant to the economy and exploitative and insensitive. The latter was characterized alternately as the victim of industrialization (and specifically, at the mercy of unscrupulous industrialists) and a major social problem due to their filth of person, homes, and environment; poor eating habits; degenerate social practices; and poor work ethic.

The question is why, in Britain, both Jewish capitalists and Jewish alien sweatshop workers came to be assigned the negative role in these dichotomies. G. C. Webber has argued that Jewish plutocrats simply became the "symbol of finance," and thus "anti-Semitism had less to do with Jews as such."[37] By extension, then, one may presume that destitute Jewish aliens became the "symbol" of all that was loathsome in the working class. Webber's approach is not convincing and merely raises the level of scapegoating. George Dangerfield's comment, however, contains the seeds of an answer:

> Whatever his political convictions may have been, the Englishman of the 70s and 80s was something of a liberal at heart. He believed in freedom, free trade, progress, and the Seventh commandment. . . . But somehow or other, as the century turned, the burden of Liberalism grew more and more irksome; it began to give out a dismal, rattling sound . . .[38]

The 1870s and 1880s were indeed the heyday of liberalism. The "dismal, rattling sound" was emitted by liberalism as its elevated principles and aims became sullied by modern capitalism; economic enterprise had gone berserk, tainting British and continental European civilization. The Jews, according to some, contributed to this transformation.

> The Rothschild leeches have for years hung on with distended suckers to the body politic of Europe. . . . a gigantic conspiracy manifold and comprehensive . . . . has been the cause of untold mischief and misery in Europe during the present century, and has piled up its prodigious wealth chiefly through fomenting wars.[39]

As long as the buoyancy of the liberal era cast the Jews in a favorable light, concerns about the Jews could get no hearing. But with a reversal of liberalism's positive image, the economic activities of the Jews indeed came under criticism. That age-old stipulation that the Jewish presence would be tolerated provided their contributions to the economy did not become a liability either through overperformance or underperformance was no longer suppressed. *This* is the point of commonality between Jewish capitalists and Jewish sweatshop workers and why both came to be assigned the negative role in the dichotomy: neither was fulfilling his prescribed role of being of economic utility. Both Jewish capitalists and Russian-Jewish aliens were guilty of overperformance: while excessive wealth was being concentrated in the hands of the former, the latter were seen to be worsening the economic lot of the British working class.

NOTES

1. Foremost advocate of Jewish emancipation Thomas Macaulay, quoted in I. Abrahams and S. Levy, eds., *Macaulay on Jewish Disabilities* (Edinburgh, 1910), 25.
2. Amongst these novels are four written by Anthony Trollope in the 1870s: *The Eustace Diamonds, Phineas Redux, The Way We Live Now,* and *The Prime Minister.* Charlotte Lea Klein, "The Changing Image of the Jew in Modern English Literature," *Patterns of Prejudice* 5, no. 1 (January–February 1971): 23.
3. "The Correspondence of an English Lady on Judaism and Semitism," quoted in Heinrich Graetz, in *The Structure of Jewish History, and Other Essays,* ed. Ismar Schorsch (New York: Jewish Theological Seminary, 1979), 192.
4. S. H. Jeyes, quoted in the *Fortnightly,* in Finestein, "New Community," 112.
5. Aronsfeld, "German Jews," 316-17.
6. Pollins, *Economic History of the Jews,* 170-71.
7. John James, quoted in Aronsfeld, "German Jews," 316-17.
8. *Yorkshire Observer* (1934), quoted in Aronsfeld, "German Jews," 317.
9. Aronsfeld, "German Jews," 317; Endelman, *Jews of Britain,* 155.
10. MP Samuel Montagu, quoted in Aris, *Jews in Business,* 69.
11. Aris, *Jews in Business,* 64-65.
12. W. S. Adams, quoted in Aronsfeld, "German Jews," 315.
13. Aronsfeld, "German Jews," 315.
14. Kurt Grunwald, "Windsor-Cassel—The Last Court Jew," *LBIYB* 14 (1969): 121.
15. Quoted in Aronsfeld, "German Jews," 315-17.
16. T. H. S. Escott [a foreign resident, pseud.], *Society in London* (1885), quoted in Feldman, *Englishmen and Jews,* 81.
17. *Daily News,* 17 January 1882, 5.
18. *East London Leader,* quoted in Holmes, *Anti-Semitism,* 64.
19. Gershom A. Knight, "The Rothschild-Bleichroder Axis," *LBIYB* 28 (1983): 43-57.
20. Sachar, *Course of Modern Jewish History,* 133-40.
21. For the following list which places Jews within the general subject of finance I have relied on Feldman's *Englishmen and Jews,* 78-80. J. Camplin, *The Rise of the Plutocrats* (London, 1978); S. D. Chapman, *The Rise of Merchant Banking* (London, 1984); P. L Cottrell, *British Overseas Investment in the Nineteenth Century* (London, 1975); L. Davis and R. A. Huttenback, *Mammon and the Pursuit of Empire, 1860-1912* (Cambridge, 1986); R. Davis, *The English Rothschilds* (Durham, N.C., 1983); M. Edelstein, *Overseas Investment in the Age of High Imperialism* (London, 1982); P. Emden, *Money Powers of Europe in the Nineteenth and Twentieth Centuries* (London, 1937);

Evans, *The City: Or the Physiology of London Business* (London, 1845); G. D. Ingall and G. Withers, *The Stock Exchange* (London, 1904); E. V. Morgan and W. A. Thomas, *The Stock Exchange: Its History and Functions* (London, 1962). See also Niall Ferguson, *The House of Rothschild: The World's Banker, 1849-1999* (New York: Viking, 1999).

22. Sidney Whitman, "The Anti-Semitic Movement," *Contemporary Review* 63 (January-June, 1893), 704-5.

23. J. A. Hobson, *The War in South Africa: Its Causes and Effects* (1900; repr., New York and London: Garland Publishing, Inc., 1972), 206-10.

24. Hobson, *War in South Africa*, 217-18.

25. J. A. Hobson, *Imperialism—A Study* (1902; repr., 2nd printing, United States of America: University of Michigan Press, 1967), 60.

26. Holmes, *Anti-Semitism*, 81.

27. Hobson, *War in South Africa*, 190-91.

28. Not only was the entire mining industry in their hands, but Jews also had a monopoly over dynamite, the liquor trade, and the horse trade. They owned most of the large commercial businesses, and furthermore, stated Hobson, "I am informed that a very large proportion of the Transvaal farmers are as entirely in the hands of Jewish moneylenders as is the Russian moujik or the Austrian peasant." Hobson, *War in South Africa*, 189, 192-94.

29. Hobson, *Imperialism*, 78; J. A. Hobson, "Capitalism and Imperialism in South Africa," *Contemporary Review* 77 (January–June 1900): 1-3.

30. Hobson, *Imperialism*, 56-58, 60.

31. Hobson, *Imperialism*, 46-48; J. A. Hobson, "Free Trade and Foreign Policy," *Contemporary Review* 74 (July–December 1898): 167-77.

32. Quoted in Holmes, *Anti-Semitism*, 68.

33. Quoted in Rubinstein, *History of the Jews*, 113.

34. Labour MP John Burns, quoted in Bernard Porter, *Critics of Empire: British Radical Attitudes to Colonialism in Africa 1895-1914* (London: Macmillan & Co Ltd, 1968), 127-28.

35. Porter, *Critics of Empire*, 129; Holmes, *Anti-Semitism*, 68-70.

36. Colin Holmes, "J. A. Hobson and the Jews," in *Immigrants and Minorities in British Society*, ed. Colin Holmes (London, 1978), 125; Colin Holmes, "Goldwin Smith (1823-1910): A Liberal Anti-Semite," *Patterns of Prejudice* 6 (September–October 1972): 25-26; Holmes, *Anti-Semitism*, 11-12, 140-43, 148; Rubinstein, *History of the Jews*, 108-111, 114.

37. G. C. Webber, *Ideology of the British Right* (London: Croom Helm, 1986), 73. The *Contemporary Review* published an article which supports Webber's assertion—but only to a point. Considering anti-Semitism "but the coarse outer shell of a deeper inner revolt of many against the materialistic tendencies of our age," the author added that it coincides with "the operations of the Hebrew." Whitman, "Anti-Semitic Movement," 712, 707-8.

38. George Dangerfield, *The Strange Death of Liberal England* (New York: Harrison Smith & Robert Haas, 1935), 7-8.

39. *Labour Leader*, quoted in Holmes, *Anti-Semitism*, 81-82.

Chapter 13
The Prewar Years

Reflecting on the years preceding the Great War, George Orwell wrote this description of attitudes towards Jews.

> It was accepted more or less as a law of nature that a Jew was a figure of fun and—though superior in intelligence—slightly deficient in 'character'. In theory a Jew suffered from no legal disabilities, but in effect he was disbarred from certain professions. He would probably not have been accepted as an officer in the navy, for instance, nor in what is called a 'smart' regiment in the army. A Jewish boy at a public school almost invariably had a bad time. He could, of course, live down his Jewishness if he was exceptionally charming or athletic, but it was an initial disability comparable to a stammer or a birthmark. Wealthy Jews tended to disguise themselves under aristocratic English or Scottish names, and to the average person it seemed quite natural that they should do this, just as it seems natural for a criminal to change his identity if possible. . . .
> The working-class attitude was no better. The Jew who grew up in Whitechapel took it for granted that he would be assaulted, or at least hooted at, if he ventured into one of the Christian slums nearby.[1]

Miss McPhail, a character in Ford Madox Ford's (Ford Hermann Hueffer), *Mr. Fleight*, "was still in a tremendous rage at having been called a Jewess." Fleight "could quite understand how trying it must be for a person half Scotch, half German, to get called a Jew in public. It was never nice to be called a Jew; he himself never liked it."[2] In Leonard Merrick's three-volume novel, *Violet Moses*, one of the characters spoke of the "difficulty about admitting oneself a Jew," because "one is always afraid the genial faces will harden, and the cheery smiles grow chilly, and fade away—we have seen it so often." Any protestation to the contrary by Christians was "all rubbish."[3] In this atmosphere, the "Jew joke" of the music halls, postcards, periodicals, and comic papers were popular, and, "However little the average intellectual may have agreed with the opinions of Belloc and Chesterton, he did not acutely disapprove of them. Chesterton's endless tirades against Jews . . . never got him into trouble—indeed Chesterton was one of the most generally respected figures in English literary life."[4]

In its weakening state, liberalism was less and less able to shield Jews from the ire of British society. The prewar years saw a growth in overt and virulent expressions of hostility towards Jews. Imagery almost indistinguishable from medieval times may be found in the literature of the period. Cosmopolitan, capitalist, alien, devil-like, disloyal, scandalous, and taking unfair advantage: these were some of the convictions held about Jews. The forcefulness of the complaints greatly alarmed some members of the Jewish community. "Anti-Semitism is spreading," warned one writer in the *Jewish Chronicle*. "We have talked. It is time to act." Another contributor described the situation as "precarious"; "neither are the times so airy as to permit us patience for . . . delicately chiselled polemics."[5]

The capitalist orientation of the Jew, which had catapulted him into a position of power, was frequently emphasized in novels.

> The capitalists would rake in the shekels, and make fortunes by buying up the wreckage. Capital, he said, had no conscience and no fatherland. Besides, the Jew was behind it. . . . If you're on the biggest kind of job and are bound to get the real boss, ten to one you are brought up against a little white-faced Jew in a bathchair with an eye like a rattlesnake. Yes, sir, he is the man who is ruling the world just now.[6]

Ford's *Mr. Fleight*, about a Jew who is chosen to be a candidate in an upcoming election, highlighted the alienage of the Jew:

> He isn't part of our country; he hasn't got our morality, but he's extraordinarily capable as a ruler. So our side takes him up and uses him. It doesn't matter to him which side he's on, because he can't begin to understand our problems or our ethics or our morality or our way of looking at things.[7]

Occasionally, references to Jewish "chicanery and greed for gain, predominat[ing] . . . as they did of old," and Jews who immerse their children in the "talk of bargains when other children talk of toys," made their appearance in the press.[8] Negative portrayals of the Jew were carried over into popular fiction, the diet of the working class. Whether as spies or anarchists, Jews (most often German Jews) were cast in roles where they threatened to undermine the security of the nation or that of modern society. Christian mythology was evoked, with the Jew as a devil-like character, as in the best-selling novels, *Men v. Devils* by T. Kingston Clare and *When it Was Dark* by Guy Thorne. Even more powerful, however, was the image conjured up of Jews as the anti-Christ. The undisputed master of this theme was Marie Corelli, most prodigious and more popular than all the other authors of this genre combined. *Barabbas: A Dream of the World's Tragedy* (1895), for example, speaks of Christ who was slain to satisfy the blood-thirstiness of the God-Elected Children of Israel.[9] In *Temporal Power: A Study in Supremacy* (1897), Jews are identified with "the rulers of the darkness of this world," a darkness which included "the blight of atheism, infidelity, callousness, and indifference to honourable principles."[10]

Author and Liberal MP Hilaire Belloc[11] was another, but more serious writer who often portrayed his characters of German-Jewish background in negative terms. The upper echelons of society were also engaged in this activity according to Leo Maxse's *National Review*, as was the *Review* itself. It denounced German Jews "who 'simply' use the hospitality and social distinctions accorded them in this country to intrigue against British interests and to work for our German enemies."[12] This statement by Maxse provides the backdrop to Belloc's series of four novels (1904-1910) which trace the progress of the main character, I. Z. Barnett (a man of German-Jewish heritage as he comes to exert increasing power and influence over the Prime Minister in his capacity as friend, confidante, and financial advisor, eventually corrupting this honest Englishman with his Jewish cosmopolitanism. Even more dire, Barnett is linked with the "fate of England;" "innocent old England" becomes increasingly corrupted by Jewish plutocrats grasping after financial and political power and Jewish Cabinet Ministers surreptitiously buying shares as a side benefit of British imperialism. Eventually—applying Macaulay's adage that wealth means power—Barnett comes to be at the forefront of British politics.

> The Duke of Battersea [Barnett] . . . lay in Battersea House not yet asleep. He was feeding internally and nourishing his soul upon Dolly [the Prime Minister] and the Indian loan. He held Dolly between his spatulated forefinger and his gross thumb. But then he did not understand blood which was not his own, nor what sympathies might arise between men of one race and one society.[13]

In 'real life,' Belloc issued this statement to the *Times* in 1910: the House of Lords was "a body which stood as a Committee for the protection of the interests of the modern Anglo-Judaic plutocracy under which they lived."[14] In the same year, he gave an interview to the *Jewish Chronicle* where he stated, "The anti-Semitic movement is essentially a reaction against the abnormal growth in Jewish power, and the new strength of anti-Semitism is largely due to the Jews themselves."[15]

Also in 'real life,' two major scandals erupted in 1912, giving sibylline overtones to Belloc's works. In the Marconi Scandal, a contract for the construction of a chain of wireless stations was forged between the government and the Marconi Company, whose managing director was Godfrey Isaacs, a brother of Sir Rufus Isaacs, attorney general. (The brothers were Jewish.) As Colin Holmes relates,

> before the contract was publicly announced or ratified, Godfrey Isaacs went to the United States and took up a parcel of new shares on preferential terms in the American Marconi company whose share capital it had been agreed to enlarge, and in April 1912, he generously offered a number of such shares to Harry Isaacs, his brother, who offloaded some to Rufus Isaacs, who in turn successfully offered some of his holding to the chancellor of the Exchequer, Lloyd George.[16]

In the Indian scandal, MP Sir Stuart Samuel and his first cousin Edwin Montagu, parliamentary undersecretary for India, were accused of making a secret contract with the Indian government to buy £5,000,000 of silver—contrary to normal procedures—for the family bullion brokerage firm. The public was made very aware of two facts: first, in the Indian scandal, all the beneficiaries were Jewish.[17] And second, "All the silver for India is financed by the House of Samuel," a statement made by Conservative Party member Major Glyn and reinforced by the economist J. M. Keynes: "There was only one firm in a position to buy large quantities of silver."[18] To many, these scandals served to confirm the existence of a 'Jewish conspiracy,' "Jewish abuse of social power," and 'Jewish domination.'[19]

Specific incidents indicating widespread antipathy towards Jews also occurred. A prime illustration is the Limerick boycott of 1904, although there had been sporadic reports of Jews being beaten up and their property destroyed in that city since 1894. One particularly severe incident occurred when a Jew was seemingly mistaken for a Protestant preacher by some Catholics. But that surely was not the whole of the story, for after the police had escorted him home, a mob three-hundred strong that had accompanied the police and the Jew proceeded to attack all the members of the Jewish community they could find and partially destroy the houses in which they lived.[20] The Limerick boycott was organized by the priest Father Creagh and was the outcome of a sermon he had preached 11 January 1904. Whereas Jews had formerly kidnapped and slain Christian children, now, he said, they "will not hesitate to expose them to a longer and even more cruel martyrdom by taking the clothes off their back and the bit out of their mouths."[21]

A week-long spate of rioting began just before midnight, on 19 August 1911, when several thousand young men mostly belonging to the "respectable working class" began a tour of Tredegar, a village in Wales, attacking Jewish shops. The shops were wrecked and their contents looted. While the village of Ebbw Vale provided the requested police reinforcements, the mob could not be restrained, and military help was asked for Sunday afternoon. Its arrival twenty-four hours later coincided with another outbreak of rioting. Rumors of attacks further afield were borne out as Jewish shops in Ebbw Vale and Rhymney were looted Monday night and Tuesday, followed by Victoria, Cwm, Waunllwyd, Abertyswg, and Brynmawr, and then Wednesday night at Bargoed in Glamorgan, and shortly thereafter, Senghennydd. Over the course of Friday and Saturday in Bargoed, the rioters fought with police and soldiers who had arrived on Thursday. About the Tredegar Riots, as they came to be known, magistrate A. L. Tallis stated that the rioters were, from the outset, targeting the Jews. These Jews were exhibiting the same pattern as their coreligionists in London,

> there being a number of this nationality in the Town, some of whom during the last few years have been purchasing slum dwellings and, it is freely rumoured, considerably raising the rents for the same. I know of no other reason other than this which would give rise to the feeling against the Jews many of whom are respectable citizens and who have been in business in Tredegar for very many years.[22]

In his report to Winston Churchill, then Home Secretary, Chief Constable Bosanquet of Monmouthshire added a few more details:

> I have the honour to report that in all the Colliery districts in this County, Jews come to settle down. Though they usually arrive apparently without means, they soon establish themselves in business and acquire house property. As soon as they become landlords they raise rents very high, and, I am told, make their tenants deal at their shops. There is in consequence a very strong feeling against them. This is the case in Tredegar and there is a determination expressed by the inhabitants to get rid of them.[23]

Of the affair, the *Jewish Chronicle* concluded: "After the events of this week nobody can again say that, as far as the anti-Jewish malady is concerned, Great Britain shows a clean bill of health. . . . Let us then dispose of the cant that the Jewish position in this country is essentially different from that elsewhere."[24]

As to how the position of the Jews might be improved,

> there is only the choice of going forward or backward. . . . Reform and Zionism are the broad alternatives. . . . It is easy to understand the antipathy which the great body of Jews naturally feel towards the prospect of assimilation. They have too much pride of race to relish the idea of complete absorption. But (at least from the Gentile standpoint) it is no less hard to see the justification than the practicability of a policy of continued separatism. . . . On the whole, if the gains and losses of assimilation could be reckoned against one another, there seems little doubt on which side the balance would be found.[25]

NOTES

1. Orwell, "Antisemitism in Britain," 337-38.
2. Ford Madox Ford, *Mr. Fleight* (London: H. Latimer, 1913), 221.
3. Leonard Merrick, *Violet Moses* (London: Richard Bentley & Son, 1891), 1:151.
4. Orwell, "Antisemitism in Britain," 336, 338. Hilaire Belloc was of Anglo-French parentage; radically Catholic; a proponent of the 'distributist' philosophy (redistribution of wealth) and the resuscitation of the guild system; and a supporter of the French Revolution. Serving as a Member of Parliament for the Liberal Party between 1906 and 1910, after this one term in office, he returned to his profession as a writer. His works were very wide-ranging. They included books on travel, religion, social matters, verse for children, and the Jews. G. K. Chesterton (1874-1936) was one of the most well-known and provocative English writers of his day. A critic, novelist, and poet, his works bear the imprint of his conversion to Roman Catholicism, to which he was devoted.
5. *Jewish Chronicle*, 24 January 1902, 9.
6. John Buchan, *The Thirty-Nine Steps* (1915; repr., London: Hodder & Stoughton Limited, 1936), 39.
7. Ford, *Mr. Fleight*, 213.
8. Quoted in Williams, "Anti-Semitism of Tolerance," 86.
9. Bryan Cheyette, "Jewish Stereotyping and English Literature, 1875-1920: Towards a Political Analysis," in *Traditions of Intolerance: Historical Perspectives on Fascism and Race Discourse in British Society*, ed. Tony Kushner and Kenneth Lunn (Manchester: Manchester University Press, 1989), 26.
10. Horace B. Samuel, ed., "The *Weltanschauung* of Miss Marie Corelli," *Modernities* (London: Kegan Paul, Trench, Trubner & Co. Ltd, 1913), 114-33.
11. Bryan Cheyette, *Constructions of 'The Jew' in English Literature and Society: Racial Representations, 1875-1945* (Cambridge: Cambridge University Press, 1993), 150-53.
12. *National Review* (1911), quoted in Aronsfeld, "German Jews," 327.
13. Hilaire Belloc, *Pongo and the Bull* (London: Constable & Company Limited, 1910), 93-94.
14. Hilaire Belloc, quoted in Bryan Cheyette, "Hilaire Belloc and the 'Marconi Scandal' 1913-1914: A Reassessment of the Interactionist Model of Racial Hatred," *The Politics of Marginality: Race, the Radical Right, and Minorities in Twentieth Century Britain*, ed. Tony Kushner and Kenneth Lunn (London: Frank Cass & Co. Ltd, 1990), 136.
15. Hilaire Belloc, quoted in the *Jewish Chronicle*, 12 August 1910, 14.

16. Holmes, *Anti-Semitism*, 70.
17. Holmes, *Anti-Semitism*, 71-80; Endelman, *Jews in the History of Britain*, 153-55.
18. Major Glyn and J. M. Keynes, quoted in Holmes, *Anti-Semitism*, 78.
19. Holmes, *Anti-Semitism*, 71-75.
20. *Jewish Chronicle*, 11 May 1894, 21; 18 April 1884, 5; 25 April 1884, 7; 2 May 1884, 9; 12 April 1889, 6; 26 August 1892, 6.
21. *Jewish Chronicle*, 22 January 1904, 9.
22. A. L. Tallis, quoted in Anthony Glaser, "The Tredegar Riots of August 1911," in *The Jews of South Wales: Historical Studies*, ed. Ursula R. Q. Henriques (Cardiff: University of Wales Press, 1993), 155, 158, 160-62; *Jewish Chronicle*, 25 August 1911.
23. Chief constable Bosanquet, quoted in Colin Holmes, "The Tredegar Riots of 1911: Anti-Jewish Disturbances in South Wales," *Welsh History Review* 11 (December 1982): 218-19. These Jewish landlords had borrowed a practice that was quite widespread among mining communities. Mine owners often stipulated that the miners, as a condition of employment, had to shop at company stores.
24. *Jewish Chronicle*, 25 August 1911, 5-6; 1 September 1911, 5-6.
25. "By a Quarterly Reviewer," "The Jew in London: A Study of Racial Character and Present-Day Conditions: Being Two Essays Prepared for the Toynbee Trustees. . . .," *Aspects of the Jewish Question* (London: John Murray, 1902), 12-13.

Chapter 14
The First World War

The outbreak of the Great War provoked much doubt in the minds of Britons as to the national loyalty of the Jews. Initially, it was Jews of German origin whose loyalty was called into question. Shortly thereafter, it was Jews from Russia, identified as aliens and reluctant participants in the war effort. Thus, the comment by the *Jewish Chronicle* that Jewish recruits were "more English than the English in their expression of loyalty and desire for service"[1] was bound not only to be disbelieved but also considered outrageous.

At the outset of the war, the *New Witness* asked if it was "proper that [Felix] Schuster [a Jew who had been born in Germany] should be allowed to remain at the head of a great banking establishment while England is at war with his native country?"[2] So widespread was this view that Sir Edgar Speyer, a Jew of German origin, felt obliged to renounce his title and resign his place in the Privy Council.[3] While Schuster's and Speyer's German origins made them potential threats to national security in wartime Britain, their image as "cosmopolitans, wanderers on the face of the earth, and indiscriminate looters of the European"[4] added a second reason to suspect these Jews of incivism. The *New Witness* reckoned that as a result of the war "there should be a fair chance of relieving this unfortunate country of the German-Jewish yoke under which we have groaned for decades."[5]

Playwright Sir Arthur Pinero submitted a letter to the *Times* suggesting that "Germans who are naturalized British citizens holding prominent positions in the country should raise their voices against Germany rather than sitting on the gate."[6] This sparked a flurry of what came to be known as "loyalty letters;" they were soon followed up by "loyalty displays" from both Anglo-German and Anglo-German-Jewish individuals. "Loyalty displays" by Anglo-German Jews ranged from merchants displaying naturalization papers and old photographs of themselves as soldiers in the army in their shop windows,[7] to the establishment of a Jewish Recruiting Committee in East London, to the interruption of the 1915 Yom Kippur service for the poor at the Pavilion Theatre, Mile End to greet and deliver a patriotic speech to the Lord Mayor—after which the choir sang 'Rule Britannia.'[8]

Throughout the war, some incidents occurred and various security measures were passed because of the presence in Britain of what was termed 'enemy aliens.' Certain wartime procedures concerning these aliens were obviously warranted. While Jews from Germany could justifiably be considered 'enemy aliens,' Jews from Russia were not; they were 'friendly aliens.' However, no distinction seems to have been made between the two, neither in law nor in the peoples' passions when they were aroused. The German sinking of the *Lusitania* in May 1915 provoked three days of extensive rioting in East End London, where not only Christians and Jews of German origin were targeted but also Russian-Jewish aliens: "Most of the shops and houses were so ransacked that only the bare walls remained," reported one newspaper.[9]

This lack of a distinction between 'friendly aliens' and 'enemy aliens' further showed up in resolutions passed by the London County Council (LCC) subsequent to the institution of the Aliens Restriction Act (5 August 1914). Inevitably, these laws redounded most of all on Jewish 'friendly aliens' because, in London, they constituted the vast majority of aliens. One of the first resolutions approved by the LCC was one which stated that it was "highly undesirable, in the interests of London, that a large number of alien enemies . . . should be allowed free access to all parts of London." Only the practical difficulties inherent in such a proposal forestalled its passage.[10] On 22 December 1914, the LCC considered the advisability of permitting children of "alien enemies" to attend "central" schools.[11] A decision was reached to allow those already registered to complete their studies, but it became policy to exclude alien children.[12] In April 1916, students already enrolled became ineligible for scholarships and other rewards,[13] and by March 1918, the LCC's Elementary Education Sub-Committee reached down to the elementary level to cancel scholarships to school children who were not British-born or who had not been naturalized before January 1914.[14] It also became policy (approved by the LCC Stores and Contracts Committee in 1915) to deny contracts to firms controlled by "enemy aliens" (exceptional cases would be considered).[15] Additionally, alien workers, though paying taxes and making national insurance contributions, found themselves deprived of benefits from the Prince of Wales National Relief Fund (a source of income many British workers found necessary to draw on when the onset of war disrupted the British economy).[16] The question cannot be avoided, since it was common knowledge that the majority of aliens were of Russian-Jewish origin: why was no attempt made in law to distinguish 'friendly aliens' from 'enemy aliens'? One must conclude, that over the course of the last three decades, when it came to classifying their new Russian-Jewish neighbors, many had rather come to consider them 'enemy aliens,' not 'friendly aliens.'

In the autumn of 1916, a call for the enforcement of Sunday trading regulations was made throughout England; explicit mention was made of Jewish businesses, and a ban was effected in many communities. This policy seems unrelated to the state of war; however, it did coincide with the economic upswing as the war went into high gear and which reversed the fortunes of a number of Russian-Jewish aliens. Accusations of "profiteering" and "job-snatching" became commonplace.[17] With money in their pockets, the trade in luxury items was brisk: fur coats, pianos, and jewelry; one shop was "crowded to the doors, so great was the press of would-be [Jewish] customers."[18] This money was also used to travel throughout Britain, where Jews found that local residents objected not only to their numbers but to their ostentation. The general determination of military tribunals which reviewed applications for military exemption was that Jews were being "allowed to strengthen their industrial position without any sacrifice."[19]

All these issues may be considered skirmishes leading up to the major battle that was to be fought over the military participation of Russian-Jewish aliens. The quarrel Britons had with these Jews was their aversion to enlist. And as we will see, this was the case. However, there was the odd circumstance, such as the situation in Hackney, where the recruitment office was found to have refused Jews for service. The following explanation was given by a recruiting officer.

> What happened was that we found a great deal of strongly developed prejudice among a certain section—not the best—against Jewish recruits. Generally they gave the Jews a rough handling in every possible way. They called them names, hustled them, distorted their foreign names and made things generally offensive. We therefore thought it best, in the interests of the Jews themselves, to refuse them.[20]

Other recruiting depots made the same decision, as did certain military units.[21]

Antipathy towards Jews may have had the effect of excluding some of them from the war effort, but the "patchy" response of many Russian-Jewish immigrants complained of by Lord Derby, the minister responsible for recruitment (before conscription) provoked an outpouring of hostility.[22] In June 1916, Jewish 'friendly aliens' were permitted to enlist; only a month later, the Government altered its position somewhat, stating that if they did not come forward to register, they would be deported.[23] However, almost none enlisted, in spite of encouragement to do so by both the Government and the Jewish community. Out of the total pool of eligible Jews from Russia, less than one per cent (fewer than four hundred as of 10 October 1916) in the London area enlisted.[24] "A great deal has been said as to the Jewish effort in the War," wrote the *East London Observer*, "but there is a strong local feeling that the 'Jew Boys', as they are termed, who hang about street corners and public houses, the cheap foreign restaurants and similar places, ought to be made to do something for the country they honour with their presence."[25]

Speaking for many of the Jews who did not come forward, one man stated that he "was opposed to warfare, his parents having left Russia so that he should not be conscripted."[26] Even many Jews of Russian origin who were born in Britain dissociated themselves from the war cause. Lacking identification with Britain, they saw no reason to fight the Germans. Lacking any appreciation for the fact that Russia was Britain's ally, they considered it grounds for indifference to the war cause. 'Jewish reasons' also played a role in the disinclination of both native-born and alien Jews to serve. Some Jews expressed feelings of solidarity with their Anglo-German and Anglo-Austrian brethren. Some considered their religion the object of their loyalty rather than the state.[27] Religious laws such as observance of the Sabbath, keeping kosher, and the interdiction against *Cohanim* being in the immediate proximity of the dead were also cited as reasons that precluded serving in the military.[28]

The Government failed to execute its threat to deport alien Jews. This failure, coupled with the decision of various trade unions, friendly societies, and Jewish Socialist groups to fight conscription and deportation, and to preserve the right of asylum in Britain through the establishment of the Foreign Jews

Protection Committee further increased the intensity of feeling among the general population. Two events gave the Government the incentive it needed to resolve the issue of alien Jews serving in the military. The first was a conference held in East London February 1917 that gathered together members of Parliament, London city councillors, and representatives from every East London borough tribunal. There they discussed the unmet demands for "equal sacrifice" in an atmosphere of undisguised hate towards the Jews.[29] The second was the outbreak of the Russian Revolution only three weeks later. As a first move, the Government formulated the Aliens Military Service Bill: stipulating enlistment or deportation, it "await[ed] for confirmation by the new Russian government." In the meantime, under the auspices of the Home Office, police chiefs and highly placed local representatives met and decided that "in the light of disorders which might take place if the public opinion in East London is still further inflamed by delay and increasing pressure," a "great police round-up of the Aliens who are of military age and eligible" should be carried out. The raid was carried out towards the end of May 1917, but figures regarding the number of detainees vary widely: anywhere from six hundred to four thousand.[30]

In July 1917, The British Workers' National League met. Presided over by Labour MP John Hodge and counting many notables among its executive, it espoused a frankly anti-alien agenda.[31] The far more significant event that month, however, was the implementation of the Aliens Military Service Bill in concert with the Anglo-Russian Convention. As part of the Bill, the Government created Jewish battalions. In an autobiographical account by Henry Myer, a Jewish soldier from a family long resident in Britain, we find that he had acceded to a request by the War Office to take up a senior post with these battalions. His account of the soldiers under his command corroborates public sentiment but contradicts the official Anglo-Jewish record, which praised Jewish participation in the war effort. Only a few of these recruits were "fine specimens;" mostly, they were "types to whom soldiers and soldiering were anathema" and who lined up in droves for sick parade. How, asked Myer, when they "owed so much to the hospitality they had enjoyed in the United Kingdom, could [they] have refrained from showing gratitude in the form of sharing burdens which fell on all Britishers."[32]

Under the Convention, more than half of the eligible Russian Jews returned to Russia, according to the *East London Observer*.[33] This figure has been hotly contested by Sharmin Kadish who concludes, after having examined a variety of sources, that there were perhaps 3,000 returnees. However, within Kadish's own documentation, there are indications that this figure might have been much higher. The *Workers' Circle Jubilee Publication*, along with other periodicals noted the "ruination" of the Jewish Social Democratic Organisation in Britain, as its membership was decimated. The *Journal of the Amalgamated Society of Tailors* wrote about the "return to Russia of thousands of tailors working in the district." If, as Kadish writes, "actual travel arrangements were made under a veil of secrecy," what assurance is there that the recorded departures constitute the total number of returnees? Furthermore, the official figure of 900 women left behind is just that—an official figure. Though the Government undertook to provide financial support for these women and their families (below), consideration must be given to comments such as Emanuel Litvinoff's, whose mother had "been left, pregnant and twenty-two, with nothing but the three of us, a sewing machine and her skill in dressmaking." It would appear that some of these women and their children simply disappeared from the official ranks to become self-sufficient or supported by family members.

Also contributing to a higher figure of returnees than Kadish would like to admit is the overlapping of the Convention with the Bolshevik Revolution, which occurred only four months later. As elsewhere, an unknown number of Jews of Russian extraction did leave for Russia to fight in the Revolution. As Robert Wilton, cited in Kadish, wrote in *Russia's Agony*, "Another lamentable feature of the revolutionary period was the constant passage of Russian and pseudo-Jew revolutionaries from Allied countries. . . . The exiles would go straight from the train to the Field of Mars and 'stir up' the revolutionary pot."[34] For how many Russian-Jewish males did the Revolution provide that extra impetus to return? How many Russian-Jewish males who were tardy in making their plans to return to Russia under the terms of the Convention might have been included amongst those who returned to fight in the Revolution?

Of their own accord and using their own finances, a large number of Jews of Russian origin, both naturalized and alien, who had been living in Britain, felt impelled to leave. The willingness, and even eagerness of these Jews to return to Russia, either under the terms of the Convention or as revolutionaries, in spite of a multitude of hardships, not the least of which was separation from their families, makes it very difficult to argue that they had assimilated in any way. At the most elemental level they had remained aliens. Arnold White's statement that Jews "have persistently refused to unite with other nationalities"—made as an observation, and not an accusation—can be said to be true in the case of these Jews.

Other complaints were soon added. Many of the families of Russian-Jewish alien males who had been returned under the Convention had remained in Britain, since their fares back to Russia had not been subsidized by the Government (although this may not have been the only reason), and their maintenance came out of the public purse, outraging a number of Britons. As well, those Russian-Jewish alien males who had chosen not to be repatriated under the Convention, they were of course now eligible for military service. However, a substantial number of them—in the range of ten thousand—made application for military exemption to the Special Tribunal, yet another sore spot for the war-weary British.[35] Shortly thereafter, they were amongst those East-End London Russian Jews (whose status varied from alien, to naturalized, to native-born) who left London for the south coast and other locations when heavy air raids targeted the city in 1917. This perceived trend provoked a number of complaints from local residents, publicized by the local and national press: that these Jews were responsible for rent increases and brought disease and dirt with them.[36] The press also turned their attention to the majority, who had remained in East-End London, reporting that they filled the air-raid shelters and underground stations before an air-raid had been confirmed, thereby spreading panic.[37]

Public anger at the failure of alien Jews to enlist contined to simmer, as the chief constable of Leeds communicated to the Home Office:

> In my opinion the chief cause of the feelings of the Christian people towards the Jewish population is brought about by the large number of alien Russian Jews of military age that we have in this city who can constantly be seen promenading about our principal streets and the various pleasure resorts . . . and members of the Christian population have been heard to ask why these men are not serving in the Army as the husbands, brothers and sons of the Christian population have had to do.[38]

Moreover, in support of Dr. Rentoul Reid's assertion that Jews were "degenerates" and Alderman Silver's description of them as "debilitated" and "sickly", the rejection rate for Jewish military recruits in Leeds was three times higher (one out of five) than the rate for non-Jews, primarily due to lung disease and myopia.[39] Thus it was that serious outbreaks of violence occurred in Leeds 2-4 June 1917. In the first episode, the *Yorkshire Post* reported that "every Jewish shop window was smashed, and the street was littered with fragments of glass and the damaged remnants of goods . . . in no case was a shop occupied by a British subject molested. . . . The unmistakable evidence of Jew-baiting was clear."[40] The only difference between the first and second incident was the numbers involved: the size of the mob had increased from one to three thousand.[41]

A warning in the *East London Observer* foreshadowed another violent outburst.

> If the Government show weakness in their determination and allow themselves to become the victims of the 'political refugee' trick, we fear the consequences will be serious. The misbehaviour of any offensive foreign bounder, or the impertinence of a Whitechapel Jew boy, may light the smoldering fires of a native feeling. To use a familiar colloquialism, East London is 'fed up'.[42]

Hence, an incident involving Englishmen and Russian-Jewish aliens on 23 September 1917 exploded the next day into a mob scene of 5,000 people in London's Bethnal Green. That the object of their anger was the Jews is clear from the police report labeled "Anti-Jewish Demonstration."[43]

The peace of Brest-Litovsk, concluded between the Bolshevik Government and the Germans in February 1918 rendered the Anglo-Russian Convention, for practical purposes, null and void, although a court ruling declared that it was still in force. Thus, the Government again began the process of recruiting, but this time made the decision to send the Russian-Jewish alien recruits to labor units or auxiliary services rather than to the front. This half-measure simply fueled the hostility towards the Jews.

By March 1918, the *Jewish Chronicle* reported that anti-Jewish sentiment had escalated "to an extent that has no precedence in modern times."[44]

Notes

1. *Jewish Chronicle*, 7 August 1914.
2. *New Witness*, quoted in Holmes, *Anti-Semitism*, 124-25.
3. Panikos Panayi, *The Enemy In Our Midst: Germans in Britain During the First World War* (New York and Oxford: Berg Publishers Limited, 1991), 188-91.
4. *New Witness*, quoted in Holmes, *Anti-Semitism*, 124-25.
5. *National Review*, quoted in Holmes, *Anti-Semitism*, 125.

6. Sir Arthur Pinero, quoted in the *Times*, in Holmes, *Anti-Semitism*, 122.
7. David Cesarani, "An Embattled Minority: The Jews in Britain During the First World War," in *The Politics of Marginality: Race, the Radical Right, and Minorities in Twentieth Century Britain*, ed. Tony Kushner and Kenneth Lunn (London: Frank Cass & Co. Ltd, 1990), 65.
8. *Jewish Chronicle*, 11 September 1914, 5, 7, 11; 1 October 1915, 6; *East London Observer*, 1 May 1915, 7.
9. *East London Observer*, quoted in Julia Bush, *Behind the Lines: East London Labour* (London: Merlin Press, 1984), 170. It may be noted that the rioting was followed up by a campaign in the press complaining about the German-Jewish yoke. Cesarani, "Embattled Minority," 64; Geoffrey Alderman, *London Jewry and London Politics 1889-1986* (London and New York: Routledge, 1989), 62-63.
10. Greater London Record Office, *London County Council Minutes*, 27 October 1914, 673.
11. These were training and technical schools to which eleven-year-old students had to be recommended in order to attend.
12. Greater London Record Office, *London County Council Minutes*, 22 December 1914, 1024, 1028.
13. Greater London Record Office, *London County Council Minutes*, 4 April 1916, 306.
14. Board of Deputies of British Jews, E3/42 (I), 'Notes of interview between Sir Stuart M. Samuel, Bart, accompanied by Mr. Charles H. L. Emanuel, and Mr. Cyril Cobb, and Sir Robert Blair,' 14 November 1917.
15. Greater London Record Office, *London County Council Minutes*, 26 January 1915, 105; 27 April 1915, 677.
16. Cesarani, "Embattled Minority," 72. Although some amelioration was eventually forthcoming, it primarily fell to the Anglo-Jewish community to subsidize them. Alderman, *Jewish Community*, 88.
17. Alderman, *Jewish Community*, 73; Holmes, *Anti-Semitism*, 135.
18. *Jewish Chronicle*, 19 March 1915.
19. *East London Advertiser*, quoted in Bush, *Behind the Lines*, 173.
20. Quoted in the *Jewish Chronicle*, 9 October 1914, 5, 17.
21. *Jewish Chronicle*, 9 October, 1914, 5, 17; 23 October 1914, 8; 4 December 1914, 12-13.
22. *Jewish Chronicle*, 9 October 1914, 5, 17; 23 October 1914, 8; 4 December 1914, 12-13; 19 November 1915, 16.
23. Bush, *Behind the Lines*, 173-76.
24. Cesarani, "Embattled Minority," 65-69; Sharmin Kadish, *Bolsheviks and British Jews: The Anglo-Jewish Community, Britain, and the Russian Revolution* (London: Frank Cass & Co. Ltd., 1992), 253.
25. *East London Observer*, quoted in Bush, *Behind the Lines*, 170-71.
26. *East London Observer*, quoted in Bush, *Behind the Lines*, 172.
27. Bush, *Behind the Lines*, 167.
28. Bush, *Behind the Lines*, 173. The Jewish people, for religious purposes, were divided into three groups: Cohen, Levi, and Israel.
29. Bush, *Behind the Lines*, 173-76.
30. *East London Observer*, quoted in Bush, *Behind the Lines*, 179-80.
31. Kadish, *Bolsheviks and British Jews*, 47.
32. Henry Meyer, quoted in Mark Levene, "Going against the Grain: Two Jewish Memoirs of War and Anti-War (1914-18)," in *Forging Modern Jewish Identities: Public Faces and Private Struggles*, ed. Michael Berkowitz, Susan L. Tananbaum, and Sam W.

Bloom (London: Vallentine Mitchell, 2003), 104-5.
33. Bush, *Behind the Lines*, 181.
34. Robert Wilton, quoted in Kadish, *Bolsheviks and British Jews*, 214, 25, 209-11.
35. Bush, *Behind the Lines*, 181-84.
36. *Jewish Chronicle*, 5 October 1917, 5, 18; 29 March 1918, 3; 19 April 1918, 6.
37. *Jewish Chronicle*, 28 September 1917, 4; 1 February 1918, 12.
38. Chief Constable of Leeds, quoted in Holmes, *Anti-Semitism*, 127.
39. Endelman, *Jews of Britain*, 136.
40. *Yorkshire Post*, quoted in Holmes, *Anti-Semitism*, 131.
41. Holmes, *Anti-Semitism*, 131.
42. *East London Observer*, quoted in Holmes, *Anti-Semitism*, 135.
43. Holmes, *Anti-Semitism*, 136.
44. *Jewish Chronicle*, 15 March 1918, 7.

Chapter 15
Anti-Alienism in Postwar Britain

Shortly after the war ended, the Aliens Restriction (Amendment) Act (1919) and the Aliens Order (1920) were approved. It may be that these bills reflected the continuation of a 'wartime mentality' that was slow in dissipating, but the codification of those who were not naturalized as potential enemies during peacetime, and even Jews whose alien lineage was one generation removed seems to serve as confirmation that the majority of Jews living in Britain were not thought to have assimilated to the point where they could be considered British.

According to the terms of the bills, aliens were to be treated the same way they were during the war: as potential enemies; even those who had been resident in Britain for years could be detained or deported on virtually any grounds.[1] (And they were: a member of the Stepney Trades Council and Central Labour Party recorded arrests and deportations of trade union officials in its annual report.[2]) The *Jewish Chronicle* preferred the former Aliens Restriction Act because it had at least rendered "aliens' liabilities in some determinate form," whereas the new one had the "arbitrary indefiniteness of Orders in Council and Orders too, made by Department officials."[3] Thus, "Department officials," in this case, from the LCC, used the current Aliens Restriction Act as a reference point in its hiring policies and academic subsidies as it had done during the war, and again, it was mostly Russian-Jewish aliens who were affected. In 1919, Councillor Major E. H. Coumbe introduced a policy barring all aliens from employment by the LCC, regardless of whether or not they were naturalized. While it was debated for just over a year, the Council's General Purposes Committee finally approved it by a narrow margin. Only foreign language teachers and other exceptions to be taken up by the Council were exempt.[4] British-born children of non-naturalized parents were excluded from educational scholarships after March 1920. As an employer, the LCC decided in June of that year to hire only British-born subjects, thus excluding naturalized Jews.[5]

While these measures reflected the perception that Russian and other Eastern-European immigrant Jews had remained completely alienated from British society—a perception solidly entrenched by their wartime performance—they affected only one segment of the Anglo-Jewish population. The world conspiracy theory, Bolshevism, and the move to create a Jewish state would do even more to define the Jew in alien terms and had an impact on all of Anglo-Jewry.

Jewish World Conspiracy

> We are ... informed, that the statue of Sir John Barnard, formerly father of this City, and a strenuous asserter of Christianity, is ordered to be taken down, and that of Pontius Pilate is to be put up in his room. Last night, the Bill for naturalizing Christians was thrown out of the Sanhedrin [the Jewish Court] by a very great majority.[6]

This prediction had been made during the Jew Bill debate in 1753. Todd Endelman has noted that it was more than a political spoof; rather, it reflected Christians' understanding of Jews as a separate people that was power seeking and hostile. In a resounding echo, this fear surfaced full-blown during the 1920s. Russian-Jewish immigrants had shown that they were aliens on one count; the war had claimed them as aliens on another. The Anglo-Jewish plutocracy, "holding the sceptre of finance," were part of a "ring of international financiers." The Bolshevik Revolution (1917), then Communist uprisings in Germany and Hungary occurred, with Jews prominent at every level. Then came the granting of the British Mandate for Palestine in 1920, which recognized the Jews as a people with their own homeland, offering more grounds for challenging the loyalty of Jews.

While the war had directed public opinion along two trajectories—that of the Jew as an alien and therefore a potential enemy, and the Jew as unpatriotic—another issue had been percolating which would inform its parameters during the postwar years. This was the idea that the Jews were behind an international conspiracy to control the world. J. H. Clarke's *The Call of the Sword* (1917) warned Britons that the nation was now in the hands of moneylenders. Ian D. Colvin's *The Unseen Hand in English History* (1917) was the "unseen hand of [foreign] organized interest."[7] Both sought to expose a Jewish plot to dominate the world. During the 1920s, this sampling grew into an avalanche of literature propagating the idea of a Jewish world conspiracy. Nesta H. Webster was a popular author and historian whose works went through numerous editions. Through books, articles, and speeches, Webster elaborated on the theme that the worldwide revolution was a Jewish conspiracy.[8] Like others immediately after the war, she believed that there was a "German-Jewish" influence on Bolshevism, which was progressively modified until only the Jews were held to be responsible as "the power far older, that seeks to destroy all national spirit, all ordered government in every country, Germany included."[9] Less serious works such as F. Britten Austin's *The War-God Walks Again* and T. S. Eliot's poem *Burbank with a Baedeker: Bluestein with a Cigar* treated this subject as well.[10]

However, the centerpiece of world conspiracy literature was the *Protocols of the Learned Elders of Zion*.[11] Described in itemized detail were the means through which "we [the Jews] shall so wear down the **goyim** that they will be compelled to offer us international power of a nature that by its position will enable us without any violence to gradually absorb all the State forces of the world and to form a Super-Government."[12] The *Protocols* seemed to confirm current events. The first English translation was at the hands of one George Shanks, a resident in Moscow until the Bolshevik Revolution. It received an official stamp of approval by virtue of its publisher, Eyre and Spottiswoode, His Majesty's Printing Office.[13] Exotic and mysterious in origin, the *Protocols* received mass exposure through the *Morning Post*, which published it as an eighteen-part serial on the causes of world unrest.[14] In response to Lady Bathurst's (owner of the *Morning Post*) fears that publishing the *Protocols* might adversely affect the reputation of the paper, editor H. A. Gwynne, replied: "We have had the reputation of being anti-Jew for the last 3 [sic] years and we have flourished."[15] "So many people seem to be convinced that they [the *Protocols*] are genuine," wrote Sir Basil Thomson, then Director of Intelligence, "that I do not see why they should not be published."[16]

So spectacular were its pronouncements that the *Spectator* called for a Royal Commission to investigate their veracity, while *Blackwood's Magazine*, not in need of such assurance, stated that wherever there was a rebellion there was a "Jewish organization to strengthen and support it."[17] The *Times*, as it ruminated over the authenticity of the *Protocols*, could not help asking:

> Are they a forgery? If so, whence comes the uncanny note of prophecy in parts fulfilled, in parts far gone in the way of fulfillment? Have we been struggling these tragic years to blow up and extirpate the secret organization of German world domination only to find beneath it another, more dangerous because more secret?[18]

Its belief in the truth of the *Protocols* was more compelling than any doubts, and the *Times* went ahead and published it.* The *Patriot* undertook to footnote its discussions with references to the *Protocols*. *Plain English* spoke plainly indeed when it denounced all those as insane who were not persuaded of the truth of this document.[19] In the event, the *Protocols* was proved a forgery, but not before there had been mass exposure to the theories it propagated, and more importantly, not before it may be seen that a large segment of British society was sympathetic to such ideas.

Bolshevism

"The man who has seen what Bolshevism really means," wrote the *Times*, "cannot rest without enlisting his wife and all his family into a crusade against it and a campaign for the enlightenment of the British public."[20] The Bolshevik Revolution roughly coincided with, and was then incorporated into the Jewish world conspiracy theory. Many of the postwar attitudes towards Jews were fed by the 'Bolshevik menace,' where the large number of Jews among Communist

---

* That the *Times* actually published the *Protocols* is not surprising given the fact that one of its contributors on Russian affairs, Stephen Graham (the correspondent in St. Petersburg), Robert Wilton, and the *Times'* editor Henry Wickham Steed had all publicly voiced their opinion that the Jews had been responsible for both the murder of the Tsar and the Bolshevik Revolution. Kadish, *Bolsheviks*, 22-32.

ranks definitely fueled the belief that they were behind the Bolshevist takeover of Russia.

In April 1919, the *Morning Post* accused Jews of wholesale collaboration with the Bolshevik agenda to advance Communism through worldwide revolution.[21] In another article, it spoke of

> the Jews [as] a great nation. . . . In their hands lies the traditional knowledge of the whole earth, and there are no State secrets of any nation but are shared also by the secret rulers of Jewry. . . . It may be doubted whether all that is best in Jewry the world over will not ere long find some cause deeply to regret what seems, in the light of the latest revelations, something like a Jewish alliance with Old Testament Germany to regain temporal power upon the earth.[22]

Winston Churchill submitted his views on Bolshevism and the Jewish involvement in this movement on more than one occasion.

> This movement among the Jews is not new. From the days of Spartacus-Weishaupt to those of Karl Marx, and down to Trotsky (Russia), Bela Kun (Hungary), Rosa Luxemburg (Germany), and Emma Goldman (United States), this world-wide conspiracy for the overthrow of civilization and for the reconstitution of society on the basis of arrested development, of envious malevolence, and impossible equality, has been steadily growing.[23]

These revolutionaries, wrote Churchill in another article, were a "league of the failures, the criminals, the unfit, the mutinous, the morbid, the deranged, and the distraught in every land."[24] According to the *Post*, Jews who aligned themselves with Bolshevism sought control; according to Churchill, they sought destruction. The Bolshevik Revolution provided fertile soil for both views to mushroom.

The Reverend B. S. Lombard, having observed the situation close up in his capacity as Chaplain of the British forces in Russia, definitively stated that "Bolshevism originated in German propaganda and was, and is being, carried out by international Jews."[25] There was also a rash of eyewitness accounts, travelogues, and contemporary histories by diplomats, members of the military, and journalists who were on the spot. Along with the *National Review* and the *New Witness*, other well-respected journals such as the *Spectator*, *Nineteenth Century and After*, the *Quarterly Review*, and the *English Review* all supported the claim that Jews had been instrumental in the Bolshevik Revolution.[26]

Gwynne of the *Morning Post* warned British Jews that they should "dissociate themselves from a cause which is doing the Jewish people harm in all parts of the world."[27] (*Jewish Chronicle* editor Leopold Greenberg, for example, had written in the spring of 1919, "The ideals of Bolshevism at many points are consonant with the finest ideals of Judaism."[28])

> It would be downright wicked to ascribe to Jewry as a whole this mad and dangerous policy [of promoting 'World Unrest']. In that direction lies the danger; the hideous danger of a violent and indiscriminate antisemitism. It must be averted by the Jews themselves. The honest, patriotic Jews must come forward and denounce . . . the revolutionaries of their race . . . for the time has come when there can be no sitting on the fence; those who are not with us are against us.[29]

This article prompted ten of England's most eminent Jews to publish a letter in the *Morning Post*, ostensibly meant to show solidarity between Anglo-Jewry and the British populace in their condemnation of "the theoretic principles of Russian Bolsheviks, as well as to acknowledge the damage done to the Jewish people everywhere when it was believed that Jews were pro-Bolshevik."[30] However, another object of the 'Letter of the Ten,' as it came to be called, may be seen from a letter published in the *Jewish World* by a member of the League of British Jews (an organization to which the 'Ten' belonged). The "object was to obtain from the *Morning Post* a cessation of its anti-Semitic writings against us Jews who belong to this country, by showing that we are truly British to the very core, and are associated heart and soul with the British people in our detestation of Bolshevism." But in doing so, these ten Jews had "betrayed their community in order to curry favour with a foreign master" and were traitors. Citing a biblical verse, "Thou shalt not go up and down as a talebearer among thy people, neither shalt thou stand against the blood of thy neighbour," this denunciation of one's coreligionists outside the protective circle of the community would afford only temporary relief; ultimately, the letter stated, their denunciation could only serve to increase anti-Jewish sentiment, engulfing them, too.[31]

Palestine: Incipient Jewish State

As the ideal of Zionism was catapulted from a spiritual concept to a political one, it too raised the hackles of many Britons. Britain, with its long tradition of promoting the restoration of the Jews was now faced with the object of its desire: approval for the creation of a Jewish state. However, the fundamental reaction to Zionism made manifest took its cue from the concern of Enlightenment thinkers such as Michaelis. Their homeland was not the country they inhabited, "which they hope one day to leave to their great happiness, and return to Palestine. A people that has such hopes will never entirely feel at home or have patriotic love for the paternal soil."[32] Zionism proclaimed the dual loyalty, at best, or the lack of loyalty, more likely, of the Jews to the state in which they resided. With the Jewish state an imminent reality, there was no room now to interpret 'Zion' as a symbol, no more imagining that once Jews were emancipated this yearning for Zion would fall by the wayside.

Some Britons actually supported the creation of a Zionist state on other than religious grounds, because it expressed their ultimate wish fulfillment: a modern day expulsion,[33] but one which, while resolving the Jewish Question, would have been achieved with the Jews' cooperation. Envisioning Palestine as a "refuge for the oppressed," Churchill considered it "a national idea of a commanding character; it was also in the best interests of both the British Empire and Europe and it would concentrate Jewish political energies in the east rather than the west—Zionism . . . as an antidote to Bolshevism."[34] Churchill was in fact articulating the position of the government.

> We are advised that one of the best methods of counteracting Jewish pacifist and socialist propaganda in Russia would be to offer a definite encouragement to Jewish nationalist aspirations in Palestine.... The question of Zionism is full of difficulties, but I should be glad ... to learn your views as to whether a declaration by the Entente of sympathy for Jewish Nationalist aspirations would help or not in so far as concerns the internal and external situation of Russia.*

For most, however, the transformation of Zionism from a spiritual concept to a political reality merely reinforced their conviction that British Jews were indeed alienated from their non-Jewish counterparts.[35] It prompted author and former parliamentarian Hilaire Belloc to formulate a thesis to account for the indelible alienage of the Jew. Whereas the usual anti-Semite is a "man who hates Jews," individuals like himself had identified a problem with Jews based on national status: they are an alien nation by virtue of their "culture, tradition, race, and religion." Being an alien body sets up "friction, which is evil both to itself and to the organism it inhabits."[36] "Recognition" of this situation on both sides was the first step in finding a solution: the best one in his estimation was a "full recognition of separate nationality that is thrust into being by morals and social conventions first, and only later into law."[37] Belloc, like many others, saw a major contradiction in the Jews' assertion that they were simply citizens of the 'Mosaic faith' while they simultaneously backed efforts to establish a Jewish state in Palestine.

The special correspondent of the *Daily Mail* expressed the popular view that in the act of settling Palestine Jews were "perpetrating a Jewish conspiracy against Christianity, Jewish legal and financial chicanery, international Jewish finance power, and Russian-Jewish-Bolshevik infiltration." Furthermore, Jews had no particular right to be there; "They were an alien people and should be treated just like any other immigrants." "It is revolting," he wrote in the concluding article of his series, "that a Christian country such as Britain is should turn the Holy Land into the domain for free-thinking Judaeo-Slavs. Our forefathers made the Crusades; but our statesmen ... hand over the country of the Redeemer to infidels such as Richard Coeur de Lion knew."[38] The point that the British taxpayer was bearing the price of a Zionist government was made by both the *Daily Express* and *Sunday Express*, among others: "Judah has washed his garments in wine and his clothes in the blood of grapes. Out of the great wine-press of the Great War, paid for by British blood and British treasure, has arisen a Jewish State."[39]

The *Morning Post* did not hesitate to divide Jews into two groups: bad, foreign Zionist Jews and good, loyal British Jews, "who are being made unpopular

---

* Extract from a government memorandum, quoted in Kadish, *Bolsheviks*, 139. In his memoirs, Lloyd George cited "considerations of war policy," propaganda, and public opinion as determinants in the drafting of the Balfour Declaration: "We had every reason at that time to believe that in [Russia and America] the friendliness or hostility of the Jewish race might make a considerable difference." This issue is much more complex than can be conveyed here. See Kaddish, *Bolsheviks*, 138-46, which not only gives a good accounting but also supplies further references.

by a Jewish Nationalist Movement and also a Jewish revolutionary movement."[40] Another dichotomy was constructed by the *Spectator*: "More regard should have been paid to the sensitivities of the Arabs" who were confronted by "hordes of passionate and distracted Jewish zealots. . . . These men have been schooled by suffering and persecution to be bad citizens . . . intolerant." Zionism, the *Spectator* argued, was provoking the Jewish Question; "Just when old distinguishing facts have become more noticeable to the public eye, a new distinguishing fact has been added. . . . Is religious and racial exclusively [sic] compatible with citizenship?"[41]

The fears expressed two decades before in the *Jewish Chronicle* had been realized: "Nationalism, so far from offering an escape from anti-Semitism, is the avenue to it."[42]

NOTES

1. Elaine R. Smith, "Jewish Responses to Political Anti-Semitism and Fascism in the East End of London, 1920-1939," in *Traditions of Intolerance: Historical Perspectives on Fascism and Race Discourse in British Society*, ed. Tony Kushner and Kenneth Lunn (Manchester: Manchester University Press, 1989), 55.
2. Smith, "Jewish Responses," 55-56.
3. *Jewish Chronicle*, 11 April 1919, 7.
4. Greater London Records Office, *London County Council Minutes*, 15 April, 13 May 1919; LCC/MIN/6273: Minutes of the General Purposes Committee, 19 May, 13, 20 October, 3 November 1919; LCC/MIN/6273: Minutes of the General Purposes Committee, 28 June 1920.
5. *Jewish Chronicle*, 20 March 1925, 19.
6. "Hebrew Journal," article in the *London Magazine*, quoted in Endelman, *Jews of Georgian England*, 100-101.
7. Ian D. Colvin, *The Unseen Hand in English History* (London: "The National Review" Office, 1917), x. Colvin contributed a series of articles on the subject of this book to the *National Review* and since 1909 he had been a lead writer at the *Morning Post*. Panayi, *Enemy In Our Midst*, 164-68.
8. Richard Griffiths, *Fellow Travellers of the Right: British Enthusiasts for Nazi Germany, 1933-9* (London: Constable & Company Ltd, 1980), 63.
9. Nesta H. Webster's *The Origins and Progress of the World Revolution*, quoted in Griffiths, *Fellow Travellers*, 64.
10. Griffiths, *Fellow Travellers*, 64; Cheyette, "Jewish Stereotyping," 27.
11. See Norman Cohn's *Warrant for Genocide: The Myth of the Jewish World-Conspiracy and the Protocols of the Elders of Zion* (Eyre & Spottiswoode [Publishers] Ltd., 1967).
12. *Protocols of the Learned Elders of Zion*, trans. from the Nilus Documents by Victor E. Marsden, ed., Clyde J. Wright (1905; repr., Houston, Tex.: Pyramid Book Shop, 1932), 21.
13. Gisela C. Lebzelter, *Political Anti-Semitism in England, 1918-1939* (London: Macmillan Press Ltd, 1975), 24.
14. The paper's editor, H. A. Gwynne would shortly publish this serial in book form, *The Cause of World Unrest: With an Introduction by the Editor of the Morning Post* (London: G. Richards Ltd., 1920). In the introduction, he wrote, "They may or may not be genuine. Their chief interest lies in the fact that . . . the Jewish Bolsheviks are today carrying out almost to the letter the programme outlined in the *Protocols*."

15. H. A. Gwynne, quoted in Keith Wilson, "The Protocols and The Morning Post," *Patterns of Prejudice* 19, no. 3 (July 1985): 9. This stance of the *Morning Post* was determined in part by Victor Marsden, their contributor on Russian affairs. Open in his reports that "Russian Jews of German extraction" had been responsible for the Revolution, he made a new translation of the *Protocols* which was published by the Britons Publishing Society. Marsden, quoted in Kadish, *Bolsheviks and British Jews*, 33.

16. Sir Basil Thomson, quoted in Richard C. Thurlow, "Racial Populism," *Patterns of Prejudice* 10, no. 4 (July–August 1976): 22.

17. *Blackwood's Magazine*, quoted in Holmes, *Anti-Semitism*, 156.

18. *Times*, quoted in Kadish, *Bolsheviks and British Jews*, 31-32. For some, attempts to disprove the *Protocols* were seen as further proof of the existence of a Jewish plot. For others, it was irrelevant to the main point: international forces were in fact undermining the British Empire and "the effect if not the intention, was a conspiracy." Thurlow, "Racial Populism," 27.

19. Holmes, *Anti-Semitism*, 156.

20. *Times*, quoted in Lebzelter, *Political Anti-Semitism*, 17.

21. *Morning Post*, 8 April 1919, 6. Such accusations had already come to the fore during the election campaign four months prior. *Jewish Chronicle*, 24 January 1919, 5; Kadish, *Bolsheviks and British Jews*, 10.

22. *Morning Post*, quoted in Lebzelter, *Political Anti-Semitism*, 15.

23. Winston Churchill, quoted in the *Illustrated Sunday*, in Lebzelter, *Political Anti-Semitism*, 19.

24. Winston Churchill, quoted in Lebzelter, *Political Anti-Semitism*, 17.

25. Chaplain of the British Forces, quoted in Lebzelter, *Political Anti-Semitism*, 15.

26. Kadish, *Bolsheviks and British Jews*, 37-38, 252.

27. H. A. Gwynne, quoted in Lebzelter, *Political Anti-Semitism*, 121.

28. Leopold Greenberg, quoted in Lebzelter, *Political Anti-Semitism*, 121.

29. Gwynne, *Cause of World Unrest*, 13-14.

30. 'Letter of the Ten,' published in the *Morning Post*, quoted in Lebzelter, *Political Anti-Semitism*, 121.

31. Quoted in Kadish, *Bolsheviks and British Jews*, 123, 120, 125.

32. J. D. Michaelis, quoted in Katz, *Out of the Ghetto*, 91-92.

33. Kadish, *Bolsheviks and British Jews*, 240.

34. Winston Churchill, quoted in Kadish, *Bolsheviks and British Jews*, 137.

35. Bernard Wasserstein, *The British in Palestine* (London: Royal Historical Society, 1978), 237.

36. Hilaire Belloc, *The Jews* (London: Constable & Co, 1928), 3-4.

37. Belloc, *Jews*, 301-3.

38. *Daily Mail*, quoted in David Cesarani, "Anti-Zionist Politics and Political Anti-Semitism in Britain," *Patterns of Prejudice* 23, no. 1 (Spring 1989): 35-38.

39. Quoted in Cesarani, "Anti-Zionist Politics," 38.

40. *Morning Post*, quoted in Cesarani, "Anti-Zionist Politics," 30.

41. *Spectator*, quoted in Cesarani, "Anti-Zionist Politics," 31, 35.

42. *Jewish Chronicle*, 14 June 1901, 17.

Conclusion

Why the British drew alienage from the common pool of attitudes towards Jews may be explained in a number of ways. Arguments could be formulated around the insularity of British society or Britain's role in the nineteenth century as an empire more accustomed to controlling than accommodating. This section could be viewed as no more than a series of well-founded complaints arising out of a trying situation. If the figure of approximately 100,000 immigrants in Britain in 1871 was one with which British society was comfortable, a steady stream over a twenty-year period, which more than trebled this number, might have overtaxed them. And had Britain not already taken in her share of Jews? In any case, the wave of immigration after 1881 was homogeneous and foreign in the extreme. Moreover, Britain was not looking for immigrants; rather, emigration of the best and the brightest Britons was an ongoing concern.

However, a truly sound argument must examine Russian-Jewish immigration in light of that factor to which it is directly related: the entrenched ethos of the right to political asylum in Britain.[1] The right to political asylum was an essential part of the British political landscape and formed the basis for opposing any change in the immigration laws, more significant than arguments positing that the Russian-Jewish aliens were *not* having a deleterious affect on British society. Those who argued against unrestricted entry had to argue their point over and against this right.[2] While all the concerns mentioned above are certainly valid, none of them would have been compelling enough to force passage of a restriction law, for none of them was hinged to the right of political asylum, the pathway used to gain entrance to Britain. It was the realization that the Jews from Russia did not conform to others who knocked at Britain's door seeking refuge from oppression and in need of political asylum, confined in number and time, that was the real impetus for seeking changes in the immigration laws. Rather, they were part of the process of a potential evacuation of the whole of Jewry from the country that contained the greatest number of them, approximately six million. This immigration of Jews was not finite; and it *would not* stop until it *was* stopped. Once the implications of this had been absorbed, the principle of the right of political asylum gave way.

Then, the British began to make assessments based on the traditional frames of reference. These 'Oriental' Jews from Russia, whether or not they had become naturalized, were now under the obligation "to be absorbed and to mingle their blood with ours."[3] But it was not only the avoidance of intermarriage (leading to the spouse's conversion, or at least the children's) that was problematic. The undermining of the labor class ethos; the housing problems brought on by 'Jewish' habits; the obsession with making money to the exclusion of all else; the traits of solidarity, social exclusiveness, and social cohesion; the practice of endogamy; the high rate of crime from which the British extrapolated that the Jew was lacking in any morality; and the Russian-Jewish aliens' manner of living in such a degraded fashion—all these issues contravened this expectation. As was feared in medieval times, these manifestations of Jewish character traits were having an adverse affect on the whole of British society. While the terms of the Anglo-Russian Convention belatedly resolved the ubiquitous problem of young 'Oriental' Russian-Jewish men perambulating the streets, it did not resolve their alien status. Unaccepted in Russia, they continued to be aliens once in Britain because they were seen to be making no efforts to assimilate. The issue of alienage climaxed when almost all Russian-Jewish males rejected the call to arms issued by the British government. It was somewhat of a denouement when so many of them returned to Russia under the terms of the Anglo-Russian Convention. By the time the Bolshevik Revolution broke out and many Russian Jews showed that they still harbored an attachment to their erstwhile 'homeland' and returned to Russia to participate in the Revolution, it could have done little more than provoke a few raised eyebrows.

Concerning the original Jewish settlers and those Jews who immigrated over the nineteenth century but were already 'pre-assimilated' in their countries of origin, both groups were at great pains to cultivate the image of 'the perfect English gentleman.' They were convinced that this was the way to gain acceptance into English society. However, cultivating this image was not enough. There was a uniform standard set for all emancipated Jews. It was the 'Occidental' Jew who showed at the time of the Balkan insurrection that Jewish solidarity was operative. Liberals expressed their expectations of assimilation through their widespread condemnation of this deviation from liberal norms. The Boer War is equally set apart from the issue of Russian-Jewish immigration. This war highlighted the existence of a Jewish plutocracy, composed of 'Occidental' Jews. It was the 'Occidental' Jew who was becoming, due to his role in national and international finance and hegemony in capitalist enterprises "a power more despotic than that of the king and all his cabinet."[4]

In what we recognize as the public forum, individuals expressed their opinions about the multiple negative influences of Russian-Jewish immigrants in Parliament, at meetings, in the press, in books and journals, and to the Royal Commission. The complaint that British society was ruled by a Jewish plutocracy was mainly transmitted through the printed medium. Underlying all their complaints was the failure of the Jews to assimilate and adopt the norms of the country. Did these individuals speak on behalf of the general public? If we may rely on the longevity of one particular folk rhyme, which made its way across much of the English-speaking world—first recorded in 1846, it was still circulating in 1892—then the answer is yes. This ditty reveals that the public had clearly grasped the issues surrounding Jewish assimilation, and that it was an ongoing concern of theirs.

> I had a piece of pork,
> And stuck it on a fork,
> And gave it to the von, von, Jew.
> > (*English Folk Rhymes*: 1892)
>
> I had a piece of pork, I put it on a fork,
> And gave it to the curly-headed Jew.
> Pork, Pork, Pork. Jew, Jew, Jew.
> > (New York: 1864)
>
> If I had a piece of pork,
> I'd stick it on a fork,
> And give it to a Jew boy, Jew.
> > (Hobart Town and Adelaide, Australia: 1846, 1848)[5]

While these rhymes lend themselves to various analyses, they all revolve around the proffering of pork to the Jew, pork being the quintessential symbol of the abandonment of adherence to Judaism. Therefore, these ditties clearly tell us that what was being asked of the Jew was to give up *all* Jewish distinctiveness and take on the attributes and norms of Christian society. Whether 'Occidental' or 'Oriental', all Jews were enjoined "to be absorbed and to mingle their blood with ours." British society was largely frustrated in this hope.

NOTES

1. Porter, *Refugee Question*, 124-25, 218-19.
2. Gainer, *Alien Invasion*, chap. 7, 144-65.
3. White, *Modern Jew*, 208-9.
4. Thomas Macaulay, quoted in Abrahams and Levy, *Macaulay on Jewish Disabilities*, 25.
5. This poem was reproduced in Jonathan Sarna's "Pork on the Fork: A Nineteenth Century Anti-Jewish Ditty," *Jewish Social Studies* 44, no. 2 (Spring 1982): 170-71.

SECTION 4

HUNGARY AND BRITAIN: A COMPARISON

Analysis

In Britain, they called them aliens; in Hungary, they said Jews were not melding in. These expressions were just two ways of saying the same thing: Jews were not assimilating. This study began with a list of reforms, the fulfillment of which many thought would lead to the assimilation of the Jews and presumably their acceptance in the broader society. One hundred years later, Hungarians and Britons were still awaiting their realization.

Both Hungarians and Britons decried the Jews' solidarity, social cohesiveness, and social exclusiveness, the latter two having emerged with emancipation, thereby expanding the program for reform. Erecting a social barrier between themselves and the rest of society, these traits were also used to gain an unfair advantage in the marketplace. Together, these three traits also contributed to the failure of Jews to become assimilated, as they were often shut out "from all table conversation, and the most agreeable intercourse in life; and by consequence, exclude[d] them from the most probable means of conversion."[1]

In both Hungary and Britain, Jewish morality was a significant issue. Jews were said to be both amoral and immoral. Amorality was repeatedly exhibited by both strata of Jews: they lacked ethics, gain being their only aim—as von Knigge had written. Kosmann's list of immoral character traits, including "rapacity, group prejudice, vindictiveness, excessive racial pride, timidity mixed with guile and cringing; idleness; suspicion" was still current, as was Goethe's assertion that the primary impulse of Jews was to "grab the purse" of Christians. Manifested in the occupations Jews that practiced and the way they practiced them, capital "had no conscience." Amongst the Galizianers in Hungary and the Russian Jews in Britain, immorality was most conspicuously displayed in the high rate of Jewish crime. Jewish criminality was discussed in the context of assimilation as well as the concrete affect it had on society, exercising both Hungarians and Britons. These Jews could only be considered "scrap material",[2] whose "low standard of life"[3] showed that they had yet to be "humanized".[4] The range of behaviors from which the British derived most of their complaints about Jewish character traits may have been narrower than the range observed by the Hungarians but the same traits were distilled from it. Clearly, the Jew "hasn't got our morality."[5]

And since moral reform was connected to occupational reform, this should mean that Jews were still engaged in their traditional occupations, as indeed, they were. "The tendency of their spiritual makeup [which] is trade, and its aim, money,"[6] underwent little, if any modification. "The greatest capital sums are in the hands of the Jews; for to the Jews all means are the same in order to attain their objective:"7 hence, Britons shared with Hungarians their grave concern over the monopolization of sectors of the economy and their influential role in finance and credit-related institutions, both domestically and as 'superpowers' in the world of international finance.

While industry, manufacturing, and trade were far less in Jewish hands in Britain, poor working Russian Jews established their own kind of monopoly in the economic sphere, dislodging English workers from their place in the workforce. Not as potent as the Jewish dominance in big business in Hungary, nevertheless, economic domination, whether at the level of the industrial magnate or the Russian-Jewish alien who appropriated a costermonger's pitch, was perceived equally by Hungarians and Britons as the manifestation of the Jewish character trait "to grab the purse," on the one hand, and an obsessive, uncontrolled work ethic, on the other. By the late eighteen hundreds, Hungarians and Britons were sharing this complaint of the *Fuggetlenseg*: "No one would have anything against Jewish emancipation. . . . if the Jews would not provoke hatred with their unlimited drive to power. . . . the rule of capital is poisoning all the spirit."8

The member of the Asiatic Brethren had been convinced that the Jews' "inclination to stand out as a distinctive crowd"9 would never be gotten rid of. Whether in the form of the "bothersome extroversion" that the Hungarian author Emma Ritook wrote of, or the Russian-Jewish aliens' conduct at home and in the workplace in the East-End neighborhoods which was at variance with British norms, Hungarians and Britons saw this trait as one of the signs that Jews stood outside of "good society," as Emil Reich put it.

In the post-emancipation era, the Jewish religion came under continual scrutiny and criticism. Quite apart from the clergy who continued to advocate conversion on theological grounds, Hungarians and Britons exhorted the Jews in letters to the editor, newspaper articles, pamphlets, petitions, and books to reform their religion or to convert; "complete absorption" could not be achieved otherwise.10 But no, Jews persisted in "set[ting] themselves off from Christianity, especially by means of their observance of the laws of *Kashrut* and ritual purity, which debase Christians and insult them."11 Around the issue of Sunday observance, which both countries brought to the fore, maintaining the Christian character of society and the problem of Christians working on Sunday for Jewish employers were discussed in Hungary, while the disturbance of the Christian rhythm of society was the focus in Britain. While many Hungarians and Britons contended that adherence to "Mosaic Law makes the full naturalization and fusion of the Jews with other peoples virtually impossible,"12 a number of Jews who did abandon the Jewish faith became iconoclasts and Communist revolutionaries in Hungary and anarchists and Communist revolutionaries in Britain. In other words, loosening ties to the Jewish religion did not necessarily promote an assimilative state of mind. Religious or non-religious, numbers of Jews were inclined to resist the adoption of societal and political norms.

In grappling with the problem of effecting reform among the Jews, many viewed conversion as the best way to bring this about. At all levels of Hungarian and British society, there was the expectation, or at least the hope that Jewish emancipation would lead to the conversion of the Jews. This expectation was largely thwarted in both countries by the refusal of most Jews to leave their community. At the same time, doubts were raised that this blanket solution was capable of solving the Jewish Question because converted Jews were still inclined to certain aspects of Jewishness, particularly social cohesion. Some Hungarians and Britons settled for intermarriage as an intermediate step to complete assimilation; its benefits, they hoped, would accrue to the children of these mixed marriages.

By 1920, there was an accumulation of examples for Hungarians and Britons to draw on which negatively portrayed the Jews' relation to the state. In both countries, Jews were accused of incivism. After emancipation, the suspicion that Jews were not loyal was first confirmed by the Jews' avoidance of conscription in Hungary in the 1880s, and in Britain, by Anglo-Jewry's response to the Balkan situation. But it was the First World War that provided a surfeit of opportunities for both to see the Jew as unpatriotic. Low enlistment, poor military performance, and profiteering were explosive issues in both countries. The Enlightenment thinkers' list—low participation in the military; Jews as a political and not a religious entity; as a mighty state; as a state within a state; and as a nation that had a homeland elsewhere—matched up with a current list: the wartime performance of many Jews discredited them as loyal citizens; many of the leaders and supporters of the Bolshevik revolutions (Russia, Hungary, Germany) were Jews; both Bolshevism and capitalism were considered just two different means to attain the goal of world domination; and the birth of a Jewish state was imminent.

While all Jews were 'tarred with the same brush' generally speaking, differentiation between Jews was a common phenomenon in both Hungary and Britain. 'Our' homegrown Jews were good Jews when contrasted with 'those' Jews, the Galizianers and the Jews from Russia, who were bad Jews. Being permitted to settle in a land where they were emancipated had not proved sufficient impetus for them to reform and become assimilated. Thus, governments in both countries sought to modify their open-door policies and regulate Jewish immigration. That Britain was somewhat successful in this effort and Hungary was not may say more about the longevity of liberalism in Hungary than in Britain.

Still, when considered on their own, 'our' Jews exhibited a host of unassimilated traits. Hungarians and Britons complained about their solidarity; social cohesiveness; social exclusiveness; the practice of endogamy; ostentation; unpleasantness; obsession with making money; a monopoly over certain sectors of the economy; international Jewish affiliations; cosmopolitanism; and that unquantifiable 'difference' of the Jew.

Both Hungarian and British parliamentarians discussed the issue of immigration and its negative effects at length. But it was a lightning rod for many other issues, and MPs thus sought resolution to the Jewish Question as a whole. British MPs may have hidden behind a qualifying statement before they embarked on their remarks, nonetheless, they raised the same points as their Hungarian counterparts: concern over immigration; the Jews' influence in the economic sphere; and criminal activity—in the course of which, Jewish morality, the Jews' cohesiveness, exclusiveness, and insufferable habits to which the entire nation was being subjected were also brought up.

Alongside government debate on the topic, organizations were formed in both countries with the express purpose of curtailing Jewish immigration. As well, the public participated: in Hungary, they signed petitions; in Britain, they made submissions to the Royal Commission. The Hungarian clergy promoted this cause in their local parishes, and the British clergy joined anti-alien associations and societies. The citizens of both countries wanted protection from the adverse affects that these Jewish immigrants were thought to be having on society.

Following Tiszaeszlar in Hungary, and the passage of the Aliens Act in Britain, comments about Jews became increasingly acerbic. Both events signaled the transformation of the Jewish Question from a social question into a political one, although political measures in Hungary were precluded by Prime Minister Tisza's iron grip on the country. The literature shows that both Hungarians and Britons drew on Social Darwinist arguments to further frame the nature of the Jewish Question debate.

Before emancipation, liberals had made it clear that they expected Jews to reform. Therefore, there was little quarrel with liberalism; it would protect the interests of the people. However, the liberal reflex of tolerance (in the expansive sense of the word) went so far as to extend special accommodation to the Jews where they were present in sufficient numbers: stock exchange closings and court adjournments on Jewish holidays in Hungary; permission to trade on Sunday and the "Jewification" of elementary schools in London's East End. Moreover, Hungarian and British Liberal governments refused to legislate any controls over monopolization. Growing opposition in both countries eventually culminated in riots and violence. Public opinion forced into passage the Aliens Act of 1905 in Britain and the *Numerus Clausus* in 1920 in Hungary: both signaled the disrepute into which liberalism had fallen.

In Hungary, the production of literature which addressed the Jewish Question is extensive. If there seems to be a dearth of populist publications on the Jewish Question in Britain, such as tracts, pamphlets, and press coverage, this deficit has somewhat been made up for by the number of novels and other books which dealt with this issue tangentially or even as the main theme.

Nor was there a shortage of individuals to articulate the nature of the problem. In Hungary, Ottokar Prohaszka and Gyozo Istoczy were the most prominent: those who "do not want to assimilate to us, become one people with us, must part with us."[13] In Britain, Arnold White and Major William Evans-Gordon were two of the most well-known figures who spoke out: "If the Jews will consent to be absorbed and mingle their blood with ours, all will be well."[14] These Hungarians and Englishmen forecast terrible consequences in the future if the Jewish Question—the failure of the Jews to unite body and soul with the host society—was not resolved.

Several circumstantial reasons mitigated the intensity of the complaints levied against Jews in Britain after emancipation, but none of them may be used to argue that Britons were innately more favorably disposed towards their Jewish population than Hungarians were. One is the abridged presence of Jews in Britain. Not only does this mean that there was less of a historical memory of marginalizing the Jews to erase, but also that their proportion in the population, compared to Hungary, remained insignificant. The special regard in which the sizeable millenarian Christian community held the Jews and the fact that they were quite influential is another factor. Furthermore, the British tended to emphasize alienage rather than the whole comprehensive package of reforms, and therefore, the rhetoric of assimilation that was pervasive on the Continent was less prominent in Britain. This had the effect of reducing the number of 'assimilatory thrusts' (the avenues used by Jews to 'assimilate' into society and which embodied their (mis)understanding of assimilation), which in turn lessened the number of complaints against the Jews. Finally, of the Jews who arrived in Britain after 1881, most stopped only long enough to arrange passage to America (although that often took some time); and both these 'temporary residents' and the relatively few who actually stayed were concentrated in one part of Britain, London's East End, making the Jewish Question fairly localized.

Notes

1. *Spectator*, no. 495, Saturday, 27 September 1753, 84.
2. Bary, *Vizsgalobiro emlekiratai*, 16.
3. Earl of Dunraven, *Parliamentary Debate*, 3rd ser., vol. 345 (1890), col. 296-7; Earl of Dunraven, "Invasion of Destitute Aliens," 993-94.
4. J. G. Herder, quoted in Barzilay, "Jew in the Literature," 91.
5. Buchan, *Thirty-Nine Steps*, 39; Ford, *Mr. Fleight*, 213.
6. Baron Schroetter quoted in Katz, *Out of the Ghetto*, 102.
7. Baron Schroetter quoted in Katz, *Out of the Ghetto*, 102.
8. *Fuggetlenseg*, 13 May 1884.132.
9. Member of the Asiatic Brethren, quoted in Katz, *Out of the Ghetto*, 84-85.
10. Russell and Lewis, "Jew in London," 12-13.
11. One of the points in the Tapolca Petition, quoted in Bary, *Vizsgalobiro emlekiratai*, 434.
12. J. D. Michaelis, quoted in Liberles, "From Toleration to *Verbesserung*," 14.
13. Istoczy, *Istoczy Gyozo orszaggyulesi*, 59.
14. White, *Modern Jew*, 208-9.

Conclusion

In 1920, Jozsef Schonfeld, editor of the *Zsido Szemle*, the establishment mouthpiece of the Jewish community (not unlike the *Jewish Chronicle* in London) wrote a tract about the position of Hungarian Jews who now found themselves living in other countries due to the imposed truncation of Hungary after the war. Schonfeld stated that culturally they would "remain identified with the Jews of dismembered Hungary." Further, "Jews, organized in the name of the Jewish national idea, will be an invisible force that will topple artificial borders while our cultural ties will establish economic connections among us."[1] Christian Hungarian society could not have failed to recognize in these sentences the proof that not only had Jews not assimilated but that even the language of assimilation was foreign to them.

Schonfeld drew attention to the fact of cultural homogeneity among Jews. Despite the exhortations to become "equal partners . . . in the common culture of humanity,"[2] they had insisted on maintaining a separate cultural identity. Alongside the religious injunction that Jews not "take their meals with us [non-Jews],"[3] the traits of solidarity, social cohesiveness, and social exclusiveness ensured that this cultural identity was held firmly in place, and Jews would remain unassimilated.

Giving voice to the notion that Jews were "organized in the name of the Jewish national idea," this statement by Schonfeld automatically severed Jews from their fellow countrymen. It proclaimed their status as a separate people, and further, conjured up an image of the Jews as a 'state within a state' and the implications to be derived therefrom: incivism and the possibility that Jews might "repudiate the laws of the state," "in the case of a conflict between its laws and the laws of the state."[4] When Schonfeld referred to Jews as "an invisible force," it was more than an admission—it was a declaration of the "unseen hand of organized interest."[5] Schonfeld then referred to "our cultural ties [that] will establish economic connections among us." The time when such international economic connections were deemed beneficial to the host society because "they are disseminated through all the trading ports of the world,"[6] was long past. Presently, these ties smacked of cosmopolitanism, supranationalism, and an international Jewish conspiracy. Moreover, the existence of such a connection gave Jews an unfair economic advantage. (The reference to "artificial borders," while it would ostensibly advance the argument presented here, is a sentiment that would have been universally supported by Hungarians in truncated Hungary.) To many, Schonfeld would have written this article as a Jew, or perhaps a pre-emancipated Jew, but not as a Hungarian.

The Jews living in their midst were not 'just like us.' No amount of protestation on the part of the Jews could convince many Hungarians—or Britons—

otherwise. Jews had failed to carry out the exacting prescription leading to assimilation into the nations in which they resided; there had never been any intention to establish grounds for accepting the Jew *as* Jew. In Britain, the response to this failure took the shape of increasing hostility to their own Jews and complete indifference to the plight of Jews elsewhere (1930s), shown by the almost total non-application of the principle of the right to political asylum. In Hungary, they agreed to institute formal measures, the *Numerus Clausus*, as a means to curb Jewish influence in society. However, this measure would prove inadequate to contain the outrage over the perceived damage done to Hungarian society on every front since the Jews' emancipation: this evoked a desire for punishment.

> My father was never an anti-Semite; he always respected in them what could be respected, especially their spiritual openness. Having been asked by Oszkar Jaszi, I did write about this question in the periodical *Huszadik Szazad*, during the war. People did think I was terribly anti-Semitic, though I was not at that time. Jews think that just because I am not totally on their side in every detail, I am anti-Semitic. We do speak different languages, so discussion was never possible. I always felt this difference in questions pertaining to love, marriage, loyalty, courage . . . even with Lukacs and Bloch. . . .
>
> Modern Jews have lost the sense of tradition. I remember how a Jewess told Ignotus next to the sculpture of Kossuth: 'What relation should I have to this sculpture?' The answer was simple: 'He was the one you can thank for being accepted by our nation.' Without traditions, they can change their positions relentlessly, like Bela Balazs, or Simmel, Bloch, Lukacs, Bergson, and Freud. . . .
>
> Father never allowed intolerance against other denominations, and even the mention of the word 'race' was taboo. Of course, I don't generalize, I feel how painful it is to those Jews we do love. But this injustice is due to the terrible suffering we went through because of Jews.[7]

Notes

1. Jozsef Schonfeld "A beke ratifikalasa es a zsidosag," [Peace Ratification and the Jewry] in *Harcban a zsidosagert* [At War for the Jewry] (Budapest: 1920): 53-54.
2. J. H. Herder quoted in Barzilay, "Jew in the Literature," 108.
3. J. D. Michaelis, quoted in Katz, *Out of the Ghetto*, 91-92.
4. E. T. von Kortum quoted in Katz, "State Within a State," 64.
5. Colvin, *Unseen Hand in English History*, x.
6. *Spectator*, no. 495. Saturday, September 27, 1753, 82.
7. Emma Ritook, Collected Papers of Emma Ritook. Unpublished Diary. Excerpt taken from the year 1927. Manuscript Department. Orszagos Szechenyi Konyvtar (Szechenyi National Library). Call Number Fond 473. Ritook (1868-1945) studied in Leipzig and Paris and earned her Ph.D. in 1906. A journalist, novelist, and poet, her prewar literary career was mainly devoted to women's issues in the feminist spirit. After the war, many of her works promoted the restoration of Hungary's prewar borders.

Epilogue

The statement made in June 2001 by a then sixty-three-year-old Hungarian Jew, Mr. Markusz[‡], whose father died days after being released from Mauthausen, is instructive: "I assimilated as much as I could; but I'm not religious." Seemingly contradictory, or worse, incoherent, when the two parts of this sentence are considered separately, it is a cogent statement and the entire issue of assimilation reaching back to the period of the Enlightenment is exposed. The phrasing of the first part of the sentence—one must assimilate (as much as possible)—acknowledges that the mandate is a whole package, but the process of assimilation has not been complete. Whether this is due to a limit he put on himself—a point beyond which he was unwilling to assimilate—or whether he tried to assimilate completely but it was never considered enough, is unknown. The protest, "but I'm not religious," is as much a statement of fact as an attempt to offset the previous admission of the incompleteness of assimilation. Having assimilated as much as he could, Markusz exhibits his Jewishness only in the following ways. He is keenly aware of all the Holocaust memorials in Budapest; he has knowledge of, and goes to Jewish sites throughout the country. He belongs to a synagogue, but takes part only in the cultural events it sponsors. He is an avid collector of books about Hungarian Jewry. He has observed only one of the Passover rites since the war: the custom of making matzah balls and eating matzah exclusively during the holiday, particularly for the sake of eating it with his coffee. While acknowledging the existence of anti-Semitism, Markusz lives in the belief that he is assimilated. Markusz is a typical Hungarian Jew. This tenacity 'unto the generations' highlights the aspiration of Jews to belong to and participate in the society in which they live, despite the body of evidence showing that Christian Hungarians rejected their tokens of assimilation.

[‡] Mr. Gyorgy Markusz consented to be quoted here. He passed away a few years after giving this interview.

Bibliography

Public Documents

Kepviselohazi Naplo
Nemzetgyulesi Naplo
Orszaggyulesi Iromanyok
Orszaggyulesi Jegyzokonyv
Orszagos Leveltar
Parliament (Commons), Royal Commission on Alien Immigration, Vol.2.
United Kingdom. Parliamentary Debates
London County Council Minutes

Books

Abrahams, I. and S. Levy, eds. *Macaulay on Jewish Disabilities*. Edinburgh, 1910.
Acsady, Ignac. *Zsido es nemzsido magyarok az emancipacio utan* (Jewish and Non-Jewish Hungarians after the Emancipation). Budapest: Weiszmann testverek, 1883.
Ady, Endre. *A zsidosagrol* (About Jewry). Reprint of the original articles 27 August 1901—12 April 1903. Nagyvarad, 1919.
Agoston, Peter. *A zsidok utja* (The Way of the Jews). Nagyvarad: A Nagyvaradi Tarsadalomtudomanyi Tarsasag, 1917.
Alderman, Geoffrey. "English Jews or Jews of the English Persuasion? Reflections on the Emancipation of Anglo-Jewry." In *Paths of Emancipation: Jews, States, and Citizenship*. Edited by Pierre Birnbaum and Ira Katznelson. Princeton: Princeton University Press, 1995.
———. *The Jewish Community in British Politics*. Oxford: Oxford University Press, 1983.
———. *London Jewry and London Politics 1889-1986*. London and New York: Routledge, 1989.
———. *Modern British Jewry*. Oxford: Clarendon Press, 1992.
———. Review of David Feldman's *Englishmen and Jews: Social Relations and Political Culture, 1840-1914* and David Cesarani's *The Jewish Chronicle and Anglo-Jewry, 1841-1991*. English Historical Review 109 (September 1994).
Almog, Shmuel. *Nationalism & Antisemitism in Modern Europe 1815-1945*. Oxford: Pergamon Press, 1990.
Altenburg, Gyula. *A valasztojog es a zsidosag* (Electoral Rights and the Jews). Budapest: *A Cel* Hornyansky Viktor, n.d.
Alter, Robert. "Emancipation, Enlightenment and All That." *Commentary* 13, no. 2 F, (1972).
Altmann, Alexander. *Moses Mendelssohn: A Biographical Study*. London: Routledge & Kegan Paul Ltd, 1973.

Anderson, Robert. "The Problem of the Criminal Alien." *Nineteenth Century and After* 49, no. 408 (February 1911).

Andrassy, Gyula. *A magyar ertelmiseg feladatairol* (On the Hungarian Intellectuals' Tasks). Budapest: Magyar Kultura, 1921.

———. "A Zsidokerdesrol" (On the Jewish Question). *Uj Magyar Szemle* (July 1920.)

Arendt, Hannah. *The Jew as Pariah: Jewish Identity and Politics in the Modern Age*. New York: Grove Press / Random House, 1978.

———. *The Origins of Totalitarianism*. New York: Harcourt, Brace, 1951.

———. "Privileged Jews." In *Emancipation and Counter-Emancipation: Selected Essays from Jewish Social Studies*. Edited by Abraham G. Duker and Meir Ben-Horin. New York: Ktav Publishing House, Inc., 1974.

Aris, Stephen. *The Jews in Business*. 1970. Reprint, London: Jonathan Cape Ltd, 1971.

Aronsfeld, C. C. "German Jews in Victorian England." *Leo Baeck Institute Year Book* 7 (1962).

Aschheim, Steven E. *In Times of Crisis: Essays on European Culture, Germans, and Jews*. Madison, Wis.: University of Wisconsin Press, 2001.

Avineri, Shlomo. "A Note on Hegel's View on Jewish Emancipation." *Jewish Social Studies* 35 (1963).

Bajcsy-Zsilinszky, Endre. *Ujjaszuletes es sajto* (National Rebirth and the Press). n.p.: Taltos, 1920.

Balazs, Bela, ed. *A klerikalis reakcio, a Horthy-fasizmus tamasza* (Clerical Reaction, the Pillar of Horthy Fascism). Budapest, 1953.

Baldwin, Peter, ed. *Reworking the Past: Hitler, the Holocaust, and the Historians' Debate*. Boston: Beacon Press, 1990.

Balla, Erzsebet. "The Jews of Hungary: A Cultural Overview." *Hungarian Jewish Studies* 2 (1969).

Balogh, Eva S. "Istvan Friedrich and the Hungarian Coup d'Etat of 1919: A Reevaluation" Ph.D. diss. Reprint, *Slavic Review* 35, no. 2 (June 1976).

Bandholtz, H. H. *An Undiplomatic Diary by the American Member of the Inter-Allied Military Mission to Hungary, 1919–1920*. Edited by Fritz-Konrad Kruger. New York: AMS Press, Inc., 1966.

Bangha, Bela. *Magyarorszag ujjaepitese es a keresztenyseg* (The Rebuilding of Hungary and Christianity). Budapest: Szent-Istvan Tarsulat, 1920.

Barany, George. "Magyar Jew or: Jewish Magyar? (To the Question of Jewish Assimilation in Hungary)." *Canadian-American Slavic Studies* 8, no. 1 (Spring 1974).

Barnett, R. D. "Anglo-Jewry in the Eighteenth Century." In *Three Centuries of Anglo-Jewish History: A Volume of Essays*. Edited by. V. D. Lipman. Cambridge: Jewish Historical Society of England, 1961.

Baron, Salo W. "Great Britain and Damascus Jewry in 1860-61: An Archival Study." *Jewish Social Studies* 2, no. 2 (April 1940).

———. "The Impact of the Revolution of 1848 on Jewish Emancipation." In *Emancipation and Counter-Emancipation: Selected Essays from Jewish Social Studies*. Edited by Abraham G. Duker and Meir Ben-Horin. New York: Ktav Publishing House, Inc., 1974.

———. "The Revolution of 1848 and Jewish Scholarship." *Jewish Social Studies* 11 (1949).

———. *The Russian Jews under Tsars and Soviets.* New York: Macmillan Company, 1964.
———. *Steeled by Adversity: Essays and Addresses on American Jewish Life.* Edited by Jeannette Meisel Baron. Philadelphia: Jewish Publication Society of America, 1971.
Barta, Istvan. *Kossuth Lajos az utolso rendi oszaggyulesen* (Lajos Kossuth in the Last Estate Parliament). Budapest: Akademiai Kiado, 1951.
Bartha, Miklos. *Kazar foldon* (In the Land of the Kazars). Kolozsvar: Ellenzeki Konyvnyomda, 1901.
Bary, Jozsef. *Vizsgalobiro emlekiratai—A tiszaeszlar bunper* (Memoirs of the Magistrate: The Criminal Case of Tiszaeszlar). Budapest, 1933.
Barzilay, Isaac Eisenstein. "The Jew in the Literature of the Enlightenment." In *Emancipation and Counter-Emancipation: Selected Essays from Jewish Social Studies.* Edited by Abraham G. Duker and Meir Ben-Horin. New York: Ktav Publishing House, Inc., 1974.
———. "The Jews in the Literature of the Enlightenment." *Jewish Social Studies* 18 (October 1950).
Bauman, Zygmunt. *Modernity and the Holocaust.* Cambridge: Polity Press / Basil Blackwell Ltd, 1989.
Baumann, A. A. "Possible Remedies for the Sweating System." *National Review* 12, no. 69 (November 1888).
Beck, Wolfgang, ed. *The Jews in European History.* Cincinnati: Hebrew Union College Press, 1992.
Beksics, Gusztav. *Magyarosodas es magyarositas: kulonos tekintettel varosainkra* (Becoming Hungarians and Turning Them into Hungarians: With Special Regard to our Cities). Budapest: Az Atheneum R. Tarsulat Kiadasa, 1883.
Beller, Steven. *Vienna and the Jews: A Cultural History, 1867-1938.* Cambridge: Cambridge: University Press, 1989.
Belloc, Hilaire. *The Jews.* London: Constable & Co, 1928.
———. *Pongo and the Bull.* London: Constable & Company Limited, 1910.
Benda, Kalman. Peter Hanak, Zsuzsa L. Nagy, Laszlo Makkai, Emil Niederhuser. Gyorgy Spira, and Karoly Voros. *One Thousand Years: A Concise History of Hungary.* Edited by Peter Hanak. Translated by Zsuzsa Beres. Translation revised Christopher Sullivan. Budapest: Corvin, 1988.
Bennett, Solomon. *Critical Remarks on the Authorized Version of the Old Testament.* London, 1834.
Bereczky, Albert. *A magyar protestantizmus a zsidouldozes ellen* (Hungarian Protestantism Against the Persecution of the Jews). 1945. Reprint, Traktatus kiadas, Magyarorszagi Reformatus Egyhaz, 1984.
Berend, Ivan T., and Gyorgy Ranki. "The Horthy Regime 1919-1944." In *A History of Hungary.* Translated by Laszlo Boros, Istvan Farkas, Gyula Gyulas and Eva Rona. Translation revised by Margaret Morris and Richard E. Allen. Edited by Ervin Pamlenyi. Budapest: Corvina Press, 1973.
Berkovitz, Jay R. *The Shaping of Jewish Identity in Nineteenth-century France.* Detroit: Wayne State University Press, 1989.
Bermant, C. *Point of Arrival: A Study of London's East End.* London: Eyre Methuen Ltd, 1975.

Bernard, Paul C. *The Limits of Enlightenment: Joseph II and the Law*. Urbana, Ill.: University of Illinois Press, 1979.
Bernardini, Paolo. "The Silent Retreat of the Fathers: Episodes in the Process of Re-appraisal of Jewish History and Culture in Eighteenth-Century England." In *Cultures of Ambivalence and Contempt: Studies in Jewish-non-Jewish Relations*. Edited by Sian Jones, Tony Kushner, and Sarah Pearce. London: Vallentine Mitchell, 1998.
Bernstein, Bela. *Az 1848/49-iki magyar szabadsagharc es a zsidok* (The Hungarian War of Liberation of 1848-1849 and the Jews). Budapest, 1898. Reprint, retitled, *A negyvennyolcas magyar szabadsagharc es a zsidok* (The 1848 Freedom Fight and the Jews). Budapest: Tabor-Kiadas, 1939. Budapest: Mult es Jovo Konyvek, 2000.
Bernstein, Michael Andre. *Foregone Conclusions: Against Apocalyptic History*. Berkeley and Los Angeles: University of California Press, 1994.
Bethlen, Pal., ed. *Numerus Clausus*. Budapest: A Magyazsidosag Almanachja Konyvkiadovallalata, 1925.
Bibo, Istvan. "Zsidokerdes Magyarorszagon 1944 utan" (The Jewish Question in Hungary after 1944). *Valasz* 10-11 (1948).
Bihar, Jeno. *Egan Edet meggyikoltak* (They Murdered Ede Egan). Budapest: Hunyadi Matyas Intezet, 1901.
Birnbaum, Pierre. *Jewish Destinies: Citizenship, State, and Community in Modern France*. Translated by Arthur Goldhammer. New York: Hill and Wang, 1995.
Birnbaum, Pierre, and Ira Katznelson. "Emancipation and the Liberal Offer." In *Paths of Emancipation: Jews, States, and Citizenship*. Edited by Pierre Birnbaum and Ira Katznelson. Princeton: Princeton University Press, 1995.
Blanning, T. C. W. *Joseph II*. New York: Longman Publishing, 1994.
———. *Joseph II and Enlightened Despotism*. London: Longman Group Limited, 1970.
Bloom, Solomon. "Karl Marx and the Jews." *Jewish Social Studies* 4 (1942).
Bonyhadi, Perczel Istvan. *Judische Delikatessen* (Jewish Delicatessen). 75 vols. A private collection of newspaper clippings 1880-1887. Orszagos Szechenyi Konyvtar Archive, OH. 750.
Bosnyak, Zoltan. *Harc a zsido sajto ellen* (Fight against the Jewish Press). Budapest: Held Janos Konyvnyomdaja, 1938.
———. *Prohaszka es a zsido kerdes* (Prohaszka and the Jewish Question). Budapest: A Magyar Kulturliga kiadasa, 1938.
Bovill, W. B. Forster. *Hungary and the Hungarians: Illus. by William Pascoe*. London: Methuen, 1908.
Bowler, Peter J. *Charles Darwin: The Man and his Influence*. Oxford: Basil Blackwell Ltd, 1992.
Braham, Randolph L. *The Hungarian Jewish Catastrophe: A Selected and Annotated Bibliography*. 2nd ed. New York: Columbia University Press, 1984.
———. *The Politics of Genocide: The Holocaust in Hungary*. Vol. 1. New York: Columbia University Press, 1981.
Breuer, Edward. *The Limits of Enlightenment: Jews, Germans, and the Eighteenth-century Study of Scripture*. Cambridge, Mass.: Harvard University Press, 1996.

Bristow, Edward. "The German-Jewish Fight Against White Slavery." *Leo Baeck Institute Year Book* 28 (1983).
Bryce, James. "The Migrations of the Races of Men Considered Historically." *Contemporary Review* 62 (July–December 1892).
Buchan, John. *The Thirty-Nine Steps*. 1915. Reprint, London: Hodder & Stoughton Limited, 1936.
Buchler, Sandor. "Zsidok a magyar egyetemen" (Jews in the Hungarian University). In *Evkonyv*. Edited by Vilmos Bacher and Jozsef Banoczi. Budapest: Az Izraelita Magyar Irodalmi Tarsulat, 1897.
Buckle, George Earl. *The Life of Benjamin Disraeli, Earl of Beaconsfield*, Vol. 6. London: John Murray, 1920.
Budavary, Laszlo. *Zold bolshevizmus* (Green Bolshevism). Budapest, 1941.
Bush, Julia. *Behind the Lines: East London Labour*. London: Merlin Press, 1984.
Cannadine, David. "The Context, Performance and Meaning of Ritual: The British Monarchy and the 'Invention of Tradition', c. 1820-1977." In *The Invention of Tradition*. Edited by Eric Hobsbawm and Terence Ranger. Cambridge: Cambridge University Press, 1983.
Carlebach, Julius. *Karl Marx and the Radical Critique of Judaism*. London, Henley and Boston: Routledge & Kegan Paul, 1978.
Carsten, F. L. "The Court Jews." *Leo Baeck Institute Year Book* 3 (1958).
Cesarani, David. "Anti-Zionist Politics and Political Anti-Semitism in Britain." *Patterns of Prejudice* 23, no. 1 (Spring 1989).
———. "An Embattled Minority: The Jews in Britain During the First World War." In *The Politics of Marginality: Race, the Radical Right, and Minorities in Twentieth Century Britain*. Edited by Tony Kushner and Kenneth Lunn. London: Frank Cass & Co. Ltd, 1990.
———. *The Jewish Chronicle and Anglo-Jewry, 1841-1991*. Cambridge: Cambridge University Press, 1994.
———. *The Making of Modern Anglo-Jewry*. Oxford: Basil Blackwell Ltd, 1990.
———. "Reporting Antisemitism: The Jewish Chronicle, 1879-1979." In *Cultures of Ambivalence and Contempt: Studies in Jewish-non-Jewish Relations*. Edited by Sian Jones, Tony Kushner, and Sarah Pearce. London: Vallentine Mitchell, 1998.
Chamberlain, Houston Stewart. *Foundations of the Nineteenth Century*. 2 vols. London: J. Lane, 1911.
Chamberlain, Joseph. "The Labour Question." *Nineteenth Century* 32, no. 189 (November 1892).
———. "Tariff Reform and Unemployment." In *Mr. Chamberlain's Speeches*. Edited by Charles W. Boyd. 2 vols. London, 1914.
Champion, Justin. "Toleration and Citizenship in Enlightenment England: John Toland and the Naturalization of the Jews, 1714-1753." In *Toleration in Enlightenment Europe*. Edited by Ole Peter Grell and Roy Porter. Cambridge: Cambridge University Press, 2000.
Cheyette, Bryan. Preface to *Between "Race" and Culture: Representations of "the Jew" in English and American Literature*. Stanford: Stanford University Press, 1996.

———. *Constructions of 'The Jew' in English Literature and Society: Racial Representations, 1875-1945*. Cambridge: Cambridge University Press, 1993.

———. "Hilaire Belloc and the 'Marconi Scandal' 1913-1914: A Reassessment of the Interactionist Model of Racial Hatred." In *The Politics of Marginality: Race, the Radical Right, and Minorities in Twentieth Century Britain*. Edited by Tony Kushner and Kenneth Lunn. London: Frank Cass & Co. Ltd, 1990.

———. "Jewish Stereotyping and English Literature, 1875-1920: Towards a Political Analysis." In *Traditions of Intolerance: Historical Perspectives on Fascism and Race Discourse in British Society*. Edited by Tony Kushner and Kenneth Lunn. Manchester: Manchester University Press, 1989.

Cheyette, Bryan, and Laura Marcus, eds. *Modernity, Culture, and the Jew*. Cambridge: Polity Press / Blackwell Publishers Ltd., 1998.

Clapham, J. H. *The Bank of England: A History*. Vol. 1. New York: Macmillan Company, 1945.

———. *An Economic History of Modern Britain*, 3 vols. Cambridge: 1930-8.

Cobbett, William. *Good Friday: Or, The Murder of Jesus Christ by the Jews*. London: The Author, 1830.

Cohen, Asher. "The Attitude of the Intelligentsia in Hungary Toward Jewish Assimilation Between the Two World Wars." In *Jewish Assimilation in Modern Times*. Edited by Bela Vago. Boulder, Colo.: Westview Press, Inc., 1981.

Cohen, Carl. "The Road to Conversion." *Leo Baeck Institute Year Book* 6 (1961).

Cohen, Israel. "The Jews in Hungary." *Contemporary Review* 11 (November 1939).

Cohn, Norman. *Warrant for Genocide: The Myth of the Jewish World-Conspiracy and the Protocols of the Elders of Zion*. Eyre & Spottiswoode (Publishers) Ltd, 1967.

Collins, Kenneth E. *Second City Jewry: The Jews of Glasgow in the Age of Expansion, 1790-1919*. Glasgow: Scottish Jewish Archives, 1990.

Colvin, Ian D. *The Unseen Hand in English History*. London: *National Review* Office, 1917.

Condorcet, Marquis de. *Outlines of an Historical View of the Progress of the Human Mind*. London, 1796.

Cowen, Anne, and Roger Cowen, eds. *Victorian Jews through British Eyes*. Oxford and New York: Oxford University Press, 1986.

Cranfield, G. A. "The London Evening Post and the Jew Bill." *Historical Journal* 8 (1965).

———. *The Press and Society*. London: Longman Group Limited, 1978.

Csernatony, Lajos. "Zsidoinkrol" (About Our Jews). Series of five articles, *Ellenor* (1874).

Cunningham, W. *Alien Immigrants to England*. Edited by Kenelm D. Cotes. Social England Series. London: Swan Sonnenschein & Co. Limd, 1897.

Daner, Bela. *Penz es hatalom* (Money and Power). Budapest: Pallas Reszvenytarsag, 1921.

Dangerfield, George. *The Strange Death of Liberal England*. New York: Harrison Smith & Robert Haas, 1935.

Deak, Istvan. "Homeless Defenders of the Homeland: The Officers of the Habsburg Monarchy." In *Hungarians and Their Neighbors in Modern Times, 1867-1950*. Edited by Ferenc Glatz. New York: Columbia University Press, 1995.
———. "Hungary." In *The European Right: A Historical Profile*. Edited by Hans Rogger and Eugen Webber. Berkeley and Los Angeles: University of California Press, 1966.
Dersi, Tamas. *A szazadveg katolikus sajtoja* (The Catholic Press at the *Fin-de-siecle*). Budapest: Akademiai Kiado, 1973.
———. *Szazadvegi uzenet* (Message from the *Fin-de-siecle*). Budapest: Szepirodalmi Konyvkiado, 1973.
Diderot, Denis. "Humanité." In *Oeuvres*, Vol. 15.
Dohm, Christian Wilhelm von. *Concerning the Amelioration of the Civil Status of the Jews* (*Über die büergerliche Verbesserung der Juden*). Translated by Helen Lederer. 1781. Reprint, Cincinnati: Hebrew Union College-Jewish Institute of Religion, 1957.
———. *Über die büergerliche Verbesserung der Juden II*. Ruprecht–Karls–Universitat Heidelberg, Germany. Call No. SWB 02442963.1783.
Don, Yehuda. "Patterns of Jewish Economic Behaviour." In *A Social and Economic History of Central European Jewry*. Edited by Yehuda Don and Victor Karady. New Brunswick, N.J. and London: Transaction Publishers, 1990.
Don, Yehuda, and Victor Karady, eds. *A Social and Economic History of Central European Jewry*. New Brunswick, N.J. and London: Transaction Publishers, 1990.
Don, Yehuda, and George Magos. "The Demographic Development of Hungarian Jewry." *Jewish Social Studies* 45, nos. 3-4 (Summer/Fall 1983).
Dubnow, S. M. *History of the Jews in Russia and Poland from the Earliest Times until the Present Day*. Translated by I. Friedlander. 1916-1920. 3 vols. Reprint, New York: Ktav Publishing House, Inc., 1975.
Dunraven, Earl of. "The Invasion of Destitute Aliens." *Nineteenth Century* 31, no. 184 (June 1892).
Dyche, John A. "The Jewish Immigrant." *Contemporary Review* 75 (January–June 1899).
———. "The Jewish Workman." *Contemporary Review* 73 (January–June 1898).
Ebredo Magyarok Egyesulete (Association of Awakening Hungarians). *Antiszemitizmus magyarorszagon* (Anti-Semitism in Hungary). Budapest, 1920.
Eckhart, Ferenc. *A Short History of the Hungarian People*. London: Grant Richards Fronto Limited, 1931.
Eighty Club. *Hungary, Its People, Places, and Politics: The Visit of the Eighty Club in 1906*. London: Unwin, 1907.
Elbogen, Ismar. *A Century of Jewish Life*. Philadelphia, 1944.
Elon, Amos. *The Pity of it All: A History of the Jews in Germany, 1743-1933*. New York: Metropolitan Books, 2002.
Emanuel, Charles H. L. *A Century and a Half of Jewish History*. London: George Routledge & Sons Limited, 1910.

Endelman, Todd M. "The Englishness of Jewish Modernity in England." In *Toward Modernity: The European Jewish Model.* Edited by Jacob Katz. New Brunswick, N.J.: Transaction Books, 1987.
———. *The Jews of Britain, 1656 to 2000.* Berkeley and London: University of California Press, 2002.
———. *The Jews of Georgian England 1714-1830.* Philadelphia: Jewish Publication Society of America, 1979.
———. *Radical Assimilation in English Jewish History, 1656-1945: The Modern Jewish Experience.* Bloomington, Ind.: Indiana University Press, 1990.
———. "The Social and Political Context of Conversion in Germany and England, 1870-1914." In *Jewish Apostasy in the Modern World.* Edited by Todd M. Endelman. New York: Holmes & Meier Publishers, Inc. 1987.
Endelman, Todd M., and Tony Kushner, eds. *Disraeli's Jewishness.* London: Vallentine Mitchell, 2002.
Engelman, Uriah Zevi. "Intermarriage Among Jews in Germany, U.S.S.R., and Switzerland." *Jewish Social Studies* 2, no. 2 (April 1940).
———. *The Rise of the Jew in the Western World: A Social and Economic History of the Jewish People of Europe.* 1944. Reprint, New York: Arno Press Inc., 1973.
Englander, David, ed. *A Documentary History of Jewish Immigrants in Britain, 1840-1920.* London: Leicester University Press, 1994.
———. *Landlord and Tenant in Urban Britain, 1838-1918.* Oxford: Clarendon Press, 1983.
Eotvos, Jozsef. *Eotvos osszes munkai* (The Complete Works of Eotvos). Edited by Geza Voinovich. Vol. 12. Budapest, 1902-1904.
———. *"A Zsidok Emancipacioja"* (The Emancipation of the Jews). In *Reform es Hazafisag, Eotvos Jozsef Muvei, Publicisztikai Irasok* (Reform and Patriotism: The Works of Jozsef Eotvos, Journalistic Writings). 1840. Reprint, Budapest: Magyar Helikon, Szepirodalmi Konyvkiado, 1978.
Essays in Liberalism: Being the Lectures and Papers which Were Delivered at the Liberal Summer School at Oxford, 1922. London: W. Collins Sons & Co. Ltd., 1922.
Falk, Gerhard. *The Jew in Christian Theology: Martin Luther's anti-Jewish Von Schem Hamphoras, Previously Unpublished in English, and Other Milestones in Church Doctrine Concerning Judaism.* Jefferson, N.C.: McFarland & Company, Inc., Publishers, 1992.
Faber, W. S. *Hungary's Alibi.* London: Lincolns-Prager (Publishers) Ltd., 1944.
Feiner, Shmuel. "Towards a Historical Definition of the Haskalah." In *New Perspectives on the Haskalah.* Edited by Shmuel Feiner and David Sorkin. London and Portland, Oreg.: Library of Jewish Civilization, 2001.
Feldman, David. *Englishmen and Jews: Social Relations and Political Culture, 1840-1914.* New Haven: Yale University Press, 1994.
Ferenc, Fejto. *Magyarsag, zsidosag* (Hungariandom and Jewry). Budapest: MTA Tortenettudomanyi Intezete, 2000.
Ferenc, Fiala, and Istvan Nyekhegyi. *A magyar sajto igazi arca* (The True Face of the Hungarian Press). Budapest: Az Osszetartas Kiadasa, 1938.
Ferguson, Niall. *The House of Rothschild: The World's Banker , 1849-1999.* New York: Viking, 1999.

Finestein, Israel. *Anglo-Jewry in Changing Times: Studies in Diversity 1814-1914*. London: Vallentine Mitchell, 1999.
———. *Jewish Society in Victorian England: Collected Essays*. London: Valentine Mitchell, 1993.
———. "The New Community, 1880-1918." In *Three Centuries of Anglo-Jewish History: A Volume of Essays*. Edited by V. D. Lipman. Cambridge: Jewish Historical Society of England, 1961.
———. *Post-emancipation Jewry: The Anglo-Jewish Experience; The Seventh Sacks Lecture Delivered on 8th June 1980*. Oxford: Oxford Centre for Postgraduate Hebrew Studies, 1980.
Fishman, William. *East End Jewish Radicals, 1875-1914*. Gerald Duckworth & Co., 1975.
———. "Jewish Immigrant Anarchists in East London, 1870-1914." In *The Jewish East End 1840-1939*. Edited by Kenneth Lunn. London: Jewish Historical Society, 1981.
Foa, Anna. *The Jews of Europe after the Black Death*. Translated by Andrea Grover. 1992. Reprint, Berkeley, Los Angeles and London: University of California Press, 2000. Originally published as *Ebrei in Europa: Della Peste nera all'emancipazione, XIV-XVIII secolo*. (Gius: Laterza & Figli, 1992.)
Frank, Dr. Mor. *Helyesen itelte-e meg Csernatony Lajos a zsidokat*? (Did Lajos Csernatony Judge the Jews Correctly?) Budapest: Wodianer F., 1874.
Frankel, Jonathan, and Steven J. Zipperstein, eds. *Assimilation and Community: The Jews in Nineteenth-Century Europe*. Cambridge, UK and New York: Cambridge University Press, 1992.
Freedman, Maurice. "Jews in the Society of Britain." In *A Minority in Britain: Social Studies of the Anglo-Jewish Community*. Edited by Maurice Freedman. London: Valentine, Mitchell & Co., Ltd, 1955.
Freifeld, Alice. *Nationalism and the Crowd in Liberal Hungary, 1848-1914*. Washington, D.C.: Woodrow Wilson Center Press / Baltimore: Johns Hopkins University Press, 2000.
Friedman, Elisha M. *Survival or Extinction: Social Aspects of the Jewish Question*. New York: T. Seltzer, 1924.
Gainer, Bernard. *The Alien Invasion: Origins of the Aliens Act of 1905*. London: Heinemann Educational Books Ltd, 1972.
Garrard, John A. *The English and Immigration 1880-1910*. London: Oxford University Press, 1971.
Gartner, Lloyd P. *The Jewish Immigrant in England, 1870-1914*. London: Allen & Unwin Publishers Ltd., 1960.
Gay, Peter. *The Enlightenment: An Interpretation*. 2 vols. New York: Knopf, 1966-69.
Gergely, Jeno. *A Puspoki Kar tanacskozasai: A magyar katolikus puspokok konferenciainak jegyzokonyveibol* (Debates of the Synod of Bishops: From the Protocols of the Conferences of Catholic Hungarian Bishops). 1919-1944.
Gilam, Abraham. *The Emancipation of the Jews in England 1830-1860*. New York and London: Garland Publishing, Inc., 1982.

Glaser, Anthony. "The Tredegar Riots of August 1911." In *The Jews of South Wales: Historical Studies*. Edited by Ursula R. Q. Henriques. Cardiff: University of Wales Press, 1993.

Glassman, Bernard. *Anti-Semitic Stereotypes Without Jews: Images of the Jews in England, 1290-1700*. Detroit: Wayne State University Press, 1975.

———. *Protean Prejudice: Anti-semitism in England's Age of Reason*. Atlanta: Scholars Press, 1998.

Goldscheider, Calvin, and Alan S. Zuckerman. *The Transformation of the Jews*. Chicago and London: University of Chicago Press, 1984.

Goldstein, Moritz. "German Jewry's Dilemma Before 1914." *Leo Baeck Institute Year Book* 2 (1957).

Gollomb, Abraham. "Jewish Self-Hatred." *YIVO Annual of Jewish Social Science* 1 New York: Yiddish Institute. (1946).

Gonda, Laszlo. *A zsidosag Magyarorszagon 1526-1945* (Jewry in Hungary 1526-1945). Budapest: Szazadveg Kiado, 1992.

Gonda, Moshe Elijahu. *A debreceni zsidok szaz eve; a martirhalallt halt debreceni es kornyekbeli zsidok emlekere* (A Hundred Years of the Jews of Debrecen: In Memory of the Debrecen and Area Jews Who Suffered Martyrdom). Haifa: Debreceni Zsidok Emlekbizottsaga, 1970.

Graetz, Heinrich. "The Correspondence of an English Lady on Judaism and Semitism," in *The Structure of Jewish History, and Other Essays*. Translated and edited by Ismar Schorsch. New York: Jewish Theological Seminary, 1979.

Gratz, Gusztav. *A forradalmak kora, 1918-1920* (The Age of Revolutions, 1918-1920). Budapest: Magyar SzemleTarsasag, 1935.

Grayzel, Solomon. *A History of the Jews: From the Babylonian Exile to the Present*. 1947. Reprint, Canada: Meridian / Penguin Books Canada Limited, 1984.

Grégoire, Henri. *Essai sur la régénération physique, morale et politique des Juifs*. 1789.

Grell, Ole Peter, and Roy Porter. "Toleration in Enlightenment Europe." In *Toleration in Enlightenment Europe*. Edited by Ole Peter Grell and Roy Porter. Cambridge: Cambridge University Press, 2000.

Griffiths, Richard. *Fellow Travellers of the Right: British Enthusiasts for Nazi Germany, 1933-9*. London: Constable & Company Ltd, 1980.

Grunwald, Kurt. "Europe's Railways and Jewish Enterprise." *Leo Baeck Institute Year Book* 12 (1967).

———. "Windsor-Cassel—The Last Court Jew." *Leo Baeck Institute Year Book* 14 (1969).

Gwynne, H. A., ed. *The Cause of World Unrest: With an Introduction by the Editor of the Morning Post*. London: G. Richards Ltd., 1920.

Gyurgyak, Janos. *A zsidokerdes Magyarorszagon* (The Jewish Question in Hungary). Budapest: Osiris Kiado, 2001.

Hajdu, Tibor, and Zsuzsa L. Nagy. "Revolution, Counterrevolution, Consolidation." In *A History of Hungary*. Edited by Peter F. Sugar. Bloomington, Ind.: Indiana University Press, 1990.

Haller, Istvan. *A zsidokerdes es a kereszteny terfoglalas vegleges megoldasa* (The Final Solution to the Jewish Question and the Christian Expansion). Budapest: A szerzo kiadas Stephaneum nyomda, 1938.
Hanak, Peter. "The Dual Monarchy 1867-1918." In *A History Of Hungary*. Edited by Ervin Pamlenyi. Translated by Laszlo Boros, Istvan Farkas, Gyula Gulyas and Eva Rona. Translation revised by Margaret Morris and Richard E. Allen. Budapest: Corvina Press, 1973.

———. "Hungary in the Austro-Hungarian Monarchy: Preponderancy or Dependency?" *Austrian History Yearbook* 3, pt. 1 (1967).

———. "Polgarosodas es asszimilacio Magyarorszagon a 19. Szazadban" (Bourgeois Development and Assimilation in Hungary in the Nineteenth Century). *Tortenelmi Szemle* 4 (1974).

———, ed. *Zsidokerdes, asszimilacio, antiszemitizmus* (The Jewish Question, Assimilation, Anti-Semitism). Budapest: Gondolat, 1984.

Hanak, Peter, Istvan Dioszegi, Karoly Voros, Gyorgy Kover, Eszter Gabor, Janos M. Rainer, Laszlo Varga, Anna Fabri, Zsofia Mihancsik, Violetta Hidvegi, Katalin Jalsovszky, and Emoka Tomsics. "Az Andrassy ut" (Andrassy Street). *Budapesti Negyved* 1, no. 1 (1993).
Handler, Andrew. *Blood Libel at Tiszaeszlar*. Boulder, Colo.: East European Monographs / New York: Columbia University Press, 1980.

———. *An Early Blueprint for Zionism: Gyozo Istoczy's Anti-Semitism*. Boulder, Colo.: East European Monographs, 261 / New York: Columbia University Press, 1989.

Haraszti, Gyorgy. *Magyar zsido leveltari repertorium: hazai leveltarak zsido vonatkozasu anyaganak attekintese a kiadott leveltari segedletek alapjan* (Directory of Archival Holdings: Relating to the History of Jews in Hungary). 2 vols. Budapest: MTA Judaisztikai Kutatoport, 1993.
Harsanyi, Laszlo. *A Szentesi Izraelita Hitkoseg tortenete* (The History of the Jewish Community in Szentes). Budapest, 1970.
Hart, Mitchell B. *Social Science and the Politics of Modern Jewish Identity*. Stanford: Stanford University Press, 2000.
Hegedus, Sandor. *A tiszaeszlari vervad* (The Tiszaeszlar Blood Libel). Budapest, 1966.
Henriques, H. S. Q. "The Civil Rights of English Jews." *Jewish Quarterly Review* 18 (1906).

———. "The Jewish Emancipation Controversy in 19th Century Britain." *Past and Present* 40 (July 1968).

———. "The Political Rights of English Jews." *Jewish Quarterly Review* 19 (1907).

Henriques, Ursula R. Q. *Religious Toleration in England, 1787-1833*. Toronto: University of Toronto Press, 1961.
Herder, Johann Gottfried. "Bekehrung der Juden." In *Herders samtliche Werke*, herausgegeben von Bernhard Suphan. Vol. 24. Berlin, 1883.

———. *Ideen zur Philosophie der Geschichte der Menschheit*. Leipzig, 1812.

Hertz, Deborah. *Jewish High Society in Old Regime Berlin*. New Haven and London: Yale University Press, 1988.

———. "Seductive Conversion in Berlin, 1770-1809." In *Jewish Apostasy in the Modern World*. Edited by Todd M. Endelman. New York: Holmes & Meier Publishers, Inc., 1987.

Hertzberg, Arthur. *The French Enlightenment and the Jews: The Origins of Modern Anti-Semitism*. New York: Columbia University Press, 1968, 1990.

———. *The Zionist Idea: A Historical Analysis and Reader*. New York: Atheneum, 1959.

Herzl, Theodor. The Jews' State (*Judenstaat*). Translated by Henk Overberg. 1896. Reprint, Northvale, N.J.: Jason Aronson Inc., 1997.

Heschel, Susannah. "Abraham Geiger on the Origins of Christianity: Wissenschaft vom Judentum As A Strategy For and Against Assimilation." In *Jewish Assimilation, Acculturation and Accommodation: Past Traditions, Current Issues and Future Prospects*. Edited by Menachem Mor. Lanham, Md.: University Press of America, Inc., 1992.

Hillerbrand, Hans J. "Religious Dissent and Toleration: Introductory Reflections." In *Tolerance and Movements of Religious Dissent in Eastern Europe*. Edited by Bela K. Kiraly. New York and London: East European Quarterly, Boulder, Colo. / Columbia University Press, 1975.

Himmelfarb, Gertrude. *Darwin and the Darwinian Revolution*. Gloucester, Mass.: Peter Smith, 1967.

Hirschfeld, C. "The British Left and the Jewish Conspiracy." *Jewish Social Studies* 41 (Spring 1981).

Hobson, J. A. "Capitalism and Imperialism in South Africa." *Contemporary Review* 77 (January–June 1900).

———. *The Crisis of Liberalism: New Issues of Democracy*. London: P.S. King & Son, 1909.

———. "Free Trade and Foreign Policy." *Contemporary Review* 74 (July–December 1898).

———. *Imperialism: A Study*. 1902. 2nd ed. Reprint, Mich.: University of Michigan Press, 1967.

———. *Problems of Poverty: An Inquiry into the Industrial Condition of the Poor*. 1891. Reprint, New York: Augustus M. Kelley Publishers, 1971.

———. *The War in South Africa: Its Causes and Effects*. 1900. Reprint, New York and London: Garland Publishing, Inc., 1972.

Hoffmann, Mor. *Zsidoinkrol! Igaza van-e Csernatony Lajos urnak vagy nem?* (About our Jews! Is Mr. Lajos Csernatony Correct or Not?) Nagy-Kanizsa: Fischel Fulop, 1874.

Holmes, Colin. *Anti-semitism in British Society 1876-1939*. London: Edward Arnold (Publishers) Ltd, 1979.

———. "East End Crime and the Jewish Community, 1887-1911." In *The Jewish East End, 1840-1939*. Edited by Colin Holmes. London: Jewish Historical Society, 1981.

———. "Goldwin Smith (1823-1910): A Liberal Anti-Semite." *Patterns of Prejudice* 6 (September–October 1972).

———. "J. A. Hobson and the Jews." In *Immigrants and Minorities in British Society*. Edited by Colin Holmes. London, 1978.

———. "The Tredegar Riots of 1911: Anti-Jewish Disturbances in South Wales." *Welsh History Review* 11 (December 1982).
Horkheimer, Max, and Theodor W. Adorno. *Dialectic of Enlightenment*. Translated by John Cumming. 1944. Reprint, New York: Continuum, 1982.
Horvath, Janos. *Aranytol Adyig* (From Arany to Ady). Budapest, 1921.
———. "Szomoryzmusok a Nemzeti szinpadjan" (Szomoryisms on the Stage of the National Theater). In *Magyar Nyelv* (Hungarian Language). Vol. 2. Budapest, 1914.
Hueffer (Ford), Ford Madox. *Mr. Fleight*. London: H. Latimer, 1913.
Hyamson, Albert M. *A History of the Jews in England: With 26 Illustrations and 2 Maps*. 2nd ed. 1908. Reprint, London: Methuen & Co. Ltd., 1928.
———. *The Sephardim of England: A History of the Spanish and Portuguese Jewish Community 1492-1951*. London: Methuen & Co. Ltd., 1951.
Hyman, Paula E. *The Emancipation of the Jews of Alsace: Acculturation and Tradition in the Nineteenth Century*. New Haven and London: Yale University Press, 1991.
Incze, Istvan. *Kereszteny vagy?—milyen lapot olvasol* (Are you Christian? What Press Are You Reading?) Budapest: Katolikus Holgyek Orszagos Sajtoegyesulete. Ev Nelkul. No publication date. The OszK received it in 1928.
Istoczy, Gyozo. *Istoczy Gyozo orszggyulesi beszedei inditvanyai es torvenyjavaslatai, 1872-1896* (Gyozo Istoczy's Speeches, Resolutions, and Bills in the National Assembly, 1872-1896). Budapest: Buschmann F. Konyvnyomdaja, 1904.
Itzkowitz, D. C. "Cultural Pluralism and the Board of Deputies of British Jews." In *Religion and Irreligion in Victorian Society: Essays in Honor of R.K. Webb*. Edited by R. W. Davis and R. J. Helmstedter. New York: Routledge, 1992.
Jacobs, Joseph. "Notes on the Jews of England." *Jewish Quarterly Review* 4 (1892).
Janos, Andrew C. *The Politics of Backwardness in Hungary, 1825-1945*. Princeton: Princeton University Press, 1982.
Jaszi, Oszkar. *The Dissolution of the Habsburg Monarchy*. Chicago: University of Chicago Press, 1929.
———. *Revolution and Counter-Revolution in Hungary*. London: P. S. King, 1924.
Jenks, William A. "The Jews in the Habsburg Empire, 1879-1918." *Leo Baeck Institute Year Book* 16 (1971).
The Jewish Chronicle 1841-1941. London: Jewish Chronicle, 1949.
Kadish, Sharman. *Bolsheviks and British Jews: The Anglo-Jewish Community, Britain, and the Russian Revolution*. London: Frank Cass & Co. Ltd., 1992.
———. *'A Good Jew and A Good Englishman': The Jewish Lads' and Girls' Brigade 1895-1995*. London: Vallentine Mitchell, 1995.
Kaiser, Gerhard. *Pietismus und Patriotismus im Literarischen Deutschland*. Wiesbaden, 1961.

Kann, Robert. "Hungarian Jewry during Austro-Hungary's Constitutional Period." *Jewish Social Studies* 7, no. 4 (October 1945)
Kaplan, Marian A. "For Love or Money: The Marriage Strategies of Jews in Imperial Germany." *Leo Baeck Institute Year Book* 28 (1983).
Karady, Viktor. "Demography and Social Mobility: Historical Problem Areas in the Study of Contemporary Jewry in Central Europe." In *A Social and Economic History of Central European History*. Edited by Yehuda Don and Victor Karady. New Brunswick, N.J. and London: Transaction Publishers, 1990.
———. "Jewish Enrolment Patterns in Classical Secondary Education in Old Regime and Inter-War Hungary." In *Studies in Contemporary Jewry*. Edited by J. Frankel. Vol. 1. Bloomington, Ind., 1984.
———. *Zsidosag Europaban a modern korban: tarsadalomtorteneti vazlat* (Jewry in Europe in the Modern Age: Sociohistorical Sketch). Translated from French into Hungarian by Laszlo Toth. Budapest: Uj Mandatum Konyvkiado, 2000.
———. *Zsidosag, modernizacio, polgarosodas: tanulmanyok* (Jewry, Modernization, Civic Development: Essays). Translated into Hungarian 1997. Budapest: Cserepfalvi Kiadasa, 1997.
Karsai, Elek. *A budai Sandor Palotaban tortent 1919-1941* (It Happened in the Sandor Palace in Buda). Budapest: Tancsics Konyvkiado, 1964.
Katz, David S. "The Hutchinsonians and Hebraic Fundamentalism in Eighteenth-Century England." In *Sceptics, Millenarians, and Jews*. Edited by David S. Katz and Jonathan I. Israel. Leiden, N.Y.: E. J. Brill, 1990.
———. *The Jews in the History of England 1485-1850*. Oxford: Oxford University Press, 1994.
———. *Philo-Semitism and the Readmission of the Jews to England, 1603-1655*. Oxford: Clarendon Press / New York: Oxford University Press, 1982.
Katz, Jacob. *Emancipation and Assimilation: Studies in Modern Jewish History*. Westmead, Farnborough, Hants, UK: Gregg International Publishers Limited, 1972.
———. *Exclusiveness and Tolerance: Studies in Jewish-Gentile Relations in Medieval and Modern Times*. New York: Schocken Books, 1961.
———. *From Prejudice to Destruction: Anti-Semitism, 1700-1933*. Cambridge, Mass.: Harvard University Press, 1980.
———. *A House Divided: Orthodoxy and Schism in Nineteenth-Century Central European Jewry*. Hanover and London: Brandeis University Press, 1998.
———. *Jewish Emancipation and Self-Emancipation*. Philadelphia, New York, Jerusalem: Jewish Publication Society, 1986.
———. *Jews and Freemasons in Europe 1723-1939*. Translated by Leonard Orschy. Cambridge: Harvard University Press, 1970.
———. *Out of the Ghetto: The Social Background of Jewish Emancipation, 1770-1870*. Cambridge, Mass.: Harvard University Press, 1973.
———. "A State Within a State." In *Emancipation and Assimilation*. Edited by Jacob Katz. Westmead, Farnborough, Hants, UK: Gregg International Publishers Limited, 1972.
———. "The Term 'Jewish Emancipation': Its Origin and Historical Impact." In *Emancipation and Assimilation*. Edited by Jacob Katz. Westmead,

Farnborough, Hants, UK: Gregg International Publishers Limited, 1972.
———. *Tradition and Crisis: Jewish Society at the End of the Middle Ages*. New York: Free Press of Glencoe, Inc., 1961.
Katzburg, Nathaniel. *Anti-Semitism in Hungary 1867-1914*. Tel Aviv: Dvir Co. Ltd., 1969.
———. "Hungarian Antisemitism: Ideology and Reality (1920-1943)." In *Antisemitism Through the Ages*. Edited by Shmuel Almog. Translated by Nathan H. Reisner. Oxford: Pergamon Press, 1988.
———. "Hungarian Jewry in Modern Times." In *Hungarian-Jewish Studies*. Edited by Randolph L. Braham. New York: Gantt Publishers Printing Representative, 1966.
———. *Hungary and the Jews: Policy and Legislation 1920-1943*. Jerusalem: Bar-Ilan University Press, 1981.
———. *Fejezetek az ujkori zsido tortenelembol magyarorszagon* (Chapters from the New Age Jewish History in Hungary). Budapest: MTA Judaisztikai Kutatocsoport—Osiris Kiado, 1999.
———. "Political Anti-semitism in Hungary in the 1880s and the 1890s" (PhD diss., Hebrew University, 1963).
———. "The Struggle of Hungarian Jewry for Equal Rights in the Nineties of the Nineteenth Century." [in Hebrew] *Zion: A Quarterly for the Study of Jewish History* 22 (1957).
Kereszteny magyar orvosbajttarsunk hiv a MONE (Our Christian Hungarian Medical Comrade, the MONE is Calling You). Budapest: 1940.
Kereszty, Viktor. "A zsidorecepcio a tudomany szempontjabol" (The Jew Reception from a Scientific Viewpoint). *Magyar Sion* 7 (1893).
Kertzer, David I. *The Popes against the Jews: The Vatican's Role in the Rise of Modern Anti-Semitism*. New York: Alfred A. Knopf, 2001.
Kiraly, Bela K. "Protestantism in Hungary Between the Revolution and the Ausgleich." In *Tolerance and Movements of Religious Dissent in Eastern Europe*. Edited by Bela K. Kiraly. New York and London: East European Quarterly, Boulder, Colo. / Columbia University Press, 1975.
Kisch, Guido. *The Jews in Medieval Germany: A Study of Their Legal and Social Status*. New York: Ktav Publishing House, 1970.
Kiss, Jozsef. "December Huszadikan" (On the Twentieth of December). In *Zsido Dalok* (Jewish Songs). 1868.
Klein, Bernard. "Hungarian Politics and the Jewish Question in the Interwar Period." *Jewish Social Studies* 28, no.2 (April 1966).
Klein, Charlotte Lea. "The Changing Image of the Jew in Modern English Literature." *Patterns of Prejudice* 5, no. 1 (January– February 1971).
Knight, Gershom A. "The Rothschild-Bleichroder Axis." *Leo Baeck Institute Year Book* 28 (1983).
Kobanyai, Janos, ed. *A zsidosag utja: esszek (1848-1948)* (The Way of the Jews: Essays [1848-1948]). Budapest: Mult es Jovo Kiado, 2000.
Kobler, Franz, ed. *A Treasury of Jewish Letters: Letters from the Famous and the Humble*. Philadelphia: Jewish Publication Society of America, 1952.
———. *Napoleon and the Jews*. New York: Schocken Books Inc., 1976.
Kobor, Tamas. "A zsido kerdesrol" (On the Jewish Question). *Mult es Jovo* (23 April 1920).

Kohler, Max L. *Jewish Rights at the Congress of Vienna (1814-1815) and Aix-la-Chapelle (1818)*. Baltimore: Lord Galtimore Press, 1918.
Kohn, Hans. *The Idea of Nationalism: A Study in its Origins and Background*. New York: Macmillan Company, 1994.
Kolosvary-Borcsa, Mihaly. *A zsido kerdes magyarorszagi irodalma* (The Literature of the Jewish Question in Hungary). Budapest: Stadium, 1943.
Komlos, Aladar. "A szazadveg koltoi" (Poets of the *fin-de-siecle*). In *Tegnap es ma* (Yesterday and Today). Budapest, 1956.
Komoroczy, Geza, ed. *Jewish Budapest: Monuments, Rites, History*. Translated by Vera Szabo. 1995. Budapest: Central European University Press, 1999.
Kontler, Laszlo. *A History of Hungary: Millenium in Central Europe*. Houndmills, Basingstoke, UK: Palgrave / Macmillan, 2002.
Komlos, Aladar [Almos Koral, pseud.]. *Zsidok valaszuton* (Jews at the Crossroads). Budapest: Eperjes, 1921.
Kosary, Dominic G. *A History of Hungary*. Cleveland and New York: Benjamin Franklin Bibliophile Society, 1941.
Kovacs, Alajos. *A csonka-magyarorszagi zsidosag a statisztika tukreben* (Rump Hungary's Jewry in the Mirror of Statistics). Budapest, 1935.
———. *A zsidosag terfoglalasa Magyarorszagon* (The Expansion of Jewry in Hungary). 1923. Reprint, Budapest: Kellner, 1935.
Kovacs, Jozsef O. *Zsidok a Duna-Tisza kozen: tarsadalomtorteneti esettanulmanyok, XVIII-XIX. szazad* (Jews in the Danube-Tisza Region: Sociological Case Studies in the Eighteenth and Nineteenth Centuries). Kecskemet: Kecskemet Monografia Szerkesztosege, 1996.
Kovacs, Maria M. *Liberal Professions and Illiberal Politics: Hungary from the Habsburgs to the Holocaust*. Washington: Woodrow Wilson Center Press, 1994.
———. " A numerus clausus es az orvosi antiszemitizmus a huszas evekben" (The Numerus Clausus and Medical Anti-Semitism in the Nineteen-twenties). *Budapest Negyed* 8 (1995/2), http://www.bparchiv.hu/magyar/kiadvany/bpn/08/kovacs1.html
Kovacs, Martin L. "National Minorities in Hungary, 1919-1980." In *Eastern European National Minorities 1919-1980*. Edited by Stephan M. Horak. Littleton, Colo.: Libraries Unlimited, 1985.
Kozma, Gyorgy. "The Background of the Denial of Anti-Semitism: Psycho-Historical Case Study of Emma Ritook, a Pre-War Hungarian Writer." masters thesis, Central European University, 2001.
Kramer, T. D. *From Emancipation to Catastrophe: The Rise and Holocaust of Hungarian Jewry*. Lanham, Md., New York, and Oxford: University Press of America, Inc., 2000.
Krudy, Gyula. *A tiszaeszlari Solymosi Eszter* (Eszter Solymosi of Tiszaeszlar). Budapest: Magveto Konyvkiado, 1975.
Kubinszky, Judit. *Politikai antiszemitizmus Magyarorszagon 1875-1890* (Political Anti-Semitism in Hungary 1875-1890). Budapest: Kossuth Konyvkiado, 1976.
Kushner, Tony, ed. *The Jewish Heritage in British History: Englishness and Jewishness*. Totowa, N.J.: Frank Cass, 1992.

———. *The Politics of Marginality: Race, the Radical Right, and Minorities in Twentieth Century Britain*. London: Frank Cass & Co. Ltd., 1990.
Landa, Myer Jack. *The Alien Problem and Its Remedy*. London: P. S. King & Son, 1911.
———. *The Jew in Drama*. 1926. Reprint, Port Washington, N.Y.: Kennikat Press, 1968.
Lang, Gyula. *A Papai zsidosag emlekkonyve: a martirhahalt papai es kornyekbeli zsidok emlekere* (In the Memory of the Jews of Papa and Vicinity who Suffered Martyrdom). Haifa: The Author, n.d.
Laszlo, Erno. "Hungary's Jewry" A Demographic Overview, 1918-1945." In *Hungarian-Jewish Studies*, vol. 2. Edited by Randolph L. Braham. New York: World Federation of Hungarian Jews, 1966-1973.
Lebzelter, Gisela C. *Political Anti-Semitism in England, 1918-1939*. London: Macmillan Press Ltd, 1975.
Lendvai, Istvan. *A harmadik Magyarorszag—joslatok es tanulsagok* (The Third Hungary: Predictions and Conclusions). Budapest: Pallas, 1921.
Lepes, Andor. *Zsidok kereszteny alarcban* (Jews in a Christian Mask). The Author, 1935.
Letter to the Right Honourable Sir Thomas Chitty, Lord Mayor of London. London, 1760.
Levai, Jeno. *Fekete konyv a magyar zsidosag szenvedeseirol* (The Black Book About the Suffering of Hungarian Jewry). Budapest: Officina, 1946.
Levene, Mark. "Going against the Grain: Two Jewish Memoirs of War and Anti-War (1914-18)." In *Forging Modern Jewish Identities: Public Faces and Private Struggles*. Edited by Michael Berkowitz, Susan L. Tananbaum, and Sam W. Bloom. London: Vallentine Mitchell, 2003.
Lewis, C. S. "The Unchristening of Europe." In *De Descriptione Temporum. An Inaugual Lecture*. Cambridge: Cambridge University Press, 1955.
Liberles, Robert. "From Toleration to *Verbesserung*: German and English Debates on the Jews in the Eighteenth Century." *Central European History* 22 (1989).
Lilly, W. S. "Illiberal Liberalism." *Fortnightly Review* 58 (November 1895).
Linehan, Thomas P. "Fascist Perceptions of Cable Street." In *Remembering Cable Street: Fascism and Anti-fascism in British Society*. Edited by Tony Kushner and Nadia Valman. London and Portland, Oreg.: Vallentine Mitchell, 2000.
Lipman, V. D. "The Age of Emancipation, 1815-1880." In *Three Centuries of Anglo-Jewish History: A Volume of Essays*. Edited by V. D. Lipman. Cambridge: Heffer, 1961.
———. *A History of the Jews in Britain since 1858*. Leicester: Leicester University Press, 1990.
———. *Social History of the Jews in England 1850-1950*. London: C. A. Watts & Co. Ltd, 1954.
Locke, John. "A Letter Concerning Toleration." In *The Works of John Locke*. Vol. 6. London: 1823.
Low, Leopold. *Die Emanzipation der Juden*. Szegedin: Dend v. Sigmind Burger, 1863.

Lunn, Kenneth, ed. *Hosts, Immigrants and Minorities: Historical Responses to Newcomers in British Society, 1870-1914*. Folkestone, Kent, UK: Wm Dawson & Sons Ltd., 1980.

Macartney, C. A. *A History of Hungary, 1929-1945*. Vol. 1. New York: Praegar, 1956.

———. *Hungary and her Successors: The Treaty of Trianon and its Consequences, 1919-1937*. London: Oxford University Press, 1937.

———. *October Fifteenth: A History of Hungary 1929-1945*. Vol. 1. Edinburgh: Edinburgh University Press, 1956.

Macaulay, Thomas Babington. *Reviews, Essays, and Poems: Including Essays from The Edinburgh Review, Lays of Ancient Rome, and Miscellaneous Writings in Prose and Verse*. London Ward, Lock: G. T. Bettany, n.d.

Machin, G. I. T. *Disraeli*. London and New York: Longman Publishing, 1995.

MacKnight, Thomas. *(The Right Honourable) Benjamin Disraeli, M.P.* London: Richard Bentley, 1854.

Mahler, Raphael. "The Austrian Government and the Hasidim During the Period of Reaction 1814-1848." *Jewish Social Studies* 1, no. 2 (1939).

———. *A History of Modern Jewry 1780-1815*. London: Vallentine, Mitchell & Co. Ltd., 1971.

Major, Robert. "The Churches and the Jews in Hungary." *Continuum*. Independent quarterly sponsored by the Saint Xavier College, Chicago, Ill. 4 (Autumn 1966).

———. *25ev ellenforradalmi sajtoja 1919-1944* (Twenty-five Years of Counterrevolutionary Press 1919-1944). Budapest: Cserepfalvil, 1945.

Marcus, Jacob R. *The Jew in the Medieval World: A Source Book; 1315-1791*. 1938. Reprint, Philadelphia: Jewish Publication Society of America, 1961.

Marczali, Henrik. *"Emlekeim"* (My Memories). *Nyugat* 22 (October 1929).

Marrus, Michael R. "European Jewry and the Politics of Assimilation." In *Jewish Assimilation in Modern Times*. Edited by Bela Vago. Boulder, Colo.: Westview Press, Inc., 1981.

———. *The Holocaust in History*. Hanover: University Press of New England, 1987.

———. *The Politics of Assimilation: A Study of the French Jewish Community at the Time of the Dreyfus Affair*. London: Oxford University Press, 1971.

———. "The Theory and Practice of Anti-Semitism." In *The Nazi Holocaust: The Origins of the Holocaust*. Edited by Michael R. Marrus. Vol. 2. Westport: Meckker Corporation, 1989.

Marschalko, Lajos. *Tiszaeszlar: a magyar fajvedelem hoskora* (Tiszaeszlar: The Heroic Age of Hungarian Race Defense). Debrecen, 1943.

Martin, Kingsley. *French Liberal Thought in the Eighteenth Century: A Study of Political Ideas from Bayle to Condorcet*. London: Phoenix House, 1962.

Marton, Erno, ed. *Az emancipacio multja es jovoje* (The Past and Future of Emancipation). Kolosvar: Fraternitas R.T., 1942.

Massingham, H. W. *The London Daily Press*. London: Religious Tract Society, 1892.

Maurois, Andre. *Disraeli: A Picture of the Victorian Age*. Translated by Hamish Miles. USA: D. Appleton & Company, 1928.

Maxwell, Elisabeth. "Silence or Speaking Out." In *Cultures of Ambivalence and Contempt: Studies in Jewish-non-Jewish Relations*. Edited by Sian Jones, Tony Kushner, and Sarah Pearce. London: Vallentine Mitchell, 1998.
Mayer, Gustav. "Early German Socialism and German Emancipation." *Jewish Social Studies* 1, no. 4 (October 1939).
Mayer, Sigmund. *Die Wiener Juden: Kommerz, Kultur, Politik 1700-1900*. Vienna, 1918.
McCagg, William O. *A History of Habsburg Jews, 1670-1918*. Bloomington, Inc.: Indiana University Press, 1989.
———. "Jewish Conversion in Hungary in Modern Times." In *Jewish Apostasy in the Modern World*. Edited by Todd M. Endelman. Holmes & Meier Publishers, Inc., 1987.
———. *Jewish Nobles and Geniuses in Modern Hungary*. East European Quarterly, Boulder, Colo. / New York: Columbia University Press, 1972.
Mearns, A. *The Bitter Cry of Outcast London*. 1883.
Meizler, Karoly, ed. *Prohaszka, a napbaoltozott forradalmar* (Prohaszka, the Revolutionary Dressed in the Sun). Vol. 1. Buenos Aires: Editorial Pannonia, 1964.
Merrick, Leonard. *Violet Moses*. 3 vols. London: Richard Bentley & Son, 1891.
Mill, John Stuart. *Utilitarianism, Liberty, and Representative Government*. 1863. Reprint, New York: E. P. Dutton, 1950.
Mendelsohn, Ezra. *The Jews of East Central Europe Between the World Wars*. Bloomington, Ind.: Indiana University Press, 1987.
Mendes-Flohr, Paul, and Jehuda Reinharz, eds. *The Jew in the Modern World*. 2nd ed. New York and Oxford: Oxford University Press, 1995.
Menes, A. "The Conversion Movement in Prussia during the First Half of the Nineteenth Century." *YIVO Annual of Jewish Social Science* 6 (1951).
Meyer, Paul H. "The Attitude of the Enlightenment Towards the Jew." *Studies on Voltaire and the Eighteenth Century* 26 (1963).
Meyers, Maurice. "Some Miscellaneous Sidelights on Anglo-Jewish Emancipation." In *Transactions of the Jewish Historical Society of England*. Vol. 6. 1912.
Mikszath, Kalman. *Osszes Muvei. kritikai kiadas: cikkek es karcolatok* (Collected Works. Critical Edition: Articles and Sketches). Vols. 62-67. 1904. Reprint, Budapest: Szepirodalmi Konyvkiado, 1971.
Miller, Michael Laurence. "Rabbis and Revolution: A Study in Nineteenth-Century Moravian Jewry" PhD. diss., Columbia University, 2004.
Mitchell, Harvey. "Hobson Revisited." *Journal of the History of Ideas* 26 (1965).
Modder, M. F. *The Jew in the Literature of England*. 1939. 2nd ed. Philadelphia: Jewish Publication Society of America, 1944.
Molino, Frances. "The Right to be Equal: Zalkind Hourwitz and the Revolution of 1789." In *From East and West: Jews in a Changing Europe, 1750-1870*. Edited by Frances Molino and David Sorkin. Oxford: Basil Blackwell Ltd, 1990.
Molnar, Miklos. *A Concise History of Hungary*. Translated by Anna Magyar. 1996. Reprint, Cambridge: Cambridge University Press, 2001.

Montesquieu, Charles Louis. *Lettres Persanes. Texte établi et presenté par* Elie Carcasonne. 1721. Reprint, Paris, 1929.
Mor, Menachem, ed. *Jewish Assimilation, Acculturation and Accommodation: Past Traditions, Current Issues and Future Prospects.* Lanham, Md.: University Press of America, Inc, 1992.
Moricz, Miklos. "Budapest amerikai kivandorlasa" (The Emigration of Budapest to America). *Nyugat* 1 (1911).
Moskovits, Aron. *Jewish Education in Hungary (1848-1948).* New York: Bloch Publishing Company, 1964.
Mosse, George L. *Germans and Jews: The Right, the Left, and the Search for a Third Force in pre-Nazi Germany.* London: Orbach & Chambers Ltd, 1970.
———. *Toward the Final Solution: A History of European Racism.* New York: H. Fertig, 1978.
Mosse, Werner E. "From 'Schutzjuden' to 'Deutsche Staatburger Judischen Glaubens: The Long and Bumpy Road of Jewish Emancipation in Germany." In *Paths of Emancipation: Jews, States, and Citizenship.* Edited by Pierre Birnbaum and Ira Katznelson. Princeton: Princeton University Press, 1995.
Murray, Robert K. *Red Scare: A Study in National Hysteria, 1919-1920.* Westport, Conn.: Greenwood Press, 1955.
Nagy, Peter Tibor. "A numerus clausus—hetvenot ev utan." (The Numerus Clausus after Seventy-five Years). *Vilagossag* 36, no. 2 (1995).
Nagy-Talavera, Nicholas M. *The Green Shirts and the Others: A History of Fascism in Hungary and Rumania.* Stanford, Calif.: Hoover Institution Press / Stanford University, 1970.
Necheles, Ruth F. "Abbé Grégoire and the Jews." *Jewish Social Studies* 33 (1971).
Nemes, Dezso. *Az ellenforradallom tortenete* (The History of Counterrevolution). Budapest, 1962.
Newman, Aubrey. *The Jewish East End, 1840-1939.* Jewish Historical Society of England, 1981.
Nezo, Istvan. *A Kisvardai zsidosag tortenete* (The History of the Jews of Kisvarda). Nyiregyhaza: Ardlea Kiado, 1998.
Oliphant, L. "The Jew and the Eastern Question." *Nineteenth Century* 12 (July–December 1882).
100 Eves a cionista mozgalom (100 Years of the Zionist Movement). Budapest: 1997.
Orwell, George. "Antisemitism in Britain." In *The Collected Essays, Journalism and Letters of George Orwell.* Edited by Sonia Orwell and Ian Angus. Vol. 3. London: Martin Secker & Warburg Limited, 1968.
Osterman, Nathan. "The Controversy over the Proposed Readmission of the Jews to England." *Jewish Social Studies* 3, (1941).
Panayi, Panikos. *The Enemy In Our Midst: Germans in Britain During the First World War.* New York and Oxford: Berg Publishers Limited, 1991.
Panitz, Esther L. *The Alien in Their Midst: Images of Jews in English Literature.* East Brunswick, N.J.: Associated University Presses, Inc., 1981.
Parkes, James W. *An Enemy of the People: Antisemitism.* 1943. Reprint, New York: American Pelican Books, 1946.

———. "The History of the Anglo-Jewish Community." In *A Minority in Britain*. Edited by Maurice Freedman. London: Valentine, Mitchell & Co., Ltd., 1955.

———. *The Jew and His Neighbour*. London: Student Christian Movement Press, 1930.

———. *The Jew in the Medieval Community: A Study of his Political and Economic Situation*. London: Soncino Press, 1938.

———. "Jewish-Christian Relations in England." In *Three Centuries of Anglo-Jewish History*. Edited by V. D. Lipman. Cambridge: Jewish Historical Society of England, 1961.

———. *The Jewish Problem in the Modern World*. London: Thornton Butterworth Ltd, 1939.

Pastor, Peter, ed. *Hungary Between Wilson and Lenin: The Hungarian Revolution of 1918-1919 and The Big Three*. New York: Columbia University Press, 1976.

Patai, Jozsef. "Zsido assimilacio" (Jewish Assimilation). In *Harc a zsido kulturaert* (Struggle for The Jewish Culture). Edited by Jozsef Patai. Budapest: Mult es Jovo Jubileumi Kiadasa, 1937.

Patai, Raphael. *The Jews of Hungary: History, Culture, Psychology*. Detroit: Wayne State University Press, 1996.

Pearce, Sarah. "Attitudes of Contempt: Christian Anti-Judaism and the Bible." In *Cultures of Ambivalence and Contempt: Studies in Jewish-non-Jewish Relations*. Edited by Sian Jones, Tony Kushner, and Sarah Pearce. London: Vallentine Mitchell, 1998.

Pearson, Karl. *National Life from the Standpoint of Science*. London, 1905.

Pelle, Janos. *A gyulolet vetese: a zsidotorvenyek es a magyar kozvelemeny 1938-1944* (The Sowing of Hatred: The Jew-Laws and Hungarian Public Opinion 1938-1944). Budapest: Europa Konyvkiado, 2001.

Pellew, Jill. "Communication: The Home Office and the Aliens Act, 1905." *Historical Journal* 32 (1989).

Perkin, Harold. *Origins of Modern English Society*. 1969. Reprint, London: Routledge, 1991.

Perry, Thomas W. *Public Opinion, Propaganda, and Politics in Eighteenth-Century England: A Study of the Jew Bill of 1753*. Cambridge, Mass.: Harvard University Press, 1962.

Pesti, Erno, ed. *Az Est-lapok 1920-1939* (The Evening Papers 1920-1939). Budapest: Repertorium, Petofi Irodalmi Muzeum, 1982.

Petrassevich, Geza. *Magyarorszag es a Zsidosag* (Hungary and the Jews). Budapest: Szent Gellert Konyvnyomda, 1900.

Petty, Sir William. "A Treatise on Taxes and Contributions." In *The Economic Writings of Sir William Petty*, 2 volumes in 1. 1662. Reprint, Fairfield, N.J.: Augustus M. Kelley Publishers, 1986.

Philipson, David. *The Jew in English Fiction*. 1889. Reprint, New York: Robert Clarke & Co., 1918.

Picciotto, James. *Sketches of Anglo-Jewish History*. London: Trubner & Co., 1875.

Pinsker, Polly. "English Opinion and Jewish Emancipation 1830-1860." *Jewish Social Studies* 14 (1952).
Pollak, Miksa. *A zsidok tortenete sopronban* (The History of the Jews in Sopron). Budapest: Franklin-Tarsulat Nyomdaja, 1896.
Pollins, Harold. *Economic History of the Jews in England*. East Brunswick, N.J.: Associated University Presses, Inc., 1982.
Porter, Bernard. *Critics of Empire: British Radical Attitudes to Colonialism in Africa 1895-1914*. London: Macmillan & Co Ltd, 1968.
———. *The Refugee Question in mid-Victorian Politics*. Cambridge: Cambridge University Press, 1979.
Porter, Roy. *The Enlightenment*. 2nd ed. Houndmills, Basingstoke, Hampshire, UK and New York: Palgrave, 2001.
Porter, Roy, and Mikulas Teich, eds. *The Enlightenment in National Context*. Houndmills, Basingstoke, Hampshire, UK and New York: Palgrave / St. Martins Press, 2001.
Posener, Solomon V. "The Immediate Economic and Social Effects of the Emancipation of the Jews in France." *Jewish Social Studies* 1, no. 3 (July 1939).
Priestly, Joseph. *A Comparison of the Institutions of Moses with Those of the Hindoos and Other Ancient Nations . . . and An Address to the Jews on the Present State of the World and the Prophecies Related to It*. Northumberland, 1799.
Prohaszka, Ottokar. *Fold es Eg: kutatasok a geologia es theologia erintkezo pontjai korul* (Earth and Sky: Research Around the Common Points of Geology and Theology). Vols. 1-2. Budapest: Szent Istvan tarsulat az apostoli Szentszek Konyvkiadoja, 1921.
———. *"Pro juventate 'catholica." Alkotmany* (26 May 1918).
———. [Dr. Petho, pseud.]. *"A zsido recepcio a moralis szempontbol"* (The Jew Reception from the Viewpoint of Theology). *Magyar Sion* 7 (1893).
Protocols of the Learned Elders of Zion. Edited by Clyde J. Wright. Translated from the Nilus Documents by Victor E. Marsden. 1905. Reprint, Houston, Tex.: Pyramid Book Shop, 1934.
Puskas, Juliana. "Jewish Leaseholders in the Course of Agricultural Development in Hungary, 1850-1930." In *Jews in the Hungarian Economy 1760-1945: Studies Dedicated to Moshe Carmilly on his Eightieth Birthday*. Edited by Michael K. Silber. Jerusalem: Magnes Press / Hebrew University, 1992.
Rabinbach, Anson. *In the Shadow of Catastrophe: German Intellectuals between Apocalypse and Enlightenment*. Berkeley Calif.: University of California Press, 1997.
Ranki, Vera. *The Politics of Inclusion and Exclusion: Jews and Nationalism in Hungary*. New York and London: Holmes & Meier Publishers, Inc., 1999.
Redwood, John. *Reason, Ridicule and Religion: The Age of Enlightenment in England 1660-1750*. London: Thames & Hudson, 1976.
Reich, Emil. *Hungarian Literature*. Boston: L. C. Page & Company [Incorporated] Publishers, 1898.
———. "The Jew-Baiting on the Continent." *Nineteenth Century* 40 (1896).
Rentoul, Robert Reid. *Race Culture: Or, Race Suicide?* 1906. Reprint, New York: Garland Publishing, Inc., 1984.

Ritook, Emma. *Collected Papers of Emma Ritook*. Unpublished Diary. Excerpt taken from the year 1927. Manuscript Department, Orszagos Szechenyi Konyvtar (Szechenyi National Library). Call Number Fond 473.
Robertson, Ritchie. *The 'Jewish Question' in German Literature 1749-1939: Emancipation and its Discontents*. Oxford: Oxford University Press, 1999.
Rogers, Colin. *The Battle of Stepney*. London: Robert Hale, 1981.
Romsics, Ignac. *Istvan Bethlen: A Great Conservative Statesman of Hungary, 1874-1946*. Boulder, Colo.: Social Science Monographs. Highland Lakes, N.J.: Atlantic Research and Publications / New York: Columbia University Press, 1995.
Rosenberg, Edgar. *From Shylock to Svengali: Jewish Stereotypes in English Fiction*. Stanford: Stanford University Press, 1960.
———. "Tabloid Jews and Fungoid Scribblers." In *Jewish Characters in Eighteenth Century English Fiction and Drama*. H. R. S. Van Der Veen. 1935. Reprint, New York: Ktav Publishing House, Inc. 1973.
Roth, Cecil. *Anglo-Jewish Letters (1158-1917)*. London: Soncino Press, 1938.
———. "Are the Jews Unassimilable?" *Jewish Social Studies* 3 (1941).
———. *Gleanings: Essays in Jewish History, Letters and Art*. New York: Hermon Press for Bloch Publishing Company, 1967.
———. *A History of the Jews in England*. Oxford: Oxford University Press, 1941.
———. *Magna Bibliotheca Anglo-Judaica*. No. B. 1, 109, 2nd ed. London, 1937.
Rothschild, Joseph. *East Central Europe between the Two World Wars*. 8th printing. Seattle and London: University of Washington Press, 1998.
Rowe, William V. "Difficult Liberty: The Basis of Community in Emmanuel Levinas." In *From Ghetto to Emancipation: Historical and Contemporary Reconsiderations of the Jewish Community*. Edited by David N. Myers and William V. Rowe. Scranton: Scranton University Press, 1997.
Rubinstein, W. D. *A History of the Jews in the English-Speaking World: Great Britain*. London: Macmillan Press Ltd, 1996.
Ruderman, David B. *Jewish Enlightenment in an English Key*. Princeton: Princeton University Press, 2000.
Rurup, Reinhard. "Jewish Emancipation and Bourgeois Society." *Leo Baeck Institute Year Book* 14 (1969).
Ruse, Michael. *The Darwinian Revolution*. Chicago: University of Chicago Press, 1979.
Russell, C., and H. S. Lewis, eds. "The Jew in London: A Study of Racial Character and Present-Day Conditions: Being Two Essays prepared for the Toynbee Trustees. . . . In *Aspects of the Jewish Question*. By "A Quarterly Reviewer." London: John Murray, Albemarle Street, 1902.
Sachar, Howard Morley. *The Course of Modern Jewish History*. 1977. Rev. ed. Reprint, Vintage Books / New York: Random House, Inc., 1990.
Sacher, Harry. *Jewish Emancipation: The Contract Myth*. London: English Zionist Federation, 1917.
Salbstein, M. C. N. *The Emancipation of the Jews in Britain: The Question of the Admission of the Jews to Parliament, 1828-1860*. East Brunswick, N.J.: Associated University Presses, Inc., 1982.
Saltman, Avrom. *The Jewish Question in 1655: Studies in Prynne's Demurrer*. Ramat Gan: Bar Ilan University Press, 1995.

Samuel, Horace B. "The Weltanschauung of Miss Marie Corelli." In *Modernities*. Edited by Horace B. Samuel. London: Kegan Paul, Trench, Trubner & Co. Ltd., 1913.

Sandor, Ivan. *A Vizgalat iratai, tudositas a tiszaeszlari per korulmenyeirol* (The Documents of the Investigation, Reporting on the Circumstances of the Tiszaeszlar Trial). Budapest: Kozmosz, 1976.

Sarkozi, Matyas. *Szinhaz az egesz vilag* (The Whole World is a Theater). Budapest: Osiris-Szazadveg, 1995.

Sarna, Jonathan D. "The Pork on the Fork: A Nineteenth Century Anti-Jewish Ditty." *Jewish Social Studies* 44, no. 2 (Spring 1982).

Sas, Meir. *Vanished Communities in Hungary*. Translated by Carl Alpert. Toronto: Memorial Book Committee, 1986.

Schatz, Jeff. *The Generation: The Rise and Fall of the Jewish Communities of Poland*. Berkeley, Los Angeles and Oxford: University of California Press, 1991.

Scheiber, Sandor. *Evkonyv* (Yearbook). Budapest: Magyar Izraelitak Orszagos Kepviselete, 1970.

———. *Magyarorszagi zsido feliratok: a III. Szazadtol 1686-IG* (Jewish Inscriptions in Hungary from the Third Century until 1686). Budapest: Magyar Izraelitak Orszagos Kepviselete kiadasa, 1960.

Schmidt, H. D. "The Terms of Emancipation." *Leo Baeck Institute Year Book* 1 (1956).

Schmidt, James, ed. *What is Enlightenment?* Berkeley and Los Angeles: University of California Press, 1996.

Schmitt, Carl. *Political Theology: Four Chapters on the Concept of Sovereignty*. Translated by George Schwab. Cambridge, Mass.: MIT Press, 1985.

Scholem, Gershom. "Jews and Germans." *Commentary* 42 (November 1966).

Schopflin, George. "Jewish Assimilation in Hungary: A Moot Point." In *Jewish Assimilation in Modern Times*. Edited by Bela Vago. Boulder, Colo.: Westview Press, Inc., 1981.

Schorsch, Ismar. *Jewish Reactions to German Anti-Semitism, 1870-1914*. New York: Columbia University Press, 1972.

———, ed. *The Structure of Jewish History, and Other Essays*. New York: Jewish Theological Seminary, 1979.

Schulvass, Moses A. *From East to West*. Detroit: Wayne State University Press, 1971.

Schweitzer, Jozsef. *A Pecsi Izraelita Hitkoseg tortenete* (The History of the Jewish Community in Pecs). Budapest, 1966.

Scult, Melvin. "The Conversion of the Jews and the Origins of Jewish Emancipation in England" Ph.D. diss., Brandeis University, 1968.

———. "Conversionism in the Age of Emancipation." *Jewish Social Studies* 35 (1973).

Seton-Watson, Hugh, and Christopher Seton-Watson. *The Making of a New Europe: R. W. Seton-Watson and the Last Years of Austria-Hungary*. Seattle: University of Washington Press, 1981.

Seton-Watson, Robert W. *Corruption and Reform in Hungary: A Study of Electoral Practice; With Numerous Documents*. London: Constable, 1911.

———. *Racial Problems in Hungary*. London: Archibald Constable & Co Ltd, 1908.
Shannon, R. T. *Gladstone and the Bulgarian Agitation 1876*. London: Thomas Nelson & Sons Ltd, 1963.
Sherard, R. H. *The Child Slaves of Britain*. London, 1905.
Sherman, A. J. "German-Jewish Bankers in World Politics." *Leo Baeck Institute Year Book* 28 (1983).
Silber, Michael K. *The Historical Experience of German Jewry and Its Impact on Haskalah and Reform in Hungary*. New Brunswick, N.J. and Oxford: Transaction Books, 1987.
———, ed. *Jews in the Hungarian Economy 1760-1945*. Jerusalem: Magnes Press / Hebrew University, 1992.
Silberner, Edmund. "Anti-Jewish Trends in French Revolutionary Syndicalism." *Jewish Social Studies* 15 (1953).
———. "The Fourierist School and the Jews." *Jewish Social Studies* 9 (1942).
Simon, Oswald John. "The Mission of Judaism." *Fortnightly Review* 50 (1896).
Sinor, Denis. *History of Hungary*. London: George Allen & Unwin Ltd, 1959.
Skinner, Patricia, ed. *The Jews in Medieval Britain: Historical, Literary and Archaeological Perspectives*. Woodbridge, Suffolk, UK: Boydell Press, 2003.
Smith, Elaine R. "Jewish Responses to Political Anti-Semitism and Fascism in the East End of London, 1920-1939." In *Traditions of Intolerance: Historical Perspectives on Fascism and Race Discourse in British Society*. Edited by Tony Kushner and Kenneth Lunn. Manchester: Manchester University Press, 1989.
Smith, Goldwyn. "Can Jews be Patriots?" *Nineteenth Century* 3 (January–June 1878).
———. "The Invasion of Pauper Foreigners." *Nineteenth Century* 23 (January–June 1888).
———. "The Jewish Question." *Nineteenth Century* 10 (July–December 1881).
———. "The Jews: A Deferred Rejoinder." *Nineteenth Century* 12 (July–December 1882).
———. "The Moral of the Late Crisis." *Nineteenth Century* 20 (July–December 1886).
Smith, John. "The Jewish Immigrant." *Contemporary Review* 76 (July–December 1899).
Sombart, Werner. *The Jews and Modern Capitalism* [Die Juden und das Wirtschaftsleben]. Leipzig: Duncker und Humblot, 1911. Translated with notes by M. Epstein. Reprint, New York: E. P. Dutton & Company, 1913.
Sorkin, David. "Emancipation and Assimilation: Two Concepts and their Application to German-Jewish History." *Leo Baeck Institute Year Book* 35 (1990).
———. "Jews, the Enlightenment and Religious Toleration—Some Reflections." *Leo Baeck Institute Year Book* 37 (1992).
———. *The Transformation of German Jewry, 1780-1840*. New York and Oxford: Oxford University Press, 1987.
Sos, Endre. *Zsidok a magyar varosokban* (Jews in the Hungarian Cities). Budapest: Lebanon kiadasa, n.d.

Southern, R. W. *Western Society and Church in the Middle Ages.* Harmondsworth, UK: Penguin Books, 1970.
Stapleton, Julia, ed. *Liberalism, Democracy, and the State in Britain: Five Essays, 1862-1891.* Bristol: Thoemmes Press, 1997.
Steinweis, Alan E. "The Holocaust and Jewish Studies." In *Lessons and Legacies.* Edited by Peter Hayes. Vol. 3. Evanston, Ill.: Northwestern University Press, 1999.
Sterling, Eleonore O. "Jewish Reaction to Jew Hatred in the First Half of the Nineteenth Century." *Leo Baeck Institute Year Book* 3 (1958).
Stern, Samu. *A zsidokerdes Magyarorszagon* (The Jewish Question in Hungary). Budapest: Kiadja, A Pesti Izr. Hitkozseg, 1938.
Stillschweig, Kurt. "Jewish Assimilation as an Object of Legislation." *Historia Judaica* 7 (1946).
Strauss, Raphael. "The Jewish Question as a Problem of Nationalism." *Historia Judaica* 12 (1950).
———. "The Jews in the Economic Evolution of Central Europe." *Jewish Social Studies* 3 (1941).
Sugar, Peter F. "Governments and Minorities in Austria-Hungary—Different Policies with the same Result IV." In *Eastern European Nationalism, Politics, and Religion.* Aldershot, UK / Brookfield Vt.: Ashgate, 1999.
Sutcliffe, Adam. *Judaism and Enlightenment.* Cambridge: Cambridge University Press, 2003.
Szabo, Dezso. *Az egesz latohatar* (The Entire Horizon). 2 vols. 1939-44. Reprint, Budapest: Puski, 1991.
———. *A magyar kaosz* (The Hungarian Chaos). Budapest: Szepirodalmi Konyvkiado, 1990.
Szabo, Ervin. *Hol az igazsag!?* (Where is the Truth!?) Budapest: Magveto Konyvkiado, 1977.
Szabo, Miklos. "Uj vonasok a szazadfordulo magyar konservativ politikai gondolkodasaban" (New Features in the Hungarian Conservative Political Thinking at the Turn of the Century). *Szazadok* (1974).
Szabolcsi, Lajos. *Ket emberolto 1881-1931* (Two Generations 1881-1931). A posthumously published memoir. Budapest: MTA Judaisztikai Csoport, 1993.
Szajkowski, Zosa. "The Alliance Israelite Universelle and East European Jewry in the '60s." *Jewish Social Studies* 4, no. 2 (April 1942).
———. "How the Mass Migration to America Began." *Jewish Social Studies* 4, no. 4 (October 1942).
———. "The Jewish Saint-Simonians and Socialist Antisemites in France." *Jewish Social Studies* 9, no. 1 (1942).
Szaraz, Gyorgy. *Egy eloitelet nyomaban* (On the Trail of a Prejudice). Budapest: Magveto, 1976.
Szatmari, Mor. *Husz esztendo parlamenti viharai* (Twenty Years of Parliamentary Tempests). Budapest: Amicus, 1928.
Szecsy, Janos. *Az itfelejtett nep* (The Forgotten People). Budapest: Magyar Enciklopedistak Tarsasaga, 1945.
Szegvari, Katalin. *Numerus Clausus*, Budapest: Akademiai Kiado, 1988.

Szekfu, Gyula. *Harom nemzedek es ami utana kovetkezik* (Three Generations and What Follows). 1920. Reprint, Budapest: AKV—Maecena, 1989.
Tannenbaum, Edward R. *1900*. Garden City, N.Y.: Anchor Press / Doubleday, 1977.
Teleki, Pal. *Grof Teleki Pal Programbeszede* (Program Speech of Count Pal Teleki). Szeged: Tevel Nyomda, 1919.
Teleki, Paul (Pal). *The Evolution of Hungary and Its Place in European History*. Edited by Bela K. Kiraly. 1922. Reprint, Gulf Breeze, Fla.: Academic International Press, 1975.
Thomas of Monmouth. *The Life and Miracles of St. William of Norwich, Now First Edited from the Unique MS.* . . . Translated and edited by A. Jessop and M. R. James. Cambridge: Cambridge University Press, 1896.
Thompson, E. P. *The Poverty of Theory*. London: Merlin Press, 1978.
Thurlow, Richard C. "The Powers of Darkness." *Patterns of Prejudice* 12, no. 6. (November–December (1978).
———. "Racial Populism." *Patterns of Prejudice* 10, no. 4 (July–August 1976).
———. "Satan and Sambo: The Image of the Immigrant in English Populist Thought since the First World War." In *Hosts, Immigrants and Minorities*. Edited by Kenneth Lunn. Folkestone, Kent, UK: Wm Dawson & Sons Ltd., 1980.
Tokeczki, Laszlo. *Magyar liberalizmus* (Hungarian Liberalism). Budapest: Szazadveg, 1993.
Toland, John. *Reasons for Naturalizing the Jews in Great Britain and Ireland on the Same Foot with all Other Nations, Containing also Defense of the Jews Against all Vulgar Prejudices in all Countries*. London, 1714.
Tormay, Cecile. *An Outlaw's Diary: Revolution*. Translator unknown. Vol. 1. London: Philip Allan & Co., 1923.
Toury, Jacob. "'The Jewish Question'—A Semantic Approach." *Leo Baeck Institute Year Book* 11 (1966).
Traverso, Enzo. *The Jews and Germany*. Translated by Daniel Weissbort. Lincoln and London: University of Nebraska Press, 1995.
Trefort, Agoston. "Riehl sociologiaja es munkassaga" (The Sociology and Works of Riehl). *Budapesti Szemle* 16, no. 53 (1862).
12 Ellen Ropirat (Twelve Counter Pamphlet). Nagyvarad: Armin Laszki, 1880.
12 Ropirat (Twelve Pamphlets). Edited by Gyozo Istoczy.
Ungvari, Tamas. *The "Jewish Question" in Europe: The Case of Hungary*. Social Science Mongraphs. Highland Lakes, N.J.: Atlantic Research and Publications, Inc. / Columbia University Press, New York, 2000.
Vago, Bela, ed. *Jewish Assimilation in Modern Times*. Boulder, Colo.: Westview Press, Inc., 1981.
Vambery, Rustem. *Hungary—To Be Or Not To Be*. New York: Frederick Ungar Publishing, 1946.
Van den Berg, J. "Priestley, the Jews and the Millenium." In *Sceptics, Millenarians, and Jews*. Edited by David S. Katz and Jonathan I. Israel. Leiden, N.Y.: E. J. Brill, 1990.
Van Der Veen, H. R. S. *Jewish Characters in Eighteenth Century English Fiction and Drama*. 1935. Reprint, New York: Ktav Publishing House, Inc. 1973.

Vardy, Peter. "Epiphanies: Hungarian Jewish Experiences and the Shoah." In *Forging Modern Jewish Identities: Public Faces and Private Struggles*. Edited by Michael Berkowitz, Susan L. Tananbaum, and Sam W. Bloom. London: Vallentine Mitchell, 2003.

Vardy, Steven Bela. "The Origins of Jewish Emancipation in Hungary: The Role of Baron Jozsef Eotvos." *Ungarn-Jahrbuch* Band 7. Jahrgang 1976. Munchen.

Vazsonyi, Vilmos. *Vazsonyi Vilmos beszedei es irasai* (The Speeches and Writings of Vilmos Vazsonyi). Budapest: Az Orszagos Vazsonyi-Emlekbizottsag Kiadasa, 1927.

Veghazi, Istvan. "The Role of Jewry in the Economic Life of Hungary." In *Hungarian-Jewish Studies*, vol. 2. Edited by Randolph L. Braham. New York: World Federation of Hungarian Jews, 1966-1973.

Venetianer, Lajos. *Magyar Zsidosag tortenete—kulonos tekintettel gazdasagi es muvelodesi fejlodesere a XIX. Szazadban* (The History of Hungarian Jewry: With Special Emphasis on Its Economic and Cultural Development in the 19th Century). Budapest: Fovarosi Nyomda, 1922.

Verhovay, Gyula. *Az orszag urai* (The Rulers of the Country). Budapest: Buschmann F. Konyvnyomdaja, 1890.

Vida, Marton. *ITELJETEK! Nehany kiragadott lap a magyar-zsido eletkozosseg konyvebol* (JUDGE FOR YOURSELVES! A Few Randomly Chosen Pages from the Book of Hungarian-Jewish Coexistence). Budapest, 1939.

Virag, Istvan. *A zsidok jogallasa Magyarorszagon 1657-1780* (The Legal Position of Jews in Hungary 1657-1780). Budapest: Sarkany Nyomda R.T., 1935.

Volgyes, Ivan, ed. *Hungary in Revolution, 1918-19: Nine Essays*. Lincoln: University of Nebraska Press 1971.

Voros, Karoly. *One Thousand Years: A Concise History of Hungary*. Edited by Peter Hanak. Translated by Zsuzsa Beres. Translation revised Christopher Sullivan. Budapest: Corvina, 1988.

Wasserstein, Bernard. *The British in Palestine*. London: Royal Historical Society, 1978.

Webber, G. C. *Ideology of the British Right*. London: Croom Helm, 1986.

Weber, Eugen. *Varieties of Fascism*. New York: Van Nostrand Reinhold Company, 1964.

Wedgewood, Julia. "The Message of Israel: The Newer Criticism and the Ancient Ideals." *Contemporary Review* 64 (July–December 1893).

Weintraub, Stanley. *Disraeli: A Biography*. New York: Truman Talley Books / Dutton, 1993.

Weisel, Elie. "Looking Back." In *Lessons and Legacies*. Edited by Peter Hayes. Vol. 3, Evanston, Ill.: Northwestern University Press, 1999.

Weszpremy, Kalman. *A zsidosagrol* (About the Jewry). Debreczen: A Szerzo Kiadasa, 1907.

Wetzlarische Nebenstunden. Vol. 3. Ulm, 1756.

Whaley, Joachim. "A Tolerant Society? Religious Toleration in the Holy Roman Empire, 1648-1806." In *Toleration in Enlightenment Europe*. Edited by Ole Peter Grell and Roy Porter. Cambridge: Cambridge University Press, 2000.

White, Arnold. *The Destitute Alien in Great Britain: A Series of Papers Dealing with the Subject of Foreign Pauper Immigration.* London: Swan, 1892.

———. *The Modern Jew.* New York: Frederick A. Stokes Company, 1899.

———. *Problems of a Great City.* London: Remington & Co., 1887.

———. "The Truth About the Russian Jew." *Contemporary Review* 61 (May 1892).

Whitman, Sidney. "The Anti-Semitic Movement." *Contemporary Review* 63 (January–June 1893).

Wilkins, W. H. *The Alien Invasion.* London: Methuen & Co., 1892.

Williams, Bill. "The Anti-Semitism of Tolerance: Middle Class Manchester and the Jews 1870-1900." In *City, Class and Culture.* Edited by Alan J. Kidd and K. W. Roberts. Manchester: Manchester University Press, 1985.

Wilson, Keith. "The *Protocols* and *The Morning Post.*" *Patterns of Prejudice* 19, no. 3 (July 1985).

Wischnitzer, Mark. "The Historical Background of the Settlement of Jewish Refugees in Santo Domingo." *Jewish Social Studies* 4, no. 1 (1942).

———. *To Dwell in Safety: The Story of Jewish Migration since 1800.* Philadelphia: Jewish Publication Society of America, 1948.

Wistrich, Robert S. *Antisemitism: The Longest Hatred.* 1991. Reprint, London: Thames Mandarin, 1992.

———. "Austrian Social Democracy and the Problem of Galician Jewry 1890-1914." *Leo Baeck Institute Year Book* 26 (1981).

———. *Between Redemption and Perdition.* London and New York: Routledge, 1990.

———. *The Dilemma of Assimilation in Germany and Austria-Hungary.* East Brunswick, N.J.: Associated University Presses, Inc., 1982.

Wolf, Lucien. *Essays in Jewish History.* Edited by Cecil Roth. London: Jewish Historical Society of England, 1934. Published posthumously.

———. *Notes on the Diplomatic History of the Jewish Question.* London: Spottiswoode, Ballantyne & Co. Ltd., 1919.

Yahil, Leni. *The Rescue of Danish Jewry.* Philadelphia: Jewish Publication Society of America, 1969.

Yerushalmi, Yosef Hayim. *Zachor: Jewish History and Jewish Memory.* Seattle and London: University of Washington Press, 1982.

Young, B. W. *Religion and Enlightenment in Eighteenth-Century England: Theological Debate from Locke to Burke.* Oxford: Clarendon Press / Oxford and New York: Oxford University Press, 1998.

Zadrvecz, Istvan Pater. *Titkos naploja* (Secret Diary). Budapest: Kossuth Konyvkiado, 1967.

Zangwill, Israel. *Children of the Ghetto: A Study of a Peculiar People.* 3rd ed. London: William Heinemann, 1897.

Zichy, Herman. *Magyar zsidok a millenniumon* (Hungarian Jews at the Time of the Millenium). Budapest: Miljkovic Dragutin, 1896.

Zimandy, Ignacz, ed. *Ebreszto hangok: a muveltebb kath. korok szamara* (Waking Voices: For the More Educated Catholic Circles). Vol. 6. Budapest: Hunyadi Matyas Intezet, 1884.

———. *Kossuth Lajos.* Budapest: Szent-Gellert Konyvnyomda, 1896.

Zimmermann, Moshe. *Wilhelm Marr: The Patriarch of Anti-Semitism.* New York and Oxford:Oxford University Press, 1986.
Zinner, Tibor. *Az bredok fenykora 1919-1923* (The Golden Age of the Awakening Hungarians). Budapest: Akademiai Kiado, 1989.
"A zsidokerdes Magyarorszagon" (The Jewish Question in Hungary). *Huszadik Szazad* 2 (1917).
Zsoldos, Jeno. *1848-1849 a magyar zsidosag eleteben* (1848-1849 in Hungarian Jewish Life). Budapest: Pesti Izraelita Hitkozseg Leanygimnaziumanak es Ipari Leanykozepiskolajanak 48-as Ifiusagi Bizottsaga 1948.
———, ed. *Magyar iroldalom es zsidosag. Koltoi es prozai szemelvenyek* (Hungarian Literature and the Jews: Selected Poetry and Prose). Budapest, 1943.
Zsolt, Bela. *Villamcsapas: (Schwartz Andras onelatrajza)* (A Stroke of Lightning: [Andras Schwartz's Autobiography]). Budapest: Pantheon, n.d.
———, ed. "A zsido" (The Jew). In Andras Bozoki, *A vegzetes toll* (The Fatal Pen). Budapest, 1992.

Index

acceptance of Jew only as non-Jew: via conversion, 9; via reforms, 9
acculturation: in the arts, 163-64; Enlightenment thinkers' views on, 48
Acsady, Ignac, 127, 206
Act of 1867: XVII, 105
Adamovics, Jozsef, 119n
Adorno, Theodor, 7
Age of Reform, 97
Agoston, Peter, 179-83 *passim*
Akers-Douglas (MP), 234
Alderman, Geoffrey, 215
alien, Jews in Britain as, 217, 275
alienage: and Anglo-Jewish plutocracy, 245-47, 276; Anglo-Jewry's involvement in Boer War, 247-48, 276; and Anglo-Jewry's support of Turkey, 225-26, 276; and Bolshevism, 269-71; in British prewar literature, 253-55; and creation of Jewish homeland, 271-72; and Jewish world conspiracy, 268-69; and low participation of Russian-Jewish aliens in war effort, 261-62, 263-64; nonassimilation of Russian Jews, 229-35 *passim*; return of Russian Jews to fight in Bolshevik Revolution, 263; separate nationality of Jews, 272, 273
alien problem, in Britain: avoidance of military service, 261-62, 263; correlation between British emigration and alien immigration, 235; criminality, 233-35; failure to intermarry, 237-38; housing-related issues, 232-33, 241n50; importing of anarchist ideology, 235; labor issues, 229-32, 240n40; loyalty of Anglo-German Jews prewar and during WWI, 253-55,

259; political stability threatened by forcing down of wages, 235; return of Russian-Jewish aliens under Anglo-Russian Convention, 262; Social Darwinist perspective on, 235-36; statistics on Russian-Jewish aliens, 227. *See also* labor issues; housing-related issues
Aliens Act of 1905: contents of, 237; Prime Minister Balfour's speech on, 237-38
Aliens Bill of 1904, 237n
Aliens Military Service Bill, 262
Aliens Order, 267
Aliens Restriction Act (1914), 260
Aliens Restriction (Amendment) Act (1919), 267
Alliance Israelite Universelle, 112
Almassy, Sandor, 150
Alsace, Jews of, 69
Altaras, Jacob Isaac, 75
anarchist movement, 234, 235
Andrassy, Gyula, 191, 203n142; and progressive demise of liberalism, 197
Andreanszky, Gabor, 135-36
Anglo-German Jews: assimilation of, 245; in business, finance, and industry, 246-47; as cosmopolitans, 254-55; as enemy aliens, 259-60; goal of, 216; and loyalty, 253-54; and monopolization of press, 247
Anglo-Russian Convention, 262-63; number of Russian-Jewish returnees under, 262-63
anonymous English merchant, 37, 59n48
anti-Semite, use of term, 5, 139
Anti-Semitic Congress, 133
Anti-Semitic League, 113
Anti-Semitic Press Company, 185

anti-Semitism, 56; essential characteristics of, 4-5; as explicit political creed, 5; historiographical analysis of factors, 2-6, 7, 29; origin of term, 12n19; religion-based, 2; term a misnomer, 139; use of term, 5
Antiszemita Kate, 133-34
Apponyi, Albert, 191
Arendt, Hannah, 2, 54, 168
Argyll, Duke of, 226
Arnold, Thomas, 221
art of self-definition: in the arts, 206; business, 206; compared to Galizianers, 207, 232; and conversion, 205-6; in the economy, 206; in education, 207; in the free professions, 206; and Jewish religion, 207; and Judaization of society, 207; and loyalty, 207; and participation in war effort, 207; and religious reform, 205-6
arts, and Jews' participation in, in Hungary, 163-64
Ashkenazi Jews. *See* Eastern European Jews
Asiatic Brethren, Order of, 42
assimilation: as culmination of reform, 39; as defined by Enlightenment thinkers, 39; failure of, 8-9; and 'golden era' of Hungarian Jewry, 9-10, 13n25, 86, 88; historians' understanding of, 83-86; increasing irrelevance of after Tiszaeszlar, 127-28; intermarriage as sign of, 169, 171-72; Jews' measurement of, 142; non-Jewish understanding of, 83-84, 183, 238; possibility of, according to Enlightenment thinkers, 39-40; post-Holocaust phase of, 11; purported success of, 88, 88-89n, 205; role of, in emancipation, 39-40; temporary success of in Hungary, 86. *See also* reform
assimilation, historiographical analysis: acculturation as component of, 83-84; differentiation between assimilation and acculturation, 83; and nationalism, 85-86; as a negative, 84; reciprocity as component of, 83, 92n16; regional approach to, 85
assimilation, institutional forms of: intermarriage, 169-72; Jews as social class, 167-69
assimilation, issues of, in Britain: character traits, 229-32; crime, 234; intermarriage, 237-38; loyalty, 225-26; patriotism, 259-61, 271-73; solidarity, 225-26
assimilation, issues of, in Hungary: acculturation, 163-64; in the arts, 163-64; attachment to German language, 111, 111n; business ethics, 141; character traits, 158-60; commerce, finance, and industry, 154-55; conversion, 140-41, 182; disproportionate attendance at university, 161-62; evasion of military service, 147-48, 181, 183-84; illegal professions, 156-57; immigration of Galizianers, 112; immorality, 158-60, 207; intermarriage, 169-72; Jewification of society, 164; land leasing, 152; landownership, 150-52; in legal profession, 155; loyalty in war, 147, 148; in medical profession, 155; monopolization of the press, 164-66; Jewish nationalism, 148; patriotism in wartime, 140, 147-48; performing preemancipation roles, 141, 148-49, 150; post-emancipation character traits, 142-43, 162; religious reform, 122, 126, 140-41, 158, 159n; 161; resistance to intermarriage, 124; resistance of Orthodox Jews to public education, 159, 159n; ritual murder, 119-26; Sabbath and festival observance, 160, 161; social cohesion, 111, 112, 182; social exclusiveness, 112; solidarity, 111-12, 182; in trade, 154; unassimilability, 160, 179-80, 181-82; unprofessional professions, 155-58; usury, 122, 142, 144, 153, 156; work ethic, 111; working on Sunday, 160

Association of Awakening Hungarians, 190-91, 200-201n92
Association of Hungarian Defense (M.O.V.E.), 190-91, 200n86
Association of the Non-Jews of Hungary, 113
Association for Preventing the Immigration of Destitute Aliens, 236
Attwood, Thomas, 222
Augustine, Saint, 17
Augustus Frederick (Duke of Sussex), 219
Austria, measures against Jews after 1848-49 Revolution, 103-4
Az Est, 165, 193

Bach regime, and laws enhancing economic utility of Jews, 104
Bajsy-Zsilinszky, Endre, 187, 193
Balfour, Arthur, 237-38
Balfour Declaration, 209-210, 272n
Balkan insurrection. *See* Bulgarian atrocities agitation
Bandholtz, H. H., 188, 191
Bangha, Bela, 185
Barnes, Julian, 7
Bartholdy, Salomon, 54
Basnage, Jacques, 41
Batthyany, Lajos, 102
Bedford Charity Case, 30, 35n75
Beksics, Gustav, 89
Bela IV (King), 23
Belgrave (Viscount), 221
Beller, Steven, 65, 84-85
Belloc, Hilaire, 253, 254-55, 257n4, 272
Benedict XII (Pope), 32n11
Bentinck, George, 222
Berenyi, Janos, 103
Bergmann, Hugo, 90
Bernolak, Nandor, 195
Bernstein, Michael, 2-3
Bethlen, Istvan, 191, 192
Bethlen, Pal, 195
Bethnal Green, Jewish anti-alien riots in, 264
Bexley (Lord), 219
bills of emancipation: The Act of 1867: XVII, 105; Act to Provide For The Relief...., 221; Act to Substitute One Oath For the Oaths...., ('Emancipation Bill'), 221; Bill About the Jews: Act IX:1849, 103, 103n; bill emancipating French Alsatian Jews, 69; bill emancipating French Sephardi Jews, 69; Parliamentary Oaths Act of 1866, 221
Birnbaum, Pierre, 3
Black Death, 18
Bleichroder, Lionel von, 247
blood libel. *See* ritual murder
Boer War: Hobson's views on, 247; as Jewish War, 247; Labour's views on, 248; Liberal's views on, 248
Bolshevik Revolution, 263; departure of Russian Jews back to Russia, 263; Jews classified as ethnic minority, 209; Jews as primary fomenters of, 269-70
Bolshevism, 269-71; Churchill on, 270; *Morning Post* on, 270
Booth, Charles, 232
Bosanquet (Chief Constable), 256
boycotts, 142
Brest-Litovsk, peace of, 264
British Brothers League, 236-237
British context: abridged Jewish presence, 216, 284-85; conversos and Marranos as 'neutral' Jews, 216; influence of millenarian Christians, 217, 219-20, 223n4, 284-85; issues expressed in terms of alienage, not assimilation, 217
British Workers National League, 262
Brody, Sandor, 9, 9n, 182
Brown (witness for Royal Commission), 229
Buda, 24, 26
Budavary, Laszlo, 191-92; and his Ten Point Program, 194, 202n121
Bulgarian atrocities agitation, 225-26, 225n; Anglo-Jewry's stand on, 225-26; Disraeli's stand on, 225; Jewish solidarity, 226; reaction of British public to Anglo-Jewry's stand on, 226
Burnett, John, 230

Callaghan, James, 232
Cassel, Ernst, 246

Catholic Central Press Company, 184-85
Catholic People's Party. *See* Neppart
census of 1871, 227
census of 1901, 227
Central Consistory, 69
Chamberlain, Joseph, 235, 237
character traits of Jews: Enlightenment thinkers' views on, 41-43; after emancipation, 111-15, 147-50, 153, 156-60, 229-32, 233-35, 256; possibility of reforming, 42-43
Charles II (King), 26-27
charters, 19
Chartists, 222
Chesterton, G. K., 253, 257n4
Christian character of state, Enlightenment thinker's views on, 51-52, 56-57
Christian Hebraists, 45, 60n56
Christian National Course, 189-90
Christian National Party, 192
Christian National Unity Party, 192
'Christian observer' (writer for *Jewish Intelligence*), 75
Christian Socialist Party, 192
Churchill, Winston: and Bolshevism, 270; and Jewish state, 271
circular orders, 133, 136, 144n3
civil marriage, as part of *Recepcio*, 137-38
Civil Marriage Bill: Church's opposition to, 129n35, 137-38; failure to pass in 1883, 124; as part of *Recepcio*, 137-38
class system, 167-69; comparison of Jews with serfs, 168-69; implications of classless status, 169, 178n158; Jews as members of a class, 168; system of ranks, 167
Clement VI (King), 18
Clerk, George Russel, 188-89
Clermont-Tonnerre, Stanislas de, 50
Cobbett, Richard, 221
Cohen, Asher, 4-5, 85
Colquhoun, Patrick, 28
Communism: reactions to in Britain, 269-70; reactions to in Hungary, 186-87; regime in Hungary, 186-87

comparisons between Britain and Hungary: conversion, 282-83; criminality, 281; disruption of Sunday observance, 282; distinctiveness of Jews, 282; financial control domestically and internationally, 282; homegrown Jews, 283; immigrant Jews not assimilating, 283; intermarriage as solution, 283; the Jewish Question, 284; the Jewish Question, 284; Jews' relationship to the state, 283; liberalism in disrepute, 284; Liberals' accommodation to Jews, 284; literature addressing Jewish Question, 284; monopolization of sectors of economy, 282; morality, 281; MPs on immigration and Jewish Question, 283; occupational concentration, 281-82; organizations to control immigration, 283-84; 'our' Jews and 'those' Jews, 283; religion, 282; social cohesiveness, social exclusiveness, and solidarity, 281; transformation of Jewish Question from social to political, 284; unlimited drive to power through capitalism, 282
Concerning the Amelioration of the Civil Status of the Jews, 66n
Condorcet (Marquis de), 37
consumers unions, 141-42; and Prohaszka, 142; launched by Vatican, 142
contextualization, historiographical analysis of, 3-4; specificity of British context, 217, 219-20, 223n4
contingency, 2-3, 9
contingency theory, 2-3
conversion, 56-57, 182-83, 188, 190; as aid in assimilation, 172, 282-83; Disraeli's, 226; and emancipation debates, 40; Enlightenment thinkers' views on, 46-48, 60n67; forced, 21; intermarriage as stepping stone to, 237; as means of acceptance, 9, 19, 140, 171-72, for professional advancement, 23,

conversion (*continued*)
  149, 205-6; promoted by secular and religious Enlightenment thinkers alike, 47-48; related to toleration of Jews, 20-21
conversionism, 20-21, 23, 28, 32n22, 219
conversos, 27, 216
Corelli, Marie, 254
costermongers, 231
Coumbe, E. H., 267
Council of Szabolcs, 23
Counterrevolution. *See* White Terror
Creagh, Father, 256
credit companies, 141-42
credit cooperatives, 153
crime: anarchist-related, 234; and British Jews in 18th century, 28; Enlightenment thinkers' views on, 41; Hungarian Jews' involvement in, 155-57; notorious murders, 234; prostitution, 234; Russian-Jewish aliens and, 233-35; white slave trade, 157, 235
Crusades, 18, 23
Csemegi Codex, 159, 192
Csemegi, Karoly, 159, 192
Csernatony, Lajos, 111
culture, in Hungary: as commodity, 164; and Jewish sensibilities, 163-64; Jews' influence on, 163-64; *utanerzes*, 163; views on, in *Huszadik Szazad* questionnaire, 180
Cunningham, W., 229

Daner, Bela, 192
Dangerfield, George, 249
Deak, Ferenc, 104
Declaration of the Moderate Oppositional Anti-Semitic Party, 136
Deism, 38, 62n104
Deists, 45
Derby, Lord, 261
Dessewffy, Aurel, 98
Diderot (Denis), 41, 45
Diet of 1839-40, 97-99; laws of overturned by 1840 Bylaw XXIX, 98-99
Diet of 1843-44, 100-2; and defeat of Jewish emancipation petition, 100

Diet of 1847-48, 102-3; and opposition to Jewish emancipation, 102
Diez, H. F., 58n16
Disraeli, Benjamin, 225-26; and stand on Bulgarian atrocities agitation, 225-26; conversion of, 226; and 1880 election, 226
D'Israeli, Isaac, 31
Dissenters. *See* Non-Conformists
dogmatic toleration, 66-67, 69, 76
Dohm, Christian Wilhelm von, 42-43, 46, 50-51, 52-53, 59n34, 62n111, 66n
domination: by Jews in Britain, 245, 247-48, 255, 268-69; by Jews in Hungary, 70, 112, 127, 131n60, 154. *See also* economy, role of Jews in; Rothschild, Nathan Meyer
Dominicans, 18
Dunraven, Earl of, 230, 236

East End Conservative Associations, 236
Eastern European Jews: criminality, 28; immigration to Britain, 27; presence of in Britain and Hungary as source for notion of 'our' Jews and 'those' Jews, 75-76, 126, 245, 283
Eastern Question, in Britain. *See* Bulgarian atrocities agitation; immigration
Eastern Question, in Hungary, 112
economic entity, Jews as, 22
economic integration. *See* occupational reform
economic overperformance, 19-20, 155, 181, 249-50
economic underperformance, 19-20, 21, 155, 249-50
economic utility of Jews, 19-20, 44, 57, 68, 93n32, 149, 155, 208; Bach regime's decrees to improve, 104; in Britain, 249-50; and ennoblements 148-49
economy, role of Jews in: finance, 28, 112, 154, 246-47, 249, 268, 272, 282; industry, 149-50, 154, 208, 208-9n, 246, 251n28; land leasing, 152; land ownership, 150-52; 1937

economy, role of Jews in (*continued*)
profile, 208-9n; Pollins on, 29; *Toleranzpatent*, 68; trade, 28-29, 43-44, 50, 122, 142, 154-55, 246

edicts, complementary to *Toleranzpatent*, 68; as embodiment of Enlightenment ideals specific to the Jews, 68

education in Britain, operating on Jewish format in London's East End, 233

education in France: limited attendance by Jewish students, 70; special schools for Jewish students, 70

education, in Hungary: behavior of Jewish university students, 162; Christian approach to, 162; enrolment patterns, 163, 176n114, 176n117; Jewish approach to, 162; Jewish high school students oriented to cultural and professional careers, 161; as means to achieve reform, 161; Orthodox Jews' resistant to secular forms of, 159n; as primary corrective to faults of Jews, 161; proportion of Jewish students at university, 161-62

Edward I (King), 26

Egan, Ede, 152-53, 153n, 173n35; on the Jewish Question, 153

1840 Bylaw XXIX, 99

1884 election, 133-35; agitations during, 133-35; and circulation of anti-Jewish tracts, 133-34; clergy's participation in, 133-34, 144n7; and Tisza's circular order, 133; Tisza's post-election speech, 135; Tisza's New Year's speech, after election, 136

1887 election, and Jewish Question raised during, 136

Eisler, Edmund, 74

emancipation: bills of, 69, 103, 103n, 105; defeat of 1848 and 1849 bills of emancipation in Hungary, 103; and dogmatic toleration, 66; Enlightenment thinkers' criteria for, 39; of French Alsatian Jews, 69; of French Sephardi Jews, 69; Hungarian Catholic Church's position on, 120-21; inquiry into revoking in France, 70; and lack of public acceptance, 96n; liberal approach to, 66; limitations placed on in France, 69-70; limited by *Numerus Clausus*, 193, 208; origin of term, 66n; and political toleration, 66; process in Britain, 219-22; process in Hungary, 97-105; renegotiation of in Hungary, 209-10; revoked after Hungarian Revolution of 1848-49, 103; terms of renegotiated in 1920, 209-10

emancipation debates in Britain, 219-21

emancipation debates in Germany, 96-97

emancipation debates in Hungary, 97-99, 100-104 *passim*, 108n35

Emancipation of the Jews (a Zsidok emancipacioja), 99-100

Emden, Jacob, 53

emigration: of Britons, connected to arrival of Russian Jews, 235; of Jews from Europe in 19th century, 74-75; of Hungarian Jews, 115n2; societies, 75

employees of state, Jews as, and Enlightenment thinkers' views on, 52-53

Endelman, Todd, 215

enemy aliens, WWI: Anglo-German Jews as, 259; London County Council's resolutions regarding, 260; Russian-Jewish aliens considered as, 259, 267

England, readmission of Jews to, 26-27

Enlightenment, 7; concepts of, 37-38; historiographical treatment of, 7; ideals of as impetus for reconsidering Jews' status, 37-38

Enlightenment ideals specific to the Jews, 7, 39, 57; debate regarding fulfillment of, 39-40; embodied in *Toleranzpatent* and edicts, 67-68; as focus of emancipation debates, 95-103 *passim*

Enlightenment thinkers on: acculturation, 48; character traits of Jews, 41-43; conversion, 47-48; crime, 41; Jewish religion,

Enlightenment thinkers on (*continued*) 44-46; Jews in government, 52; Jews in the military, 52-53; Jews' increased participation in the economy, 43-44; Jews as a nation, 48-49; Jews' relation to the state, 48-53; Jews as a state within a state, 49-50; maintaining Christian character of the state, 51-52; moral reform connected to occupational reform, 43-44; overestimation of Jewish population, 41; possibility of reform among Jews, 39; reform, before or after emancipation, or impossible, 40; separation of Church and state, 51-52
ennoblements: innovations in process of granting, 149; disproportionate number offered to Jews, 149-50; as reward for economic utility, 149
Eotvos, Jozsef, and his views on Jewish emancipation, 99-100
Epstein, M., 2
era of liberalism: beginning with *Toleranzpatent*, 67-68; British period of, 219, 220, 222, 248-50; French revolutionary period of, 69-71; Hungarian period of, 91, 99, 122-23, 126, 151, 160-61; Jewish migration and Zionism coinciding with, 72-74; ending with *Numerus Clausus* in Hungary, 194-95, 197
era of the millennium: assessment of Jews' assimilation during, 140-43; consumers unions and credit companies, 141-42; patriotism of Jews, 140; signs of antipathy to Jews, 141, 143
era of Toleration, 7; in Britain after readmission, 26-31; determined by Church doctrine, 17; determined by secular authorities, 19-20; in Hungary, 23-26, 106n9; Jewish condition, 17-22
Ereky, Karoly, 194
Escott, T. H. S., 247
essay contests, in France, 40, 71
ethnic minorities. *See* nationalities

Evans-Gordon, William, 234, 236, 237
expulsion, 21-22; from England, 27; from Hungary, 23-26 *passim*

Factory Act of 1859, 104
Feher Kereszt Kavehaz. See White Cross Café
Fejervary, Geza, 149
Feldman, David, 3
Fichte, Johann Gottlieb, 40, 42, 45, 49, 74n
finance. *See* economy, role of Jews in
Finestein, Israel, 215
First International Anti-Jewish Congress, 124
Fleury (Cardinal), 44
Foncesca Brandon, Joshua and Jacob de, 29
Ford, Ford Madox, 253, 254
Foreign Jews Protection Committee, 261-62
foreshadowing, 10
Fourteen Points (Woodrow Wilson's), and Jews included in Minorities Treaties, 209
Franciscans, 18
Frankfurt Tradition: Internationalization, 247
Freak, Charles, 231
Freedom of the City, 31
Freeman, Edward, 226
Freund, Ismar, 51
Friedlander, David, 72, 150, 150n, 207
Friedrich, Istvan, 188, 192, 194
friendly aliens, 259, 260
Fuggetlenseg, 87, 87n

Galizianers, 75, 76, 98, 112, 116n6, 126, 153, 180-81, 189, 206. *See also* Eastern Question; Ede Egan; Hasids; *Huszadik Szazad* questionnaire; immorality; petitions
Gawler, George, 220
Geiger, Abraham, 97
General Pachtung, 152
German trends, as influences on emancipation debates in Hungary, 95-97
ghetto histories, 3
ghettos, 18-19; in Rome, 18-19

Gilam, Abraham, 215, 216
gimnazium. *See* high school
Gladstone, William, 220, 225; and 1880 election, 226
Glyn, Major, 255
Goethe, Johann von Wolfgang, 41, 45-46, 47, 49
golden era of Hungarian Jewry, 9-10, 13n25, 86
Goldstein, Moritz, 207
Gombos, Gyula, 190
Graetz, Heinrich, 95
Grant, Robert, 219
Grattenauer, Karl Wilhelm, 43, 47, 48, 51-52
Greenberg, Leopold, 270
Grégoire, Henri (Abbé), 40, 40n, 41, 44, 45, 49, 51
Guenée, Antoine (Abbé), 47
Guizot, François, 71, 75, 79n36
Gwynne, H. A., 269, 270
Gyurgyak, Janos, 83-84

Hackney recruitment office, 261
Halevy, Elie, 240n40
Haller, Istvan, 188-89; and his end of liberalism speech, 194-95
Handler, Andrew, 167
Harnack, Adolf von, 95, 106n3
Hartley, David, 50
Hartmann, Friedrich Traugott, 46, 50, 52
Hase, Karl August von, 95
Hasids, 98, 107n22
Hatvany, Lajos, 140, 182
Hebrew language, 67
Heine, Heinrich, 96, 106n6, 182
Hell, François, 59n34, 61n87
Henry III (King), 20, 26
Herczeg, Ferenc, 197
Herder, Johann Gottfried, 37, 43, 48
Herman, Otto, 123
Herzl, Theodor, 72n, 79n43, 177n137, 237
Hess, Moses, 73
Hezel, Wilhelm Friedrich, 47
high schools, 163, 175n101
Hirsch, Baron de, 227
Hitel, 97
Hobhouse, John Cam, 219
Hobson, J. A., 230, 247-48; Holmes and Rubinstein on, 248-49

Hofjuden, 168; Sir Ernst Cassel, last of the, 246
Holmes, Colin: on Hobson and Smith, 248-49; on the Marconi Scandal, 255
Holocaust, 1, 6-7
Horkheimer, Max, 7
Horvath, Boldizsar, 105
Horvath, Janos, 164
Hounsditch murders, 234
Hourwitz, Zalkind, 40, 58n19
housing-related issues, and Russian-Jewish aliens: health hazards, 232-33; increase in East-End rents, 232; habits of Jewish neighbors, 232-33; relations with neighbors, 233; relocation of local residents, 232, 241n50; social cohesiveness, social exclusiveness, and solidarity of Russian-Jewish aliens, 233, 238
Hueffer, Ford Hermann. *See* Ford Madox Ford
Humboldt, Wilhelm von, 51, 51n, 55
Hungarian Christian Society Union, 127, 130n56
Hungarian Defense Union, 124
Hungarian 1848-49 Revolution, 102-3, 105; emancipation bills during, 103; Jews separately blamed and punished for, 103-4; rioting against Jews during, 108n44
Hungarian Military Jewish Archive, 183
Hungarian Social Alliance, 190
Hungarian University and High School Students Countrywide Union. *See* MEFHOSZ
Hungarianization. *See* Magyarization
Hungarianization offices, 114
Hungary: in Austro-Hungarian empire, 106-7n9; during the Commune (Dictatorship of the Proletariat), 186-87; in the Dual Monarchy, 104; post-WWI-1920, 187-93; during the prewar years, 143-44
Huszadik Szazad, questionnaire, in, 179-83

immigration: of Eastern European Jews to Central-Western Europe, 48; of Galizianers to Hungary, 98, 112;

immigration (*continued*)
of Russian Jews to Britain, 226-28; of Russian Jews related to right of political asylum, 228, 228n, 275; and statistics on Russian Jews, 227
Immigration Reform Association, 237
immigration restriction in Britain: Aliens Act of 1905, 237; Aliens Act of 1905 and Balfour's rationale for, 237; investigations into, 228; parliamentary debates on, 228; right of asylum now a matter of discretion, 237; Royal Commission on, 229; Select Committees on, 228
immigration restriction in Hungary, 112, 116n6, 121
immorality of Jews, 43, 45, 68, 100, 157, 158-60, 207, 238
Imperial Chancery, 68
Imperial Decree of 1806, 69-70, 78-79n28
Imperial Patent of 1853, 104
Indian Scandal, 255; and Jewish plutocracy, 255
Indignation meetings, 227
industry. *See* economy, role of Jews in
Infamous Decree. *See* Imperial Decree
Inglis, Robert, 221
Innocent IV (Pope), 18
Inquisition, 18
interactive theory, 3
intermarriage, 112; from Christian perspective, 171; conditions affecting rate of, 170-71; definitions of, 170; from Jewish perspective, 171; low rate of as rationale for Aliens Act of 1905, 237; as mechanism for assimilation, 171-72; Christians receptive to, 171; as sign of assimilation, 169, 171-72; Hungarian statistics on, 169, 169n
Iranyi, Daniel, 123
Isaacs, Godfrey, 255
Isaacs, Rufus, 255
Israelite Women's Association, 140-41
Istoczy, Gyozo, 65, 112n, 126; on immigration restriction, 112; on the Jewish Question, 112; and

"Restoration of the Jewish State in Palestine" speech, 113-14
Istvan I (King and Saint), 9, 9n, 22-23
Itzkowitz, David, 215

Jack the Ripper murders, 234, 241-42n64
Jansenists, 46
Jaszi, Oszkar, 165; and *Huszadik Szazad* questionnaire, 179
Jew Bill of 1753, 29
Jewification of society. *See* Judaization of society
Jewish battalions, 262
Jewish Chronicle, 96, 218n7, 225, 235, 237, 238, 239n16, 241-42n64, 254, 255, 257, 259, 264, 267, 270, 273
Jewish condition, religious basis for Augustinian view, 17; consequence of failure to accept Jesus and responsibility for his death, 17; conversion only means of acceptance, 19
Jewish Condition, secular basis for: monarchies' regulations based on Jews' economic utility and Jews as chattels, 19-20
Jewish Emigration Society, 75
"Jewish Lady," 245
Jewish Laws of Frederick II the Bellicose, 23
Jewish Question in Britain, 238-39, 271, 273; factors mitigating intensity of, 284-85
Jewish Question, in Hungary, 2, 84, 112, 122, 123, 126, 127, 134, 136, 138, 153, 156, 184; 189, 191, 193, 197; *Huszadik Szazad*, questionnaire on, 179-83; Istoczy on, 112, 113-14; Liberal government's stand on, 91, 112, 141; as political question, 138; related to intermarriage, 171-72; as social question, 208; from social to political question after Tiszaeszlar, 127-28, 208; and Verhovay, 87
Jewish state: British government's support of, 271-72, 272n; Churchill's support of, 271;

Jewish state (*continued*)
  contradiction between Jews' support of and as citizens of Mosaic faith, 272; and issue of divided loyalty, 272-73; as part of Jewish conspiracy, 272; as reinforcement of alienage, 272
Jewish Territorial Organization, 237
Jewish world conspiracy, 268-69; and literature about, 268; and *Protocols*, 268-69; as widespread conviction in postwar Britain, 268-69
Jeyes, S. H., 235, 245-46
job-snatching, 260
John (King), 26
Jokai, Mor, 122
Joseph II (Emperor), 49
Judaization of society, 121, 181, 190, 206, 207
Judaizing, 21
Judische Delikatessen, 86-87; 90-91

Kadish, Sharmin, 262-63
Kalischer, Zvi Hirsch, 73
Kant, Immanuel, 38, 47, 49
Kaplan, Marian, 83, 170-71
Karady, Viktor (Victor), 169-70, 171
Karolyi, Mihaly, 186
Katolikus Neppart. *See* Neppart
Katz, Jacob, 9-10, 53, 54, 55, 84
Katznelson, Ira, 3
Khazars. *See* Galizianers
Kiss, Jozsef, 111, 115n2
Klapka, Gyorgy, 123-24
Knigge, Adolf von, 41-42
Kortum, Ernst Traugott von, 49
Kosmann, George, 41
Kossuth, Lajos, 102, 103, 105; views on Galizianer immigration, 98; reform of Jewish religion, 100-101
Kun, Bela, 186-187

labor issues arising from Russian-Jewish presence: cheap pool of labor, 229-30; competitiveness, 230; deterioration of labor standards, workers' standard of living, and workers' standard of wages, 230; job displacement, 230; low-quality sweatshop commodities related to falling markets and unemployment, 231; sweatshop conditions, 231; sweatshop owners, 231; unionization, 231
Lacratelle, Louis, 39
Lajos I (King), 21, 23
Lajos II (King), 23
land: auctioned off by Jews, 151; auctioned off to Jews, 153; as capitalist venture, 151; as corrective to Jewish character traits, 43; Hungary's economic stability based on, 151; leased by Jews, 152, 173n31; mortgaged to Jews, 152; and occupational reform, 150; ownership of by Jews, 150-52
Laszlo V (King), 23
Lavater, Johann Caspar, 46-47
Law 1920.XXV. *See Numerus Clausus*
Law of Jewish Emancipation (France), 69
Leeds, anti-Jewish riots in, 264
Lencz, Geza, 197
Lesznai, Anna, 171-72
Letter of the Ten, 271
letter killing, 33n39
Letter to the Brethren, 72, 72n
Levi (Levy), David, 72
liberal era. *See* era of liberalism
liberalism, 65-66, 91; characterized by 'political' toleration, 76; constraints of, 229; definitions of, 65n, 65-66; demise of in Hungary, 196-97, 207; dichotomy inherent in, 66, 66-67, 76; evolution of, 76, 208; French Revolution, as mature, 69-71; Holmes and Rubinstein on, 248-49; in Hungary, 65, 111, 141, 161; in mid-nineteenth century Hungary, 77n3; nascent state of in Britain, 219; and *Numerus Clausus*, 194-95; in second half of nineteenth-century Britain, 77n3; and Tiszaeszlar, 126; *Toleranzpatent* as nascent, 67-68; transformation of, 249-50; values of at odds with anti-Semitism, 248-49. *See also* era of liberalism

Limerick: boycott, 256; incidents in, 256
Lipski, Israel, 234
Lisles de Sales, Jean Baptiste Nicolas de, 39
literature, British prewar, and Jews: Anglo-German Jews as spies and anarchists, 254; capitalistic orientation of, 254; as cosmopolitans, 255; financial power of, 254-55; medieval imagery in, 253-54; political power of, 255; social nonacceptance of, 253; undermining nation and society, 254-55
Lloyd George, David, 272n
Locke, John, 38
London County Council (LCC), resolutions of, 260, 267
Londoners' League, 236
loyalty, of Jews: Anglo-German during WWI, 259-60; and Bulgarian atrocities agitation, 225-26; compromised by textual references to Zion, 48, 50-51; in doubt with creation of Jewish state, 271; and ennoblements, 148-49; and evasion of military service in Britain, 261-64; and evasion of military service in Hungary, 147-48, 183-85; Friedlander on, 150; and Jews as a people, 148; and return of Russian-Jewish aliens to fight in Bolshevik Revolution, 263; and return of Russian-Jewish aliens under Anglo-Russian Convention, 262-63; and Russian-Jewish aliens, 261-64; and superficial displays of, 147, 259; and voting *en bloc*, 148
loyalty displays, 259
loyalty letters, 259
Ludovika Military Academy, 194
Lusitania, 260
Luther, Martin, 21

Macaulay, Thomas, 222
Magyar Israelite Literary Society, 140
Magyarization: government policy of promoting Hungarian language and names, 114, 114n; Jews' motives for Hungarianizing their names, 114-15; public education as aid in, 161
Marconi Scandal, 255
Maria Theresa (Empress), 21, 25-26
Markusz, Gyuri, 289
Marr, Wilhelm, 12n19
Marranos. *See conversos*
Marrus, Michael R., 2
Marxist theory, 3
matricula, 148
Matthias Corvinus (King), 23
McCagg, William O., 149
Medina, Solomon de, 28
MEFHOSZ, 193, 201n109
Mendelsohn, Ezra, 86
Mendelssohn, Moses, 46; and his deviations from traditional Judaism, 53; as target for conversionists, 53-54
Men of Szeged, 189-90, 190; goals of, 190; ideology of, 189-90; leitmotif of, 189
Messianism, 50
Michaelis, Johann David, 39-40, 41, 44-45, 46, 50, 53
migration of Eastern European Jews, 74-76, 79n47; as barometer of public sentiment and progress of legal emancipation, 74-75, 80n56; factors influencing, 76; Russia and others' agreement to, 75, 80n53
Miklos, Andor, 165-66
Mikszath, Kalman, 10, 205
military service, Enlightenment thinkers' views on, 52-53, 62n111
military service, WWI, Britain: avoidance of by Russian-Jewish aliens, 261-62, 263-64; exemption from, for Russian-Jewish aliens, 260-61; exclusion from, 261; government measures to increase enlistment among Russian-Jewish aliens, 261, 262, 264; Jewish battalions, 262; opposed by Foreign Jews Protection Committee, 261-62; performance of Russian-Jewish recruits, 262; public's reaction to avoidance of, 261-62, 264
military service, WWI, Hungary and evasion of, 183n, 183-84

millenarianism, influence of on emancipation, 46, 219-20, 223n4
millennium. *See* era of the millennium
millet system, 24
Mills, John, 220
mining towns, exclusion of Jews from, 25
Minorities Treaties, 209, 210, 210n
Moderate Oppositional Anti-Semitic Party, declaration of, 136
Mohacs, 24
Montagu, Edwin, 255
Montagu, Samuel, 246
moneylending. *See* usury
monopolization. *See* domination
Montefiore, Moses, 75, 247
Montesquieu, Charles Louis, 44, 45
moral reform, connected to occupational reform, 43
Moreau, Agricole, 71
Morning Post: on Jews as Bolsheviks, 270-71; on the *Protocols of the Elders of Zion*, 269
Morris, William, 226
Mosaic Judaism, as impediment to emancipation, 44-45
Moser, Justin, 96
Mosse, George, 3
M.O.V.E., 190-91, 200n86. *See also* Awakening Hungarians, Association of
Müller, Adam, 55
Myer, Henry, 262

Napoleon, Bonaparte, 8, 55, 66, 69-70
National Anti-Semitic Party, 127, 133, 135, 146n43
national contexts, comparative study of, 4
National Review, 254
nationalities, and attitudes towards Jews, 166-67
Naturalization Bill of 1753. *See* Jew Bill of 1753
Nedtvich, Karoly, 125
Neolog Jews, 206, 206n
Neppart, 141-42; and boycott of Jewish enterprises, 142; and consumers unions, 141-42; and credit companies, 141-42
New Christians, 21, 22
Noah, Mordecai, 74-75

Non-Conformists, 220
numerus clausus: support for expansion of idea, 194; in universities, 193; as way to settle the Jewish Question
Numerus Clausus Law 1920. XXV, 193-96; aimed at Jews, 209; arguments opposing, 195-96; difficulties in framing law, 195; way of imposing assimilation, 208-09; methods of enforcing, 194; way of neutralizing Jewish domination, 208; purpose of, 193; reclassification of Jews as race in, 209; support for, 193-94
numerus nullus, 194, 201n111

oblava. *See* raids
Occidental Jew, 276
occupational reform: Agoston on, 181; Enlightenment thinkers' views on, 43-44, 59n35; as determining factor in improving Jews' status, 43; possibility of, 43
Oktober Diploma, 104
October Revolution, 186
organizations: to control Jewish domination, 113, 124; formation of, postwar, 190-91; protection of non-Jews from Jewish competition, 113; to restrict immigration, 113, 236-37
Oriental Jew, 275
Orwell, George, 1, 253
Oszi, Kornel, 165
Ottomans: millet system, 24; occupation of Hungary, 24
ownership of Jews, 19-20, 33n39

Palestine, restoration of: connected to Jewish emancipation, 219-20, 223n4, 271-72; as solution to Jewish Question, 74n, 113-14, 271; as solution to presence of Jews in Europe, 74n, 113-14, 271. *See also* Jewish state; millenarianism; Zionism
papal bulls, 17
papal statutes, 18
Paris Peace Conference, 186, 188, 191, 209

Parkes, James W., 5, 83
Patent Roles of 1274, 26
patriotism: lack of among Hungarian Jews during WWI, 183-85; overdramatic displays of, 147, 148. *See also* loyalty
Paul III (Pope), 24
Paulus, H. E. G., 50
Pearson, Karl, 236
Perczel, Istvan Bonyhadi, 86-87, 90
Pereira, Francis, 28
pergamen, 168, 178n156
petitions, 121-24; Liberal MPs' debates on, 122-23; Szatmar, 121; Tapolca, 122
Petrassevich, Geza, 148, 150, 151, 158, 164
Philo-Judean Society, 219
philo-Semitism, 5, 12n18, 20-21
philosophes. *See* Enlightenment thinkers
Pietism, 96
Pinero, Sir Arthur, 259
Pinsker, Leo, 73-74
Pinto, Isaac de, 47
political anti-Semitism, 2, 5
political asylum, right of: as basis for opposing immigration restriction, 228, 228n, 275; discretionary after Aliens Act of 1905, 237; Russian-Jewish immigration not in conformity with concept of, 275
political stability, threatened by: forcing down of wages, 235; number of Jews in anarchist movement, 235
political toleration, 66, 69, 76
Pollins, Harold, 29
population estimates, of Jews: Istoczy's figures, 112, 116n8; exaggeration of during Enlightenment, 41; Russian Jews in Britain, 227
Potter, Beatrice, 230
Poujol, Louis, 70
press, Jewish monopolization of: Andor Miklos, 165-66; and Anglo-Jewish finance, 247; and Boer War, 247; Hungarian liberal, 87-88; effects of on Hungarian society, 164-65; newspaper editors, 164; press monopolies, 165; printers, 177n128

prewar years: in Britain, 253-57; in Hungary, 143-44
Priestly, Joseph, 223n4
Prince of Wales National Relief Fund, 260
profiteering, WWI: in Britain, 260; in Hungary, 184
progress, notion of, 37-38
Prohaszka, Ottokar, 5, 138-39, 188; biography, 139n; and Christian National Course, 189-90; and Jews' wartime participation, 183; and participation in consumers unions, 142
Protocols of the Learned Elders of Zion, 268-69, 273n14, 274n18

Rabbi (Central Synagogue), 226
raids, government-sanctioned, 184
ranks, system of, 167-68
readmission of Jews, to England, 21, 27
realist histories, 3; and uniqueness of accommodation of the majority to the minority in Britain, 216; sidestepping emancipation debates, 215-16
Recepcio, 137-40, 139-40; Catholic Church's objections to, 138-39
Red Terror, 186-87
reform: and acculturation, 48; of character traits, 41-43; constituent parts of, 41-53; Enlightenment ideals specific to the Jews, 7, 39; failure of Jews to, 8-9, 69-71; 140-41, 205-08; of Jewish language, 49; Jews' relation to the state, 48-53; moral, 43; moral connected to occupational, 43-44; occupational, 43-44, 59n35; Palestine (Zion) as homeland, 50-51, 56; reduced to expectation or hope by liberals, 66; religious, 44-48, 55, 158; thwarted by Jews' approach to education, 161, 162-63. *See also* assimilation; Enlightenment ideals specific to the Jews
Reformation, 20-21
regional histories, 4
Reich, Emil, 142-43
religious reform, 122, 126, 140-41, 158-59, 159n, 161; Enlightenment thinkers' views on, 44-48

Rentoul, Robert Reid, 236
Report of the Finance and
    Parliamentary Committee of the
    Stepney Borough Council, 241n50
reproduction rate, among Jews, 116n8
residency charters, 20
Ritook, Emma, 288, 288n7
ritual murder, 18; in Britain, 26; in
    Tiszaeszlar, 119-20, 124-25
ritualized humiliation, 19
Roebuck, Arthur James, 220
Rohling, Augustus, 158
Roman Catholic Church's position on:
    emancipation, 120-21; evasion of
    military service during WWI, 184-
    85; *Recepcio*, 138
Roth, Cecil, 225
Rothschild, A. M., 75
Rothschild, Lionel de, 220, 247
Rothschild, Nathan Meyer, 246
Royal Commission on Alien
    Immigration 1902-03, 229, 230,
    231, 233, 237
royal free cities, exclusion of Jews
    from, 25
Royal (Habsburg) Hungary, 24
Royal Society for Arts and Sciences,
    essay contests, 40-41, 71
Rubinstein, W. D., on Hobson and
    Smith, 248-49
Rupert, Rezso, 194
Russian-Jewish aliens: and Anglo-Russian
    Convention, 262-63; and Bolshevik
    Revolution, 263; as cause of British
    emigration, 235; crime among, 233-
    35; and dirt and disease, 229, 230,
    232; and evasion of military service,
    261-64; and housing issues related
    to, 232-33; as immigrants to Britain,
    227-28; not in conformity with
    concept of political asylum, 275; and
    immigration restriction, 228-29;
    initial reaction to, 227; and labor
    issues, 229-32; Parliamentary
    debates on, 228; population statistics
    on, 227; Royal Commission on, 229;
    social cohesiveness, social
    exclusiveness and solidarity of, 233;
    threat to political stability, 235; and
    unions, 231; war-related complaints
    against, 260-64

Russian Revolution. *See* Bolshevik
    Revolution
Ruthenians: and Ede Egan's program,
    153; indebtedness to Jewish usurers,
    153; loss of lands to Jews, 153
Sabbath and festival observance, 28,
    43-44, 160, 161, 233, 261
Salbstein, M., 217
Salomons, David, 247
salons: and impending emancipation,
    54-55; as a neutral society, 54;
    vital function of, 54
Salvador, Joseph, 28
Samuel, Stuart, 255
Sasinek, Peter, 166
Scharf, Jozsef, 125
Schelven, A. A. van, 66
Schleiermacher, Friedrich, 47
Schlettwein, Johann August, 59n35
Schnitzler, Arthur, 90
Scholem, Gershom, 2
Schonfeld, Jozsef, 287
schools: behavior of Hungarian Jewish
    university students at, 162; limited
    attendance at French public, 70;
    operating on a Jewish format in
    London's East End, 233;
    proportion of Hungarian Jewish
    students in, 161, 163; Saturday
    attendance by Hungarian Jewish
    students, 161; special for French
    Jewish children, 70. *See also*
    Toleranzpatent; university
Schopflin, George, 83, 85
Schroetter (Baron), 50
Schuckmann, F. von, 96n
Schuster, Felix, 259
Schwarcz, Salomon, 125
secularization, 2, 40-41n, 109n50
Select Committees, 228
self-definition. *See* art of self-definition
separation of Church and state, as
    related to Jews: Enlightenment
    thinkers' views on, 51, 56-57
Sephardi Jews, after readmission to
    England, 27; affluence of, 28-30,
    245; in business, finance, and
    industry, 28, 246-47; goal of, 216;
    images of, 27, 29-30; role of in
    trade, 28-29
Seton-Watson, Robert, 144

Shaftesbury (Lord), 221
Sherard, J. H., 230
Shneur Zalman (Szerencses [Fortunatus]), 24
sideshadowing, 3
Sigismund (King), 23, 33n39
Silver, James Lawson, 232, 233, 235-36
Simonyi-Semadam, Sandor, 191
Smith, Goldwin, 226; Holmes and Rubinstein on, 248-49
social cohesiveness, 42, 112, 116n5, 148, 182, 206, 207, 233, 281, 283
Social Darwinism, as determinant in immigration policy, 235
social exclusiveness, 71, 111, 116n5, 206, 207, 281, 283
social functionality, 2
Society for the Suppression of the Immigration of Destitute Aliens, 236
solidarity, 111-12, 120, 123, 126, 148, 182, 206, 207, 226, 233, 261, 271, 276, 281, 283, 288
Solymosi, Eszter, 89n, 119
Sombart, Werner, 1-2, 28
Sorkin, David, 83, 84
South African Conciliation Committee, 248
Southern, R. W., 2
Soviet Republic of Hungary: Jews involved in, 186-87; radical nature of, 186; and Red Terror, 187; White Terror as response to, 187-92
Spanish Inquisition, 21
Special Tribunal, 263
Speyer, Sir Edgar, 259
state, Enlightenment thinkers' views on Jews' relation to, 48-52, 55-57; 62n111; 153, 181, 185, 283, 287
status in statu. See state within a state
state within a state, Jews as, 49-50, 153
Steiner, Jozsef, 89
Stephen (Saint), 7, 7n. *See also* Istvan I
student unions, 162, 193, 194, 210n109
Sunday trading regulations: targeting Jewish businesses during WWI, 260; waived for Jewish costermongers, 231

sweatshops, 231
Synod of Bishops, 187
Szabo, Balazs, 193-94
Szabo, Dezso, 197
Szabolcsi, Lajos, 140
Szechenyi, Istvan, 89, 97, 101-2
Szeged, 10-11, 88, 88-89n9, 205
Szemnecz, Emil, 121
Szep, Erno, 180
Szmrecsanyi, Gyorgy, 194
Szorengi, Lipot, 162

Tapolca petition, and others: points contained in, 121-22; discussion of in Parliament, 122-23; discussion of, in the press, 123-24
taxation, 22, 28; tax profile of 1735, 25
tax evasion, 157
Teleki, Pal, 189, 192, 193, 194, 201n105
Tests and Corporation Acts, 30
Theobald of Cambridge, 20
Thièry, Adolphe, 40, 58n18
Thomson, Sir Basil, 269
Thought of Szeged (*Szegedi Gondolat*), 189
Times (of London): on Bolshevism, 269; on the *Protocols*, 269, 269n
Tisza, Istvan, 149
Tisza, Kalman: and 1885 New Year's Speech, 136; and Acsady, on historical reconstructions, 127; on anti-Semitism, 126-27, 135, 144n3; on Catholic clergy, 120; on morality, 159; on religion, 126
Tiszaeszlar, 128n1
Tiszaeszlar ritual murder case, 89n, 128n4; Church's response to, 120, 125; countrywide agitations during, 120-21, 125-26; incorporated into the Jewish Question, 126; Jewish solidarity highlighted, 120, 126; Liberal government's response to, 120-21, 122-23, 126; petitions provoked by, 121-22; signals transformation of Jewish Question from social to political, 127-28; trial, 124-25, 129n37
Titus Aemilius. *See* Szemnecz, Emil
Toland, John, 41, 44

Toleranzpatent, as embodiment of Enlightenment ideals specific to the Jews, 67-68, 78n14
toleration, Augustinian view of, 17; definition adhered to in this study, 7; religious basis for, 17; secular basis for, 19-20
Toleration, era of. *See* era of Toleration
Toleration Tax, 5, 25, 97, 102, 106-7n9
Tormay, Cecile, 181, 185, 186
Trades Union Congress, 248
Traverso, Enzo, 83, 84
Treaty of Vienna, 80n56
Tredegar Riots, 256-57, 258n23
Trefort, Agoston, 104, 105, 135, 161, 176n103
Turul, 193, 194, 201n109
12 Ellen Ropirat, 88
12 Ropirat, 17, 112n, 113,117n121

United Christian League, 192
Universal Anti-Jewish Alliance, 136
Universal Anti-Semitic Congress, 136
universal emancipation: as prod to emancipate Jews in liberal era, 66
universal humanism: as impetus to improve Jews' status in Enlightenment era, 37-38
unprofessional professions, 156-58
usury, 22, 23, 33n32, 33n38, 69-70, 122, 138, 142, 144, 153, 156, 158, 166-67, 221
utanerzes, 163-64
utilitarianism, notion of, 38

Vambery, Rustem, 65-66, 196
Vazsonyi, Vilmos, 184, 209
Verhovay, Gyula, 87
Veszprem, Bishop of, 120
Vincent, Howard, 234
Voltaire (François-Marie Arouet), 45
voting: patterns, 148; women obtaining vote, 163

Way of the Jews (a zsidok utja), 179
Webber, G. C., 249
Webster, Nesta H., 268
Wekerle, Sandor, 186
Wenckheim, Bela, 112
Whately, Richard, 220

White, Arnold, 6, 233, 236, 237, 238-39, 284
White Cross Coffeehouse, 140
white slave trade, 157, 235
White Terror, 187-93; in Budapest, 188-89; in the countryside, 188; government support of, 188, 191-92; Jewish Question as basis for, 189; organizers of, 189; purge of Jewish and non-Jewish Communists, 187-88; reign of Red Terror as basis for, 187
Wiesel, Elie, 7
William III (King), 28
Wilton, Robert, 263
Wistrich, Robert, 2, 5
world conspiracy. *See* Jewish world conspiracy
WWI in Britain, and the Jews: Anglo-German Jewry and incivism, 259; Government's efforts to promote enlistment of Russian-Jewish aliens, 261-64 *passim*; refusal of most Russian-Jewish aliens to enlist, 261; riots protesting Russian-Jewish aliens, 264; Russian-Jewish aliens as 'enemy' aliens, not 'friendly' aliens, 259-60
WWI in Hungary, and the Jews: abuse of war contracts, 184; black market, 184; Church's attack on incivism, 184-85; desertion, 184; evasion of military service, 183-85; hiding and hoarding, 184; profiteering, 184; raids as part of government efforts to control incivism, 184

Yiddish, 49, 49n, 67

Zakany, Gyula, 191
zikzene-zakzene music, 127, 130n54
Zimandy, Ignac, 133-34
Zionism, 148; Enlightenment thinkers' views on, 50-51; factors influencing, 72-74, 76. *See also* Palestine, restoration of
Zionist literature, five phases of, 73-74

www.ingramcontent.com/pod-product-compliance
Lightning Source LLC
Chambersburg PA
CBHW020829160426
43192CB00007B/577